Founding Mothers of the Indian Republic

Founding Mothers of the Indian Republic begins with the momentous task of demolishing the prejudices attached with the phrase 'founding fathers' that has held an immense sway over constitutional interpretation. It shows that women members of the Indian Constituent Assembly had painstakingly co-authored a Constitution that embodied a moral imagination developed by years of feminist politics.

This book traces the genealogies of several constitutional provisions to argue that, without the interventions of these women framers, the Constitution would have been much lesser than the celebrated document of rights and statecraft that it is. Situating these interventions in the larger trajectory of Indian feminism in which they are rooted, in the nationalist discourse with which they perpetually negotiated, and in the larger human rights discourse of the 1940s, it shows that the women members of the Indian Constituent Assembly were much more than the 'founding mothers' of a republic.

Achyut Chetan teaches at St. Xavier's University, Kolkata. He has received a Fulbright Fellowship at Columbia University and the South Asian Studies Fellowship at Cornell University for his research on the history of Indian feminism and the Indian Constitution. He taught the marginalized students of Santhal Parganas, India, for several years.

SOUTH ASIA IN THE SOCIAL SCIENCES

South Asia has become a laboratory for devising new institutions and practices of modern social life. Forms of capitalist enterprise, providing welfare and social services, the public role of religion, the management of ethnic conflict, popular culture and mass democracy in the countries of the region have shown a marked divergence from known patterns in other parts of the world. South Asia is now being studied for its relevance to the general theoretical understanding of modernity itself.

South Asia in the Social Sciences will feature books that offer innovative research on contemporary South Asia. It will focus on the place of the region in the various global disciplines of the social sciences and highlight research that uses unconventional sources of information and novel research methods. While recognising that most current research is focused on the larger countries, the series will attempt to showcase research on the smaller countries of the region.

General Editor
Partha Chatterjee
Columbia University

Editorial Board
Pranab Bardhan
University of California at Berkeley

Stuart Corbridge
Durham University

Satish Deshpande
University of Delhi

Christophe Jaffrelot
Centre d'etudes et de recherches internationales, Paris

Nivedita Menon
Jawaharlal Nehru University

Other books in the series:

Government as Practice: Democratic Left in a Transforming India
Dwaipayan Bhattacharyya

Courting the People: Public Interest Litigation in Post-Emergency India
Anuj Bhuwania

Development after Statism: Industrial Firms and the Political Economy of South Asia
Adnan Naseemullah

The seal of the Constituent Assembly.

Source: From the letterhead of the Constituent Assembly.

Founding Mothers of the Indian Republic

Gender Politics of the Framing of the Constitution

Achyut Chetan

CAMBRIDGE
UNIVERSITY PRESS

CAMBRIDGE
UNIVERSITY PRESS

Shaftesbury Road, Cambridge CB2 8EA, United Kingdom

One Liberty Plaza, 20th Floor, New York, NY 10006, USA

477 Williamstown Road, Port Melbourne, vic 3207, Australia

314 to 321, 3rd Floor, Plot No.3, Splendor Forum, Jasola District Centre, New Delhi 110025, India

103 Penang Road, #05–06/07, Visioncrest Commercial, Singapore 238467

Cambridge University Press is part of the University of Cambridge.

It furthers the University's mission by disseminating knowledge in the pursuit of education, learning and research at the highest international levels of excellence.

www.cambridge.org
Information on this title: www.cambridge.org/9781108832564

© Achyut Chetan 2022

First published 2022
Reprint 2023 (thrice), 2024, 2025

Printed in India by Repro India Ltd.

A catalogue record for this publication is available from the British Library

ISBN 978-1-108-83256-4 Hardback

For Maa–Babuji

As I stand here at the moment, I imagine myself to be somewhat dreaming. Today the memory of those days comes to my mind when I was a student and perused the part played by Hamilton, Jefferson and others in framing the Constitution of the United States of America. Then I used to wonder if there will ever come a stage when India would emerge from slavery to assume an independent status. I also wondered if we shall ever be competent to frame our own constitution. By the grace of Providence that occasion has come and it is my good fortune that I am indulging in self-praise for being fortunate to play a part Sir, I feel proud to submit that our Constitution has, at last been framed.

—Durgabai Deshmukh
Provisional Parliament of India, 1 February 1950
From *Parliament of India: Official Report of the First Session of Parliament*, Vol. I, 1950, Part II: Proceedings other than Questions and Answers, p. 82

Lakshmikant Maitra: Do not think that I am a hater of women, that I am a misogynist, or that I have no feeling for women.

An honourable member: He is a married man.

Lakshmikant Maitra: Yes, I am a married man. I have a humble wife married according to Hindu Shastric rites, a simple, unsophisticated lady, brought up and nurtured in the ideas of our Hindu homes.

The Hon'ble B. R. Ambedkar: What a pity!

Lakshmikant Maitra: It is pity! May be. But I have not much of love or liking for the lavender, lipstick and vanity bag variety of that sex.

Constituent Assembly (Legislative) of India, 1 March 1949, *CA(L)D* II: 996

Contents

Images

Preface

This book has long been in search of an author and it seems worth sharing with my readers how I stepped into that role. It was the summer of 2005. After my final university exams I had returned to my isolated hometown in Jharkhand – a town that had yet not arrived on the railway map of India – whose growing squalor was encircled by the heart-stopping beauty of a river passing through ancient hills and dense forests. It was here that my father, a bibliophile and an old-school lawyer had painstakingly built over years, a sprawling house. The pride of place was a large airy library, which, given his slender fortunes, was incredibly well-stocked. This was the library that had inculcated in me a curiosity about the world. So, I grew up reading not only story books but also encyclopedias and dictionaries, biographies and histories. It was here that I had encountered as a child the 13 volumes of the *Constituent Assembly Debates*, well-thumbed and underlined in pencil by my father. Little did I know at that age that these volumes would become indispensable for my research and I would pour over them, train my eyes to read their densely printed pages, and sometimes feel exasperated at the volubility of the participants of the Constituent Assembly – they had so much to say. But that was much later, and I must not run ahead of my story and return to the moment when it all began.

One evening we sat in the library and read in companionable silence till my father shut the volume he was reading, rubbed his tired eyes, and asked me what I knew of the women members of the Constituent Assembly? His reason for asking me this question, I realized later, was because I often spoke of feminism, of women activists, writers, and historians – issues that preoccupied me in those days. But his question took me by surprise. I had never heard or read about women participating in the debates of the Constituent Assembly. All the discussions revolved around the 'Founding Fathers' of the Constitution, a group of powerful male politicians like Jawaharlal Nehru, Vallabhbhai Patel, Rajendra Prasad, and of course, B.R. Ambedkar. As he looked at my nonplussed expression, my father shook his head in dismay that his son belonged to that ilk who had read history, law, and political science but continued to remain ignorant of the basic facts. This was indeed the case and baffled me further as I discovered that these were prominent women in their times.

That evening my father lamented, as we all must, that 'We, the People' of India had forgotten the most exceptional women who had given the Constitution to 'ourselves'. He spoke with a degree of confidence about their exceptionality.

Curious, I prodded his memory only to be surprised by what he remembered. They were highly educated women who were intelligent, charming, and had great courage. To my amazement, he recounted the hostilities that Renuka Ray had faced during her campaigns for reforms in Hindu law and described in astounding detail her meeting with President Rajendra Prasad, whose reservations against the Hindu Code Bill were well known, to win him over to her own camp.

He remembered, with some gratitude, his medical treatment at the All India Institute of Medical Sciences (AIIMS) and spoke of Amrit Kaur, India's first Health Minister, responsible for establishing AIIMS and several other institutions of national importance. Amrit Kaur, the princess of Kapurthala, was used to fine silk and precious jewelry, which my father recalled she dropped after becoming an energetic feminist and a widely respected voice of the Indian women's movement. At the time of her death, a few months before Jawaharlal Nehru's, she had several honorary doctorates, including a Doctor of Law from Princeton University. These and other memories were created from a distance, partly imagined, partly from news-reports that had once floated in public memory, but almost always, full of admiration: inaccurate, impressionistic, even irrelevant, yet inviting, and opening new gateways to the past. How could we have forgotten them?

I got some hints of an answer some years later, when I spoke to an eminent Indian historian of my father's generation about these women. To my surprise, her memory spoke differently. She had met some of them in her childhood and youth. She felt they were demure and may not really have added much besides a symbolic, decorative value to the Constituent Assembly. Her condescending remarks about the women founders reflected the attitude that the men of the Constituent Assembly must have had about their female colleagues. Other scholars have expressed similar views asking more counter-historical questions about the absence of these women rather than making queries about their presence: what if these women had not been there? What difference would it have made even if some women had participated in framing the Constitution? These were preemptive questions, suggesting that there was not much of value in my lamentation. A cultural theorist, seemingly influenced by the skewed poststructuralist notion of the 'text', told me that the Constitution is all we have and there is nothing outside its text. Given the prominence of the women founders in the public sphere for several decades, it is difficult to believe that the scholars I was meeting were not aware that they were important figures. What I was, therefore, seeing was a denial of female agency so bold that it seemed willing to deny evidence, or, when confronted with it, misconstrue it. And then there were scholars who, in spite of knowing about the women members, continued to ignore them, relegating them to occasional and imprecise footnotes.

The divergence between my father's memory and that of the eminent historian set the template of the inquiry for me. On the one hand, was a common *man* – a 'common reader' of the Indian Constitution, who, in Virginia Woolf's felicitous description, is 'guided by an instinct to create for himself, out of whatever odds and ends he can come by, some kind of whole',[1] and on the other hand, were well-known academics who smugly assumed that the whole did not really matter. I realized that unencumbered by the need to conform to contemporary critiques of the Constitution, the memory of the common reader is protected by a positive nostalgia. In contrast, the academic, a specialized reader, driven solely by current political/ideological concerns, has already conceived the past as woefully lacking and is prepared to preclude historical enquiry. In this judgmental position, any aura of 'extra'-ordinariness that may have lingered around the women members of the Constituent Assembly erodes in conjunction with the reading of the Constitution. Consequently, women founders become a victim of the text that they had produced in 'those' times.

I had retained my faith in the common reader also because as a student in a literature department, I had under come under the influence of an exceptional faculty member. Since this book is also an act of rebellion against the politics of anonymity, I name her here. Swati Ganguly, the only feminist faculty member in a large literature department was exceptional in the conflation of her two identities as a reader – the common and the uncommon reader at once. As a common feminist reader, she had shown us how to read women's voices in texts produced by, for, and against women. But it was as an uncommon feminist reader that she gave us, both in her lectures and informal discussions, what emerged as valuable for my work: to be alert to the pitfalls of a feminist criticism that fails to recognize the distinction between will and consent. Feminist genealogies, especially those pertaining to social and political thought, have been impervious to this distinction, and often confuse what was a response to a specific occasion with the general design of the women's movement. This has made it difficult to appreciate the ingenious modes in which feminist ideas have developed in the context of the Constitution and its framing.

Women's engagement in the three-year long framing process, in times of great turbulence that generated compelling ethical questions, can only be understood if sufficient attention is paid to the specific context in which they made their enunciations during the making of the Constitution. It is through the dynamics of will, consent, and, frequently enough, dissent, that women members carried the feminist movement through and beyond the Constituent Assembly. Each article of the Constitution, therefore, is a point of diffraction in the history of Indian feminism. The Constitution is drafted not just by the consent of women but also by their will.

This work does not make any claim to be an exhaustive account of women's participation in the making of the Constitution of India. Indeed, such a task is impossible given the staggering range of their interventions in the framing debates, several of which I have not even been able to touch upon; for instance, the language question. I think of this book as an invitation to historians, constitutional scholars, feminists, political theorists, and other readers to think about the Constitution. The invitation is to pay attention to women's constitutional politics – a politics of petitions, charters, and memoranda; to examine the discursive spaces of the Parliament, which was once also occupied by feminists; to notice the unique contexts in which feminist thought developed in India. Constitutional theorists may find something of value in the idea of originalism.

I return the counter-historical gaze by drawing attention, whenever possible, to the damage that we have incurred by forgetting and misremembering the founding mothers. Over the years I have come to the conclusion that forgetting is less injurious than misremembering. The course of unforgetting that I have undertaken has been accentuated by my emphasis on clearing some theoretical prejudices and also developing a healthy scepticism about its indispensability.

When I began my forays into this field of enquiry, I was enamoured by poststructuralist ideas of author and text, author function and its relationship with authority that presented me with a seductive matrix of reading. This I decided would be my theoretical framework for understanding the author function of the Constitution. I may have pursued my study along these lines had I not been called by the archives. The archives completely transformed the direction of my inquiry and I began seeing the past like a feminist historian. As I read their letters, notes, and other documents preserved in files, a fascinating narrative began to emerge. Since most women members were familiar with constitutional politics in their own organizations, they were adept at writing petitions, notes, and documents; adept at strategizing to put across their ideas in an overwhelmingly masculine set-up of powerful male politicians and lawyers. But the archives also revealed that these women were strong allies, whose bonds were of sorority and affect. They spoke on behalf of each other in meetings, guarded each other's secrets, and wrote endearing letters to each other, signing off 'with love'. As I read these letters and notes, these women – authors of the book of the nation – gradually began to come alive in my imagination. They were characters in search of an author who would *discover* and *remember* them. Since I became that author, I may only hope that this book will lead the common and the uncommon reader alike to the 'contrived corridors' of the founding narrative, following, as it does, the footprints of the mothers of the republic.

NOTE

1.   Virginia Woolf, *The Common Reader* (London: Vintage, 2003; originally 1925), 1.

Acknowledgements

In Kafka's other story about metamorphosis, 'A Report to an Academy', Red Peter, an ape, reports to a conference of scientists on the process of his becoming one with human beings, and attaining the average education of a European, including music, with an effort that had no parallels in the history of either of the two species.[1] The effort was put in as much by his human teachers, some of whom themselves became apes in the process, as by the ape. For me, the writing of this book has been a journey from apedom into the 'freedom' of academia, a journey of 15 years: 'not much perhaps in calendar terms, but an eternity to have had to gallop through as I have done, variously helped on my way by persons, advice, applause or orchestra music – all of them excellent'.[2]

For Red Peter, the desire to perfect the habits of human beings come from the desire to be free. This desire was ambivalent for me since my unfreedom was a result of my own choice of teaching students from the most underprivileged sections of my hometown in a marginal corner of the state of Jharkhand. Bringing constitutional values, especially the feminist ones upheld by the founding mothers, into one's pedagogy even as one was rediscovering them through research was a challenge for which, unfortunately, I had no training. The fact that this book has been finally written against unspeakable hostilities and obstructions makes all the people I want to thank, named and unnamed, very special in my life. That this list is still so long, and incomplete is evidence of hope. There is no intellectual debt as I realize from my experience in these long years in which is not an emotional debt, and vice versa.

Professors Sudipta Kaviraj and Partha Chatterjee have been intellectual custodians of the work from its very beginning and it is my great fortune that they have continued to rescue me from intellectual follies. Sudipta-da helped me untie several interdisciplinary knots that had blocked my work, and gave me the necessary courage to enter fields that were formidably closed to me in the initial days of my research. Partha-da showed similar faith and guided me to the most relevant archives at a time when I was finding myself at the dead ends of many misplaced enquiries. It is an expression of his faith in my work that this book is being published. I must add the name of Professor Gayatri Chakravorty Spivak whose keen insights into the nuances of feminist, deconstructionist reading of the archives, and faith in the reader of literary texts to venture into uncharted fields have been a source of strength for me. I thank the three Columbia professors named above for never letting my location in the marginal non-academic space of Dumka obstruct my access to their support and encouragement.

Many years after my reading of Geraldine Forbes's volume on women in modern India – each of its footnotes leading to several passages of historical enquiries – I found my way through some of them through her collections at the British Library archives. Later I had opportunities to have warm conversations about Indian women and feminist historiography with her that helped me to correct a few problems with my perspective. She read through the entire manuscript with an editor's diligence, a scholar's sharpness, and a teacher's empathy. Personally, for me, to thank her would be both impertinent and impossible, yet I would like to express my gratitude to her on behalf of all scholars of modern women's history of our generation.

Professor Abhijit Sen of the Department of English, Visva-Bharati, and Janaki Bakhle, Professor of History at Columbia University (currently at the University of California at Berkeley), had been my official advisors during my doctoral research, and deserve my thanks for keeping the work anchored during that period.

I am indebted to the two anonymous reviewers for their precious comments on both the content and form of the work. Several oversights that could have led to profound loopholes in my readings have been avoided because of their suggestions. Scholars who read earlier drafts or parts of it have improved it with their valuable suggestions. They include Kalpana Kannabiran, Paromita Chakravarti, Nandini Sundar, and Kavita Panjabi. Conversations with Sarmishta Dutta Gupta, Nicholas Dirks, and Vivek Kumar have also helped with some important formulations. I thank each one of them. I thank Aziz Rana of Cornell Law School for sharing his thoughts on originalism in the context of Indian Constitutionalism. Stimulating discussions with Rajdeep Konar provided important insights into the performative aspects of the Constituent Assembly.

Archival research for this work has been supported by fellowships and grants by institutions to which I am indebted. Sir Ratan Tata Trust made possible an early research in the specialized library of the School of Women's Studies, Jadavpur University. Work at the archives of the Women's Library at the London School of Economics and at the British Library, London was made possible thanks to a Charles Wallace India Trust Fellowship and the British Council. The Fulbright Fellowship at Columbia University, New York was of immense help in shaping the work in the foundational stage. The South Asian Studies Fellowship at Cornell University, last year, brought me what has so far been the most uninterrupted stretch of writing and research in my life. Iftikhar Dadi and Daniel Bass, the Director and Manager of the wonderful South Asia Program at Cornell are remembered with a gratitude that borders on nostalgia for the ambience that only a campus like Cornell's could provide.

The libraries at the School of Women's Studies, Jadavpur University, Kolkata and the Indian Council of World Affairs, New Delhi; the Nehru Memorial Museum and Library, New Delhi; the National Archives of India, New Delhi; Butler Library and Lehman Library, Columbia University, New York; and the New York Public Library, New York, deserve my heart-felt gratitude. A major portion of this work was written at the Kroch Library of Cornell University, a library that holds a special place in my heart. Alison Cummerson of the London School of Economics Library and Jyoti Luthra of the Nehru Memorial Museum and Library deserve special thanks for their support in providing access to rare resources at very short notices.

I am grateful to several institutions for inviting me to speak about my work while it was still in progress. These include the Seagull Foundation for the Arts; Takshila Education Society; Presidency University, Kolkata; Jawaharlal Nehru University; University of Hyderabad; and Ashoka University in India; University of Texas at Austin; Columbia University; Brooklyn College; and Cornell University in the USA. The contribution of the incisive comments I received from the audience during these talks in shaping my thoughts is gratefully acknowledged.

I also wish to put on record my gratitude to St. Xavier's University, Kolkata for its support. To the Vice Chancellor, Rev. Father Felix Raj, S. J., I owe my sincerest gratitude for agreeing to grant me leave in the middle of a hectic semester to work on the final draft of the book. My colleagues in the Department of English – Antara, Ananya, Indira, Medha, Prayag, Prodosh, and Sonali – have been the most supportive of colleagues, always willing to accommodate my whims and needs so that I could complete the work in the most grueling of circumstances. I am grateful to each one of them. Among my colleagues at my previous institution,

I am particularly grateful to Professors Prashant, Swatantra Kumar Singh and Ajoy Sinha for their support and Amita, Varsha, and Mihir for their camaraderie and academic solidarity.

The book has taken me to cities where I discovered and rediscovered souls whose care – often parental – gave me sustenance in crucial ways at crucial times. K. P. Das and Gautami Das, Sudipta and Nilanjana Kaviraj, and Arijit and Swapna Banerjee in New York; Arundhati Lahiri and Anirban Lahiri in London; and Antonia Shouse at Ithaca gave me homes away from home. I am profoundly indebted to their kindness and support.

At Cornell, where I could do the most rigorous work that has gone into the making of this book, I had the support of two of the most amazing friends, Antonia Shouse, conscientious world citizen who gives new meaning to the words 'right' and 'care' with every yes or no that she utters, and Nipun Prabhakar, artist, photographer, activist ever-brimming with new ideas and thought. Among the people whose gratitude the book has incurred at Cornell, I must name Professors Kaushik Basu and Alaka Basu for their warm support, and Anya Golovkova, Abdullah Shahid, Palashi Waghela, and Rewa Palshikar for their friendship. In Kolkata, thanks to Amitesh Mukherjee, I have the most conducive home one could have to complete a draft in a pandemic stricken city. 'Usharko' at Santiniketan – the residence of Bratindranath Chattopadhyay and Srilekha Chattopadhyay – has nurtured me in ways for which I owe them my deepest gratitude.

My former and current students have fortified me with an unassailable care against assaults that were savage enough to have nearly destroyed the work. Over the years, I have learnt to think of them as my children and listing them here would be nothing short of belittling these young friends. Yet I would like to place on record my debt to the exceptional courage and ethical discretions of Horen Hansdak, Joanna Tudu, Anju Baskey, Nikita Hembrom, Saul Soren, Sushila Murmu, and Prity Kisku who vindicated my faith in my idea of constitutional morality when confronted with difficult choices. To Divya, Chanchala, Raju, Shweta, Deepshikha, Abu Solhe, Lalit, Naman, Rishabh, Deepak, Megha, Sunandita, Aditya, Kunal, Shivam, Ganesh, Shristi, Sagar, Swati, Jitesh, and Shambhavi I owe special gratitude for sustaining the feminist teacher in me against the odds of a deeply misogynist pedagogy. Since this is also a record of solidarity, I must add the names of Soma Mukhopadhyay and Shromona Das to this list. My fondest thanks to all of them.

Kainaat Ghazal, Anindita Patra, Namrata Pandey, and Sanghamitra Baladhikari relentlessly worked as a team of dependable research assistants who kept me supplied with the relevant references and curated archival notes on demand through exchanges of emails during an unprecedented lockdown. Raghav Mani and Kanchan Maji know what they have done is incomparable and my debt to them cannot be put in words. Apart from painstakingly verifying all the endnotes, they also helped me in preparing the chronology for the Appendix. Preparing the final draft of the book in times of such crisis as the unprecedented lockdown and paralyzing pandemic have brought in would not have been possible without their help. To this, I must add the names of Father Devraj, Paloma Chaterji, Priyanka Bharadwaj, Ayesha Salma, Priyashi, Manasi Patra, Lovely Majumdar, and Gennia Nuh. Arijit has been a taskforce unto himself, always ready to fulfil my relentless demands and extend all possible technical support. My students at SXUDE have also been a great support in these overwhelming times. I profusely thank of all of them.

I have only a few friends who have supported me emotionally over the decades. I thank them without naming them. They know who they are. Yet a special word of thanks to Neha Hui, friend for two decades, who has been my online library, ever ready to hunt articles and books and make them available to me all the way from London. Nitesh Hemraj, childhood friend, knows what I owe him.

At one level, this volume is about the production of a book, and about women's hand in it. It could not be more fitting that from the very day that the rough draft of the manuscript arrived at her desk and to the moment it sees the light of the day, it has been in the hands of a team comprising mostly women – Anwesha Rana and Anwesha Roy – and led by the ever-dependable Qudsiya Ahmed, whose friendship has been a unique gift to the author. It is Qudsiya's faith in my ability to complete the work in the most distressing of circumstances – a pandemic that has gagged even our right to mourn, her own ability to cheer others up while dealing with stressful conditions herself, and diligently planning strategies that could defeat all adversities – that has made the book possible in the most literal sense of the term. I am ever grateful to Aniruddha De providing me the help of a most meticulous research assistant. Had it not been for his support, there would have been many more errors in the book than there are now!

At Dumka, my home is bigger than the town. The squalor of the town and the fossils and the forests that surround it make my home look like the work of a miracle. My parents, Lalita Sinha and Balram Sahay, have built a house against the grain: bricked with books and suffused with an anomalous love for learning in a place hostile to academic pursuits. Like the missing mothers who are the protagonists of this book, my mother has also perfected the art of laying foundations in silence. As the youngest, I was spared the hardships that my siblings had to endure, often on my behalf. My brother, Achyut Keshav, a lawyer, legal commentator, and scholar in his own right, has continued the family tradition in his own ways and has been of great support in the writing of the book, especially in my understanding of the judicial pronouncements and nuances of constitutional law. My sisters, Atima Smiti and Shuchismita, have provided moral support and encouragement throughout the period. Atima Smiti, in fact carried tonnes of books for me from Mumbai, including the multi-volume writings of B. R. Ambedkar. The children in the family, Abhijit, Akshay, Satyarth, and Alakshya, deserve special affection and thanks for the support that they did not understand they were providing. This is not true for Satyarth, who with his precocious emotional intelligence stood by me in times of severe stress. The book emerges from the same home, partly as a token of gratitude and partly as an anomaly my work has always been.

In the decade-long course of this research, I have been unfairly fortunate in getting the support and care of Swati Ganguly: exemplary feminist, extraordinary friend, exceptional reader. She set me deadlines, patiently revised numerous clumsy drafts, and together we thrashed every idea in the book. Having been there from its most uncertain beginnings to the completion of the work, she resurrected the work on many occasions when I lost faith in it. This is as much her book, as it is mine – if not more. The faults, of course, are my notes of dissent. Besides standing with me in all crises mentioned and unmentioned, she has exemplified feminist solidarity like nobody else and has lived by a constitutional faith that may be deserves to be called the basic argument of the founding mothers: an inviolable conviction in the possibility of bringing love and justice together.

NOTES

1. Franz Kafka, 'A Report to an Academy', in *Metamorphosis and Other Stories*, trans. Michael Hofmann (London: Penguin Books, 2015).
2. Ibid., 195.

Abbreviations

AICC	All India Congress Committee
AIIMS	All India Institute of Medical Sciences
AIR	All India Reporter
AISCF	All India Scheduled Castes Federation
AIWC	All India Women's Conference
CSWI	Committee on the Status of Women in India
ILO	International Labour Organization
CAD	*Constituent Assembly Debates*
CA(L)D	*Constituent Assembly of India (Legislative) Debates*
NCWI	National Council of Women in India
NMML	Nehru Memorial Museum and Library
RSS	Rashtriya Swayamsevak Sangh
SCC	Supreme Court Cases
SCR	Supreme Court Reports
UDHR	Universal Declaration of Human Rights
UN	United Nations
WIA	Women's Indian Association

Introduction

Towards a Feminist Reading of the Making of the Constitution

The original Indian Constitution, handwritten in brilliant calligraphy and adorned with motifs and sketches on the margins of the pages by the great artist Nandalal Bose and his students, was finally self-dedicated by representatives of 'We, the people' on 24 January 1950. The signatories on this much-adorned document that day, one discovers, included 11 women. They were: G. Durgabai,[1] Ammu Swaminathan, Amrit Kaur, Dakshayani Velayudhan, Hansa Mehta, Renuka Ray, Sucheta Kripalani, Purnima Banerji, Begum Qudsiya Aizaz Rasul, Kamala Chaudhri, and Annie Mascarene.[2] More than their signatures on the adorned version, it is their presence on the Constitutional text – traces of their valuable interventions in the writing of the Constitution – that I seek to recover in this book. Historical records and the official documents of the Constituent Assembly show that women's presence in this momentous process was indeed an act of will, a comprehensive act of commitment to principles and ideals that they articulated through the text that was enacted to inaugurate the republic.

Though they were only a few in number, we need to *re-turn* to these forgotten women and *re-member* them as integral to the Constituent Assembly as its 'missing mothers'. In so doing, I address, among other issues, the politics of their erasure, and then attempt a revisionary account of their significant contributions to the making of the Constitution. These contributions were not limited only to addressing and redefining what is understood as the 'woman question' but extended, among others, to debating on and shaping the very fundamental principles that constitute the ideals of Indian democracy. An account of their participation can neither be a footnote to the narrative of constitution-making in India nor to the history of Indian feminism.

The Constituent Assembly first met on 11 December 1946 and had 169 sessions before its members finally put their signatures on the document on 24 January 1950. Its members met on an equal number of occasions

Image I.1 On the same page. Signatures of some members of the Constituent Assembly. Those clearly identifiable are of Amrit Kaur, Vallabhbhai Patel, Jagjivan Ram, B. R. Ambedkar, and Syama Prasad Mookerjee; in the right column are Dakshayani Velayudhan and B. Shiva Rao.

Note: Signatures on this page of the original copy of the Constitution, literally and metaphorically, showcase the entire diversity of positions that came together in its framing.

in sessions when it performed the role of a legislature – the Constituent Assembly (Legislative) – from 15 August 1947 to the day of the adoption of the Constitution. Its career, thus, spanned a period of more than three years. In the course of the framing of the Constitution, thousands of documents, including questionnaires, status reports, memoranda, and amendments, were produced by the Assembly and its numerous committees. The Assembly's work generated a considerable number of reports and discussions in the Indian and international media, which influenced its decisions. The framing was a wide and complex process that involved an enormous number of people, who spoke – formally and informally – in the name of 'We, the People' (Image I.1).

Who spoke for 'We, the People'? At first glance this question does not appear to be puzzling and indeed has a ready response in the collective as well as official memory of the nation: B. R. Ambedkar, Jawaharlal Nehru, Vallabhbhai Patel, and the other members of the Constituent Assembly. They were the unquestioned 'founding fathers' of the republic. However, if one ponders over the phrase 'founding fathers', which seems ubiquitous and unquestionable in current discourse, it is possible to harbour a sceptical response. This hermeneutic informs this book and invites a resisting reader to journey through the mazes of constitutional history with an affirmative suspicion.

A FEMINIST *RE-MEMBERING*: THE WOMEN MAKERS OF THE REPUBLIC

Women had striven hard to get elected to the Constituent Assembly, employing ingenious methods of democratic politics and feminist propaganda. They formed a distinct group in that august body, spoke in a distinct feminist parlance, and shared a constitutional vision of justice to such an extent that they can collectively be called the 'mothers' of the Indian Constitution. One can discover threads of authorial intentions that converged on the women members' overlapping desires to address women's issues and to contribute to the founding of a democracy which must treat women as citizens with equal rights and complete opportunities for self-expression.

Hansa Mehta, Amrit Kaur, Renuka Ray, Aizaz Rasul, Ammu Swaminathan, Purnima Banerji, and Sucheta Kripalani had been at the vanguard of the All India Women's Conference (AIWC) since its foundation in 1927, and G. Durgabai and Dakshayani Velayudhan in their own ways had been actively engaged in expanding the ambit of the woman question before they had joined the Constituent Assembly. Together, they engaged with the central problematics of feminist politics of their times and endeavoured to find solutions that would suit the best interests and ideals of a democratic state envisaged by the Constitution. Not only did they aspire to frame a Constitution that would make the state 'a great moral agency' but articulated the content of its agency, often circumscribing it with feminist demands and cautions.[3]

Even when they offered different solutions, they framed the problems in one voice, an inheritance of a women's movement whose organizational and intellectual history provided a robust background to their interventions in the founding process. The task that I set in this book is to establish these women framers, especially those associated with the AIWC, as authors of the Constitution of India, deliberately presenting them, in a lavish stroke of counter-rhetorical performance, as 'the mothers' of the Constitution. This is not to reduce them to their gendered identities and imply that all their interventions during the constitution-making process were made as women; nor is it to suggest that all of them converged on all issues and their differences did not matter to the framing process. This is also not exactly to construct these women as what Michel Foucault calls an author-function: as a 'principle of a certain unity of writing' that 'serves to neutralize the contradictions that may emerge in a series of texts'. While the women framers can serve as an alternative author-function, they must not be seen as just another tool to regulate the meaning of the constitutional text. Instead, their recovery should lead to the exposure of such processes through which interpretive fields have been neglectful of women's presence in the past.[4]

My purpose is to designate them as authors of the text of the Constitution, who, as historically situated individuals, came together into a negotiation regarding the rights of women with other actors at a moment that is waiting to be discovered for feminist politics. More precisely, it is an attempt to identify modes in which these women and their voices can inflect discourse on the Indian Constitution. Fortunately, the energy with which feminist and postcolonial literary theory raise doubts about the transparency and innocence of all knowledge has made it is impossible to take this received understanding about the Constitution on faith. Further, there is a suspicion of metaphor, particularly a public metaphor, 'that common substratum of the representation of institutions', and its metaphorical field that subsumes our understanding and makes us complicit in a play of power.[5] The figure of the 'founding fathers' is a profoundly disturbing metaphor with its ideological residue and immense hold on the postcolonial imagination. This book is provoked by the endurance of this metaphor and its ability to inflect the disciplines of constitutional history and law within a certain compass. Its implied asymmetry, naturalised within the idioms of the postcolonial nation-state, does not merely dislocate and erase women, or 'mothers', but invests a phallocentric logic at the heart of the narrative of its founding.

Why have these women not figured in discussions about the framing of the Constitution? Is it because of an a priori understanding that their roles were negligible and hence not worthy of attention? Was it understood that these token women had managed to gain membership of the Constituent Assembly not by virtue of their ability but solely because of the benevolence of powerful patriarchs? Do such assumptions not loudly proclaim the gender politics of scholarship itself? What would an alert feminist researcher discover if she or he paid attention to their presence and took cognizance of their engagement and contribution by going to the archives neglected in history?

The erasure of women from constitutional history has been the result of a double assault on their memory from two different theoretical approaches: the poststructuralist enterprise of the de-centring of the subject, and the social contract theory in the liberal tradition. The former (discussed in the next chapter), in denying any primacy to authorial agency of the male or female subject, precludes the possibility of remembering women as subjects who contributed to the Constitution. Works in the latter tradition continue to think of the male members of the Constituent Assembly as the sole liberal humanist subject invested with agency and authority. The eternally perpetuated narrative of the social contract, as Carole Pateman has shown, is a patriarchal fiction, 'a modern story of masculine political birth'.[6] The story presupposes that women who are 'naturally deficient in a specifically *political* capacity, the capacity to create and maintain political right', are incapable of entering into a contract.[7] The story is 'an example of the appropriation by men of the awesome gift that nature has denied them and its transmutation into masculine political creativity'.[8]

By agreeing that it is the founding fathers who gave us the Constitution, we submit our imagination to this political fiction. By circulating it further, we invest the act of paternity with the social authority that motherhood has been denied in the realm of politics. Most importantly, we imagine that unlike natural birth which could produce a male or female child, the act of political creativity, invested solely in men, produced a Constitution after the image of only the fathers, and read within its text a tapestry of 'vicious patriarchal logic'.[9] The theoretical presumption that the logic of constitution-making is inherently patriarchal and it 'perpetuates women's legal subordination'[10] does not allow historians who approach the framing from a social contract framework to think of searching for empirical evidence that proves the contrary. They readily think of the Constitution as a text of compromise rather than as an expression of women's will. One of these scholars, Christine Keating, writes:

> the Constituent Assembly struggled to reconcile their commitment to an egalitarian polity with their efforts to build consent for the political authority of the new Indian state ... the assembly settled on a *compromise*, what I call the postcolonial sexual contract, to resolve that dilemma: they established equality in the public sphere as a fundamental right for women yet sanctioned discriminatory personal laws that maintained women's subordination in the family in order to secure fraternal acquiescence to centralized rule.[11]

This compromise, Keating argues, is 'the central component of a postcolonial social contract, a new form of the social contract that both advances and compromises gender, caste and minority group rights'.[12] Not once in her explication does she grant the possibility that, at its originary moment, this contract was between 'the founding fathers' and 'the founding mothers'; instead she seems to assume that the 'compromise' was between men.

EXAMINING THE CATEGORY 'FOUNDING MOTHERS'

Though few in number, these women played a significant role in the *Constituent Assembly Debates*, either through direct interventions, comments, or rejoinders on the floor of the assembly, or by evolving strategies among themselves to ensure that certain issues were brought up in the debates.

I use the phrase 'missing mothers' for these women, who have been virtually erased from history through a gender politics of scholarship on the making of the Constitution. 'Missing mothers' serves as a reminder of the sexism inherent in a constitutional discourse which is suffused with paternalist metaphors and patriarchal prejudices, and reclaims the space for a feminist politics. One might also read the phrase as a reminder of the rhetorical value assigned to women as mothers within the nationalist discourse that had culminated in the making of the Constitution, and deploy it as a corrective to the skewed view of an event that is of momentous significance – the birth of the nation. I deliberately use the phrase 'missing mothers' for the chapter in which I introduce them and substantiate my claims about their considerable achievement. Thereafter, the thrust of my work is to move toward establishing them as the founding mothers of the republic (Image I.2).

Capable and courageous, these founding mothers conferred with each other and evolved strategies to present a consolidated women's position to challenge patriarchy. This is not to deny or erase the complexity involved

Image I.2 A few women amongst men. All members of the Constituent Assembly
sitting together towards the end of its sessions, probably around November
1949.

Source: Photos of the making of the Constitution, Department of Justice, Ministry of Law and Justice,
Government of India (https://doj.gov.in/page/photos-making-constitution, accessed on 17 June
2021).

in the women's negotiations among themselves since their class, caste, and
community affiliations were richly different. For instance, the dimension
of class that seems to have somehow disappeared from discussions on the
Constituent Assembly emerges prominently in the case of Qudsia Aizaz
Rasul. A member of a landed Muslim family, Rasul wanted to protect the
interests of her class as is borne out by the debates between her on the one
hand and socialist women like Renuka Ray and Purnima Banerji on the other.

Also difficult is locating the voice of Dakshayani Velayudhan, the sole Dalit
woman in the Constituent Assembly. Her bold assertions against the British
combined with her critiques of the collective wisdom of the Constituent
Assembly on some issues are evidence of a distinct subjectivity that refuses to
be drowned in any dominant narrative. In spite of her own reservations about
what she perceived as the elitism of the women's movement, on questions
of gender equality and the desirability of a decentralized socialist state, she
reached the same conclusions as her other female colleagues and spoke *with*
them even if not exactly in their words. It might be worth mentioning that her
positions ran contrary to Ambedkar's on separate electorates and reservations.
Dakshayani wanted to enhance the representative potential of the Dalit, who,
she claimed, could represent the entire Hindu community.[13]

For upper-caste women, too, the standard strategy and ethic of participation was the same as Dakshayani's. In their search for an acceptable constitutional morality, the upper-caste women would often project 'lower caste' social practices as ideal models for legal and social reform, and culled rationales from these that could be woven into the fundamental principles of the Constitution. Individual women often took distinct positions and negotiated with the Assembly on questions about the definition of 'minority', the autonomy of communities, and the measures for social reform within the framework of class, community, and caste. Nevertheless, a discernible gendered perspective informed all their interventions. Being alert to these differences and remembering how gender identities are necessarily constituted within these intersections, a sensitive reading of the archives also reveals the possibility of feminist solidarities at a critical juncture of Indian history – the making of the republic. Women's interventions during debates on questions of class, religion, caste, minority, and citizenship reveal several interesting configurations of these possibilities and need to be explained with reference to their proper historical contexts.

Reading their interventions juxtaposed with B. R. Ambedkar's positions on these issues in a historicized context shows the strategic and conceptual overlaps between their views. For women, the challenge was to eschew positions derived from their caste and class associations in order to present a consolidated women's position, a task in which they achieved significant success. This is not surprising given the fact that in spite of the diverse composition, most of the women came from similar backgrounds, were engaged in a feminist movement of solidarity, and had established women as an important constituency for both the colonial government and nationalist politics in the years prior to formal decolonization and constitution-making. An understanding of this earlier history is crucial to recognize that these women brought in a feminist authorial voice to the Constituent Assembly and gendered the debates that went into the Constitution of India.

Conventional constitutional theory eschews an engagement with questions of contingency and indeterminacy of the collective proper noun 'We, the people', and instead relies upon the straightforward connection between the historical facts of the framing and the normative authority of constitutions. Leading theorists of constitutional authorship are uncomfortable with the author–reader frame of interpretation of constitutional history and fear that a search for a historical authority for the legitimacy of a constitution may prove to be infinitely regressive. In India, for example, the case for the Constituent Assembly as a legitimate source of authority is built on the historical sanctity of the nationalist movement and its demand for constitutional autonomy.

A Dalit critique may locate this authority in the pre-Independence Indian movement against caste inequality. This could either, like Periyar, through 'painstaking descriptions and interrogations of the proceedings of the Constituent Assembly' reject the Constitution of India for 'enabling and legitimizing the persistence of caste',[14] or seek to emphasize the authority of B. R. Ambedkar in the drafting process. Similarly, a feminist project in search of the authority–authorship of the Constitution may locate it in the women's movement that preceded the formation of the Constituent Assembly. In turn, a Dalit feminist position may critique this authority by challenging the claims of representation of the women's movement and exploring the caste-politics implicit in its modes of operation.[15] It may also build upon collapsing the binary of the public politics of Ambedkar as an author of the Constitution and the gender politics of his private life.[16] None of these would be accurate and possible without a historized assertion of women's place in the august Assembly of the founders of the nation-state. The project of such an assertion, so far, has been half-hearted and severely compromised by theoretical premises that need to be examined.

Such an assertion can only be performed in full awareness of the contingency of the origins of constitutions, particularly in postcolonial contexts like India.[17] It is a task that requires a constant search for the empirical evidence of women's participation and also a certain scepticism about any methodological boundary that is grounded in inherited categories of classifying their discourses.

FRAMING THE FEMINIST INQUIRY: THE STRUCTURE OF THE BOOK

There are several stages through which I attempt to address the failure of historiography and constitutional discourse to come together in such ways as can recognize women as important actors in the making of the Constitution. The preliminary step is to identify the theoretical and empirical prejudices that have blocked women from view. These prejudices – discussed in detail in the next chapter – are contained in the phrase 'founding fathers', the persistence of which in Indian constitutional discourse, both classic and contemporary, confirms the patriarchal pattern of constitutional studies. Since these prejudices inform significant academic contributions, it is important to engage with them critically. I do this, first, by denaturalizing the myth of paternity and showing the male members of the Constituent Assembly as embedded masculine subjects with their own interests and rationality and, second, by challenging the gendered assumptions regarding women's abilities and inclination.

The second step in this project of reclaiming the Constitution's authorship for women has entailed the pushing of the limits of the archives. A statist perspective on what constitutes the archive reinforces the amnesia towards women. Therefore, a revisionist work like this must also revise the defined territories of the archives. If authorship involves the articulation of a set of principles and giving a determinate shape to a moral imagination, then its authority must be traced to those principles and imagination as well as to the author's attempts to explicate them. The archives of women's constitutional authorship must be painstakingly built from private correspondence, petitions, memoranda, journalistic writings, speeches, and other forms of discourse through which a set of democratic and constitutional ideals were consolidated by these women much before they entered the portals of the Constituent Assembly. The intellectual histories of the women members must try to reconstruct the caste, class, and community configurations of their ideas and experiences, as women as well as members of the anti-caste movement or as opponents of fundamentalist forces. These arguments constitute the second and third chapters of the work where I show the complexity of women's struggles – both individual and collective – to get elected to the constitution-making body and its implications. The third chapter visits the preparatory phase of the 1930s and 1940s and traces their moral imagination that was shaped by their constitutional politics of these decades.

Recovering women's interventions in the Constituent Assembly is the next step. The fourth chapter elaborates on the necessary modes in which this can be done. This involves a critical reading of women's strategies to inscribe their voices in the framing discourses, particularly regarding issues related to women. Our failure to listen to women's voices during the framing is a result of our inability to look for them in the right places. This is partly because serious attention has not been paid to the interior spaces of the Assembly and women's location in its intricate architecture. Closely looking at the smaller, more formal spaces of the Committees of the Assembly, this chapter recovers women members' articulations of the most fundamental propositions regarding the fundamental rights and directive principles. I also argue that a complete recovery of the authorial intention of women members of the Constituent Assembly – or, for that matter, of its male members as well – is not possible without examining their parallel performance in the Assembly when it served as a legislature.

A close reading of women's interventions seeks to establish both an epistemological continuity in their moral imaginary throughout the decades of the 1930s and 1940s, including the years of the framing, and an internal consistency in their moral voice. The fifth chapter examines women's interventions in the Constituent Assembly on questions of rights, state, federalism, secularism, and education. They spoke as a collective and brought into the framing of India's Constitution a distinct moral vision. Some of their interventions did not achieve the desired results, yet they persisted tirelessly to bend the moral arc of the text in the direction they wanted.

The sixth chapter takes the reader to the heart of 'the woman question' and its proposed resolution by the founding mothers. The Constitution was framed in times of great turbulence. Debates on the 'Partition' and the attendant violence on women of the two newly created nation-states, the furious arguments on the codification of Hindu personal law and the contested redefinition of woman as daughter–wife–mother, and the emergence of the new woman as a rights-bearing citizen took place in the Constituent Assembly in its parallel legislative sessions. Women's interventions in these sessions gave an entirely new meaning to the woman question, and inflected the constitution-making discourse in significant ways which we need to recover in these times more than ever.

Finally, I examine the possibility of interpreting the Constitution in ways the founding mothers would have done. This is a process they had themselves initiated as soon as the Constitution had been framed and continued doing so until the end of their lives. The immense archives of women's voices in the Constituent Assembly go far beyond the interventions that are examined in this work. Women participated with great vigour in debates on the fundamental right to property, brought in their unique pan-Indian and inter-regional perspective on the contentious question of language, debated on the need and relevance of the Upper House of the Legislatures, intervened in debates on the representative potentials of the members of legislative houses, contributed to discussions on the appointment of Governors, and offered constructive advice on the independence of the judiciary. Through their interventions, they left indelible marks on the Constitution, waiting to be re-examined from several perspectives so that their full semantic forces can be explored in the wider interests of the republic. A first step in this direction, this book invites us to turn towards a feminist reading of the making of the Constitution of India.

NOTES

1. Gummidithala Durgabai. After her marriage to Chitamani Deshmukh, in January 1953, known as Durgabai Deshmukh. In this book she is referred to as Durgabai or G. Durgabai.

2. In its initial election, the Constituent Assembly had fifteen women members, six of whom – Malati Choudhury, Vijayalakshmi Pandit, Sarojini Naidu, Begam Jahanara Shahnawaz, Leela Roy, and Begum Shaista Ikramulla – resigned from its membership at different stages. Two women, Renuka Ray and Anne Mascarene, were elected in the middle of its sessions.

3. Amrit Kaur, *Challenge to Women* (Allahabad: New Literature, 1946), 153.

4. Michel Foucault, 'What Is an Author?', in James Faubion (ed.), *Essential Works of Michel Foucault: Aesthetics, Method, and Epistemology*, 206–222 (London: Penguin, 2000), 215.

5. David Punter, *Metaphor* (London and New York: Routledge, 2007), 46.

6. Carole Pateman, *The Sexual Contract* (Stanford: Stanford University Press, 1988), 102.

7. Ibid., 96.

8. Ibid., 102. For a robust and provocative feminist critique of the patriarchal prejudices embedded in the social contract tradition and accounts of political creativity, see Carole Pateman, 'Genesis, Fathers, and the Political Liberty of the Sons', which is chapter 4 of *The Sexual Contract*, 76–115.

9. Upendra Baxi, 'The (Im)possibility of Constitutional Justice', in Zoya Hasan, E. Sridharan, and R. Sudarshan (eds), *India's Living Constitution: Ideas, Practices, Controversies*, 31–63 (New Delhi: Permanent Black, 2002), 53.

10. Christine Keating, 'Framing the Postcolonial Sexual Contract: Democracy, Fraternalism, and State Authority in India', *Hypatia* 2, no. 2 (2007): 130–145, 130.

11. Ibid., 131 (emphasis mine).

12. Christine Keating, *Decolonizing Democracy: Transforming the Social Contract in India* (Pennsylvania: Pennsylvania State University Press, 2011), 16.

13. Dakshayani Velayudhan, Constituent Assembly of India, 24 January 1947, *Constituent Assembly Debates* (hereafter *CAD*), II: 342–343.

14. V. Geetha and S. V. Rajadurai, *Towards a Non-Brahmin Millennium: From Iyothee Thass to Periyar* (Calcutta: Samya, 2008), 309.

15. See Sharmila Rege, *Writing Caste/Writing Gender: Reading Dalit Women's Testimonies* (New Delhi: Zubaan, 2006), 74–75. See also descriptions of the Annual Conference of the AIWC held at Nagpur in December 1937 and the subsequent founding of the Ramabai Ambedkar Women's Sangh and the All India Untouchable Women's Federation, in Urmila Pawar and

        Meenakshi Moon (trans. Wandana Sonalkar), *We Also Made History: Women in the Ambedkarite Movement* (New Delhi: Zubaan, 2008), 39–156.

16. I have in mind Sharmila Rege's reading of a popular poster depicting the wedding reception of Ambedkar and Ramabai that shows Ramabai sitting next to Ambedkar who has, in his lap, a book, presumably the Constitution of India. The image, Rege suggests, 'registers an imagination that sees Ramabai as central to Ambedkar's political contributions – be it the Constitution or the conversion to Buddhism'. Sharmila Rege (ed.), *Against the Madness of Manu: B. R. Ambedkar's Writings on Brahmanical Patriarchy* (New Delhi: Navayana, 2013), 34.

17. Gayatri Chakravorty Spivak, 'Constitutions and Culture Studies', *Yale Journal of Law and the Humanities* 2, no. 1 (1990): 133–147, 135.

1

In the Shadow of the Founding Fathers

We are not merely technically, the inheritors of the fathers of the Constitution. We really shaped it and hammered it after years of close debate.
—Jawaharlal Nehru, *Speech in the Parliament of India*, 1951

Patriarchal discourse pervades mainstream scholarship about the Constitution and its making. One assumption which recurs in most writing, including much of the existing feminist scholarship on the making of the Constitution, is that all its architects were male. Evidence of this is the ubiquitous phrase 'founding fathers' of the Indian Constitution. This implies that there were no women involved in the framing of the most crucial document concerning the republic, in spite of very obvious empirical evidence to the contrary.

FOUNDING FATHERS: THE AMERICAN HERITAGE

The term 'founding fathers' reinforces assumptions about the political structures of society, relegating women away from the sphere of decision making. In consonance with the conventional vocabulary of political thought, this idiom fails to assign women autonomous political selves that can exceed the so-called separate realms of the private and the public. The persistent and longstanding presence of the term in academic and popular discussions reinforces many patriarchal modes of narrative and contributes to the silencing of voices whose protection, ironically, is the legitimate task of the system of justice framed by the Constitution.

The Indian framers had borrowed some significant provisions and juristic concepts from the American Constitution. One of these was the term 'founding fathers' reverently reserved for 'thirty-nine of the continent's most eminent men' who had met at 'a special conclave held in Philadelphia during the summer of 1787'.[1] When these men had put their 'names on the page, they had put their reputations on the line'.[2] A canonical moment in the history of the phrase can be traced to Alexis de Tocqueville's classic study of the American democratic system, *Democracy in America* (1840). Tocqueville himself does not use the phrase but lays the ground through his influential discussion of the American Constitution. Tocqueville denies the moment of independence its celebratory status and confers, instead, the glory on the moments of constitution-making. 'The spectacle of a nation battling vigorously to achieve its independence', for Tocqueville, is banal since 'every century has displayed [it] to our eyes'.[3] The American War of Independence, contained less heroism than it is credited with, the received account of the courage of American armies and the patriotism of its citizens being 'greatly exaggerated'. It was in the framing of the Constitution that 'America showed itself capable of rising for a few moments to that lofty degree of renown which the proud imagination of its inhabitants would constantly reveal to us....'[4] The tone for the description of the revolutionary founding moment not just for American but all human history was set in these lyrical, yet insightful words, of the French raconteur:

> But what is new in the history of societies is the sight of a great nation, warned by legislators that the workings of the government are grinding to a halt, turning its attention without haste or fear, upon itself, sounding out the depths of the ill, standing still for two whole years, in order to uncover the remedy at leisure and, on discovery of the remedy, submitting to it voluntarily without its costing humanity a single tear or drop of blood.[5]

The founding fathers, 'all the great men' the Revolution had created were 'the finest minds and the noblest characters that have ever emerged in the New World'.[6] Nehru's extraordinarily poetic description of the moment of the founding, 'the magic in this moment of transition from the old to the new, something of that magic which one sees when the night turns into day' is reminiscent of Tocqueville's brilliant description of the founding moment as that of a nation turning its attention upon itself, 'sounding out the depths of the ill'.[7] Both are striking, the extraordinariness of the moment and the greatness of the founders.

Bruce Ackerman's extremely sophisticated account of the American Constitution is probably the most influential and robust attempt to reconcile the understanding that constitutions are products of their historical times and the obligatory nostalgia rendered in praise of the great founders. Ackerman's ingenious formulation is that constitutions are produced (and profoundly edited/amended) not in moments of normal politics but in extraordinary moments that 'occur rarely, and under special constitutional conditions'.[8] It is in these moments when the creative genius of a people finds supreme expression, and all their talents are mobilized, that constitutions are made. Among the things that define these moments is 'the remarkable act of authority', on the part of the founding fathers, to ratify the constitution in the name of 'We, the people'.[9] Ackerman looks at the authority of the framers in terms of generation. While he posits 'the generation' as the basic unit of constitutional evolution – the founders being a spiritual entity – constitutional law, for him, is constituted by a 'conversation between generations'.[10] More importantly, it is through this inter-generational conversation that 'We, the people' is defined, legitimized, and recreated at every stage of historical time. As a people, Americans' commitment to being ruled by themselves implies that they continue a dialogue with the generation of the founding fathers, and not just respect them.[11]

The phrase 'founding fathers' is not limited to the members of the Philadelphia Convention. It has become synonymous with any set or group of brilliant, dedicated men who participate in the legal, deliberative processes of constitution-making in their respective countries. In the histories of modern nations, which claim to have a written constitution, it works like a trope in standard narratives, especially if these men happen to have continued shaping the nation long after the framing. The American founding fathers, defined narrowly as men who either signed the Declaration of Independence or crafted the Constitution, were figures of great eminence in the life of the nation, even beyond the task of the framing.

The double entrenchment in the Indian context

Interestingly the phrase 'founding fathers' is also used for their Indian counterparts, creating no ripples in the historical imagination of Indians who use it in academic and popular discourse alike to designate the members of the Constituent Assembly of India.

Part of the reason why the phrase is acceptably used for the Indian framers is the same as it is for the American founders. Most of these men occupied the highest offices of the state that the Constitution created: the first President and almost the entire cabinet of Prime Minister Nehru, including

B. R. Ambedkar had been members of the Constituent Assembly. Ambedkar, whose figure has accumulated around itself a formidable social and political force, has been deified as the 'father' of the Constitution. In the people's imagination, Ambedkar's name has become synonymous with the Constitution and some of its principles that have had profound implications for the nation. Most importantly, he symbolizes the very idea that the law of the nation comes not from 'sacred', 'transcendental' sources but from the people whose lives it purports to change. As a founding father, Ambedkar continues to crystallize certain social meanings of the Constitution that are, not inaccurately, attributed to his authorship. Even while arguing that Constitutionalism can be a deterrent to the 'Dalit' revolution, Arundhati Roy circulates the metaphor, calling him 'the Father of the Indian Constitution' presumably in order to underscore that writing the Constitution was 'a radical act' for Ambedkar.[12]

The other framers, too, have been assigned a great role by historians, making it impossible to think that the Constitution could have survived, let alone been drafted without them. 'Would the best of constitutions have survived Nehru's early disappearance from the scene?',[13] asks Granville Austin, summing up a line of thought that claimed that the Constitution was a success because among 'the circumstances that conspired to allow it to work well' was a 'charismatic leadership' who had 'in themselves been a point of focus for the nation'.[14] The founding fathers did not merely frame the Constitution but maintained it. Indeed, it took the Indian leaders themselves some time to transcend the paternal love they had for the Constitution.[15] During the debate on the First Amendment Bill, 1951 in the Lok Sabha, Nehru evoked the collective pride of the members reminding them that 'it is we, we who sit here, or nearly all of us ... we after all, who were the Constituent Assembly and who drafted the Constitution' (Image 1.1).[16] The founding fathers may not have had the legal or constitutional authority that the courts have, Nehru argued, for it is the 'right and privilege of the highest courts of the land ... to interpret it in the light of the law and with such light as *they* can give it'[17] but they had a *moral* authority by virtue of being its fathers:

> there is no doubt that this House has authority. There is no doubt about that, and here, I am talking not of the legal or constitutional authority, but of moral authority, because it is, roughly speaking, this House that made the Constitution.[18]

The identification of themselves as the fathers of the Constitution, and hence endowed with a moral authority, was extended further to entrench

Image 1.1 Commemorating Plaque for the Constituent Assembly in the Central Hall of the Parliament.

Source: Photos of the making of the Constitution, Department of Justice, Ministry of Law and Justice, Government of India (https://doj.gov.in/page/photos-making-constitution, accessed on 17 June 2021).

the discourse on constitutional justice with the intention of the founding fathers – the original intent of the framers, not just as it was exercised in the act of the framing but also as it should have been exercised:

> it becomes our duty to see whether the constitution so [judicially] interpreted was rightly framed and whether it is desirable to change it here and there so as to give effect to what really in our opinion, was intended or should be intended.[19]

The double entrenchment of the original will is clear from these statements. The Constitution is to be interpreted in such light as the judicial offices can throw upon it, and yet it must be judged in the light of the original intention. The original intention in Nehru's speech has to be understood in its dual temporality, both as it was available during those precise dates of the working of the Constituent Assembly and in the ought-ness in which the founding fathers see it *now* – the moment of Nehru's assertion. The original intention has not been entirely absent from the judgments of the court. The court claims to rely on the canons of statutory interpretation, and has generally been reluctant to turn to historical material for the justification or substantiation of its judgments. Yet, as late as in 2001, the Supreme Court affirmed, 'It is a settled position that the debates in the Constituent Assembly may be relied upon as an aid to interpret a constitutional provision because it is the function of the Court to find out the intention of the framers of the Constitution.'[20]

The original intention of the founding fathers found explicit reference and commendation from the court in the landmark *Kesavananda Bharati* judgment, also known as the Fundamental Rights Case (1973).[21] Despite disagreement on the right tools to discover the original intention of the framers, almost all the thirteen judges, divided into a majority of seven versus a minority of six, drew from the historical records of the founding moment to arrive at their respective conclusions. Apart from being the longest constitution in the world, meant for a diverse and large population, it was praised for being 'chiselled and shaped by great political leaders and legal luminaries, most of whom had taken active part in the struggle for freedom'.[22]

While trying to establish a proper juristic relation between the fundamental rights and the directive principles, the judges on the bench took pains to understand the mind of the founding fathers. They read the fundamental rights chapter of the Constitution to suggest that 'the founding fathers were equally anxious that it should be a society where the citizen will enjoy the various freedoms and such rights as are the basic elements of those freedoms without which there can be no dignity of the individual'.[23] The judgment that the two chapters should be read harmoniously was substantiated by the understanding that 'our founding fathers were satisfied that there is no anti-work between the Fundamental Rights and the Directive Principles. One supplements the other.'[24] The hermeneutic traditions of the court may not prefer to rely on the probatory data of the Constituent Assembly, sparing itself from the difficulty of understanding 'the inarticulate mental process behind' the acts of the founding fathers, but its respect and occasional dependence on their wisdom have remained intact.[25] The 'faiths of the founding fathers'[26] have percolated down to the jurisprudential discourse of the country. The Constitution being an organic document, the fiction of its monogenic origins has continued to grow with it.

As a category of self-description, the figure of the founding father had animated the Indian Constituent Assembly itself. In his famous speech while presenting the Objectives Resolution, Jawaharlal Nehru placed the Constituent Assembly in the tradition of constitution-making bodies of the past and spoke of the founders as fathers – fathers not merely of a constitution but of a great nation and its future.

I think also of the various Constituent Assemblies that have gone before and of what took place at the making of the great American nation when *the fathers of that nation* met and fashioned out a constitution which has stood the test of so many years, more than a century and a half, and of the great nation which has resulted, which has been built up on the basis of that Constitution.[27]

The curious mixing of the metaphor of parenting with revolutions and constitution-framing continued when Nehru remembered the French Revolution and the subsequent constitution. His mind went back to that mighty revolution which took place over 150 years earlier, and to the Constituent Assembly that met in Paris, and its many difficulties.[28] Nehru reminded the house of the Oath of the Tennis Court, recalling the legendary efforts of the revolutionaries to fashion their own Constitution amid the violent and vigorous obstruction. In the same breath, he remembered the more recent revolution in Russia, 'not only a mighty country but for us in India, a neighbouring country'.[29] Nehru's descriptions evoked a series of glorious historical images of men as agents of revolutions and founding something new. When he said, 'we shall advance … in spite of obstructions and difficulties, and achieve and realise the dream that we have dreamt so long',[30] women members of the Assembly had already slipped out of the metaphorical baggage of the first person collective pronoun.[31] Ironically, he continued describing the 'psychological moment in India's history' in terms implicitly referring to the birth pangs of the nation. The emotive appeal was to the maternal act of reproduction, locating the founders 'on the verge of this passing age, trying, labouring, to usher in the new'.[32] Nehru was finding it difficult to speak, his voice trembled, and his mind seemed full of images from the past:

> I tremble a little and feel overwhelmed by this mighty task. We have come here at a strange moment in India's history. I do not know but I do feel that there is some magic in this moment of transition from the old to the new, something of that magic which one sees when the night turns into day and even though the day may be a cloudy one, it is day after an [*sic*], for when the clouds move away, we can see the sun later on.[33]

Nehru's narrative refers to the labour pain of the authorship, while at the same time assuming authority as the 'fathers' of the text. The moral claims and legitimacy of the authorship are asserted by placing the framers in the long tradition of male law-givers; the glorification of the act is done by evoking the labour of the woman, which is immediately appropriated by the authoritative figure of the founding father. It would hardly be an exaggeration to conclude that with this appropriating self-definition produced on 'the fifth day of this first session of the Constituent Assembly'[34] began the act of erasure of the figure of the mothers of the Constitution. It is a reflection of the gendered nature of our faith that we continue to erase women from our constitutional narrative while being faithful to the founding fathers. In the following three sections I shall provide brief critical reviews of the existing literature.

Though 'Indians do not have an exulted mythology of the founding fathers', barring perhaps the glorified status of B. R. Ambedkar as one, discussions on the Indian Constitution are replete with references to these figures.[35] That 'benighted moment',[36] to borrow Salman Rushdie's inimitable phrase, was suffused with the aura of its great founding fathers: 'heroes of the independence movement'.[37] The eminent historian of the Constituent Assembly, Granville Austin describes its most influential members in these terms:

> Nehru, Prasad, Patel and Azad, in fact, constituted an oligarchy within the Assembly. Their honour was unquestioned, their wisdom hardly less so. In their god-like status they may have been feared; certainly they were loved. An Assembly member was not greatly exaggerating the esteem in which his colleagues held these men when he said that the government rested in the hands of those who (were) utterly incapable of doing any wrong to the people. The oligarchy's influence was nearly irresistible....[38]

A fairly diverse range of Indian scholars has been uncritically using the term 'founding fathers'. They repeat the narrative pattern of the constitutional story developed so elegantly in the American context. The list includes historians, political scientists, jurists, lawyers, parliamentarians, and professional journalists. Subhash Kashyap, an expert on the Indian Parliament and an eminent constitutionalist uses the term as freely as his American counterparts. 'Our founding fathers *gave* us a Constitution which has stood the test of time', says Kashyap in a passage that throws into relief the salient points about the trope discussed above:

> Its basic features, objectives and values *were* most unexceptionable. The Constitution *deserved* respect from all of us. It *was* a symbol of our national unity and integrity. It should be kept above the marsh and mire of party-politics.[39]

The use of past tense in the passage is emphasized here to draw attention to the fact that Kashyap is the editor of a volume of archival materials about the framing process. In his account, the actions of the founding fathers and the text are relegated to a past for which we must have reverence but which can still be described in glaringly patriarchal terms. His complete amnesia about the women framers becomes all the more remarkable given the fact that Kashyap has done extensive research on the framing of the Constitution. The passage reflects his historical approach to the Constitution, which he considers a historical object.

Other instances of such 'forgetful' usage and uncritical acceptance of the term are to be found in works by the jurist Fali S. Nariman, Uday Singh Mehta, and other scholars.[40] An interesting occurrence of the phrase is contained in an incisive little book about the Indian legal system by the constitution expert and lawyer Fali S. Nariman in the course of his analysis of the constitutional provisions on positive discrimination. Nariman summarizes the force behind the groundswell of opinion against reservations in these words: 'an increasing resistance to the view that the sins of generations of our forefathers in the higher castes should be expiated here and now, in a couple of generations'.[41] The critics of the reservations with whom he seems to be in a brief dialogue remind us that even the doctrine of 'pious obligation' 'requires the Hindu son to meet the financial obligations only of his father, not of the forebears of his father'.[42] Complaining that the courts have not been consistent in their approach towards the method settled by the Constitution to achieve an egalitarian society, Nariman reassures the readers that 'Whatever the nation's karma, the founding fathers cannot be faulted for a lack of idealism; nor can Providence'; the problem 'is not in our stars but in ourselves'.[43] The discourse is about fathers and sons inhabiting the prescribed terrain by the same 'inegalitarian' *shastra* (Hindu law) with providential attributes that the Constitution seeks to displace.

By one verbal slip, the framers of the Constitution – which include women who raised a vociferous protest against the (uncodified) Hindu Law and the legendary campaigner against it B. R. Ambedkar – are brought into the same syntagmatic order of traditional 'sacred' patriarchy. Nariman's use of the phrase and the field within which it operates confounds the general understanding that the Indian Constitution had demolished 'the belief that a polity or society should be founded upon or sanctioned by a religious or divine order, by inherited social practice, or simply by forcible conquest'.[44] It is ironic that Ambedkar had spoken about the relation between the author and the reader in the Brahmanical tradition in terms of 'filial obligations':

The Brahmin scholar has a twofold interest in maintaining the sanctity of this literature. In the first place, being the product of his forefathers, his filial duty leads him to defend it even at the cost of truth. In the second place, as it supports the privileges of the Brahmins, he is careful not to do anything that will undermine its authority.[45]

The figure of the father in Indian discourse, then, is not just a result of a historiographical error, a temporary amnesia, or an oversight. The framing of the Constitution is a revolutionary act occurring in 'magical time' and meant to achieve 'revolutionary ends' by unusual methods, to use S. Radhakrishnan's words.[46] The law it gives to the nation constitutes a new morality voicing 'the silent immaculate premise of our [modern] outlook' for a society which is 'so orthodox, so archaic in its thought and its social structure'.[47] The figure of the founding father, etched as it is in historical memory even before the act of the founding, appears to be a meta-discursive burden that drags this 'revolution' to a long patriarchal tradition of author, authorship, and authority. As a figure of re-appropriation, it smothers the possibility of the radical inscription of women in the foundations of justice, perpetuating the 'law of the father' through the numerous discursive shifts of so-called social and constitutional revolution.

THE INTELLECTUAL PREJUDICES IN ACADEMIC LITERATURE

If theoretical orthodoxy and the received history of the Constitution have forgotten these women, it is largely due to a gendered perspective on the process and a pervasive masculinist bias in the discourse surrounding the Constitution. Therefore, before embarking on a detailed examination of these records and understanding the gender politics of the entire framing, it becomes imperative to question the theoretical assumptions and prejudices that have contributed to the exclusion of these women from constitutional discourse in India. This critical scrutiny of the received narrative of constitutional history that has safely buried these women in the archives will serve as a pre-emptive conceptual strategy before they are retrieved for a faithful historical memory.

My attempt at this retrieval both at a conceptual and an empirical level treats the Constitution as a text and the members of the Constituent Assembly as its authors. This necessarily means asking interdisciplinary questions about a text that is not literary and is usually a preserve of legal scholars and political theorists. These questions – historical, feminist, semantic, and legal – situate the founders of the Constitution in relation with the readers of the Constitution, who constitute an 'interpretive community' which as Stanley

Fish conceptualizes them is 'not so much a group of individuals who shared a point of view, but a point of view or way of organizing experience that shared individuals'.[48] The 'distinctions, categories of understanding, and stipulations of relevance and irrelevance'[49] that form the consciousness of the interpretive community are central to the conceptual questions that are essential to the treatment of the Constitution as a text. Who or what is the author of the Constitution? Does the fact that the Constitution was framed by an assembly of representatives of an incipient nation have a bearing on this question? What are the continuities between the readers and writers of the Constitution? These questions become crucial and remarkable because the answers given to them have had no reference to the women representatives in the Constituent Assembly. There must be something amiss in the hermeneutic processes of revisiting the framing that has erased the contribution of women to the founding discourse of the republic (Image 1.2).

The term 'contribution of women' immediately invites problematization: what does it mean to contribute to a work of collaboration? What does it mean to attribute authorship to a miniscule minority of women in a gathering of male authors? What does it mean for women to be originators of some ideas or involved in 'a set of linked activities (authemes)' performed in collaboration and with compromises?[50] What does it mean for women to contribute to an assembly of representatives chosen on the basis of their community? Who attributes authorship and under what compulsions? Does 'to contribute' mean 'to represent'? For women, did it mean to put up resistance to another act of recasting women and reconstituting patriarchy at the emergence of a postcolonial nation-state?[51] These are the questions that this work seeks to answer.

The search for women's authorial voice means posing these questions before a cluster of texts at the core of which is the Constitution of India; the others in the cluster include the body of writings related to the making of the Constitution, namely, the *Constituent Assembly Debates*, the reports of the various committees in the Constituent Assembly, the debates of the Constituent Assembly in its role as the provisional parliament, the archive of correspondence, memoirs, official notes, reports, memoranda, petitions, and numerous other documents produced by the women members and their collaborators in the Assembly. The interpretive community under whose authority the Constitution is illuminated has a zealous interest in controlling these archives, in making some of these visible and relegating others to a secondary status. The discovery of women's voices problematizes the stable

Image 1.2 The Nightingale of India and the Iron Man. Sarojini Naidu seated and in animated conversation with Vallabhbhai Patel who is standing during one of the early sessions of the Constituent Assembly.

Source: Photos of the making of the Constitution, Department of Justice, Ministry of Law and Justice, Government of India (https://doj.gov.in/page/photos-making-constitution, accessed on 17 June 2021).

authorship of the Constitution and inscribes a narrative of gender politics in the venerable discourse of and about the Constitution.

In the following sections I make detailed critical appraisals of the secondary sources on the Constitution and its making in order to gain an understanding of the implications of this amnesia on scholarship.

Patriarchal patterns in dominant discourses

With its 395 articles and 10 schedules, the Indian Constitution is the largest constitutional text in the world and has naturally spawned numerous commentaries around itself, several of them running into volumes.

The most respected among these is H. M. Seervai's magisterial *Constitutional Law of India* which approaches the Constitution through nuanced analyses of judicial pronouncements and legal doctrine, and rarely touches on historical issues.[52] The three-volume work begins with a brief history of the framing of the Constitution but the account seldom refers to the complex social dynamics of the Constituent Assembly or the circumstances in which it framed the text. The only members of the Constituent Assembly who find any mention are B. R. Ambedkar and, very occasionally, Jawaharlal Nehru and Vallabhbhai Patel. The equally influential and more voluminous one by D. D. Basu is similar to Seervai's in its approach to the historical moment of the Constitution's founding.[53] Basu's commentary runs into 12 thick volumes but sums up the framing process in three neat paragraphs.[54] It maintains a clinically detached distance from the murky and complex world from which the Constitution emerged. Other commentaries do not even touch upon the question of the framing process, and make no mention of the Constituent Assembly.[55]

The smaller texts on the Constitution sometimes come with a note on its framing paying homage to the toil and tribulations of the founding fathers.[56] These commentaries significantly shape the reception of the Indian Constitution and mark the trajectories of its operation. Their impact is not impeded by the fact that they say nothing new about the past or about the relationship between the past and the text. Their novelty lies, to use Michel Foucault's astonishing claim about 'the principle of commentary' not in 'what is said, but in its reappearance'.[57] Commentaries on the Indian Constitution fill rows of bookshelves and in the process, drown the primary text, the Constitution itself, in the 'multiple or hidden meanings with which it is credited, the reticence and wealth it is believed to contain'.[58] These commentaries fulfil their role, which in Foucault's words, ironically is:

> to say *finally*, what has silently been articulated *deep down*. It must – and the paradox is ever-changing yet inescapable – say, for the first time, what has already been said, and repeat tirelessly what was, nevertheless, never said.[59]

The magnificent commentaries on the Indian Constitution, therefore, repeat the tenebrous silence about the mothers of the Indian Constitution; their comments on the articles and judicial interpretations rediscover what is already discovered, and make no space for a retrieval of women's voices inscribed in the text.[60]

The academic scholarship on the Indian Constitution, too, contains little by way of historical enquiry. According to the editors of a recent reference work on constitutional scholarship in India, it comprises little more than a scattered genre that has 'ebbed and flowed with the passage of particular scholars, and has focused on certain areas of constitutional law, while largely ignoring others'.[61] The ignored area, of course, includes the historical context of the framing and the details of the process. Most scholarship is impervious to the idea that the Constitution originally is 'an extra-legal text'[62] and its meaning lies in the complexities of the interaction of several forces not immediately visible in the text. Works on the Indian Constitution have been extraordinarily indifferent to these origins. Two decades ago, Sumit Sarkar pointed out that this crucial transitional period between 1947 and 1949 when the Constitution was framed remains virtually unexplored due to a division of labour between historians who stopped at 1947 and political scientists who study the developments after the Constitution came into force.[63] Enormous intellectual energy has gone into investigating the Partition and its consequences, though very little attention has been paid to its impact on the three-year-long framing process. Women members of the Constituent Assembly, for instance, were actively engaged in projects of recovery and rehabilitation of women during the partition riots and took several positions regarding the agency and citizenship rights of victim women. These activities have escaped the attention of scholars of the Constitution who have mostly visited the Constituent Assembly Debates through a teleological lens, paying more attention to the selective amnesia of the constitutional text towards the moment of Partition arguing that 'constitutionalism "forgets" episodes that do not fit within nationalist narratives, in view of the nexus between constitution writing and the nationalist project'.[64]

Important works of constitutional law have paid scant attention to the politics of exclusion and inclusion, of speech and silence, and of language, representation, and subjectivity. Granville Austin's classic work, *The Indian Constitution: Cornerstone of a Nation*, identifies democracy, social revolution, and the unity and integrity of the nation as weaving a seamless web which dominated the constitution-making process.[65] His influential conceptualization of the social revolution hardly ever stresses upon the profound implications of the principle of equality of the sexes, and relevant debates in the Assembly. Austin had also hinted at the possibility of a study of the personal location of the members of the Assembly in the appendix of his book, suggesting that a critical work on the constitution-making process could be done on the pattern of Charles Beard's influential work, *An Economic Interpretation of the Constitution of the United States*, that had studied the economic imperatives of the American founding fathers.[66] Works that took up the suggestion, however, remained under the shadow of Austin's seamless web of social revolution, democracy, and national integrity, and made reductive studies of the class composition of the Constituent Assembly without exploring the implications of class disparities for the Constitution of India.[67] Upendra Baxi brought into focus the problematics of imposing such overarching patterns upon a varied gathering of politicians.[68] This seamless web gives the Constitution a teleological orientation and has obscured the many complexities underlying the very long and intense process of its framing.

The debate that Austin and Baxi introduced in studies of the making of the Constitution, could not, however, initiate a process of interrogation of the so-called neutrality of its members. Moreover, they never recognized gender as an important axis around which some of their arguments turned. In his own later work, however, Baxi read the founding in no less teleological terms than Austin and made sweeping judgements that rendered the voices of women founders inaudible. Pronouncing his judgement on the Constitution, which, he argued, 'coolly contemplates a male dominated society ... [and] does not see patriarchy as problematic, [but] perceives it as natural',[69] Baxi, apparently, based his ideas on a reading of the framing that is blind towards the woman question and the presence of women in the Constituent Assembly. 'From a suffering feminist perspective', he argues, 'the foundational violence against women enacted during the moment of constitution-making, iterates itself, over and over again, through fifty long years of unfoldment of its vicious patriarchal logic'.[70] Such pronouncements project contemporary readings of the Constitution onto its history about which they have a gender-blind idea, and thus relegate women's voice to a vicious cycle that does not just assume an absence of women but also perpetuates a blindness towards them.

Thus it is not surprising that feminist legal scholars like Flavia Agnes assume that 'the issue of gender and women's rights did not figure'[71] during the debates on the uniform civil code in the Constituent Assembly and conclude that 'while laying the foundation of a new nation, the scheme of women's liberation had to be relocated within the master scheme of national integration and became subservient to it in all later developments'.[72] In her reading, there was 'a marked absence of discussion about the significance of the UCC *for women* ... the overarching concern of the *founding fathers* was the formation of the new nation-state and its smooth governance'.[73] The appearance of the phrase in such important feminist works is symptomatic of the entrenchment of the patriarchal bias and is disconcerting for the impact it might have on scholarship.

Recent works that claim to make 'a deeper examination of the Indian founding as embodying the result of a successful exercise of popular sovereignty by the Indian people'[74] do not see any connection between the early-twentieth-century women's movement in India and women's participation in the founding process. Madhav Khosla's short introduction to the Indian Constitution begins with 'the winter of 1946' when 'over three hundred men and *women* had come together'[75] to form the Constituent Assembly. Their 'assignment was one that would take them almost three years, and make them participants in an extraordinary experiment in history'.[76] Yet women find no further mention in his exposition as framers of the Constitution or as its subjects. In his attempt to 'stimulate debate about our constitutional culture and encourage engagement with this fascinating text',[77] he fails to engage with the question of gender equality.

Khosla returns to constitution-making in a recent book, *India's Founding Moment: The Constitution of a Most Surprising Democracy*, that seeks to examine the 'overlooked origins' of Indian constitutionalism and why it is surprising that the founders of the Indian republic chose constitutional democracy. He disagrees with the idea that this choice was a natural culmination of the evolution of the Indian legal structure under the colonial government. He also takes scholars to task for an 'impoverished reading of legal documents' which are presented as forerunners of the Constitution.[78] The problem with these readings, he argues, is that they fail to acknowledge the shifting semantic planes on which these legal texts were grounded. 'All words do not have the same value',[79] Khosla argues and delves into several non-legal texts – written prior to, during, and even after the foundation of the republic in 1950 – by a host of important members of the Constituent Assembly and the leaders of the nationalist movement, to create an intellectual history of the Constitution. He pays special attention to approaches towards codification and ideas about the centralized state and political representation, focusing on how these ideas came together to make it possible for the founders to constitute 'democracy in an inhospitable environment'.[80] His readings of Gandhi, Nehru, Ambedkar, Radhakamal Mukerjee, and M. Visvesvaraya push the early history of constitutional thought back to the late-nineteenth century, and trace its lineage from the available liberal inheritance.[81] This is a welcome departure, and invites us to look beyond the Constituent Assembly to recover the reasons for the legitimacy of the voices that mattered in its discourses.

Yet, like Austin, he too projects an overarching interpretive framework of the Constitution to produce a narrative structure for its history. In Khosla's case, the three aspects of what he calls 'the founding schema' are 'codification, centralization, and representation', each of which had important gendered dimensions that became invisible because of an amnesia towards the women members of the Constituent Assembly.[82]

The women's movement was significantly involved in the codification processes, notably the Hindu personal law reforms formalized by the Hindu Law Committees of the 1940s that preceded the Constituent Assembly.[83] Their primary purpose was to create a common (not uniform) legal system, synthesized from what they considered the most progressive, gender-just, and rational traditions operating within the jurisdictions of Hindu Law. As I hope to show in this book, for women as well as for Dalit leaders like Ambedkar, this implied going beyond existing codes in the interest of gender justice whenever necessary. Having thus invested in codification, a good deal of their attempt in the Constituent Assembly, as evident from their interventions during the framing of the 'freedom of conscience and free profession, practice and propagation of religion', was to preserve their past victories and build upon them.[84] Codification and the continuity of it, for the women framers, was a compulsory exercise, and inasmuch as it was meant to identify and re-inscribe the progressive elements and preclude the hermeneutics of 'reactionary pandits and priests' and conservative British endorsements, it was a radical gesture as well.[85] The phrase for the filial authority of priests and pandits is used by Renuka Ray, one of the founding mothers, to describe the challenges for gender-just readings of law.

Similarly, the women members' views on the centralized state were also developed through years of negotiation with a colonial state and the limited democratic governments formed in 1937 and 1946. The question of representation was deeply intertwined with the constitutional politics through which the women's movement had consolidated itself as a pan-Indian force, fraught with dilemmas about the rival claims of communities that were asserting their identities through the same means. Women members of the All India Women's Conference (AIWC), Amrit Kaur and Jahanara Shahnawaz, both elected to the Constituent Assembly (the latter, a member of the Muslim League, did not join the Constituent Assembly of India but went on to become the Vice President of the Constituent Assembly of Pakistan), had conflicting views on the question of the descriptive representation of women during the negotiations on constitutional reforms at the Round Table Conference of 1932. Kaur had supported joint electorates for women whereas Shahnawaz advocated separate electorates and yet, interestingly, both believed that theirs was the best way to represent all women of all classes and communities![86]

Surprisingly, most narratives of the Constituent Assembly that treat it as a site of contest or contract have not paid enough attention to the people who participated in signing the contract. Granville Austin's proposal for biographical studies of the members of the Constituent Assembly in order to understand the deeper confluences of the historical circumstances and individual preferences that contributed to the framing of the Constitution went completely unheeded. The Beardian framework of history proposed by Austin assumed that 'our fundamental law was not the product of an abstraction known as "the whole people", but a group of economic interests'.[87] Austin himself expanded on Beard's suggestion of preparing 'economic biographies' of all the important members connected with the framing and provides a more composite background of the framers. In the appendix to his book he expressly mentions the party, community, caste, region, and educational qualification of each of the Assembly's members. However, gender as an ascriptive identity does not appear important to him. This can be explained partly by the fact that Indian constitutionalism, as Upendra Baxi, argues, 'does not essentialize the identity of all Indian women as it does ascriptive caste communities, indigenous peoples and the impoverished peoples'.[88] We can read this as another example of writing the history of the Constitution through the prism of one's present reading of the text.

Evoking the death of the author: the poststructuralist trap

Writing five decades ago, Austin presumably did not have access to feminist historiographical projects of tracing the woman's voice, nor was he touched by the nascent poststructuralist theories about reading and texts that have blocked the inquiry into the presence of women founders. Scholarship that values the origins of the Constitution also does not engage with the historical authors of the text. The editor of an important collection of recent essays on the Constitution believes that to a large extent the original intentions can be captured. Though 'we may now be suffering from amnesia' about them and 'somewhere down the road we began taking them for granted', in order

> to get a handle on the current constitutional practices, to grasp their values and meaning, we may have no option but to go back in time to the *Constituent Assembly Debates* and perhaps even further back to the colonial era.[89]

Yet in the same volume, the feminist scholar Nivedita Menon argues that 'It is futile to attempt to uncover the "real" meaning intended by the author'.[90] For her, the meaning of texts lies embedded in a network of other porous texts and not their authors.[91] She eschews a turn to the author because the authorial intention has little consequence for the present. Her arguments are based on her reading of Roland Barthes famous essay 'The Death of the Author' from which she quotes this 'celebrated passage':

> the text is not a line of words releasing a single theological meaning (the message of an Author–God) but a multidimensional space in which a variety of writings, none of the original, blend and clash. The text is a tissue of quotations drawn from the innumerable centres of culture.[92]

This displacement of the author in her argument is purportedly aimed at giving more power to the reader to whom 'the meaning of the text is available … *only in the present*'.[93] The origins of the Constitution, therefore, are irrelevant for her enterprise.

In an eponymous essay in the same volume, Aditya Nigam makes the provocative claim that the Constitution is 'A Text without Author' produced not by historically circumstanced individuals but by the logic of the event.[94] It is not very clear from Nigam's essay whether he is proposing that the Constitution does not have one author but many, as Granville Austin's work suggests, or if he is trying to imply that texts like the Indian Constitution do not have authors. In either case, his theoretical positions make little space for the women founders. In the first sense – that the text has many authors – his essay betrays the patriarchal biases that are ingrained in the constitutional discourse. He conceives of the framing process as a site of settlement between such embedded subjects for whom 'existential and community attachments are constitutive of ethical beings' whose notions of the future are 'voiced in terms of cultural autonomy and difference'.[95] These embedded subjects, according to him, came together to the site of framing, in diverse currents and diverse groups, 'under the compulsion of the logic of power, to hammer out a negotiated settlement'.[96] Women members, as we shall see, problematized the notion of community attachments that they frequently presented as impediments to the idea of constitutional justice. Even when women did speak as members of caste or minority communities, Dakshayani Velayudhan and Aizaz Rasul for example, they hardly considered their community associations as the core constituent of their ethical choices. The second interpretation – that texts like the Indian Constitution do not have authors – leaves no scope for the recognition of women framers.

Both Nigam's and Menon's positions are grounded in the idea that constitutions antedate the constitution-makers since constitutions 'are already there in a sense, even before they are formally written – and we know that they need not ever be written'.[97] Such approaches dispossess the women framers of their authorship even before it has been attributed to them. They do not register the fact that Barthes is not supporting any practice of 'forgetting' the author; instead, he is asking for a radical rediscovery of the author. The 'Author' that he seeks to displace is not an actual, historical person but the 'hypostases: society, history, psyche, liberty' that have accumulated around this figure.[98] 'The Death of the Author', in effect, argues for a reading that completely frees itself from any preconceived notions about her (a deliberate use here), notions that may have gained a certain authority. When he says that 'a text's unity lies not in its origins but in its destination', he is appealing to the reader who is as impersonal and multiple as the text itself. 'The reader is without history, biography, psychology' he says, suggesting that reading must not have historical, biographical, psychological – and let us add, patriarchal – prejudices.[99] The Author, whose death Barthes in pronouncing, is an effect of these prejudices. Understood in these terms the 'poststructuralist' disavowal of the framers of the Indian Constitution seems to be repeating the same prejudices in the most un-Barthesian manner. If the death of the author, in this reading, means anything it is this: the history of the Constitution needs to be revisited shedding all preconceived notions contained in the idea of the founding fathers. The author needs to be understood and rediscovered. The women founders and the men framers have to be given their historical credit, but not under the authority of the figures of the 'fathers'.

One can trace a clear pattern in the evolution of Indian constitutional history. In its early form, untouched by the concept of the death of the author, it attributed an important role to the actors in the Constituent Assembly. These, almost unexceptionably, were men who were influenced by their social and economic backgrounds and who worked as powerful agents of these factors. We can call it the patriarchal theory of authorial agency reflected accurately in the phrase 'founding fathers'. In its later and contemporary forms, partly under the shadow of theories of text, the authors' agency has been taken away. Instead of claiming a place for the founding mothers, these recent shifts take away credit from even the founding fathers. The entire thrust of contemporary hermeneutics of the Constitution, one can argue, is towards a dispossession of the authors of the Constitution under what Jane Gallop calls the 'slogan-effect' of Roland Barthes' essay.[100] The pitfall of such a position is that it has contributed to the neglect of the crucial historical process of the framing of the Constitution. While both these positions seem to be afflicted by a crude conception of power, they still retain a possibility to return to the actual site of the production of the Constitution. At this site we find 16 women, waiting for discovery and restitution, a task to which this work is dedicated.[101]

Indian constitutional discourse, thus, does not examine the archival sources in relation either with the process of decolonization or in their gendered components. It does not even seek to delve deeper into the unpublished archives to retrieve moments of resistance to the violence of the postcolonial transformation, or to discover voices of gendered alterity. Works on the Constituent Assembly struggle to arrive at a defined and sustained approach, owing to their vulnerability to multiple interpretations, including the formidable ones by the judiciary. These are omissions of staggering proportions considering the otherwise prodigious work on the Constitution in the traditions of commentary and judicial critique. The growing unease with this narrow canon among scholars who seek to read the Constitution radically is a welcome sign. Yet despite complaints against a protocol 'that is limited to a surface reading of the constitutional text, a surface comparison with colonial legal instruments, and a surface contextualization of the pre- and post-constitutional political framework', there is hardly any recognition of the need of a gendered history of the Constitution.[102] Even when scholars visit the Constituent Assembly with the partial purpose of freeing the field from 'the mystique imposed upon "founding fathers"', they do not recognize that the site was also marked by the presence of a feminist politics.[103] Most scholars limit themselves to glimpses of the proceedings, confining themselves to one or two of the many questions that had vexed the founders, and rarely move beyond the heavy presence of the multiple volumes of the *Constituent Assembly Debates*. Not interested in the question of how to read these debates – which, in any case, are not all that is there to the Constituent Assembly, they rarely suspect that women's authorship has any real value for their hermeneutic endeavours. These scholars take one of the three approaches – 'discursive, political, or institutional' – to the reading of the debates, thus reducing the actors of the Assembly to subjects of hegemonic processes or mere political agents.[104] They, therefore, miss the profound implications of the notions of authorship, textuality, postcoloniality, and the gendering of the constitution-making process and nearly erase women's historic contributions.

The burgeoning academic literature on law, postcolonialism, and the state is often a response to the changing topicalities of issues like the uniform civil code, secularism, women's representation, minority rights, and affirmative action. The feminist acknowledgement of the postcolonial status of the Indian Constitution is a mere glimpse of the Constituent Assembly and presents an incomplete picture of the founding moment. These discourses are already informed by the postcolonial critiques of the universalizing tendencies of Western discourse. Their conceptual scheme locates the framing of the Constitution in a paradigm of derivation, dislocation, and violence. 'In postcolonial societies such as ours where the law was a product of the exigencies of colonial administration', Nivedita Menon argues, 'it cannot be granted the same emancipatory force it might have had in Europe during the transition from feudalism to capitalism'.[105] 'Rights', in her account, were produced by the 'transformation of indigenous judicial discourse', through an act of violence and dislocation.[106] Such perspectives tend to reach the conclusion that this transformation necessarily involved acts of violence and dislocation that foreclose possibilities of emancipation through a discourse.[107] They pay scant attention to the feminist women, many elected to the Constituent Assembly, who played an important part in reclaiming and redefining the idea of rights that, to use the words of one of the founding mothers, Hansa Mehta, 'existed before the Charter of the United Nations and will exist even when the Charter has ceased to exist'.[108]

Such inattention serves to diminish the expectations of feminist historiography that, in turn, does not feel particularly enthralled by the promise of finding much of significance in the archives of the Constituent Assembly beyond an occasional footnote or two. These footnotes, in an instance of affirmative irony, swell into the chapters that follow.

NOTES

1. Akhil Reed Amar, *America's Constitution: A Biography* (New York: Random House, 2006), 5.
2. Ibid., 6.
3. Alexis de Tocqueville, *Democracy in America: and Two Essays on America*, trans. Gerald E. Bevan (London: Penguin, 2003), 132.
4. Ibid.
5. Ibid.
6. Ibid., 133.
7. Ibid., 132.
8. Bruce Ackerman, *We the People: The Foundations* (Cambridge MA: The Belknap Press of Harvard University Press, 1993), 6.
9. Bruce Ackerman, 'The Storrs Lectures: Discovering the Constitution', *The Yale Law Journal* 93, no. 6 (1984): 1013–1072, 1017.

10. Bruce Ackerman, 'A Generation of Betrayal?', *Fordham Law Review* 65, no. 4 (March 1997): 1519–1536, 1524.

11. This is my summary of Frank Michelman's discussion of Ackerman's complex ideas. Frank Michelman, 'Constitutional Authorship', in Larry Alexander (ed.), *Constitutionalism: Philosophical Foundations*, 64–98 (Cambridge: Cambridge University Press, 1998), 76–77.

12. Arundhati Roy, 'The Doctor and the Saint', in B. R. Ambedkar, *Annihilation of Caste: The Annotated Critical Edition*, ed. S. Anand, 17–179 (New Delhi: Navayana, 2014), 44.

13. Granville Austin, *The Indian Constitution: Cornerstone of a Nation*, 2nd ed. (New Delhi: Oxford University Press, 1999), 329.

14. Ibid., 328.

15. Even Ambedkar who is supposed to have expressed dissatisfaction with the Constitution was nevertheless attached to it: 'The Constitution was a wonderful temple we built for the gods but before they could be installed the devils have taken possession'. Ambedkar in the Rajya Sabha, PTI News Service, 20 March 1955, cited in Eleanor Zelliot, *Ambedkar's World: The Making of Babasaheb and the Dalit Movement* (New Delhi: Navayana, 2013), 257n47.

16. Jawaharlal Nehru, Lok Sabha Debates, May 1951. From extracts cited in Samaraditya Pal and Deepan Kumar Sarkar (eds), *India's Constitution: Origins and Evolution*, Vol. 3 (New Delhi: Lexis Nexis, 2015), 192.

17. Ibid.

18. Ibid.

19. Ibid. For an interesting account of Nehru's possessive, almost paternal claims on the Constitution and his right to change it, see Tripurdaman Singh, *Sixteen Stormy Days: The Story of the First Amendment to the Constitution of India* (New Delhi: Penguin Random House India, 2020).

20. *S. R. Chaudhari* v. *State of Punjab*, (2001) 7 SCC 126.

21. *Kesavananda Bharati Sripadagalavaru* v. *State of Kerala*, (1973) Supp. 1 SCR (henceforth, *Kesavananda Bharati* Case).

22. Shelat and Grover, JJ, *Kesavananda Bharati* Case, 218.

23. Ibid., 286.

24. Hegde and Mukherjea, JJ, *Kesavananda Bharati* Case, 344.

25. Mathew, J, *Kesavananda Bharati* Case, 780.

26. Chandrachud, Bhagwati et al., JJ, *Minerva Mills Ltd* v. *Union of India* (1981) 1 SCR 209.

27. Jawaharlal Nehru, Constituent Assembly of India, 13 December 1946, *CAD*, I: 61 (emphasis mine).

28. Ibid., 61.

29. Ibid.

30. Ibid.

31. This can hardly be read as referring to the women's collective sitting in the Assembly. Nehru is reported to have once dismissed the AIWC, the organization most of the women framers belonged to, as a 'tea-party organization'. Mrinalini Sinha, *Spectres of Mother India: The Global Restructuring of an Empire* (Durham and London: Duke University Press, 2006), 247.

32. Jawaharlal Nehru, Constituent Assembly of India, 13 December 1946, *CAD*, I: 61.

33. Ibid.

34. Ibid., 59.

35. Sandipto Dasgupta, 'Conflict, Not Consensus: Towards a Political Economy of the Making of the Indian Constitution', in Udit Bhatia (ed.), *The Indian Constituent Assembly: Deliberations on Democracy*, 38–57 (London and New York: Routledge, 2018), 38.

36. Salman Rushdie, *Midnight's Children* (New York: Random House, 2011), 1.

37. Austin, *The Indian Constitution*, 18.

38. Brajeshwar Prasad, *CAD*, VII: 760–761, cited in ibid., 21–22.

39. Subhash Kashyap, *Indian Constitution: Conflicts and Controversies* (New Delhi: Vitasta, 2010), 190 (emphasis mine).

40. Uday Mehta, 'Constitutionalism', in Niraja Gopal Jayal and Pratap Bhanu Mehta (eds), *The Oxford Companion to Politics in India*, 15–27 (New Delhi: Oxford University Press, 2011), 19; Rohit De, *A People's Constitution: The Everyday Life of Law in the Indian Republic* (Princeton: Princeton University Press, 2018), 7.

41. Fali S. Nariman, *India's Legal System: Can It Be Saved?* (New Delhi: Penguin, 2008), 61.

42. Ibid.

43. Ibid., 61–62.

44. Sunil Khilnani, 'The Indian Constitution and Governance', in Zoya Hasan, E. Sridharan, and R. Sudarshan (eds), *India's Living Constitution: Ideas, Practices, Controversies*), 64–82 (New Delhi: Permanent Black, 2002, 67.

45. B. R. Ambedkar, 'Castes in India: Their Mechanism, Genesis and Development', in Valerian Rodrigues (ed.), *Essential Writings of B.R. Ambedkar*, 241–262 (New Delhi: Oxford University Press, 2003), 252.

46. S. Radhakrishnan, Constituent Assembly of India, 20 January 1947, *CAD*, II: 269.

47. B. R. Ambedkar, Constituent Assembly of India, 17 December 1946, *CAD*, I: 235.

48. Stanley Fish, *Doing What Comes Naturally: Change, Rhetoric, and the Practice of Theory in Literary and Legal Studies* (Durham and London: Duke University Press, 1989), 141.

49. Ibid.

50. Harold Love, *Attributing Authorship: An Introduction* (New York: Cambridge University Press, 2002), 39.

51. Vasantha Kannabiran and K. Lalitha, 'That Magic Time', in Kumkum Sangari and Sudesh Vaid (eds), *Recasting Women: Essays in Colonial History* (New Delhi: Zubaan, 2006; originally Kali for Women, 1989), 180–203.

52. H. M. Seervai, *Constitutional Law of India*, 3 vols (Delhi: Universal Book Traders, 1991).

53. Durga Das Basu, *Commentary on the Constitution of India*, ed. Y. V. Chandrachud, S. S. Subramani, and B. P. Banerji, 10 vols, 8th ed., Vol. 1 (New Delhi: LexisNexis Butterworths Wadhwa, 2008), 25–26.

54. Ibid.

55. M. P. Jain, *Indian Constitutional Law*, 6th ed., rev. Ruma Pal, and Samaraditya Pal (Nagpur: LexisNexis Butterworths Wadhwa, 2010).

56. Gopal Sankaranarayanan (ed.), *The Constitution of India* (Lucknow: Eastern Book Company, 2016).

57. Michel Foucault, 'The Discourse on Language', in *The Archaeology of Knowledge and the Discourse on Language* trans. A. M. Sheridan Smith, 215–237 (New York: Pantheon Books, 1972), 221.

58. Ibid.

59. Ibid. (emphasis original).

60. An exception to this rule is Samaraditya Pal and Deepan Kumar Sarkar, *India's Constitution: Origins and Evolution*, 10 vols (Gurgaon: LexisNexis, 2014–2016). With relevant extracts from the *Constituent Assembly Debates* (but rarely from the committee proceedings) attached to each article, it manages to insert some framers into the discourse but so far as women members of the Constituent Assembly are concerned, they are largely absent from these volumes.

61. Sujit Choudhry, Madhav Khosla, and Pratap Bhanu Mehta (eds), *The Oxford Handbook of the Indian Constitution* (New Delhi: Oxford University Press, 2016).

62. John W. Salmond, *Salmond on Jurisprudence*, ed. P. J. Fitzgerald, 12th ed. (New Delhi: Universal, 2003).

63. Sumit Sarkar, 'Indian Democracy: The Historical Inheritance', in Atul Kohli (ed.), *The Success of India's Democracy*, 23–46 (New Delhi: Cambridge University Press, 2001), 23.

64. Kanika Gauba, 'Forgetting Partition: Constitutional Amnesia and Nationalism', *Economic and Political Weekly* 51, no. 39 (2016): 41–47, 47.

65. Austin, *The Indian Constitution*, 6.

66. Ibid., 337. Charles. A. Beard, *An Economic Interpretation of the Constitution of the United States* (New York: The Free Press, 1935; first published 1913 by The Macmillan Company).

67. Shibani Kinkar Chaubey, *Constituent Assembly of India: Springboard of Revolution*, 2nd ed. (New Delhi: Manohar, 2000; first published 1973).

68. Upendra Baxi, 'The Little Done, the Vast Undone: Some Reflections on Reading Granville Austin's *The Indian Constitution*', *Journal of the Indian Law Institute* 9, no. 3 (1967): 323–430.

69. Upendra Baxi, 'Patriarchy, Law and State: Some Preliminary Notes' (paper presented at the Second National Conference on Women's Studies, Trivandrum, 1984), cited in Ratna Kapur and Brenda Cossman, *Subversive Sites: Feminist Engagements with Law in India* (New Delhi: Sage, 1996), 76n21.

70. Upendra Baxi, 'The (Im)possibility of Constitutional Justice: Seismographic Notes on Indian Constitutionalism', in Zoya Hasan, E. Sridharan, and R. Sudarshan (eds), *India's Living Constitution: Ideas, Practices, Controversies*, 31–63 (Delhi: Permanent Black, 2002), 53.

71. Flavia Agnes, *Law and Gender Inequality: The Politics of Women's Rights in India* (New Delhi: Oxford University Press, 1999), 72.

72. Ibid., 71.

73. Flavia Agnes, *Family Law: Family Laws and Constitutional Claims* (New Delhi: Oxford University Press, 2011), 149–150 (emphasis mine).

74. Sarbani Sen, *The Constitution of India: Popular Sovereignty and Democratic Transformations* (New Delhi: Oxford University Press, 2007), 3.

75. Madhav Khosla, *The Indian Constitution* (New Delhi: Oxford University Press, 2012), xi (emphasis mine).

76. Ibid.

77. Ibid., xix.

78. Madhav Khosla, *India's Founding Moment: The Constitution of a Most Surprising Democracy* (Cambridge, MA: Harvard University Press, 2020), 16.

79. Ibid.

80. Ibid., 20.

81. See ibid., 72–109.

82. Ibid., 21.

83. See Chitra Sinha, *Debating Patriarchy: The Hindu Code Bill Controversy in India (1941–1956)* (New Delhi: Oxford University Press, 2012).

84. Title of article 25 of the Constitution of India which guarantees to all persons the right 'freely to profess, practise and propagate religion'.
85. Renuka Ray, 'Women's Movement in India', Typescript, 1948, Speeches/ Writings by Her, File no. 88, Renuka Ray Papers, Nehru Memorial Museum and Library, New Delhi (hereafter NMML).
86. Begam Jahan Ara Shah Nawaz, *Father and Daughter: A Political Autobiography* (Nigarishat: Lahore, 1971).
87. Beard, *An Economic Interpretation of the Constitution of the United States*, 17
88. Upendra Baxi, 'Siting Secularism in the Uniform Civil Code', in Anuradha Dingwaney Needham and Rajeshwari Sunder Rajan (eds), *The Crisis of Secularism in India*, 267–293 (Ranikhet: Permanent Black, 2007), 271.
89. Rajeev Bhargava, 'Introduction: Outline of a Political Theory of the Indian Constitution', in Rajeev Bhargava (ed.), *The Politics and Ethics of the Indian Constitution*, 1–41 (New Delhi: Oxford University Press, 2008), 12.
90. Nivedita Menon, 'Citizenship and the Passive Revolution: Interpreting the First Amendment', in Rajeev Bhargava (ed.), *The Politics and Ethics of the Indian Constitution*, 189–210 (New Delhi: Oxford University Press, 2008), 189.
91. Ibid., 189–190.
92. Roland Barthes, 'The Death of the Author', cited in ibid., 189.
93. Ibid., 189 (my emphasis).
94. Aditya Nigam, 'A Text without Author: Locating the Constituent Assembly as Event', in Rajeev Bhargava (ed.), *The Politics and Ethics of the Indian Constitution*, 119–139 (New Delhi: Oxford University Press, 2008).
95. Ibid., 137.
96. Ibid., 137.
97. Ibid., 120.
98. Roland Barthes, 'The Death of the Author', in Vincent B. Leitch (ed.), *The Norton Anthology of Theory and Criticism*, 1466–1470 (New York: WW Norton & Company, 2001), 1469.
99. Ibid., 1469.
100. Jane Gallop, *The Deaths of the Author: Reading and Writing in Time* (Durham and London: Duke University Press, 2011), 4.
101. The number of women who eventual signed the Constitution is 11. For more accurate details, see pp. 42–43 and 59.
102. Gautam Bhatia, *The Transformative Constitution: A Radical Biography in Nine Acts* (New Delhi: Harper Collins, 2019), xxxiii.
103. Udit Bhatia (ed.), *The Indian Constituent Assembly: Deliberations on Democracy* (London and New York: Routledge, 2018). None of its contributors takes women's presence in the Constituent Assembly seriously.

104. Udit Bhatia, 'Introduction', in Udit Bhatia (ed.), *The Indian Constituent Assembly: Deliberations on Democracy*, 1–9 (London and New York: Routledge, 2018), 2.

105. Nivedita Menon, *Recovering Subversion: Feminist Politics beyond the Law* (Ranikhet: Permanent Black, 2004), 8.

106. Ibid.

107. Ibid.

108. Hansa Mehta, 'The International Bill of Rights', Hansa Mehta Papers, 1st Instalment, Speeches/Writings by Her, File no. 7, NMML.

2

In Search of the Missing Mothers

The future constitution of the country will affect both men and women equally. Women, therefore, have as much interest in it [Constituent Assembly] as men have, perhaps *more*, for women would like to see that the new constitution is based on democratic principles and that no disability attaches to any citizen on the grounds of caste, creed or sex and that it provides equal rights and equal opportunities for women in all spheres of human activities.

—Hansa Mehta, 1946[1]

The conventional narrative of the formation of the Constituent Assembly praises the Congress for taking a great deal of pain to ensure that the Assembly had representatives of all social and political groups. The party, in the words of the official version, had to be 'the mirror of the nation',[2] and ensure that all shades of public opinion were represented in the Constituent Assembly.[3] In Austin's words, 'The Constituent Assembly was a one-party body in a one-party country. The Assembly was the Congress and the Congress was India.'[4] For Austin, who also repeats this version, women got some seats in the Assembly through the generosity of the Congress. He bases his claim on the limited archival support of a circular issued by the All India Congress Committee on 4 July 1946, asking that all provincial Congress legislatures elect some 'specific' women candidates to the Constituent Assembly.[5] The elections to the Constituent Assembly were to be held between 11 and 22 July 1946.[6] It was 'certain that the provincial assemblies would elect the individuals recommended by the high command'.[7]

When the Constituent Assembly was finally formed, 15 of its members were women. These were Begum Aizaz Rasul, Begum Jahanara Shahnawaz, Begum Shaista Suhrawardy Ikramullah, Ammu Swaminathan, Dakshayani Velayaudhan, G. Durgabai, Sucheta Kripalani, Vijayalakshmi Pandit, Purnima Banerji, Kamala Chaudhri, Sarojini Naidu, Hansa Mehta, Rajkumari Amrit Kaur, Leela Roy, and Malati Choudhury, women who have been nearly erased from the memory of the nation in the same way that women have been omitted or erased from history; but these women can be found in the archives. Some of these women are remembered for other reasons, but hardly ever as framers of the Constitution. Two more women were elected to the Constituent Assembly: Renuka Ray from West Bengal when fresh vacancies were created after constituencies from Bengal went to East Pakistan in July 1947, and Annie Mascarene as a representative of Travancore–Cochin in December 1948.[8] All in all, 17 women were elected to the Assembly, most of whom were deeply involved in the debates on the drafting of the Constitution of India.[9] For them, securing a foothold in the dominant patriarchal territory ruled by male politicians, statesmen, and lawyers – the founding fathers – was not an easy task (Image 2.1).

Image 2.1 The founding mothers. Women members of the Constituent Assembly seated for a photo session during the framing process. *Back row (standing), from left*: Kamala Chaudhari, Sucheta Kripalani, G. Durgabai, Qudsiya Aizaz Rasul, Purnima Banerji, Dakshayani Velayudhan. *Front row (sitting), from left*: Renuka Ray, Hansa Mehta, Rajkumari Amrit Kaur, Annie Mascarene, Ammu Swaminathan.

Source: Meera Velayudhan, personal collection.

Note: The image is included in *Women at the Midnight Hour*, calendar issued by the Centre for Women's Development Studies, New Delhi, 2018, curated by Malavika Karlekar (https://www.cwds.ac.in/wp-content/ uploads/2018/06/Calendar2018.pdf, accessed on 25 May 2020). The calendar acknowledges Meera Velayudhan for providing this photograph from her precious family photographs. Interestingly, as late as in 2018, the curators of the album failed to recognize Kamala Chaudhary and Purnima Banerji in the photograph.

Indeed, contrary to the narrative that women had entered the Constituent Assembly thanks to benevolent patriarchy, history bears witness to the fact that women worked hard for places in the Assembly, and actively shaped the Constitution of India. A majority of the women in the Constituent Assembly had participated in the women's movement for years and the All India Women's Conference (AIWC) had campaigned to ensure that they were elected. However, all the women were not members of the AIWC. Dakshayani Velayudhan, the only Dalit women member of the Constituent Assembly, most notably, was not an AIWC member and the story of her election deserves special attention. For women members of all affiliations, what constituted the crux of the matter was an attempt to negotiate and counter the issue of separate electorates and plead instead for a joint electorate. It is this narrative that one must unravel before an exploration of the struggle of women who fought fiercely to be elected to the Constituent Assembly.

SEPARATE AND JOINT ELECTORATES

The Cabinet Mission Plan had fixed the number of representatives to the Constituent Assembly belonging to different communities for each Province.[10] Hansa Mehta met the Cabinet Delegation a month before it published the plan that devised the mechanism for the formation of the Assembly and strongly protested against the inherent separatism of such a plan and the 'separate electorates that had been imposed upon us in spite of our warning'.[11] In her meeting she indicted the British policy for introducing the 'communal virus' in the ranks of the AIWC, whose members were already 'twenty-five thousand this year', and which number was growing.[12] The accelerated demand for Partition and the Muslim League's refusal to join the Constituent Assembly gave some force to the centrifugal movements in the AIWC, resulting in the resignation of several Muslim members. The most notable of these was Jahanara Shahnawaz, who demanded separate electorates against the dominant position of the AIWC and joined the Muslim League's demonstrations for Pakistan. In doing so, she 'faced tear gas and *lathi* attacks, and was eventually imprisoned'.[13] She was one of the 15 women elected to the Constituent Assembly, as listed above, but never joined it. In fact, after Partition, she became a member and then Vice President of the Pakistani Constituent Assembly.[14]

As an organization, the AIWC refused to accept the privileging of communal affiliation as a basis for national identity and clearly stated that it stood for a united India.[15] In April 1946, when the Cabinet Mission had asked

Hansa Mehta about the number of Muslim numbers, she clearly told them that 'we did not think in terms of Hindu members and Muslim members', and went on to remind them that the AIWC had protested against the introduction of separate electorates which had the effect of a 'communal virus' in the organization.[16] She had to underline before the Cabinet Commission that the AIWC had members in 'most parts of India including the Muslim areas; that our general secretary is a Muslim; one of our Vice-Presidents is a Muslim; and two of our presidents – I should have said three – were Muslims'.[17]

Mehta's deposition claiming that the AIWC was opposed to the Partition and separate electorates was not supported by all the members of the AIWC. The Muslim members of the Surat branch challenged her position and asked for an explanation from her. They passed the following resolution:

> We the Muslim members of the All India Women's Conference (Surat Branch) with regret bring to the notice of the conference that the President Mrs. Hansa Mehta has presented emphatically her views in an interview with the Secretary of State for India, Lord Pethic Lawrence of the effect that all members of this Conference unanimously support the idea of United India (Akhand Hindustan) and of Joint electorates. The fact is that AIWC is a non-political body, hence the President has no rights to express her views on behalf of the Conference, with reference to the present political matters of India.[18]

It is in these ruptures that the AIWC's endeavours to gain a foothold in the Assembly must be located. The Conference was struggling with communal fissures and at the same time its leadership, which included Amrit Kaur, Hansa Mehta, and Renuka Ray, was attempting to get some women elected to the Assembly. The fault lines were clearly communal, defining politics in patriarchal terms that segregated women along community lines, while the Conference was projecting women as a unified and distinct representable group. In her refutation of the two-nation theory based on communal identity before the Cabinet Mission, Hansa Mehta had added the equality of status for women as the most important element in their imagination of the nation. The idea of 'equal status as defined by us'[19] was articulated in several documents that the AIWC produced in the two decades of its existence and participation in constitutional politics, a movement for legal and social changes carried out primarily by appealing through petitions, canvassing in legislatures, making charters, and bringing in Bills.

The discourse on women's status also had another axis of internal pull which the women leaders had to deal with during this period. This was a prominent ideological fissure that formed the background of women's electioneering for the Constituent Assembly. The notion of political neutrality with which the Conference claimed to be working was perceptively threatened by Communism during the period under concern. As evident from the correspondence between Hansa Mehta, Amrit Kaur, Hajrah Begum, and Kitty Shiva Rao, the AIWC leadership was keen on protecting the non-political nature of the AIWC. At stake, in this case too, was the definition of 'political'. An increasing suspicion of members whose 'first loyalty is to the party', posed a complex problem for the Conference. Responding to complaints that 'We are handing over the Conference to the Communists',[20] Hansa Mehta as the AIWC President clearly stated:

> The All India Women's Conference is neither for the Congress women nor for the Communists. We wish to unite all women on certain common issues, viz., on problems that affect women, their status and position in society. I believe time has come when we must define it clearly. I would, therefore, not like the AIWC to be made a political cockpit and forget the real issue.[21]

Mehta's reference was to the tug of war between the Congress and the Communist women inside the Conference that had the potential to turn it into 'a political cockpit'. Manikuntala Sen, in her memoirs speaks of 'the intense anti-Communist feelings of the handful of Congress women who were connected with the association'.[22] The English edition of *Roshni*, the Conference's journal aimed at becoming 'a reliable Indian journal dealing with Indian women's problems by Indian women' based on 'women's support'.[23] However, the editor of its Hindi–Urdu edition was Hajrah Begum, a dedicated Communist activist, who some suspected of using the journal for 'political propaganda'.[24] She was repeatedly reprimanded for publishing issues 'which might seem communist' and censured even for the advertisements she was obtaining for the magazine.[25] The number of Communists in the AIWC had significantly increased during this period leading to an ideological schism that formed another important context from which women members to the Assembly were to be nominated. It must, however, be made clear that some of the chosen women, most importantly Renuka Ray and Purnima Banerji, had socialist inclinations which were frequently articulated during the debates in the Assembly.

For women, to select the most favourable set of representatives involved negotiating with various ideological cross purposes working within the framework provided by the Cabinet Mission Plan of 1946. According to its stipulations, the very basis of the Assembly's formation was communal representation provided to divide the provincial allocation of seats between the main communities in each Province in proportion to their population; [and] to provide that the representatives allocated to each community in a Province shall be elected by the members of that community in its Legislative Assembly.[26]

This had vital implications for women's campaigns for election to the Constituent Assembly since it ensured that Muslim women could only be elected by Muslim legislators (of both sexes) from any province, and perhaps led to the exclusion of several Muslim women for whom the AIWC had campaigned. Among these was Shareefah Hamid Ali, a former Chairperson and twice President of the AIWC, a pioneer of Hindu–Muslim unity, and a champion of the idea of joint electorates. Hamid Ali had campaigned ardently for reforms in the Hindu personal law, especially the promulgation of the Child Marriage Restraint Act of 1928, and was a co-delegate on behalf of the AIWC at the Round Table Conferences of 1931 and 1933. Along with Amrit Kaur, she had had fought hard for the official position of the AIWC in favour of joint electorates since the days of the Lothian Committee (1932). When Hansa Mehta had moved to the United Nations (UN) Commission on Human Rights in 1946, it was Hamid Ali who had replaced her as an Indian and AIWC representative on the UN Commission on the Status of Women, a role that she had played with robust grace and energy (Image 2.2).

From the perspectives of these leaders of the women's movement, women could speak for all women regardless of community and ideology. The idea that women from one community could represent women from another had been at the core of their feminist practice, of which Hamid Ali's campaign for reforms in Hindu Law is just one example. To be accurate, there was opposition from within the ranks of the women's movement to this idea articulated both by prominent figures like Radhabai Subbarayan and Jahanara Shahnawaz and by lesser members of the AIWC, but the official position of the AIWC was always against reservations and separate electorates. This was the normative logic of representation upheld by nearly all the women members of the Constituent Assembly.[27]

The idea of separate electorates was a source of what women repeatedly called the 'communal virus' in their negotiation with the colonial government and during their interventions in the Constituent Assembly.[28] To be divided on a communal basis for purposes of further enfranchisement would weaken their unity and allow male leaders to reorder their priorities. Women like Shahnawaz for whom separate electorates should have been accepted 'since their menfolk supported' it and 'because it would promote religious harmony'

**Image 2.2 Begum Hamid Ali at the United Nations Commission on Status of
          Women, 1948,** Second Session, 15 February 1948, New York. With her
          is Sara B. de Monzon of Guatemala. The 15-member organ of the United
          Nations Economic and Social Council prepares recommendations and reports
          to the Council on promoting women's rights in political, civil, social and
          educational fields.

Source: UN Photo Digital Asset Management System, Unique Identifier: UN7526232 NICA
ID326869 (https://dam.media.un.org/CS.aspx?VP3=DamView&VBID=2AM94S52JUV1&SMLS=
1&RW=1334&RH=747, accessed on 12 November 2020).

could not convince the dominant leadership of the women's organization.[29]
Women's support of joint electorates was not limited to their thoughts
on electoral representation but was an expression of their larger project of
transforming women from members of communities and castes to citizens.
Implicit in this idea was also the recognition that political citizenship was a
necessary first step for social transformation and for the achievement of freedom
from oppressive boundaries like caste and male-dominated communities. The
idea of joint electorates, therefore, for women leaders represented a democratic
model which allowed Hindu women to speak for Muslim women, upper-caste
women to speak for women of the depressed classes, and vice-versa.

Although this ideal had not factored in differences and asymmetries
between these relations, it was not totally oblivious to the interlocking grids

of women's representation. The primary objective was to make it possible for women to speak to each other without the paternalistic intervention of male community leaders. However, in certain specific cases, one's location within a certain minority – the 'depressed classes' or 'untouchables' – carried a different significance and alliances would be formed with male Dalit politicians, especially if that person was the charismatic Dalit ideologue B. R. Ambedkar.

The election of Daksyahani Velayudhan

Ambedkar and the All India Scheduled Castes Federation (AISCF) had tried hard to negotiate with the Cabinet Commission and put pressure on the British Government to provide for separate electorates for the Scheduled Castes for the election to the Constituent Assembly. This included making appeals to Winston Churchill to protest against 'the shameful betrayal by the Cabinet Mission to the cause of the sixty millions of Untouchables' of India, an appeal to which Churchill had responded with an assurance that he and his Party will do 'its utmost to protect the future of sixty million Untouchables whose melancholy depression by their co-religionists constituted one of the gravest features in the problem of the Indian sub-continent'.[30] Accounts of these negotiations and the protests appeared in the weekly journal of the AISCF, *Jai Bheem*, published from Madras, to which Dakshayani was a regular contributor.[31] It was in the pages of this weekly that some of Dakshayani's most stringent criticisms of the Indian National Congress and its leadership were published. In its inaugural issue published in January 1946, she had written:

> It is a foregone conclusion that Congress will burst into pieces when it takes the entire administration of the country. Congress is the least fitted party to rule over India on a democratic basis. The Congress government will be a Government of the Caste Hindus and the Capitalists. The Congress government will never satisfy the aspirations of the masses. The Congress Government cannot give freedom of thought and action to the people. The awakened masses of India will soon realize that they have done a folly in supporting the Congress.[32]

In this article, published only six months before her election to the Constituent Assembly from the Madras Provincial Assembly, she had chastised C. Rajagopalachari as the 'man who is supposed to be reinstated as the Prime Minister of Madras', for his refutation of Ambedkar. She wrote that Rajagopalachari, 'the clever Brahmin opportunist[,] has to be taught at his late age, the A, B, C, D, of the progressive political ideologies'.[33] She compared the movement led by Ambedkar with 'the beginning of the social revolution of the untouchables which will end only in the destruction of the suzerainty of the Caste Hindus' and called for a mass movement to lead it to its proper end, that is, the acceptance of the untouchables as 'part and parcel of the Human Society'.[34] 'If death is essential', she exhorted untouchables to 'accept it honourably. Courage should be the watchword of our forward march.'[35]

Courage, indeed, was the theme of her life and when the Cabinet Mission Plan was announced three months later, she found her ideas at variance with those of Ambedkar and the AISCF. The 18 June 1946 issue of *Jai Bheem* reported her response:

> In her statement on the Cabinet Mission's Proposals, she rejoiced that 'the Separate electorates for the Scheduled Castes have been given a decent burial' which according to her 'may not be liked by the communal reactionaries who are nourished and nurtured by the British Government'. She proceeded to prophesy that 'the Harijans would, in the long run, realise the wisdom of the Cabinet Mission in coming to this judgement'.[36]

Not only had Dakshayani opposed the idea of separate electorates, she had also opposed the AISCF's call for a Direct Action, a massive civil disobedience movement against the Cabinet Mission's proposal that could, in the words of the *Jai Bheem* contributor, 'paralyze the whole economic structure of the country'. No matter how one evaluates her position vis-à-vis joint or separate electorates – and that touches on a deep debate on the normative and actual aspects of the politics of representation – one can't help notice her courage in taking these stands in the middle of a mobilization of Dalit anger against the Mission's plan. Her courage was not taken lightly by leaders of the Dalit movement, and she was denounced as a 'traitor', 'an unworthy creature', a 'turncoat,' and a woman who had fallen into 'the depths of moral turpitude'.[37] 'Any direct action launched by the Scheduled Castes', the article threatened, 'will be aimed in the first instance to deal with undesirable creatures like her amongst them'.[38] Her disagreement with Ambedkar and the Dalit movement's resolution was presented as the worst possible act a Dalit *woman* could have committed:

> But while the rest of her like are bending their heads *in shame for their inability* to join hands with Dr. Ambedkar in championing the just cause of the Scheduled Castes, Mrs. Velayudhan, to *the utter disgrace of womanhood in India*, has *the audacity* to attack Dr. Ambedkar and his followers. While the Scheduled Castes can pardon all such helpless renegades, they can never pardon an unworthy creature like Mrs. Velayudhan.[39]

The attack on Dakshayani was couched in terms of shame and disgrace, evoking notions of honour that were to be upheld by women in battle, in this case of communities, led by men. More than her disagreement with the official position of the Federation, it was her audacity to disagree that was the subject of these attacks. Also implied in the opposition was the fear that she may not speak in the best interests of the community, defined, of course, by the official leadership.

These verbal attacks were carried out a month before the nominations to the Constituent Assembly were made, on the pages of a mouthpiece of the AISCF edited by Rao Bahadur N. Sivaraj, a former President and one of the founders of the Federation. A leading light of the Dalit movement, he was also her rival in the elections to the Constituent Assembly, pointing to the complexity of her situation. A trained lawyer and a former professor of law, Rao Bahadur Sivaraj had nearly 20 years' experience of legislative politics and was, at the time of the campaigns for the Constituent Assembly, the Mayor of Madras. In comparison, Dakshayani lacked his class privilege and had significantly fewer political resources. She had lost the election to Sivaraj on the first declaration of the results on account of some miscalculation of 'the transfer of surplus votes' which when remedied had found her a seat in the Constituent Assembly.[40]

Being female and a Malayali in Madras multiplied her difficulties. Members of the Federation Depressed Classes League of Madras protested against her selection as 'a Harijan candidate, thus depriving the Madras Harijans of one seat'.[41] G. Arulappan, a male Harijan activist began a fast unto death demanding that she be replaced by a Harijan from Madras. The President of the Federation Depressed Classes League made representations against Dakshayani's election to the Constituent Assembly before the Madras Premier, T. Prakasam and the Congress party, urging that they reconsider this choice. The fast was reported to Jawaharlal Nehru and he was requested to redress the grievance of the Madras Harijans.[42]

The fiercest opposition to Dakshayani's election to the Constituent Assembly, however, came from members of the Madras Congress. Her fearless criticism of the Congress leadership was used to discredit her in the eyes of the Congress high command. Malicious attacks on her were framed in the same misogynist framework that had informed the AISCF's campaign against her. The high command of the Congress had recommended nine representatives to be elected by the Madras Legislative Assembly to the Constituent Assembly.[43] Three of these were women, including G. Durgabai, who played important roles in several committees of the Constituent Assembly, Kamaladevi

Chattopadhyay, whose nomination was later withdrawn because of the Socialist Party's refusal to join the constitution-making body, and Dakshayani herself as a Scheduled Caste woman from Cochin state. Her earlier criticisms of the Congress and of C. Rajagopalachari in particular were immediately brought to the notice of the latter who tried to prevent her selection by asking T. Prakasam, the Madras premier, to withdraw her name.[44] Since she was a nominee of the high command of the Congress, desperate letters were written to Vallabhbhai Patel and Jawaharlal Nehru, urging them to dispatch urgent telegrams to prevent her selection. Her support to Ambedkar was cited and it was argued that electing her would be 'a sin before God and a lasting shame to the Congress'.[45] Within a space of less than one month of the vitriolic attack on her by the Dalit leadership, Patel was urged not to select her to the Constituent Assembly for that would give 'Dr. Ambedkar the strongest weapon of his life to attack the Congress'.[46] Patel was told:

> The most shameful thing which is a matter of disgrace for any Political Party in any country is the selection of a Harijan *woman* from the Cochin state who till the day of the Cabinet Mission's Statement was showering abuses both in the Press and the platform in the most filthy language unworthy of any person anywhere of culture and civilization on Mahatmaji, on Yourself, on other great leaders and on the Congress.[47]

I emphasize 'woman' to highlight the suspicion that communities could have on the abilities of women, who could either bring grace or disgrace to deliberative platforms but would not be valued for the ideas and values that they might place on the table. The aligned contours of these prejudices are revealed further on reading the following remarks from the same letter addressed to Patel:

> The Congress leaders are known to have decided to get the best suited persons for the Constituent Assembly and for this purpose even reactionaries of the Imperialist production have been selected by the Working Committee. But was this principle to be confined only to the non-Harijans in the Madras Presidency? In this Presidency where Congress Leadership has degenerated to the last, the seven Harijans selected by the Congress Legislative Party includes two persons who do not know English and do not know the A.B.C. of Politics. Are these the people who are going make the future Constitution of India?[48]

Thus, one can see an implicit notion of the suitability of some people – male, English speaking, upper class, conversant in politics – for the task of writing the future Constitution. The letter, evidently written by a male opponent of Dakshayani, draws parallels between the Harijan and non-Harijan representatives to the Constituent Assembly and sees the latter as the norm. This was destabilized by the presence of Dakshayani Velayudhan, both as a woman and as a Dalit in her selection, and her interventions during the framing of the Constitution. Records show that despite her differences on policies like reservation and separate electorates, Dakshayani took a keen interest in representing the cause of the Dalits in the Constituent Assembly, the Constituent Assembly (Legislative), and other legislative bodies. She frequently raised questions about the education of the Dalit community, scholarship schemes for Scheduled Caste students including those meant to sponsor education in foreign countries, the protection of Dalits against upper-caste violence, and most significantly, drawing attention to the Dalit woman's labour and safety.[49]

Her interventions were not limited to the caste question and the question of the interest of a community but extended to a call for a socialism that would lead to 'an economic revolution in the fascist social structure existing in India'.[50] Alert to the dangers of communalism, she characterized the Rashtriya Swayamsevak Sangh (RSS) as 'a strong fascist organization which has got support in influential quarters both inside and outside the Government', and warned the members of the Constituent Assembly of the 'spirit of violence' that the 'RSS movement' had unleashed and was 'spreading into the vitals of our national life'.[51] She repeatedly critiqued the new state for being excessively dependent on capitalists who, she argued, were 'the greatest enemies of the country'.[52] 'To hope to raise the standard of life of the people with the help of the industrialists and the capitalists', she had asserted while commenting on the third Annual Budget of independent India, 'will be like entrusting the lamb to the wolf'.[53]

THE SUITABLE WOMEN: SELECTING MEMBERS FOR THE CONSTITUENT ASSEMBLY

The AIWC had taken the initiative to find the names of women who could most effectively represent the diversity and opinion of women in the Constituent Assembly. A month before the elections, it sent individual letters to the premiers of the provincial legislative assemblies, and presumably also to the Congress Working Committee, suggesting the names of suitable women candidates. Several provincial assemblies responded, mostly in agreement. The Premier of Bombay, B. G. Kher, replied saying he 'completely agree[d] that there should be women on the Constituent Assembly' and that 'the matter will be fully considered'.[54] The Government of the United Provinces, after having received a reinforcing instruction from the Congress Working Committee, replied that two of the names suggested by the AIWC had also been recommended by the party high command, and their 'selection seems to be certain'.[55] The Premier of Orissa, to whom no such letter was sent, took umbrage that the 'you have excluded Orissa from your list of provinces from which you have recommended women representatives for election to the Constituent Assembly'.[56]

These recommendations were prepared at the intersection of the ideological and political currents discussed above, after consultation. The challenge was to find, as Amrit Kaur (Image 2.3) had put it, suitable women who could deal with 'such intricate problems as constitution-making'[57] and at the same time correspond to the definitional social categories which were stipulated by procedures set by the Cabinet Mission Plan. There was no easy consensus between the various parties and the British Government about the method by which the Constituent Assembly should be formed and carry out its work. In a statement issued on 16 May 1946, the Cabinet Mission and the Viceroy admitted that despite the labours of the British Government and the Indian parties and their hopes that the 'Indian people' themselves would agree upon the method of framing the new constitution, it had not been possible. The Constituent Assembly had emerged as a vulnerable compromise, offered 'at this supreme moment in Indian history statesmanship', to arrive at 'independence in the shortest time and with the least danger of internal disturbance and conflict'.[58] The Mission's Plan was approved by the Congress after much deliberation and the Muslim League's refusal to join the Assembly. In fact when women were proposing names to the provincial legislatures, Jinnah was still 'strongly' urging upon the Viceroy 'that the elections to the Constituent Assembly should be postponed'.[59] It was in a state of anxiety and uncertainty that Amrit Kaur and her colleagues initiated their plans to join the Assembly, 'if it comes off', as she wrote to Hansa Mehta while proposing her list of probable candidates.

Knowing the tussle surrounding its formation, she thought that there is no point in 'agitating for it so that we might appear to be putting an extra spoke in the wheel' but went on to suggest that the Congress President should be urged to elect women to the Constituent Assembly if the party has to be 'true to its ideal of representing every class'.[60] She suggested a panel of names featuring experts and women who could represent every province and community.[61] The list included Kamaladevi Chattopadhyay, Renuka Ray,

TIME
THE WEEKLY NEWSMAGAZINE

AMRIT KAUR (1947)
Championing an independent India

Image 2.3 'Amrit Kaur: championing an independent India'. Amrit Kaur on *Time* magazine's special cover celebrating 100 exceptional women since 1920.

Source: Time 100 Women of the Year: Amrit Kaur (https://time.com/5793532/amrit-kaur-100-women-of-the-year/, accessed 1 January 2022).

Vijayalakshmi Pandit, Lakshmi Menon, Begum Hamid Ali, Kulsum Sayani, Radhabai Subbarayan, Aruna Asaf Ali, Ammu Swaminathan, Rani Rajwade, Lady Rama Rau, Kitty Shiva Rao, Hannah Sen, Rameshwari Nehru, Leilamani Naidu, Jethi Sipahimalani, Hansa Mehta, and Sucheta Kripalani. She requested the AIWC to send 'a panel of names preferably from each province of such women as we feel will put up a good show'.[62]

The correspondence between the leaders of the women's organizations reveals that when several names were discussed as possible candidates, two names emerged as favourites. These were Hansa Mehta, who through her efficient handling of the AIWC as its president had emerged as a reliable representative of women's issues, and Kamaladevi Chattopadhyay, the previous president of the AIWC and a stalwart socialist leader who had prepared several major drafts of charters and petitions for women's organizations.

Kitty Shiva Rao, herself a sharp legal brain working for the women's movement, considered these two to be indispensable representatives of the women of India.[63] As wife of B. Shiva Rao, and sister-in-law of B. N. Rau, eminent constitutionalist who was at the centre of constitution-framing and legal drafting in India since the 1935 Government of India Act and the Constitutional Advisor to the Constituent Assembly, she was alert to the historical–legal circumstances of the time. She was sceptical about women's efforts to win seats in the Constituent Assembly. Referring to the mandatory 'Advisory Committee on the rights of citizens, minorities, and tribal and excluded areas'[64] in Paragraph 20 of the Mission's plan, she suggested that 'Even if we have no women in the Constituent Assembly in that Committee you and Kamala ought to be there, since it will deal with Fundamental Rights'.[65] Her choice was based on the legal expertise and jurisprudential vision of these two women, the authors of the Women's Charter of Rights and Duties which articulated women's vision of the fundamental rights.

The deliberations among the women leaders point to an anxiety to strike a balance between a comprehensive representation of women from all regions and all communities of India and the need to send women who could act as effective negotiators in an Assembly that would deal with legal matters. Despite Amrit Kaur's suggestion that 'it will be difficult to find women who know something about such intricate problems as constitution making' Kitty Shiva Rao insisted upon maintaining the principle of representation. 'We should have somebody from the Punjab group and from the … group', she told Hansa Mehta, 'as otherwise these groups may be without representation'.[66] This politics of representation was not confined merely to regional affiliations but extended to community as well, creating demands for women representatives at least from the Muslim, Christian, and Parsi communities. Lakshmi Menon thought that the list prepared by Hansa Mehta was not sufficiently representative of the minority religious communities, particularly the Parsis and the Christians. She observed that, 'recent tendencies have been to alienate' the Parsis.[67] Among the Parsi women associated with the AIWC, the names of Perin Bharucha, Mithan Lam, and Gulsitan Billimoria were also circulated as potential members of the Constituent Assembly. It was not without a political purport that Hansa Mehta expressed deep satisfaction at the election of three Muslim women to the Constituent Assembly.[68] Interestingly, if Kitty Shiva Rao and Amrit Kaur saw women as minorities who must at least have a place in drafting the fundamental rights that would protect their interests, women's status as a minority group was also exploited by the Congress, which conflated their community identity with their gendered identity while making its selection for the Assembly.

Amrit Kaur's membership of a religious minority – she was Christian – was used to cast her as representing both women and Christians. In his instructions to the Premier of the Central Provinces regarding candidates from various religious minorities, Vallabhbhai Patel recommended Amrit Kaur's name so that she could serve both the purposes: 'For a woman whom you have got to provide, Rajkumari Amrit Kaur may be taken, in which case you may not have to provide separately for a Christian seat'.[69] Amrit Kaur and her women colleagues, including Aizaz Rasul (the sole Muslim woman in the Assembly), had long resisted privileging religious identity over methods of self-definition, and destabilized such binaries as between religious majority and minorities. During the framing process, Amrit Kaur, who occupied 'a *Christian* seat' and Aizaz Rasul, who occupied a Muslim seat, were enabled by the discursive arrangement of the Constituent Assembly to sometimes attenuate and negotiate with the representative force of religious minorities from a gendered perspective. Both of them took strong positions against the demands of their male minority representatives. It is important at this point to remember that in the official male constitutional discourse of rights, women's interests were already framed as minority interests, a position which women did not necessarily disagree with. In fact, 'the term "minority" periodically became associated with women or applied in the same breath'. Women, nonchalantly accepted such practices.[70] Constitutions, by definition, are supposed to protect the rights of groups disabled either by their numbers or due to disabling and discriminatory social structures and practices. It was in the latter sense that Amrit Kaur had described women as technically the largest minority during the framing process.[71]

The search for a probable group of women leaders considered the representative value of individual women, their legal acumen, their proximity to influential male leaders, and presence in the public sphere. The name of Prabhawati Jayaprakash Narayan, wife of the socialist leader, was suggested owing presumably to her proximity to the Gandhian group in the Congress, most notably Rajendra Prasad, who became the President of the

Constituent Assembly.[72] From the socialists, Kamaladevi's name was agreed as among the most suitable women for the task of constitution-making. She had been the President of the AIWC and author of numerous petitions, charters, and reports about women's status in India, and was widely admired for her abilities both inside and outside of women's organizations. Despite her ardent wish to be a part of the framing, and collaborate with the Congress in the momentous task, she was not elected to the Assembly since the socialists had chosen to stay away from it. By the time they had changed their position, circumstances had gone against them. Later in her life Kamaladevi regretted the decision of her party, calling it 'a psychological blunder' and felt that the socialists should have offered to 'collaborate from *within* instead of leaving the crucial constitution-making to non-politicals, moderate professionals like lawyers, doctors, and even some conservative elements that the Congress collected to broad-base the Constituent Assembly resulting in several unhappy results'.[73]

One of the complaints of women members like Renuka Ray, a close collaborator with Kamaladevi on the Indian Women's Charter of Rights and Duties, was against the Right to Property as it was adopted by the Constituent Assembly. As late as in March 1949, Renuka Ray lamented the absence of socialist members in the Constituent Assembly, arguing that if men of the calibre of Shri Jayaprakash Narayan and Acharya Narendra Deo and women like Kamaladevi Chattopadhyay were helping the country in this emergency, it would be all to the good.[74] Kamaladevi too, complained that the refusal of 'the original Socialists' to participate in the framing process resulted in a Constitution wrapped in the 'garb of a bogus socialism', a 'grandiose garb'.[75]

However, Kamaladevi Chattopadhyay collaborated with her women colleagues working in the Assembly from *outside* and offered them her advice on several constitutional issues. Having vigorously but unsuccessfully pleaded to Jayaprakash Narayan to join the Constituent Assembly and collaborate with Nehru during the framing, she had offered herself as the 'Socialist Party's sacrificial goat' and worked as a member of the Working Committee of the Congress Party.[76] In all probability, she played some role in ensuring that women's names were recommended to the Constituent Assembly. This work will have little to say about her in the following pages; yet the intellectual and organizational support that she provided to the women members of the Constituent Assembly and her articulation of the collective constitutional vision for them are so significant that she can be considered as one of the founding mothers.

The original 15 members elected to the Assembly did not participate evenly in its proceedings. Following the displacements caused by Partition and the joining of the new representatives from the princely states, the composition of the Assembly was slightly altered. Two of the Muslim women left for Pakistan; Leela Roy, unhappy with the Congress's acceptance of the Partition resigned in protest; Vijayalakshmi Pandit resigned to become India's first Ambassador to Soviet Russia; Sarojini Naidu died a year before the Constitution came into existence; and another member, Malati Choudhury, resigned when she realized the work did not suit her. Thus, on the day the Constitution was signed by the members, there were only 11 women who could officially put their signatures on the grand document of the Indian republic.

Among those who had left the Assembly was Malati Choudhury, a member from the Orissa Legislative Assembly. A dedicated social worker, who was then the President of the Utkal Pradesh Congress Committee, she ran Gandhian projects including hostels for children of the deprived classes in the coastal town of Angul. Malati was unhappy with the legal bickering in the Constituent Assembly. In her letter in Hindi sent to the President of the Assembly, Rajendra Prasad, citing the reasons for her resignation, she explained that she felt more suited for the rigorous Gandhian programme that she was running back at home. The branch's work would be crucial for the Swaraj which 'we will be establishing after the 15th of August'.[77] Staying away from the place of her work for long periods would cause immense damage to her project. The other reason that she cited was more interesting:

> To my mind the most important reason is that there is no suitable work for me in the Constituent Assembly. Where brains like Sri Alladi Krishnaswami ji, Munshi ji, Gopalaswami ji, etc are working what is left for people like me? I had asked Patel ji to relieve me from it in the first meeting of the Constituent Assembly; but looking at the circumstances he asked me to stay on for some more days.[78]

The men she was referring to were formidable lawyers – Alladi probably the most formidable of them all – who were soon elected to the Drafting Committee. The other women members, however, were not daunted by the presence of great lawyers and towering figures. They had experience of constitutional politics of years and had dealt with knotty questions of social and legal reforms, represented women's issues on several national and international platforms, debated issues in legislatures, and above all, had been running large women's organizations on constitutional and democratic principles. Constitution-making they knew was about establishing a democratic order, whose fundamental ethical principles were to be carved out after debates in the Assembly. Soon after the inception of the Constituent Assembly, in a note presumably written for publication in the AIWC's mouthpiece *Roshni*, Hansa Mehta expressed a deep sense of satisfaction with the election of 15 women to that august body.[79] Fifteen among 300, 'about five percent of the total membership', she knew was a paltry number in a body that was supposed to arrive at decisions through voting.[80] But it was still a victory 'considering the great scramble for seats by men'.[81] As the President of the AIWC, the most representative body of Indian women, she was aware of the grounds on which men competed for seats in the Assembly. The Constituent Assembly was no easy destination, it was a field of contestation between many interest groups and identities which were trying to rush through its narrow gates, moved presumably by the 'accelerated temporalities of the state'.[82]

Membership in the Assembly was extremely coveted. Those who could not or did not want to be elected still wanted to influence its decisions by indirect means. There is evidence that a section of his supporters wanted even Vinayak Damodar Savarkar to address the Assembly.[83] Other men kept campaigning to be elected to one or the other of its various committees. Men had to struggle to be elected to the Assembly, and felt humiliated when left out of it. Sarangadhar Das of Orissa, for example, resigned from the Orissa provincial legislature, because he could not get elected to the Constituent Assembly. Sardar Vallabhbhai Patel clearly told him that his expectation of getting elected to the Constituent Assembly or any of its committees was mistaken.[84] The leader of the Orissa Legislative Assembly, Harekrushna Mahtab was asked to 'better relieve him instead of keeping him as a disgruntled leader'.[85] Before the instructions were sent to the provincial houses, Patel had clearly explained what kind of people they wanted in the Constituent Assembly: 'men who can make a good contribution to the complicated task of constitution-making or drafting and we certainly want men of ability and experience'.[86] Women were of course, not thought of as people with ability and experience capable of valuable contribution. Anyway they were few in number.

Even the three seats vacated by the death of Sarojini Naidu and resignation of Vijayalakshmi Pandit and Malati Choudhury were filled up by men, much to the disappointment of women members who told the Constituent Assembly that 'women could have also filled up these places with equal merit and they should have been invited'.[87]

The Constituent Assembly in these early stages was still a vulnerable body, whose legitimacy was put to question from many corners. It had taken Jayaprakash Narayan a year before he could accept its validity and request Jawaharlal Nehru to induct new members like Narendra Deo, Ram Manohar Lohia, and Ashoke Patwardhan.[88] Jayaprakash also included in this list Kamaladevi Chattopadhyay and Aruna Asaf Ali, socialist women who later regretted that they could not participate in the framing of the Constitution. In her note on the formation of the Constituent Assembly in 1946, Hansa Mehta spends considerable energy defending its legitimacy and, by implication, her own place in the historical body that would lay down the foundations of the nation: 'it would be foolish to minimize the importance of the body', she says, asserting that 'even if the election had been on the basis of adult franchise the results would not have been very much different'.[89] Women's presence in the Constituent Assembly was a result of their eagerness to be a part of the founding process, to give – in the most legitimate manner – the will of the nation, a voice of their own. Once the Constitution was framed, they took legitimate pride in having spoken for the 'We, the people,' during that momentous project.

Women had in fact taken an immense interest in the Constituent Assembly and its formation. In her inaugural speech in the Assembly on 19 December 1946, Dakshayani Velayudhan reflected on the Objectives Resolution and expressed very high hopes of the Constitution addressing the idea of freedom from social fetters and caste discrimination. 'To frame a constitution is an easy job', she had said, 'because there are many models for us to imitate. But to renew a people on a new foundation requires the synthetic vision of a planner. The Independent Sovereign Republic of India plans a free society.'[90] It was a new Constitution for which there were no models from the past, one in which 'the power will come from the people' and 'there will be no barriers based on caste or community'.[91] Speaking in a nationalist vein, Velayudhan chastised Winston Churchill and the colonial masters for having done nothing significant 'to improve the social status of the Harijans' and hoped that the new Constitution will lead to 'the removal, immediate removal, of our social disabilities. Only an Independent Socialist Indian Republic can give freedom and equality of status to the Harijans.'[92]

The socialist democratic Constitution and its values of equal rights and opportunities were matters of great importance for women, and long before the Congress issued its circular, they had campaigned for their election. They were elected to the Assembly because of their sustained engagement in constitutional politics and a jurisprudential vision of the future of the nation.

THE EXCEPTIONAL LIVES OF THE 'MISSING MOTHERS':
INDISPENSABILITY OF BIOGRAPHY

The work does not pretend to catalogue every single contribution of all the women members of the Constituent Assembly. It limits itself to the contributions of Amrit Kaur, Hansa Mehta, Renuka Ray, G. Durgabai, Purnima Banerji, Aizaz Rasul, Dakshayani Velayudhan, and Sucheta Kripalani – women who worked in interrelated ways and significantly shaped the original text of the Constitution. These women illuminated the debates with their distinct insights into some of the key ideas that animated the framing process, made subtle alliances with supporting ideological forces, moved crucial amendments, raised questions of great significance, introduced phrases and verbal changes of far-reaching implications, and affected the framing process in numerous other ways in the course of the three years of the Assembly's functioning. Though they had differences among themselves, they worked together to form a distinct ideological group, adding a gendered dimension to some of the central ideas of the Indian Constitution. Since these women form the principal protagonists of this work, it would be pertinent to recollect certain biographical narratives from the mostly untapped historical memory. Indeed, the intellectual and biographical profiles of these women are deeply intertwined with their performance in the act of framing, not just in terms of its content but also in terms of their faith and conviction in the principles they were representing.

Rajkumari Amrit Kaur (1889–1964) lived, chronologically, a life exactly parallel to Jawaharlal Nehru, with whom she was associated closely during her work as India's Health Minister and also during the formation of the Constituent Assembly. It is an interesting co-incidence that her maternal grandfather was Rev Golaknath, whose descendants were party to one of the most historical cases that changed the course of the Indian jurispridence. Her parents, including her father Raja Sir Harnam Singh, of the Kapurthala estate, were Presbyterians who inculcated in her a love for austerity and a spirit of high-minded humanism. Amrit Kaur went to school in England and was partly educated at Oxford. She was a member of the AIWC since 1929, and as an erstwhile president and influential member had worked hard to ensure that Hansa Mehta was elected as the President of the AIWC during the crucial period of the making of the Constitution.[93] A leader of the women's movement, she worked as a link between the old guard and the younger activists, and also facilitated work with Mahatma Gandhi. She was a Minister in the Interim Government of Nehru during the framing period and facilitated the framing on many accounts. She was one of the founding spirits behind the All Institute of Medical Sciences (AIIMS) in New Delhi. In the Constituent Assembly, besides her role in the Fundamental Rights Sub-Committee and the Minorities Sub-Committee, she intervened frequently on questions related to the status of health in the federal structure of the state.

Hansa Mehta (1897–1995) was an unusual woman in many ways (Image 2.4). Daughter of Sir Manubhai Mehta, himself an educationist and philosopher of repute, she studied philosophy at Baroda, journalism in London, and many other subjects on her own. As the first Vice Chancellor of the MS University, Baroda, a post that she held for nine years, she touched the life and works of some of the country's most important academics. India's preeminent sociologist, M. N. Srinivas, whose academic career and research

Image 2.4 Hansa Mehta during an early meeting of the UN Sub-Commission on the Status of Women, Hunter College, New York, May 1946. *From left to right*: Hansa Mehta, India; Way Sung New, China; Fryderyka Kalinowski, Poland; Angela Jurdak, Lebanon; Marie Helene Lefaucheux, France; and Bodgil Begtrup, Denmark and Chairman of the committee.

Source: UN Photo Digital Management Asset System; Unique ID: UN7617890 (https://dam.media. un.org/CS.aspx?VP3=DamView&VBID=2AM94S52JUV1&SMLS=1&RW=1334&RH=747#/ DamView&VBID=2AM94S52I895&PN=1&WS=SearchResults, accessed on 20 May 2021).

she nourished, recalled, 'Under her leadership, the MS University began to be recognized by the cognoscenti as an innovative centre of learning.'[94] She had an unusual love for travelling and sociological field research which informed all her interventions in the women's movement. Her marriage to Dr Jivraj Mehta in 1924 was a *pratiloma* marriage – an inter-caste marriage that resulted in hypogamy, in which the husband is from a caste or class lower than that of the wife – and had caused a huge furore. She had radical ideas about Hindu laws and custom. She began participating in the constitutional reforms and attempts at the codification of Hindu law in the 1930s, deposing before several commissions, writing tracts on women under Hindu law, and envisioning a social reconstruction based on her ideas of justice and equality. She was one of the pioneers of the post-war human rights movement, a fact that has only recently been recognized.[95] With Kamaladevi and Renuka Ray as collaborators, she also authored the Indian Women's Charter of Rights and Duties, which constituted the foundational document of Indian women's campaign for constitutional rights and human rights. During the framing of the Constitution, she was dividing her time between the Indian Constituent Assembly and the UN, where she played a crucial role in the Sub-Commission on the Status of Women, and later in the drafting of the Universal Declaration of Human Rights in 1948. As a member of the Central Advisory Board of Education and later as the Chairperson of the Committee on the Differentiation of Curricula for Boys and Girls, she propounded a sophisticated gender-sensitive vision of education at all levels. Mehta was also an acclaimed Gujarati playwright and a versatile translator who translated into Gujarati English plays by Shakespeare, two French plays by Molière, and the Sanskrit epic, the Ramayana.

Renuka Ray (1904–1997) had a B. Sc. in Economics from the London School of Economics, where she was a pupil of the socialist political philosopher Harold Laski, whose ideas on history and politics influenced her. Daughter of an Indian Civil Services officer and married to another, she was also influenced by her mother, Charulata Mukherjee, a founding member of the AIWC and one of its presidents. She was an important campaigner for the removal of legal disabilities of women, especially in labour and family rights. At the request of the International Alliance of Women, she drafted the Memorandum submitted on behalf of Indian women to the League of Nations. The only woman in the Central Assembly to represent women's views on the Hindu Code Bill in 1943–1945, she had developed her independent understanding of women's lives at the intersection of law and customs. This had also allowed her to develop a close working relationship with B. N. Rau, later the Constitutional Advisor to the Constituent Assembly whom she regularly consulted. She had accompanied Mahatma Gandhi in his visits to Noakhali. She was a member of the Select Committee under the Chairmanship of B. R. Ambedkar that drafted the Hindu Code Bill, which was later modified and passed piecemeal by the Parliament. Renuka was a sound social thinker, whose many important published and unpublished articles on issues related to social structure and the relation between law and society are crucial to an understanding of the constitutional vision of the women framers.

G. Durgabai (1909–1981) had a brilliant legal practice at the Madras High Court, when she came to the Constituent Assembly. Her name was not part of the list that women had proposed for the Constituent Assembly. By her own account, she was elected to the Constituent Assembly for her 'service to the country', and because 'I had equipped myself with the legal background and field work'.[96] At the time of her election, she was among the most promising lawyers at the Madras High Court where even 'the judges, both European and Indian' thought that instead of being a part of the Assembly, she must continue her legal practice.[97] In the Constituent Assembly, however, as a member of the Steering Committee, she worked closely with B. N. Rau, Alladi Krishnaswami, and other legal luminaries who were so impressed by her legal abilities that she was entrusted with the task of moving most of the 700 amendments. This resulted in a creative dialectic of textual framing/formation between her and Ambedkar, who as the Chairman of the Drafting Committee had to defend the text against the amendments moved by her.[98] It is reported that thanks to her numerous interventions, B. R. Ambedkar referred to her as 'a woman with a bee in her bonnet'.[99] Her sharp legal perception and access to the inner working of the Assembly helped the women members significantly. After the Constitution was promulgated, she chose to contest the Lok Sabha elections, in place of becoming a judge in a High Court. Losing the election, she became a member of the first Planning Commission and established the Central Social Welfare Board.

She had chosen to study law in order to help women, having had intimate interactions with women convicts as a political prisoner at Vellore in 1932. In her own words:

> I tried to know under what circumstances these women had committed the crimes for which they were convicted. Some of them were sentenced to life imprisonment. Their narration left a deep impression on my mind. Being uneducated and illiterate, some of them pleaded guilty to the charges even though they did not commit the crime. I had then decided to take up the study

of law so that I could give such women free legal aid and assist them to defend themselves. I felt that *just as a woman patient would take a woman doctor in confidence and reveal all her ailments freely, if an accused woman had the assistance of a woman lawyer, she would narrate her case freely and fearlessly.*[100]

Durgabai's life is illustrative of the ways in which these women brought a certain feminist motive to their work and strove towards making the instruments of modernity – law, in particular – useful for them. Women's experience had to be voiced in a language that was used and introduced by modernity in such ways that these institutions do not collaborate with traditional patriarchy in marginalizing them further. Durgabai's engagement with the structure and independence of the judicial system while it was being framed in the Constituent Assembly was, partly, an extension of this project. Similarly, her keen interest in social welfare which for her was the ethical core of the state, was translated into her sustained advocacy for the directive principles throughout the framing. Durgabai was a keen social worker for whom social work was not merely activism but a manifestation of a constitutional vision in whose authorship she had participated. The relationship between the state and its machinery, as well as that between the state and civil society were crucial issues that she addressed as a Member of the first Planning Commission and as the chairperson of the Central Social Welfare Board.

Begum Qudsia Aizaz Rasul (1905–2001) was elected to the Constituent Assembly on a Muslim League ticket, and had refused many requests to migrate to Pakistan where her ancestral family had an influential status. Married into a feudal family of the United Provinces – her husband was the taluqdar of Jalalpur estate in Sandila, a small town on the outskirts of Lucknow[101] – she had huge landed interests in India, which may have determined some of her interventions in the Assembly. Rasul was a long-time member of the AIWC, and its Vice-President in the late 1930s. She was a member of the United Provinces Legislative Assembly in 1938, and a member of the United Provinces Provincial Assembly at the time of the framing. As the sole Muslim woman involved in the framing process, she was at the centre of several controversies on questions of representation at the interstices of class, gender, and community.

Unlike the majority of privileged upper-caste women members of the Constituent Assembly, Dakshayani Velayudhan (1912–1974) was born in the slave-caste of Pulaya on an obscure island off the Cochin coast. She had, in the words of her daughter, Meera Velayudhan, 'many firsts in her life':

the first girl to wear an upper cloth, the first Dalit woman graduate in India, a science graduate, a member of the Cochin Legislative Council and of the Constituent Assembly. She also resisted by not walking with shoulders bent or making way for upper castes when walking.[102]

Dakshayani's struggle against the double jeopardy of being a Dalit and a woman was played out against the desire to 'annihilate' caste, in the backdrop of a sea that 'did not have a caste'. The phrase is from her description of the formation of the Pulaya Mahajan Sabha, the Cochin-based movement of anti-caste cultural politics that had inspired her in her youth. Its first meeting, in her words,

> was held with country boats tied together in the sea in Bolghatty – the sea did not have a caste. In Kochi, the untouchables were not allowed to hold a meeting 'in my land' by the Maharaja. The raft was made by joining together a large number of catamarans with the help and support of the fisherfolk.[103]

The metaphor of a caste-less sea and bridges made of wooden boats summarizes Dakshayani's persistent negotiations with several movements against the caste system. Her marriage with the Dalit leader R. Velayudhan was presided over by Gandhi and Kasturba in Sevagram at Wardha and she retained Gandhian sympathies all her life (Image 2.5). The opposition to separate electorates was an important item in her moral imagination and as is evident from the snippets of her memoirs available in English, she recounted it with discernible pride in her later years as well.[104]

Dakshayani's political education as a young woman took place in the shadow of the Poona Pact of 1932 between Mahatma Gandhi and B. R. Ambedkar which determined that there would be no separate electorates for the Depressed Classes but reserved seats for them in joint electorates. Yet in ideological terms she refused to take sides: she advanced sincere reconciliatory gestures to the apparently incompatible Gandhian and Ambedkarite responses to the caste question, and never felt encumbered by group pressures of any kind. She never joined the AIWC despite her feminist politics, and even though rooted firmly in the Congress in the 1940s,[105] she participated in the activities of the AISCF in Madras. She was not shy of criticizing Congress leaders for failing to attend to the task of social transformation and, when she felt so, did not spare the Drafting Committee for preparing a Constitution that was 'barren' of the 'ideas and principles' that were regularly professed by the great leaders.[106]

Image 2.5 A 'Dalit' wedding. A painting of the wedding ceremony of Dakshayani and
R. Velayudhan presided over by Mahatma Gandhi and Kasturba.

Source: Meera Velayudhan, personal collection.

The three women who were elected from the United Provinces were
Sucheta Kripalani (1907–1974), Purnima Banerji (1905–1952), and Kamala
Chaudhri (1908–1970). Purnima, who passed away soon after the Constitution
came into being, was an avowed socialist and trade union leader. She took
special interest in the constitutional provisions about labour, secular education,
and property rights. She, along with Renuka Ray, was a key strategist in the
campaign against the fundamental right to property led by the group of socialist
leaders in the Assembly. Sucheta who later on became the first woman chief
minister (of a state) in independent India, was a great organizer and debater.
A brilliant student of political science at St. Stephen's College, Delhi, she was
briefly a lecturer in constitutional history at the Benaras Hindu University.
Sucheta was occupied with refugee rehabilitation during the framing process
and so could not participate in the debates as much as she had wanted to.
Yet she would make special interventions in the debates on the Hindu Code
Bill when the Constituent Assembly functioned as the central legislature.
Kamala Chaudhri, a rather quiet member of the Assembly who made very few
interventions apart from occasionally during the Hindu Code Bill debates, of
course in support of the reforms, was a moderately recognized feminist
short-story writer at the time of her election. The editors of a landmark
anthology of women's writing in India describe her fiction as carrying a

'distinctive feminist edge'.[107] Apart from writing short stories that portray the inner worlds of women's lives, she had also written some satire and translated Omar Khayyam into Hindi.[108] Although the problematic that informs this book does not permit biographical readings of women's interventions as individuals, it does make an implicit argument for the need of biographical studies of each one of them.[109]

The women framers of the Constitution were not always successful in getting their views accepted by the rest of the members of the Assembly. However, as a small group, they formed a distinct cluster whose views could not be completely ignored either. They were strategists who knew their weaknesses and strengths and acted accordingly. They were women who had worked together under a common programme of the women's movement, especially constitutional politics. They had sufficient experience of working in small and powerful committees, and were adept at articulating their ideas in a language which would be acceptable to the majority members of the Assembly. Accordingly, they got themselves inducted into some of the most important committees which would address specialized issues. It has been argued by eminent constitutional experts that the most important decisions of the Constituent Assembly were taken in these committees and their proceedings should be given precedence over the Constituent Assembly Debates in any search of the collective intention of these women.[110] If these women have been missing from our knowledge of the making of the Constitution, it is because scholars have failed to look at the right archives, namely, the proceedings of such committees and not necessarily the formal Constitutional Debates.

I would like to argue that the women's position in the framing process must be understood not with a pre-determined view from the perch of the Constitution as it was adopted. It is my submission that the archives of constitution-making in India should not be limited to the Constituent Assembly Debates. They must include the preceding and surrounding discourses in which the framers were involved; the correspondence and personal discussions between the members; the formations, proceedings, and the decisions of the various committees; and the deep textual structure in which they were all related to each other.

Indeed, I wish to suggest that the archives that also need to be explored belong to a period prior to which women became members of the Constituent Assembly. Following my earlier argument that most of the 'missing mothers' of the Constitution were also prominent members of the AIWC, I would like to posit that it is crucial to understand the conceptual and ideological core of women's politics in the period between 1927 (when the AIWC was founded) and 1946, the beginning of the formal working of the Constituent Assembly. These years were marked by the intense engagement that women in the AIWC had, through debates and discussions, about certain ideas and ideals that should guide the relationship between the individual and the state. I identify the entire gamut of the discourse on rights and duties as integral to their notion of this relationship. Further, I propose that the arguments advanced by women had a moral dimension which is of considerable significance as is the mode through which they articulated it.

In this period before coming to the Constituent Assembly, members of the AIWC had engaged with a constitutional form of colonial government. After the final phase of formal decolonization, the government of independent India, too, adopted this mode of constitutional politics. Hence there was no real rupture between modes of political mobilization. In the following chapter, I shall show that women who had acquired their skills in constitutional politics during the pre-Independence phase found themselves in a particularly enabling condition when they became members of the Constituent Assembly. Therefore, one of my major arguments in this book is that before coming to the Constituent Assembly the women members had developed a keen belief in constitutionalism and had already staged a performance of constitution writing. This involved a collective act of translation of their moral ideas which had been shaped during two decades of the women's movement into the language of constitutional law. It was inevitable that their participation in the framing process repeated, albeit in a more condensed and intense manner, this act of translation of the moral imaginary.

NOTES

1. Hansa Mehta, 'The Constituent Assembly of India', Typescript in 'Writings by Her', Subject File no. 8, Hansa Mehta Papers, I Instalment, NMML.
2. Jawaharlal Nehru, 'Unity of India' (1939), quoted in Granville Austin, *The Indian Constitution: Cornerstone of a Nation*, 2nd ed. (New Delhi: Oxford University Press, 1999), 11.
3. Austin, *The Indian Constitution*, 13.
4. Ibid., 8–9.
5. Ibid., 12n42.
6. Ibid., 12.
7. Ibid.
8. Renuka Ray joined the Constituent Assembly on 14 July 1947. *CAD*, IV: 538; Annie Mascarene joined the Assembly on 29 December 1948. *CAD*, VII: 1099.

9. Of these, Shaishta Ikramulla, Jahanara Shahnawaz, and Leela Roy lost their seats on Partition, though Jahanara Shahnawaz and Shaista Ikramulla went on to work in the Constituent Assembly of Pakistan. Sarojini Naidu and Vijayalakshmi Pandit resigned from their membership of the Assembly on being assigned roles as Governor of the United Provinces and Ambassador to Moscow, respectively. For Leela Roy's feminism, especially for the way she shaped the Bengali monthly *Jayashree* in the 1930s, see Sarmistha Dutta Gupta, *Identities and Histories: Women's Writing and Politics in Bengal* (Kolkata: Stree, 2010), 100–140. For Leela Roy's election and contribution to the National Planning Committee, see ibid., 121–122.

10. For a reproduction of the Table of Representation prepared by the Mission, see Austin, *The Indian Constitution*, 332.

11. Hansa Mehta, Letter to Branch Representatives of the AIWC, 29 April 1946, Papers, IV Instalment, File no. 58, NMML.

12. Ibid.

13. Geraldine Forbes, *Women in Modern India* (Cambridge: Cambridge University Press, 1996), 198.

14. Ibid.

15. Ibid.

16. Hansa Mehta, President, AIWC, Letter to the Branches reporting her meeting with the Cabinet Mission, 11 April 1946, AIWC Papers, IV Instalment, File no. 58, NMML.

17. Ibid.

18. Extract from the resolution forwarded by Mandakini Munsif, Joint Secretary, AIWC (Surat Branch) to Hansa Mehta, undated, Hansa Mehta Papers, Subject File no. 10, 196, NMML.

19. Hansa Mehta, President, AIWC, Letter to the Branches reporting her meeting with the Cabinet Mission, 11 April 1946.

20. Kitty Shiva Rao to Rajkumari Amrit Kaur, 3 January 1946, Hansa Mehta Papers, Subject Files, File no. 6, NMML.

21. Hansa Mehta to Kitty Shiva Rao, 14.01.1946. Subject File no. 6, Hansa Mehta Papers, NMML.

22. Manikuntala Sen, *In Search of Freedom: An Unfinished Journey* (Calcutta: Stree, 2001), 56.

23. Lakshmi Menon, then editor of the English *Roshni*, to Hansa Mehta, 19 January 1946. Hansa Mehta Papers, Subject Files, File no. 6, NMML

24. See also Hajrah Begum, *Why Should Women Vote for Communists?* (Communist Party Publication, 1962).

25. Hajrah Begum to Amrit Kaur, 7 May 1947, File no. 74, AIWC Papers, IV Instalment, NMML.

26. Paragraph 18 of the Cabinet Mission Plan, 1946. Reproduced in B. Shiva Rao, ed., *The Framing of India's Constitution: Select Documents*, Vol. 1, 209–218 (Delhi: Universal Law Publishing Co., 2004; originally The Indian Institute of Public Administration, 1967), 214.

27. Even Dakshayani Velayudhan, who was otherwise critical of the elitism of the AIWC, had taken a position against separate electorates for women or Muslims or the Depressed Classes (the official term for Dalits). I elaborate on her position during relevant discussions in this book.

28. Amrit Kaur's cross-examination by B. R. Ambedkar for the Indian Franchise Committee, 29 July 1933. *Dr. Babasaheb Ambedkar: Writings and Speeches*, Vol. 2 (Mumbai: Govt. of Maharashtra, 1982–2003), 700.

29. Forbes, *Women in Modern India*, 109.

30. *Dr. Babasaheb Ambedkar: Writings and Speeches*, Vol. 17(2), 210.

31. Extracts from Ambedkar's response to the Cabinet Mission published in *Jai Bheem* are collected in *Dr. Babasaheb Ambedkar: Writings and Speeches*, Vol. 17(2).

32. Dakshayani Velayudhan, 'The Task Ahead: Organize Federation in Every Village', *Jai Bheem* 1, no. 1 (31 January 1946): 1.

33. Ibid., 5.

34. Ibid., 1.

35. Ibid.

36. M. Dharamaiah, 'Mrs. Velayudhan's Foul Play', *Jai Bheem* (18 June 1946): 5–6, 5.

37. Ibid.

38. Ibid., 6.

39. Ibid., 5 (emphasis mine).

40. 'Madras and Bihar Results: Constituent Assembly Elections', *Times of India*, 24 July 1946, 9. Dakshayani called her election to the Constituent Assembly 'interesting and historical' as she had won after a recount. Meera Velayudhan, 'Linking Radical Traditions and the Contemporary Dalit Women's Movement: An Intergenerational Lens', *Feminist Review* 119 (July 2018): 106–125, 114.

41. 'Madras Harijan on Fast unto Death', *Times of India*, 17 July 1946, 5.

42. *Times of India*, 17 July 1946.

43. 'The Constituent Assembly: Congress Candidates from Madras', *Times of India*, 14 July 1946, 8.

44. Letter written by Raghavan Manikkan to Vallabhbhai Patel, 12 July 1946, Sardar Patel (Private) Papers, File no. II-72-4, National Archives of India, New Delhi (hereafter NAI).

45. Ibid.

46. Ibid.

47. Ibid. (emphasis mine).

48. Ibid.

49. Her interventions in the Constituent Assembly in its role as constitution-maker and as a legislative assembly deserve an entire chapter, which is beyond the scope of this book. I discuss her interventions on behalf of the Dalit woman worker in the concluding chapter.

50. Dakshayani Velayudhan, Constituent Assembly of India, 1 May 1947, *CAD*, III: 480.

51. Dakshayani Velayudhan, Constituent Assembly (Legislative) of India, 4 March 1949, *CA(L)D*, II (II): 1096.

52. Ibid., 1096.

53. Ibid.

54. Letter from B. G. Kher to Hansa Mehta, dated 22 June 1946, Hansa Mehta Papers, Subject File no. 10, NMML.

55. Office of the Premier of the United Provinces to Hansa Mehta, Hansa Mehta Papers, Subject File 10, 130, NMML.

56. Harekrushna Mahtab to Hansa Mehta, Hansa Mehta Papers, Subject File 10, 126, NMML.

57. Kitty Shiva Rao citing Amrit Kaur, Letter to Hansa Mehta, 19 June 1946, Hansa Mehta papers, Subject File no. 6, 103–107, NMML.

58. Statement by the Cabinet Mission and the Viceroy, 16 May 1946, reprinted in Rao, *The Framing of India's Constitution*, Vol. 1, 209–218, 217.

59. Jinnah to Viceroy, 28 June 1946, reprinted in Rao, *The Framing of India's Constitution*, Vol. 1, 283.

60. Amrit Kaur to Hansa Mehta, 12 June 1946, Hansa Mehta Papers, Subject File no. 6, NMML.

61. Among those whose names were regularly recommended by the AIWC leaders were Kamaladevi Chattopadhyay, Renuka Ray, Vijayalakshmi Pandit, Lakshmi Menon, Begum Hamid Ali, Kulsum Sayani, Radhabhai Subbarayan, Aruna Asaf Ali, Ammu Swaminathan, Kitty Shiva Rao, Hansa Mehta, Sucheta Kripalani, Perin Bharucha, Prabhawati Devi, and Amrit Kaur. Most of these women had been extremely active in the constitutional politics in which women participated in the late 1930s and 1940s and hence well versed in the dynamics of representation.

62. Amrit Kaur to Hansa Mehta, 12 June 1946, Mehta Papers, Subject File no. 6, NMML.

63. Kitty Shiva Rao citing Amrit Kaur, Letter to Hansa Mehta, 19 June 1946, Hansa Mehta papers, Subject File 6, 103–107, NMML.

64. Cabinet Mission Plan, cited in Rao, *The Framing of India's Constitution*, Vol. 1, 216.

65. Kitty Shiva Rao to Hansa Mehta, 19 June 1946, Hansa Mehta Papers, I Instalment, File no. 8, NMML.

66. Ibid.

67. Lakshmi Menon to Hansa Mehta, 6 July 1946, Hansa Mehta Papers, Subject File no. 6, NMML.

68. Hansa Mehta, 'The Constituent Assembly of India', unpublished typescript, written probably for the August issue of *Roshni*, the AIWC mouthpiece, Hansa Mehta Papers, I Instalment, 'Writings by Her', Subject File 8, NMML.

69. Vallabhbhai Patel to Ravishankar Shukla, 27 June 1946, in Durgadas (ed.), *Sardar Patel's Correspondence*, Vol. 3, 150–151 (Ahmedabad: Navajivan, 1971), 151.
    Vallabbhai Patel to Harekrushna Mahtab, 16 September 1946, in ibid.

70. Wendy Singer, *A Constituency Suitable for Ladies* (New Delhi: Oxford University Press, 2007), 56.

71. Amrit Kaur, 'Memorandum on Minorities', 20 March 1947, reprinted in Rao, *The Framing of India's Constitution*, Vol. 2, 309–312, 310.

72. Amrit Kaur to Hansa Mehta, 21 June 1946, Hansa Mehta Papers Subject File 10, NMML.

73. Kamaladevi Chattopadhyay, *Inner Recesses Outer Spaces: Memoirs* (New Delhi: India International Centre & Niyogi Books, 2014; originally 1986), 216 (emphasis original).

74. Renuka Ray, Constituent Assembly (Legislative) of India, *CA(L)D*, 4 March 1949, Vol. II(II): 1082.

75. Chattopadhyay, *Inner Recesses Outer Spaces*, 329.

76. Ibid., 299.

77. Malati Choudhury to Rajendra Prasad, 11 July 1947, Rajendra Prasad Papers, 6-C/47, NAI (my translation).

78. Ibid.

79. Mehta, 'The Constituent Assembly of India'.

80. Ibid.

81. Ibid.

82. Aditya Nigam, 'A Text without Author': Locating the Constituent Assembly as Event', in Rajeev Bhargava (ed.), *The Politics and Ethics of the Indian Constitution*, 119–139 (New Delhi: Oxford University Press, 2008), 137.

83. Telegram of Secretary, Hindu Sabha, to Rajendra Prasad: 'Pray Invite Veer Savarkar the Indian Revolutionary to Address Consembly on 15th', Rajendra Prasad Papers, 3M/47, Col 2, NAI.

84. Vallabhbhai Patel to Sarangadhar Das, 16 August 1946, reprinted in Durgadas, *Sardar Patel's Correspondence*, Vol. 3, 147.

85. Vallabhbhai Patel to Harekrushna Mahtab, 16 September 1946, in ibid.

86. Vallabhbhai Patel to Nichaldas C. Vazirani, 2 June 1946, in ibid., 106.

87. Purnima Banerji, 11 October 1949, *CAD*, XI: 23.

88. Jayaprakash Narayan to Jawaharlal Nehru, 3 July 1947; Nehru to Rajendra Prasad, 5 July 1947; Nehru to Jayaprakash, 5 July 1947. Rajendra Prasad Papers, File no. I-E/47, NAI.

89. Mehta, 'The Constituent Assembly of India'.

90. Dakshayani Velayudhan, Constituent Assembly of India, 19 December 1946, *CAD*, I: 151.

91. Ibid., 152.

92. Ibid.

93. Letter from Amrit Kaur to Hansa Mehta, 31 October 1944, Hansa Mehta Papers, Correspondence with Amrit Kaur, NMML.

94. M. N. Srinivas, 'My Baroda Days', in *The Oxford India Srinivas*, 609–622 (New Delhi: Oxford University Press, 2009), 621.

95. Manu Bhagavan, *The Peacemakers: India and the Quest for One World* (New Delhi: Harper Collins, 2012).

96. Durgabai Deshmukh, Oral Transcripts, 9, NMML.

97. Ibid., 8.

98. This is not to suggest that either Ambedkar or Durgabai were the authors of the text that they had respectively framed and sought amendments to. Yet the relation between a text and its amendment cannot be entirely reduced to a plane of legalistic battles.

99. Kamala Mankekar, 'Durgabai Deshmukh', in Sushila Nayar and Kamla Mankekar (eds), *Women Pioneers in India's Renaissance*, 380–388 (New Delhi: National Book Trust, 2002), 385.

100. Durgabai Deshmukh, *Chintamani and I* (Delhi: Allied, 1981), 11 (emphasis mine).

101. Aizaz Rasul, *From Purdah to Parliament* (New Delhi: Ajanta, 2001), 20.

102. M. Velayudhan, 'Linking Radical Traditions', 116.

103. Ibid., 113. These are snippets from the much-awaited translation of Dakshayani's memoirs by her daughter Meera Velayudhan.

104. Ibid., 114n15.

105. The British Intelligence Report on the members of the Constituent Assembly describes her party affiliation as 'pro-Congress'. See IOR/L/P&J/10/62, Part 1, India Office Records, British Library, London, 177.

106. Dakshayani Velayudhan, Constituent Assembly of India, 8 November 1948, *CAD*, VII: 310.

107. Headnote to Kamala Chaudhri. Susie Tharu and K. Lalita (eds), *Women Writing in India: 600 BC to the Present*, Vol. I. (New Delhi: Oxford University Press, 1991), 472.

108. Dhirendra Verma (ed.), *Hindi Sahitya Kosh*, 2nd ed., Vol. 2 (Varanasi: Jnan Mandal Limited,1986), 69.

109. The internet has recently been filled with blogs about 'the fifteen women' often presenting history as a pageant with random quotations picked up without analysis of the contexts in which they were stated. I can recommend the websites only with the above caveat. Published autobiographies and memoirs of the women members are listed in the bibliography of this book.

110. H. M. Seervai, *Constitutional Law of India*, Vol. 1 (Delhi: Universal Book Traders, 1991), 201.

3

Women's Moral Imaginary and Constitutional Politics

1927–1946

The women of India are no longer willing to submit to standards, whether local, political or ethical, which have been set for them by the male conscience of the community.

—Amrit Kaur, speech in Jullundur, 1932

Three major women's organizations were founded in India after the First World War: the Women's Indian Association (WIA) founded by the Irish theosophist and feminist Margaret Cousins in 1917, the National Council of Women in India (NCWI) founded by Mehribai Tata and her associates in 1925, and the All India Women's Conference (AIWC) founded in 1927.[1] According to Geraldine Forbes, 'the presence of the self-respect movement [led by Periyar] had helped limit the appeal of the WIA in southern India to high-caste women'[2] while the NCWI 'failed to grow and become a vital national organization because of its elitism'.[3] The AIWC, the last to be formed, was 'the most truly Indian of the three organizations' and by the time of the formation of the Constituent Assembly, was the most recognized platform of the women's movement in India.[4]

The most active women members of the Assembly had all been important members of the AIWC, playing significant roles in its committees of legal disability, labour, economic rights, education, and constitutional principles. Kamaladevi Chattopadhyay, Hansa Mehta, and Amrit Kaur were among the AIWC's founding members, and had regularly served on its Standing Committee. Hansa Mehta herself was the President of the AIWC at the time of her election to the Constituent Assembly, an office that Amrit Kaur had held more than once in the past. Qudsia Aizaz Rasul had been its Vice President and Renuka Ray had led the AIWC's legal reform movement.

These women and other members of the AIWC had contributed to a significant realignment of the social and the political through a sustained exercise of redefinition of these categories. Half a century after its foundation, when Kamaladevi Chattopadhyay recounted the history of the women's movement in India, she had described the AIWC as 'the earliest national body of women which funnelled women's aspirations, plans, projects, and focussed its achievements and failures'.[5] She called it the voice of 'a concise, authentic national women's movement from the twenties'.[6]

While Kamaladevi claimed the AIWC spoke for Indian women, others criticized the organization's internal and external practices. One instance of this was the Dalit women's report of the practice of caste-prejudice in one of its meetings.[7] However, it would be hard to deny that in the years that led to the Constituent Assembly, the AIWC generated some of the most important ideas about the relationship between the state, society, and the citizen. The figure of the Indian woman was re-imagined radically and thoroughly at its portal. According to the *Report of the Sub-Committee on Woman's Role in Planned Economy*, an early feminist manifesto, the desire of the members was nothing short of a radical reimagination of the social structure:

> We would like to displace the picture so deeply impressed upon the racial imagination of man striding forward to conquer new worlds, woman following wearily behind with a baby in her arms. The picture which we now envisage is that of man and woman, comrades of the road, going forward together, the child joyously shared by both. Such a reality we feel cannot but raise the manhood and womanhood of any nation.[8]

The nation was robustly imagined by the Committee as a planned economy with 'Woman as the focus'. She would 'contribute to all aspects of the nation's wealth and the people's well-being'.[9] The Committee had tried 'to make a very aggressive and unfamiliar individuality for women acceptable in a society which was totally unfamiliar with the idea'.[10] The report of the Committee imagined a new Indian female subject with 'a complete individuality and self-sufficiency'.[11] Drawing its moral inspiration from the declaration on fundamental rights by the Indian National Congress at Karachi in 1931, the report's new female subject was already placed in the semantic fields emerging from a constitutionalist discourse. The women leaders, several of whom like Hansa Mehta helped draft the *Report on Woman's Role in Planned Economy*, were alert to the political potentials and risks in times of transition.

They were aware of the dichotomy between the Soviet socialist experiments in planning and the liberal constitutional framework of democracy towards which they were moving:

In the world today great changes are taking place; and, we are told, that this is a period of transition; so also in India where a new order is being born, not only political but also social and economic.... The change from what is old and established to something new and untried always contains an element of danger.[12]

The entrenchment of the ideas of equality and freedom in the language of constitutionalism allowed women to think in terms of a creative membership of society. This is what Amrit Kaur had identified as 'constructive citizenship' produced by 'the daily exercise of these rights and duties and in the opportunities which the state affords to the individual of developing his or her faculties'.[13] In establishing these ideas, Amrit Kaur and the other women had activated a new moral vocabulary for the imagining of the nation. Terms of this moral imagination were consistently presented, refined, and recast in the language of constitutional politics (Image 3.1).

Image 3.1 The princess and the fakir. Amrit Kaur receiving Gandhi on his arrival at Shimla to meet the Cabinet Mission delegation, 2 May 1946.

Source: Gandhi Heritage Portal (https://www.gandhiheritageportal.org/datalink/files/ghp_photos/simla_01.jpg, accessed on 20 April 2021).

THE CONTOURS OF WOMEN'S CONSTITUTIONAL POLITICS

Constitutional politics may be defined as a specific kind of politics that takes law as a central element in the realization of the necessary changes. The sense in which I use 'constitutional politics' in my work stresses its character as a unified movement which works through negotiations, rather than confrontation with the state, made in terms that are compatible with the available constitutional framework. With reference to the women's movement in this period, the characteristics of this politics need to be defined in order to appreciate the centrality that it achieves in the constitutional history of India.

During the freedom movement, the Constitution was envisioned as a law that would give the nation a set of rules to follow. The demand for a Constituent Assembly had been part of the official agenda of the Indian National Congress from 1934, and was reiterated persistently until the Assembly was finally convened in 1946. In 1934, K. M. Munshi described the demand for the Constituent Assembly as an expression of the hope for 'the dignity of an enfranchised nation'. Through the Assembly, the nation could 'fashion its will to self-determination, and find its own soul to express it through fundamental laws'.[14] With the promulgation of the Government of India Act in 1935, this demand gained further momentum and was, in Nehru's words, 'full of big possibility'.[15] In his presidential address at the Faizpur session of the Indian National Congress, in 1936, he maintained:

> our positive demand for a Constituent Assembly ... that is the very corner-stone of Congress policy today and our election campaign must be based on it. This Assembly must not be conceived as something animating from the British Government or as a compromise with British imperialism. If it is to have any reality, it must have the will of the people behind it and the organized strength of the masses to support it, and the power to draw up the Constitution of a free India.[16]

Though the British administration had not thought of the 1935 Government of India Act as a 'foundational or constitutional document',[17] in the nationalist discourse, it had the status of a Constitution. According to the Congress Resolution against it, it was 'designed to facilitate and perpetuate the domination and exploitation of the people of India and is imposed on the country to the accompaniment of widespread repression and the suppression of civil liberties'.[18]

In the documents of the AIWC, the 1935 Government of India Act is regularly referred to as the Constitution of India, which even at the stage of its drafting had aroused hopes for women and compelled them to change the nature of their politics. 'With a new Constitution of India on the anvil', Kamaladevi recounts, it had become 'imperative to win equality in citizenship' and therefore, the AIWC had amended its own Constitution allowing its members to engage in 'political activity of a non-party and constructive nature'.[19] While this suggests that the AIWC harboured constitutional aspirations and believed in the efficacy of constitutional methods, they did not have the same eagerness and enthusiasm for the idea of the immediate convention of a Constituent Assembly. Ever sceptical and keenly observant of the nature of politics, leaders of the AIWC were aware of the challenges in convening a Constituent Assembly. In her presidential address at the All-India Socialist Conference of 1936, Kamaladevi Chattopadhyay examined 'the relationship between Imperialism and its Indian allies such as the princes, landlords, capitalists, middle-men, money-lenders, etc.'[20] She expressed anxieties about a Constitution produced at the intersection of imperialism, anti-colonial nationalist movements, and the asymmetrical class-structure of the society. She argued that a genuinely democratic constitution could only be achieved after the masses achieved a minimal economic status. Failing this, the Constitution would become an oppressive tool, not an instrument for 'a radical change in an entire system'.[21] Spoken more than a decade before the inception of the Constituent Assembly, her remarks carry the weight of an admonition and the ring of prescience:

> We thus find that the composition of the Constituent Assembly is determined by the class-basis of the national movement and the constitution by the social composition of the Constituent Assembly. The talk of convoking it at this stage with the sanction of Imperialism is sheer delusion. It would be anything but a Constituent Assembly. In fact, it will be a positive danger, for under the name of Constituent Assembly, a puppet of Imperialism will come into being to lead to further strengthening of its domination.[22]

The most serious drawback of such a Constituent Assembly, she went on to complain, would be that 'it will lack both mass sanction and composition'.[23] While Kamaladevi did not participate directly in the framing of the Constitution, her observations articulated a sense of pragmatism that informed women's engagement with constitutionalism for the entire period. In the subsequent years, while the AIWC and other women's organizations in India campaigned for several pieces of social legislation and towards a comprehensive reform in the codes of personal laws, it became clear to them that the social composition of legislative bodies and the presiding colonial power over them would force them to make compromises at every step. Therefore, they realized that more than the giving of the law, it was the *justification* of the law that had to be secured first in order to ensure legal changes. Aware of the inevitably asymmetric composition of the future Constituent Assembly, they turned towards grounding their movement in a moral justification of law which would produce a collective identity of women defined as rights-bearing citizens. Kamaladevi's remarks, made at a socialist congregation, echoed the feminist suspicion towards the Constituent Assembly's neutrality while inviting women to intervene in the process of its making. The hypothetical Constituent Assembly was a warning to reorient their politics to ensure that effective alliances were developed for the variety of constitutional politics in which the women's movement was anchored.

It is, therefore, no surprise that the women's movement represented by Kamaladevi and other leaders of the AIWC perceived itself as a collaborative venture. 'The Indian Women's Movement', as characterized by Kamaladevi in 1939, had 'met with comparatively little organized opposition' unlike in the United Kingdom where it took the form of militant warfare.[24] According to its own narrative, the Indian women's movement had 'fairly smooth sailing'.[25] Its roots, like that of women's movements in other parts of the world, were traced to 'democratic revolutions such as the French Revolution' and would inevitably have taken the path of constitutional politics. 'Had India been left to herself', argued Kamaladevi, 'she might have worked out a democratic revolution for herself, after the decline of the Moghul Empire, and destroyed the tottering feudalism'.[26] British Imperialism 'propped up a dying society',[27] and helped to perpetuate patriarchal discriminations. Women's movements emerged as a response to this imperialism, and hence, was 'not merely against conservatism but also against the State, which undoubtedly favours in its own interests, the continuance of reactionary forces'.[28] It was in the course of this opposition to the state that the women's movement in India resorted to a democratic, constitutional politics. While it 'became an integral part of the freedom movement in India',[29] it also carefully chose strategies for its success. As Kamaladevi was to explain later, the compulsion of their movement was 'patience and forbearance with wisdom and tact so as not to kill an opportunity or outrage sentiments that would recoil'.[30] In times like those, 'the technique of change had to be "reformist" piecemeal'.[31]

Women's collaboration with male reformers

In these crucial decades before the framing of the Constitution, the women's movement chose negotiation rather than confrontation. It refrained from directly opposing the government and repudiating its machineries through acts of civil disobedience and other forms of spectacular, verbal, and corporeal forms of expression. Instead, it mobilized the state's powers through the means of written petitions and requests for reforms. While women were on the leading ranks of nationalism's picketing forces, they were also producing numerous documents for the legislative processes that were adopted by the colonial state for social reforms. They collaborated actively with male jurists, lawyers, and politicians and were involved in various processes of law-making which would transform the lives of women and, more importantly, would gain legitimacy for principles that would inform the future Constitution of India.

An interesting example of such collaboration would be women's concerted effort in the reforms of Hindu Law. The endeavour was to create a discursive field for reforms in the public sphere and within the Hindu Law Committee, while supplementing their reformist stance with constructive readings of the shastric texts and the judicial pronouncements of the colonial state. Renuka Ray, who was the only woman member of the Hindu Law Committee (1943) regularly cited modern legal text books on Hindu Law during the Committee's proceedings, exercising skills of negotiation that she had learnt from eminent constitutionalists like B. N. Rau. Inside the Committee, she would collaborate with sympathetic male members like V. V. Joshi who shared her anxiety about 'the countrywide reactionary campaign against the Bill'.[32] Joshi reminded her of the opposition that the Bill would meet, especially from the Hindu Mahasabha which had 'chosen the Bill as the fit calamity it should combat with'. The revivalist organization, Joshi explained to her, had earned an unpopularity through its 'inaction and communal bias', and was looking forward to campaigning against the Bill to achieve some prominence,[33] In response, Renuka Ray attempted to mobilize progressive male leaders in support of the Bill, who could influence public opinion and persuade the Committee to think in terms of women's rights. As a member of the Committee she wrote to B. C. Roy that 'it is very essential that the progressive element amongst which our men in Bengal, including lawyers, should also make them felt in support of the Bill'.[34] This, she argued 'will help me fight the case better'.[35]

Renuka Ray's position, both inside and outside the Committee, was based on her strategic privileging of the idea of 'absolute estate' for women, no matter what their share in property was to be. Thus, for her it was crucial that women got an absolute right on property that was not subject to any limitations, conditions and restrictions. This, in turn, was an extension of the idea of indissoluble rights of women in the sphere of family and inheritance, which was again an extension of the notion of equality of the sexes. However, she carefully employed tactics to extend the fundamental concept of rights in her submissions in the initial stages of the Hindu Code debates. Instead of pushing for absolute equality in inheritance between sons and daughters, she concentrated on getting the Committee to agree to an absolute estate first. This was a tactical step which was best understood and endorsed by B. N. Rau himself, whose advice she had taken at every step of her career, prior to and during the framing of the Constitution. Rau had advised her to stick to her strategy:

> I am glad that you were able to persuade [the Committee] that there should be no whittling (down) of the absolute estate. The other compromise – giving ¼ share to the daughter and 1/8 to the widowed daughter-in-law – is a comparatively minor matter and may be accepted if it helps to allay opposition. Whether you should record a minute of dissent is a matter of 'tactics' – see what the opposition does and then decide. It is a point on which you need not make up your mind until the whole Bill has been disposed of.[36]

Rau's advice was to ensure that there was an agreement on the idea of an absolute estate, not the share. As Ray later celebrated, the vital issue was 'not the quantum of property but the right of women to be recognized'.[37] Rau's advice had always been of strategic benefit for the women members in their long association with him, this being one example of many. It illustrates the way women used *tactics* at several levels in the course of their constitutional politics. They paid meticulous attention to the terms of the discourse, selecting aspects that were to be projected during a particular moment, and deciding the nature of emphasis to be placed on them.

The idea was to secure a theoretical foothold first and wait for the right moment to get it translated into a practice whose range could be expanded. It was not an entirely radical exercise, depending as it did on available generic structures, but was sufficiently capable of creating a powerful semantic field within which women could later participate inside the Constituent Assembly. The non-confrontational politics of constitution-making, built around this dynamic engagement with the reflexive nature of the genre of constitutions, prepared women for an effective role in the framing of the Indian Constitution in more than one way.

Women's ingenious engagement with the language of constitutions must be central to any examination of their participation in the founding of the republic. This examination must not treat the language of women's politics as transparent, positive facts of history but as evidence of a compelling act of translation and meaning-making through which women tried to deal with the jargon of constitutionalism and redefined it to suit their needs. Working within the generic rules of constitutional texts, women had to create specific discursive categories in which they could mobilise their own demands. Such terms as 'legal disability', 'women's status', 'minorities', and 'constructive citizenship' were either borrowed or invented and invested with specific meanings oriented towards constitutional notions of rights and equality before they could engage with the discursive regime of colonial and postcolonial constitutions. The genealogical specificities of these terms and their historical implications will help us understand how women evolved their own modes of constitutional politics and how the choice and usage of these terms constituted ingenious acts of borrowing, appropriation, re-appropriation, and translation.

This also helps us to understand the reasons why women's constitutional politics continuously kept shifting in tone and demands. These shifts were part of a shrewd understanding of the dependence of their politics on the more dominant modes of resistance and nation building. Women were motivated by concerns of social reconstruction and attached an instrumental value to such politics. They were new to it and constituted a relatively weak group among warring factions driven by narratives like nationalism and socialism. By the time they had arrived on the scene, to use Partha Chatterjee's formulation, the 'women's question' was already resolved within the nationalist discourse. This resolution, according to him, led to 'the refusal of nationalism to make the women's question an issue of political negotiation with the colonial state'. [38] Chatterjee argues that the lives of middle-class women changed

> in the colonial period mostly outside the arena of political agitation, in a domain where the nation thought itself as already free. It was *after* independence, when the nation had acquired political sovereignty, that it became legitimate to embody the ideas of reform in legislative enactments about marriage rules, property rights, suffrage, equal pay, equality of opportunity etc.[39]

Women's participation in constitutional politics, however, brings a different perspective to the story of reform; women involved themselves in legislative reforms, in areas considered the private sphere.

What is important for the purpose of this book is to understand that in this field of constitutional and legislative discourse, women's real contest was to gain legitimacy for 'the idea of reform'. This would enable them to influence the deliberations in the Constituent Assembly with their limited numerical strength. In my reading of women's active performance within the generic field of constitutionalism, women did make a strong claim for legitimacy of these reforms in the years leading to the framing of the Constitution. This was achieved by translating their particular expediencies into the discourse of constitutional rights and nationalism that had attained the status of the universal. The fact that women's constitutional politics sought to borrow from and often coloured their ideas in the vocabulary of nationalism may give the mistaken impression that their inclinations were predominantly and exclusively nationalist. They had to code their statements in the idioms and linguistic frame of the dominant nationalist movement, and occasionally, of the promissory constitutional discourse of the colonial state and the contemporaneous language of human rights.

The most significant feature of any movement based on constitutional methods is its heavily textual character. Such a politics demands a certain dissolution of individual presences in the formalities of written texts that ensures individuals do not attract claims of leadership in the same manner as, for example, a movement of civil disobedience does. Moreover, it is characteristically an organization-based politics which develops its own corpus of texts, a steady resource for reference, to which the movement is moored even in its most radical moments. These resources stabilize the demands of the movement and are suffused with a vocabulary whose registers are unique to it. Women associated with the written-ness of such a politics form a pool of experts who are adept at representing women's issues in its terms. The AIWC, itself a democratic body with a federal structure and a defined constitution, provided such women with the necessary office through which these texts were produced, preserved, transmitted, and dispersed. An intellectual history of the AIWC, as opposed to the official accounts of its social service acts will necessarily discover patterns of intertextual evolution in the dozens of documents that it produced in this period. Remarkably, the women authors of these documents were part of a wider international feminist movement which included membership in various bodies of the ILO and UN. Moreover, they were also members of provincial and central legislatures of the colonial state. The women members of the Constituent Assembly were a committed and proficient pool of constitutional activists.

The AIWC had emerged as the pre-eminent women's organization in the 1930s and 1940s not because of its increasing membership or expansive welfare activities, but by creating a well-argued and internally consistent intellectual grid of reformist documents. From its inception in 1927, beginning with the campaign for the Child Marriage Restraint Act of 1929, it pursued a series of reforms in personal laws, legal reforms for improving the conditions of labouring women, educational reforms, and other wide-ranging reforms that generated a set of documents that collectively constituted the archives of women's moral imagination and anticipated women's role in the framing of the Indian Constitution. These archives must necessarily include, among others, the Women's Charter of Rights and Duties (1945/6), the *Report of*

Image 3.2 Hansa Mehta with J. Marguerite Bowie of the United Kingdom at the Fifth Session of the Human Rights Commission, 9 May 1949, New York.

Source: UN Photo Digital Management Asset System; Unique ID: UN7478390 (https://dam.media. un.org/CS.aspx?VP3=DamView&VBID=2AM94S52JUV1&SMLS=1&RW=1334&RH=747#/ DamView&VBID=2AM94S52I895&PN=1&WS=SearchResults, accessed on 20 May 2021).

the Committee of the Role of Women in Planned Economy (prepared 1939/40, published 1947), the Legislative Programme of the AIWC (1938), the AIWC's memorandums to the Hindu Law Committee, its memorandums to the ILO, and the numerous representations by women members at the meetings of agencies of the United Nations (UN) during this period. The host of texts, and these must include the ones produced by other women's organizations as well – petitions, charters, committee reports, journalistic pieces, speeches, correspondence – during this period embody a well-developed jurisprudential, social, and political vision.

These women had borrowed contingently from a variety of discourses but also invented a language of their own, whose persuasive powers lay both in rational arguments and rhetorical choices. For instance, there are striking parallels, both formal and substantial, between some of these texts, the Indian Constitution, and the Universal Declaration of Human Rights (UDHR). They must not just be seen as evidence of a uniformity of legal language but as the result of these women's effective participation in the historical production of these texts. These texts must form a discourse, an imaginary, and a system, often in a dialectical relation with hegemonic elements contemporaneous with them. Collectively they articulate the moral imaginary of the women's movement from whose ranks the mothers of the Constitution of India were chosen (Image 3.2).

Challenging the 'male-conscience of the community': Re-imagining the nation's women

In a speech delivered in 1932, Amrit Kaur came closest to formulating the task of women's movement as one of comprehensively contesting patriarchal ideology as it permeates all the spheres of society. Although she does not use the term, patriarchy, she clearly identifies it as a discursive force that has to be challenged. Her statement announces the long-term programme of the Indian women's movement, its constitutional politics, and characterizes the Indian social structure as deeply androcentric:

> The women of India are no longer willing to submit to standards, whether local, political or ethical, which have been set for them by *the male conscience of the community*; we are passionately aware that such standards have often been allowed to imply the complete subordination or even degradation of whole classes of women; we are aware of the necessity of finding and being judged by our own standards of free human beings, voluntarily accepted; we are determined to face the facts of life, to fight the battles of our sex and take the risks.[40]

She explicitly identifies the ideological roots of society as determined by the 'male conscience of the community' and emphatically demands that the new social code be based on women's *own standards* of free human beings. This marks the beginning of a two-pronged movement. On the one hand there is a recognition of the value of deconstructing the masculine ideal which masquerades as universal but subordinates women; on the other, is a programme of creating a standard, an ethical norm, and practical scheme based on women's own experience. Amrit Kaur's statement gives us the crucial clue to the importance of the moral imaginary of the women's movement in the framing of the Indian Constitution. If the Constitution, as several commentators have remarked, is 'a social revolutionary statement … a modernising force',[41] then in Kaur's statement are visible the most complimentary spirits for its foundation. The women members of the Constituent Assembly were all aware of this contingent and historical nature of morals and law. Although there were persistent references to the unchanging ideals of the nation, the implicit belief was in the possibility of legal reform in the interest of the best ideals available to the members, both individually and collectively.

The ground for legal reform had to be based on empirical evidence about the real condition of Indian women. But since this data was unavailable, it was necessary to make a full appraisal of women's conditions using numerous investigative teams of women's organizations. The appraisal was based on extensive surveys, often drawing on government reports, and for the period after the Census of 1931, involved sophisticated and comprehensive statistical accounts of women's status in the various aspects of their lives. Reports of such surveys were presented in the wider public discourse with the hope that they 'will stimulate greater interest and will lead to a better understanding of Indian women and their problems'.[42] These status surveys fulfilled several very important strategic functions in earning a logical place for women in the constitutional scheme. The significance of the surveys lay in vindicating women's assertion that patriarchal society disadvantaged women; the term which the women members of the AIWC used to denote this was 'disability.'

Historicizing a gendered notion of 'disability' and 'minority'

The task of the reforms was therefore the removal of the disabilities attaching to women. The epistemological framework of the women's movement presented them as material beings of a minority status afflicted by numerous disabilities. These were not disabilities that they had been naturally cursed with but ones that they had incurred in the course of their social roles.

Economically, the status of women was measured in terms of women's employment and attendant conditions, and the inferior legal rights to property and inheritance; socially, in terms of the consequences of patriarchal prejudices, their health, and education; politically, in terms of women's rights of representation at all levels – in all these aspects women were presented as having been afflicted with disabilities due to the patriarchal practices and structures of society. Custom, 'even more than law' was considered 'injurious to women'.[43] Women's organizations during elections to the legislatures in 1937 claimed that they would request women to 'exercise their vote in favour of those candidates who will fight for the [removal of] disabilities – legal, social and economic, under which women suffer'.[44] Even the Karachi Resolution of the Congress on Fundamental Rights had declared 'no disability to attach to any citizen by reason of his or her religion, caste, creed or sex'.[45]

This, then, was the dominant framework of constitutional discourse within which women placed themselves as fitting the category of the disabled and injured, hence a minority in the ethical constitutional scheme. This was a strategy they carried to the Constituent Assembly. Identifying themselves as a minority was not a completely irregular practice in the period of constitutional politics of the women's movement.[46] It was not a conscious choice of asking for any compassionate privileges but an attempt to locate the category of women properly within the framework of constitutionalism, as a socially produced minority – injured and disabled. Most women, as evidenced in the debates on the Hindu Code Bill in the Constituent Assembly (Legislative), worked within this framework denying any inferiority caused by biological differences. Interestingly though, K. T. Shah in his Introduction to the *Report of the Sub-Committee on Woman's Role in Planned Economy* called women 'an ineffable minority' based on 'biological differentiation fixed by Nature'. The committee's report, however, does not suggest that any disability that women have is natural and hence irremovable.[47] The very association of the idea of socially incurred disability in their discourse conceptually anticipates the underlying social construction of gender difference.[48] Amrit Kaur told the Minorities Sub-Committee of the Constituent Assembly, 'Women may be said to be technically the largest minority in India. Not only have custom and usage dealt harshly with us, but even the law has militated and continues to militate against us'.[49] The deep implication of this strategy was to co-opt the constitutional vision to right the wrongs done to women. Many of these elements were best articulated in the Women's Charter of Rights and Duties that Hansa Mehta and her colleagues had framed in 1946, crystallizing and blending what we have called the 'constitutional politics' and the 'moral imaginary' of the women framers.

WOMEN'S CHARTER OF RIGHTS AND DUTIES

The original suggestion for the Charter was made by Hansa Mehta at the 18th Annual Conference of the AIWC at Hyderabad. This was followed by a rigorous process of consulting and collective thinking. Hansa Mehta and her team[50] had composed a draft of the Women's Charter of Rights and Duties which became crucial to her contributions to the draft of the UDHR, worked on the same time as Indians were defining their nation through a Constitution built around the notion of fundamental rights.

The first draft of the Charter was prepared in collaboration by Kamaladevi Chattopadhyay, Kitty Shiva Rao, Hannah Sen, and Renuka Ray.[51] A blueprint of this Charter was submitted to the central and provincial governments, as well as to the Cabinet Mission before the setting up of the Constituent Assembly. In May of 1946, Hansa Mehta had submitted the Charter at the UN Sub-Commission on the Status of Women, and subsequently in August 1946, it was presented at the Fourteenth Congress where she was elected the vice-president of the International Alliance of Women.[52] The international trajectory of the Women's Charter of Rights and Duties points to the strong Indian connection with international women's rights movements and the formulation of the UDHR.

The historical location of the Women's Charter

In the margins of the draft copy of the landmark 1931 Karachi Indian National Congress Resolution on Fundamental Rights is an anonymous note, about the implications of a rights-based Constitution. The chapter on fundamental rights may appear unscientific to jurists, the note says, but it constitutes 'a public confession of faith as to the direction in which the new regime wants to move. It counteracts suspicion and creates faith.'[53] A Constitution made according to these principles 'supplies standards and prescribes limits for the legislature, the executive and the administration of justice'.[54] Such a Constitution will contain 'prospective gifts for everybody'. In the words of the writer of these pencil-written notes, those who have long suffered under arbitrary executive authority – among whom we may include women – will seek 'the moral aid of declarations of rights and liberties' that the Constitution will make.[55]

These informal remarks belong to the period prior to the Indian Constitution but resonate with the rationale and configuration of women's engagement with the Constitution during its framing and after. They might well have been influenced by the presence of the women's movement, if not written by one of its active leaders. Though women's programme of a code of rights and duties had begun during their legislative struggle for specific reforms, the full articulation of their demands, however, followed the Karachi Resolution of the Indian Congress. In standard narratives, the textual history of the moral core of the Constitution begins with the adoption of the Karachi Resolution. These narratives usually acknowledge the Congress Working Committee, and primarily Jawaharlal Nehru as the author of the Resolution. Reba Som argues:

> If to Gandhi goes the credit of having drawn out Indian women from their cloistered protected environment to join the national movement for freedom, to Jawaharlal Nehru surely goes the credit for having recognised the need formally to grant equality between the sexes and to enshrine it in the Fundamental Rights drawn up at the Karachi Congress of 1931.[56]

She claims that it was at Nehru's behest that the Congress agreed to accept the principle of equality in the fundamental rights set out at Karachi.[57] In what reads like a typical 'founding father'-centric narrative, she presents Nehru as the key author of the Karachi Resolution, who saw in 'the symbolic victory of women in their fight for recognition of equal status and civic rights, a significant victory for which women of England had to fight with great bitterness for generations'.[58] The editors of the authorized multi-volume collection of Nehru's works also attribute the drafting of the Resolution to Nehru with 'changes by Mahatma Gandhi'.[59]

An entirely different narrative, however, emerges from Kamaladevi Chattopadhyay's memoirs (Image 3.3). In her memoirs, Kamaladevi claims the fundamental rights resolution that became 'the basis of the Fundamental Rights Resolution of the Congress' first appeared in a draft prepared by Nalinakshi Sanyal, 'an active youth worker of Bengal'.[60] Kamaladevi recounts several 'fables' woven around the 'mysterious' author of the Resolution including the idea that M. N. Roy had drafted it. She claimed that as a member of the All India Congress Committee (AICC), she had personally given the draft to Nehru who had 'made only slight verbal changes' to it before presenting it at the session.[61] She admits that Nehru was the author of the Economic Policy Resolution but expresses dismay at the assumption that the Fundamental Rights Resolution also 'flow[ed] from the same source'.[62]

With limited evidence, it may not be possible to attribute the authorship to either of these figures but it is clear that women were 'most anxious' to see their rights enunciated in a document. Their investment was not limited

Image 3.3 Kamaladevi Chattopadhyay and Sarojini Naidu at the Shimla Conference, 1945.

Source: Gandhi Heritage Portal (https://www.gandhiheritageportal.org/datalink/files/ghp_photos/simla_37.jpg, accessed 1 January 2022).

to the enunciation of these rights but they were also concerned with the words in which the rights were expressed. Thus, as a member of the AICC, Kamaladevi had objected to the use of the word 'protection' in article 4 of the Resolution that had declared 'Protection of women workers, and specially adequate provisions for leave during maternity period' as a fundamental right. At the meeting of the AICC in Bombay on 8 August 1931, Kamaladevi had demanded that the word 'protection' should be replaced by the word 'attention' and the article may be reframed accordingly. She asserted that women would not 'tolerate protection from anybody, not even the State', as it denoted an inferior position.[63] Her point was completely misinterpreted by Jawaharlal Nehru, who failed to understand 'what [wa]s humiliating in protection'.[64] For him, 'there could be no better instance of inferiority complex than Mrs Kamaladevi's objection to the word "protection"'.[65] For Kamaladevi, however, rights were to be recognized as expressions of the full dignity of women and not granted as the benevolence of the nationalist patriarchy or the state that it aspired to create. This was one of the many instances when women paid close attention to the connotations of terms in which rights were articulated. In any case, women acknowledged the resolution as being a source of many of their own demands, and based their strategies on it. Thus, during the elections to the provincial legislatures in 1937, women were pressing for the implementation of fundamental rights passed by the Congress in the Karachi Resolution. This demand was not only pressed before the colonial government but it was repeatedly expected that Congressmen 'translate this resolution into practice when the time comes'.[66] Women were already conscious of the role these fundamental rights would play in removing 'the *disabilities* – legal, social, and economic under which women suffer'.[67]

The AIWC had a separate office that worked towards the removal of legal disabilities of women which worked by persuading the various legislative bodies – the Central Legislative Assembly, the provincial assemblies, and councils – to bring bills that could implement equality. Within a decade of the Karachi Resolution, however, women's politics was consolidating its demands towards a 'wholesale change in the status of women'[68] that could only be achieved through a comprehensive application of the principle of equality instead of piecemeal changes that had so far been the practice. Kamaladevi lamented:

> The commitment made solemnly in 1931 was embodied in the constitution of free India framed and adapted by the Indian Constituent Assembly in 1949. In this context, the long years of continued effort and vigorous struggle by the women toward this goal should not be minimized as it often is.[69]

Among the various episodes of 'vigorous struggle' that Kamaladevi referred to, the most important were related to women's demands in the field of family laws. Although, as Amrit Kaur had initially conceived it, the demand was to have a common but optional code of laws for all Indian women – which they should themselves frame – by the end of the 1930s, it was restricted to only Hindu women. The half-yearly report of the Legal Disabilities cell of the AIWC in 1939 stated 'the present piecemeal method of dealing with the subject [reforms in the personal laws of Hindus] is not of much good and ... the matter must be investigated thoroughly'.[70] The demands for reform of Hindu personal law were made in order to achieve an 'improvement in the rights of women', an extension of the constitutional politics built around the idea of equality that was quickly gaining a specific shape of its own in women's moral imagination. The Hindu Law Committee of 1941, assembled under the chairmanship of B. N. Rau, envisaged a new and comprehensive code of

Hindu law influenced presumably by women's demands, 'which shall recognize that men and women are equal in status with appropriate obligations as well as rights'.[71]

The idea of equality of the sexes was one of the most important features, in fact, the only social principle that the Committee considered worth mentioning in the future Code. The Committee was 'greatly impressed' by the earnestness of women's demands and objections to 'legislation in small doses'.[72] What women wanted, in the words of the Committee, was a 'comprehensive, coordinated solution' and not quick remedies.[73] The Committee's report was an important, albeit paternalist, endorsement of the shift in the tone of women's demands:

> Those who know anything of Hindu women know that their lives are usually a round of duties, leaving little room for thoughts of rights. When, therefore, even a few of them ask for better rights, no one can wish to be anything but helpful.[74]

I shall return to the Committee later while discussing the uniform civil code; here, however, it must be noted that one of the ideas that animated the Hindu Law Committee was that of a rational and comprehensive codification of the plural realities of Hindu women's legal status. This codification was not about reaching uniformity but comprehensive reform, and eventually about creating an independent legal personhood for Hindu women. The Women's Charter was prepared in the same continuum, responding as much to this desire for a singular personhood as to speak in a united voice for an Indian electorate of women.

The Women's Charter, therefore, was conceived as a crystallization of all the demands that had emerged during the period of constitutional politics. The Charter was the ethical self-expression of the composite demands of the constituency of Indian women that had evolved in the two decades of constitutional politics and the AIWC resolutions adopted for the improvement of the status of women, between 1927 and 1945. In the words of Hansa Mehta:

> The object of the charter is to crystallise these resolutions with a view to give a clear picture of the ideals for which we stand; to form a basis for future remedial legislation; and for the creation of opportunities to women for service for their attainment. These demands as embodied in the charter are by no means final, nor do they claim to be exhaustive. Changing circumstances and conditions may necessitate corresponding changes.[75]

Granville Austin has identified six important documents of rights as precursors to the fundamental rights chapter of the Indian Constitution. He considers article 16 of The Constitution of India Bill, 1895 as the 'first explicit demand for fundamental rights' which was followed by 'a series of Congress resolutions adopted between 1917 and 1919'.[76] The next important development in this series of documents was 'the drafting of the seven fundamental rights provisions of Mrs. Besant's Commonwealth of India Bill of 1925'.[77] The fourth important precursor, according to Austin, was the Swaraj Constitution of India, also known as the Nehru Report of 1928 after Motilal Nehru who was chairman of its drafting committee.

The fundamental rights of the Nehru Report, Austin tells us, were reminiscent of those of the American and the post-War European constitutions, and were in several cases taken word for word from the rights listed in the Commonwealth of India Bill. Several clauses, though, had a particularly Indian origin.[78] This was followed by the Karachi Resolution of 1931. The last important document on rights before the Constituent Assembly was formed was the *Sapru Report*, prepared by Sir Tej Bahadur Sapru and his committee, which conceptualized rights as justiciable and non-justiciable, the precursor to the Constitution's classification of fundamental rights and directive principles. Austin's list of the documents of rights is based on his understanding of the Constitution and its history, and naturally does not mention the Charter of Women's Rights and other documents and memoranda produced by the Indian women's movement of the period.

Recent scholars, too, have tried to trace alternative trajectories of such 'constitutional aspirations' but have not recognized that important strands of the women's movement too embodied them.[79] In his search for what he calls 'the other major source of constitutional imagination', Rohit De traces the aspirations of 'different groups of the Indian public', citing Ram Mohan Roy and Tej Bahadur Sapru.[80] Though he recognizes the 'active participation of several members of the future Constituent Assembly in the drafting and reception of these earlier documents', he fails to mention these women, who envisaged a constitutional order and negotiated with contemporary constitutional aspirations within and outside mainstream nationalism.[81] In her detailed genealogy of the framing of the social and economic rights in the Constituent Assembly – what she calls 'the unsocial compact' – Niraja Gopal Jayal discusses several documents, even charting their implied desire for gender equality but does not mention any of the feminist memoranda, petitions, or charters.[82] Part of the reason for this amnesia has been the failure to recognize that there had been a perpetual and collective participation of women in constitution-making and authorship. Unlike the socialists or other ideological interest groups within the Congress, women did not function as a group but worked continuously to refine their vision with an unflinching and reasoned conviction in constitutionalism.

The Women's Charter is an antecedent of the Constitution, an exemplary site at the congruence of the moral imaginary and the constitutional politics of the women's movement. It must, therefore, be read as one of the most important documents of rights preceding the Indian Constitution. In many ways it anticipated and informed the content of the Constitution, especially its chapter on directive principles, and in some of its demands proved to be in advance of the constitutional vision of the Constituent Assembly. An examination of the Charter's demands will reveal its sweeping range and inclusive character. Many of its articles, for example those emphasizing women's rights to limit the size of their families, recognition of women's work as homemakers, and demands for crèches for working women, among others, anticipate many of the later-day demands of the women's movement in India and beyond.

Women's Charter: Genealogy of an Indian document on human rights

Two important aspects of the Charter need to be emphasized. First, generically, the Charter was designed in the tradition of several documents of human rights that had shaped liberal discourse on liberty and equality. Second (which was linked to the first) was the manner in which the Charter eschewed – with a double bind – reference to the affective aspects of the nationalist discourse which had foregrounded emotional bonds and shared cultural memory as the basis of national integrity. The nation, as understood by the women who drafted the Charter, was a modern democratic society in which their identity was that of citizens. It is also worth remembering that the Charter was presented as an *Indian* Charter for an international audience that included Western feminist organizations as well as international human rights organizations. When Hansa Mehta submitted a draft of the Charter to the UN Sub-Commission of the Status of Women in May 1946, it mentioned the duties of Indian women that included fighting 'against the social evils which retard the progress of this country such as child marriage, purda, polygamy, caste communalism, untouchability'[83] but also 'to strive to the utmost for world peace'.[84] For the drafters of the Charter, the two were not disconnected, and were constituents of the larger pursuit of social freedom. Kamaladevi Chattopadhyay, Mehta's predecessor as the President of AIWC, in her Presidential address delivered at the AIWC's annual Bombay conference in 1944 had emphasized the broadening of domestic concerns with clarity and force:

> Our insular peninsular outline has widened into the global, with an increasing awareness that we and the rest of the world are but part of a single sphere, that our destinies are inevitably linked, our paths interlocked. Therefore, world policies and events are as much our concern as our affairs…. Just as national freedom is but an extension of social freedom the Conference is fighting for, the establishment of the same principle all the world over is of equal interest to us.[85]

These principles animated the Women's Charter, the interventions by the women members in the Constituent Assembly, and their participation in the UN discourses around the framing of human rights documents. These documents laid stress upon the inevitable connection between what came to be known variously as the first and second generation of rights or the civil and political rights, and the social and economic rights. The emphasis was on the rights that naturally accrue to men and women, rights that were essential to 'human' development. Its preamble commenced with truths that were considered uncontestably universal, and laid down the theoretical framework behind the rights enunciated therein. These truths, emphasized by the full generic and jurisprudential import of the word 'whereas', formed the raison d'etre of the rights, expressed without qualifications, though, as Hansa Mehta said in her foreword to the draft of the Charter, the demands were subject to changes corresponding to circumstances and conditions. Framed within the dialectic of the universal and the particular, these rights, in their details, therefore were changeable and contingent, but were meant to be expressions of transcendental values and principles.

   Since the objective of this book is to reconstruct the authorial intentions of the women framers, situating them in the context of the discursive exercises with which they engaged must include their interventions in the framing of the UN's human rights documents. The key figure in this narrative, of course, is Hansa Mehta who, unlike avowed socialists like Kamaladevi Chattopadhyay and Renuka Ray, had almost obstinately stuck to the ideal of ideological neutrality as a feminist and as a champion of human rights. A comprehensive look at her remarkable career suggests her stance protected her from being interpellated by any camp. A member of the National Planning Committee that drafted that the *Report on Women's Role in Planned Economy* in 1939, she had drafted several pamphlets on civil liberties and the uniform civil code before drafting the Women's Charter, and moving on to the UN Sub-Commission on the Status of Women and the UN Commission on

Image 3.4 Hansa Mehta with Carlos Garcia Bauer of Guatemala at a meeting of the UN Commission on Human Rights, 1 June 1949, New York.

Source: UN Digital Archive, Unique Identifier: UN7478214 (https://dam.media.un.org/CS.aspx? VP3=DamView&VBID=2AM94S52JUV1&SMLS=1&RW=1334&RH=747&FR_= 1&W=1328&H=746#/DamView&VBID=2AM94S51YS8U&PN=1&WS=SearchResults, accessed 1 January 2022).

Human Rights.[86] As a translator of major European classics into Gujarati and writer of children's books, she drafted a document with impressive clarity and attended to minute linguistic and syntactical details. In early discussions on the framing of the UDHR, Mehta had demanded that an Indian representative – herself – be included in the Drafting Committee (Image 3.4). Although her demand was not approved, she made significant contributions to the draft of the Declaration. She recommended that the 'The Declaration, which laid down general principles, must be as precise as possible if it was to be understood by the common man'.[87] The 'moral force and support of world opinion', depended on the ability of the document to 'reach and be understood every member of the public…. The Declaration aimed at defining the rights of individuals, not the rights of States. It must have human appeal, and should not be too condensed or too terse.'[88] The advice guided the drafters of the Declaration to the degree that 'whenever they worried about their draft becoming too long, they would cut it back because, as Hansa Mehta of India said, "it was to be understood by the common man".'[89]

Image 3.5 The two champions. Hansa Mehta with Eleanor Roosevelt at the UN
Commission on Human Rights, 1 June 1949, New York.

Source: UN Photo Digital Management Asset System; Unique ID: UN7499124 (https://dam.media.
un.org/CS.aspx?VP3=DamView&VBID=2AM94S52JUV1&SMLS=1&RW=1334&RH=747#/
DamView&VBID=2AM94S52I895&PN=1&WS=SearchResults, accessed on 25 May 2021).

Mehta's attention to the language of the declaratory enunciations was astute,
and her successful objection to the 'non-inclusive' language in the draft of the
Universal Declaration has already been noted by scholars.[90] In comparison with
Eleanor Roosevelt, whose feminism was 'ardent but pragmatic and subordinate
to her broader social concerns', Mehta was 'particularly vigilant concerning
women's rights' (Image 3.5).[91] While it has generally been acknowledged that
it was partly due to her intervention that the word 'men' in article 1 of the
Universal Declaration was replaced by 'human beings', the full import of her
interventions can only be appreciated in the context of her insistence that rights
accrue universally to all individuals and must not be inflected by patriarchal
notions of family. She objected to 'the wording 'all men' or 'and should act

towards one another like brothers'.[92] These, she felt 'might be interpreted to exclude women, and were out of date'.[93] Several important features of her intellectual and historical location of Indian women's contributions to the rights discourse become visible by examining her attention to the language of the texts. Evidently, she was alert to the interpretive possibilities of a legal text and was aware of the socio-legal implications of sexist language. While disagreeing with Eleanor Roosevelt that 'the word "men" used in this sense was generally accepted to include all human beings',[94] she grounded her arguments on fear of a restrictive interpretation of the words in the future. Declarations of human rights being 'a new way of thinking for many States and people, we should like it, at certain paragraphs … [that it] be underlined that these rights and duties should be equal for men and women'. In an early speech at the Commission on Human Rights she had demanded:

> Moreover, we should like the idea of equality stressed in the Preamble and, you may perhaps say *for the sake of security, have a note somewhere saying*:
>
> When a noun or pronoun denoting a male sex is used in respect of any provision contrived in the following Bill of Human Rights, such provision shall be taken to apply without discrimination to the female sex.[95]

At the core of these statements was a realization that legal documents, at their very foundation, weave possibilities of discrimination that are then perpetuated with greater force in the future, committing foundational violence against women. The documents, Indian feminists knew, were only to give legal endorsement to an ideology against which they were struggling.

Indian feminists had been alert students of modern Western history and observed the contemporary women's movements too well to ignore the gap between declared ideals and practices produced by restrictive interpretations and ideological prejudices. During her campaigns for reforms in Hindu personal laws, Renuka Ray had often presented women who opposed these reforms as interpellated in the patriarchal ideology. 'There have been slaves who did not favour the abolition of slavery', she had reminded the readers of a piece of feminist propaganda she had written in 1945,

> women who violently opposed franchise rights for their own sex in England. Even today, in the USA there are one or two women's associations such as the National Catholic Women's Council, the Jewish Women's Association who are opposed to the amendment recognizing equal rights for men and women under the American Constitution.[96]

Six months after the UN adopted the Universal Declaration, during the television talk-show 'Vanity Fair' hosted by Dorothy Doan, Eleanor Roosevelt remembered Hansa Mehta's objection to the use of the word 'men' in the document and her demand to replace it with 'person'. Roosevelt had said that the word 'everyone' instead of 'every man' was demanded by women representatives from parts of world where women had not yet gained equality. A quick repartee came from Hansa:

> I think the complaint came from women in this country that in spite of the fact that all women are equal in the Declaration [of Independence], still distinction is made with regard to rights.[97]

The idea that women in 'backward' countries like India were deprived of equal rights was a persistent refrain in international conventions formulating human rights in those days. Indian women framers regularly referred to the ongoing framing of the Constitution as a reminder of their own feminist credentials as well as of the discordance confronting Western feminism. Thus, on the repeated stereotyping of the Koran and Shariat law as regressive, Hamid Ali, who had replaced Hansa Mehta as the representative of Indian women on the Commission on the Status of Women, protested saying this was akin to accusing 'the United Kingdom of being medieval because it did not allow women in the House of Lords'.[98] She referred to India's Constitution, which was 'still on the anvil' but would ensure equal rights for women. Having twice been the president of the AIWC and an endorser of the Women's Charter, she was hopeful that the Constitution will create an ideal of gender justice in India and promised that

> if by the next year anything were still wanting in the condition of women in India, she would lay the facts frankly before the Commission. No government could achieve perfection, even to the end of the world, but each could learn from *all of the others*.[99]

It is important to pay attention to the contours of this discursive space – at the intersection of women's rights, human rights, and fundamental rights – within which the women framers participated in the framing of the Constitution. Compounded with this was the pull that warring ideological groups created between civil rights that privileged the individual above the collective and the social and economic rights that privileged the collective above the individual. Even before she attended the first meeting of the Fundamental Rights Sub-Committee of the Constituent Assembly in New Delhi, during the initial meeting of the Commission on Human Rights, Hansa Mehta had recommended a pragmatic approach of keeping an ideologically neutral stand. She made her intervention during the debate between Marxist ideologues from the Communist blocs and the liberal members that produced 'the lengthiest and most heated discussions' and what was perhaps 'the Commission's first big argument' about the nature of human rights.[100] 'We are here', she said,

> to reaffirm faith in fundamental human rights, whether the human person comes first or the society. I do not think that we should discuss that problem now. Our object should be to uphold the dignity and worth of the human person. What are the rights which we should recognize, which will carry out this purpose? I think we should not enter into *this maze of ideology* at this stage.[101]

She was immediately rebuked by the Lebanese philosopher Charles Malik who argued that one 'must have ideological presuppositions' before formulating these rights, and told that 'no matter how much you may fight shy of them, they are there, and you either hide them or you are brave enough to bring them out in the open and see them and criticize them'.[102] Hansa Mehta, however, maintained her position of neutrality, a strategy that she had perfected during her leadership of the AIWC. In her preparatory notes for the Constituent Assembly and the Commission on Human Rights, was the UNESCO memorandum on the theoretical bases of human rights. This document presented the evolution of human rights in two different contexts: the 'truly revolutionary' eighteenth-century conception of 'individual human rights as absolute and inherent' and the nineteenth-century conception of human rights, developed under the influence of Marxist theory and a belief that rights, 'whether of individuals or of groups, can be properly considered only in relation to the conditions of time and place'.[103] The memorandum traced the development of these two concepts in relation to 'different sorts of social circumstance', mostly Western, and recommended their reconciliation as an ideal solution:

> The one started from the premise of inherent individual rights, and with a bias against a strong central authority and against government interference, while the other was based upon Marxist principles and the premise of a powerful central government, and early wedded to total planning (which automatically magnifies the central power) and to one-party Government....

> One of the major tasks immediately ahead of us is thus clearly to find some common measure for the future development of the two tendencies, or in the terms of the Marxist dialectic to effect a reconciliation of the two opposites in a higher synthesis.[104]

As a feminist advocating property rights and better working conditions for women, Mehta understood the conflict between group rights and individual women's rights. Living under a colonial regime that deprived its subjects of basic civil liberties, she was uniquely positioned to respond to this state of affairs in the field of human rights. She knew that choosing civil and political rights over social and economic rights or vice versa would weaken both sets of rights. In her 1945 pamphlet on civil liberties, she had characterized Roosevelt's four freedoms to be guaranteed by any democratic constitution – freedom from fear, freedom from want, freedom of worship, and freedom of speech or expression – as 'civil liberties in Constitutional Law'.[105] The very purpose of the state, she argued was to protect these rights of the individual, and hence she made regular pleas, both in the Commission on Human Rights and the Constituent Assembly, to ensure mechanisms to do so. As the Chairperson of the Working Group on Implementation of Human Rights of the Commission on Human Rights she had argued that 'A procedure for implementing an international Convention was essential in order to assure the non-violation of human rights by States themselves'.[106] The Standing Committee that she had proposed must be empowered to listen to complaints against states lodged by individual citizens.[107] She wrote that to merely declare a set of rights that could not be implemented would be 'to frustrate the hopes of millions in this world'.[108] Responding to critics who raised the question of the feasibility of these rights, she said that we must 'not reject the principle because we feel that we cannot devise such a machinery'.[109] Of utmost importance for her was the idea that rights – human and constitutional – must, in principle, be enforceable and should be recognized as such. She argued with force and clarity, her idea informed by a suspicion of the state as easily corruptible and involved in a Hobbesian state of war with other states:

> I take the floor once again, because I feel that this is a very important question, and on the decision on this question we will raise the hopes or frustrate the hopes of millions in this world. If we allow only States to enter complaints, it is quite possible, as Professor Cassin pointed out that the States may not complain against each other from fear of making it a political question and also the fear of retaliation from another State. *After all, each State, I believe, has a skeleton in its cupboard and would be afraid to complain against the other for fear of being complained against*, and therefore, if you allow only States to complain, it is quite possible that there may be no agency to take up the cause of *the aggrieved humanity*.[110]

This conviction partly informed her interventions on the status of the directive principles in the Constitution. In the Commission on Human Rights she had, however, conceded that the 'implementation of economic rights and even some social rights would depend on the financial conditions of a State'. This was cited as a reason why in

> the Constitution recently passed by the Constituent Assembly of India, these rights are not justiciable. They are not included in Part III which deal with the Fundamental Rights, but in Part IV i.e., in the Directive Principles of state policy wherein rights are defined which are not enforceable by law.[111]

Yet during the framing of the Constitution, she argued strongly for the recognition of the directive principles as fundamental to the constitutional vision. Additionally, she co-authored the note of dissent to the Fundamental Rights Sub-Committee in the Constituent Assembly demanding the directive principles of state policy be considered as 'fundamental' to the governance of the country. This note became the source of the crucial article 37 of the Constitution of India.[112] For the women framers, the implementation of the rights by the state was framed within the conceptual relationship between rights and duties, which, in the aftermath of the retreat of Fascist (and colonial) governments, had acquired special dimensions. Demands for women's rights were also treated as against the spirit of national culture and accused of being:

> inclined to emphasize our rights too much to the detriment of our duty; that our culture lays more stress on duty – dharma – than on right – adhikara. We would not be true, therefore, to our culture if we stress the rights more than the duties.[113]

Mehta responded to such critics by reminding them that we condemn the Nazi and Fascist state

> because in a totalitarian state, the individual had all duties and no rights. The individual was loaded with duties while he had no freedom i.e., no civil rights. The individual was reduced to the state of a robot. He had no will of his own.... The result was disastrous.[114]

The balance of rights and duties leads to full freedom:

> A life of duties alone without rights means an existence of a slave; while rights without duties would mean a state of anarchy i.e., more license than freedom.

It is only where rights and duties are properly balanced and integrated that we can get an ideal society where freedom in the true sense of the term can flourish.[115]

The full political–theoretical and jurisprudential import of women's interventions in the debates on the making of the Indian Constitution can only be appreciated by reading all these arguments together and as situated at the intersection of several discursive spaces. Many of the 'rights' demanded by women were overdetermined – their trajectories not always linear, their sources varied – and waited for the Charter to gain their first systematic articulation within a comprehensive, constitutional framework that wove them together as emanating from one universal ethic. Compared with the Sub-Committee's *Report on Woman's Role in Planned Economy*, the Women's Charter laid greater emphasis on women's identity as rights-bearing citizens. While the former derived strength for its arguments on the *contribution* of women to the nation conceived as an economy, the Woman's Charter derived its demands from more universal notions of an inherent moral dignity of men and women, akin to arguments presented by the human rights discourse. The underlying principle behind the entire Charter was that all human beings had the rights of freedom and equality which they must share equally with each other. The ultimate goal of these rights was to develop their full personality, which is the necessary condition of the 'wellbeing and progress of society'; it is only when a woman is allowed to contribute 'as a free and responsible member' of society that she can play a role in building 'a free, healthy, prosperous and moral society'.[116] Women framers believed, in the words of the Charter, that society's progress depends on the ability of men and women to be 'cognizant of their responsibilities to themselves and to each other'.[117] Each of these aspects of social wellbeing had a direct correlative in the rights of women that were enumerated in the Charter.

Taking their first steps towards legal reform, equality and non-discrimination were the most important ideals in women's constitutional discourse and were given the status of fundamental rights in their Charter. The Charter depicted the recognition of human equality as the most fundamental value of a democratic society and 'affirmed' that 'all citizens are equal before law, irrespective of caste, creed or sex; and no disability attaches to any citizen by reason of her religion, caste, creed or sex....'[118] It was this fundamental value of equality that was to be translated into other aspects of women's participation in society, in matters related to both the public and the domestic sphere. Though the Charter respected women's long-standing refusal of any form of positive discrimination, it was explicit in demanding no discrimination against women in 'public employment, office of power and honour, and in exercise of any trade or calling'.[119] The Charter demanded that equal civic rights be given to women and men, and therefore, 'every woman and man of twenty-one and above … shall have a right to vote'. A woman was to be treated as independent citizen.

Going beyond the ordinary demands of parliamentary democracy, the Charter demanded that women be represented on legislative bodies, committees, commissions, conferences, and delegations. This was a part of their general strategy of demanding representation on bodies selected on the basis of expertise and public eminence. As we have seen, even during their elections to the Constituent Assembly, their strategy was to ensure positions in committees for fundamental rights and minorities, in case they failed to get elected to the Assembly.

The right to education and health

If women had to develop their full human potential, their rights had to be fashioned in such a manner that their handicaps and disabilities were completely removed. The two lengthiest and most detailed sections of the Charter pertain to the rights to education and health, both described as enabling positive rights for women and society. The conceptualization of these two rights for women was the most sophisticated extension of the concept of women as a minority afflicted with disabilities. The right to education, therefore, was characterized as 'one of the essential freedoms' rather than as a right to a public good. Education was conceived as a liberating and enabling entity, 'freedom from ignorance', ignorance – like the lack of health – being a major disability that obstructs the realization of the full potential of the individual and the nation. It was a 'fundamental right that has not been vouchsafed to the millions and millions of men and women in this country',[120] yet for women the handicap was socially afflicted and was in need of urgent solution. By citing the abysmally low percentage of literate women in society, 2 per cent in comparison with 13 per cent for men, the Charter alluded to the minority status of women that formed the crucial theoretical justification for constitutional rights. 'Education as freedom' was framed as an overarching human rights demand which subsumed other demands that were explicitly recognized as women's rights.

Thus, the Charter demanded that 'the Government should through legislation, if necessary, make immediate efforts to eradicate the evils of child marriage, child labour, purda and untouchability which come in the way of education and specially of girl's education'.[121] By bringing these issues long identified within the rubric of 'the woman question', the authors of the Women's Charter were speaking in the dominant, universalist language available to them. It was natural that they spoke about education in terms of the advancement of the nation and argued that 'no nation can go forward' if education is not ensured to all its citizens.

The rhetoric that women are the mothers of the nation and hence their education will lead to better education of its children was not repeated even once by the Charter. The Charter clearly stated that 'there shall be no difference between the education of men and women as their duties as citizens are the same'.[122] The goal of education was to enable citizens to perform their duties; there was no special burden on women by virtue of their gender. Of course, there were additional obstacles in the way to women's education that needed to be removed and the Charter enjoined the state to provide special scholarships and other assistance to girls whose parents were not willing to invest in their education, create conditions to attract women teachers, provide social insurance schemes for them, and make women's health an important part of their education.

Other items under the section on the right to education were designed to put the state under a positive obligation to make education at all levels and in all its forms including vocational training, physical education, and even teachers' education available to women. While there was sufficient stress on home science and the care of children, these subjects were by no means confined to women or the only course of education envisaged for them. Education was the most important element in women's imagination, for it was the only way in which women could be trained for what Amrit Kaur had called constructive citizenship in which a woman is 'not merely one who is a member of a state or obeys its laws but one who has an active sense of being an integral part of it'.[123] Remarkably, the Charter mentions citizenship training as part of the curriculum of health education for rural adult women, clubbing it with such matters as 'pertaining to village life including model homes, hygiene, sanitization, care of children, kitchen, gardens, etc.'[124]

While the constitutive principle behind the Charter's formulation of the right to education remains equality, as exemplified in its position that 'there shall be no basic difference between the education of men and women', its regulative features allowed for the contingencies of viability and context. Thus, having argued in favour of co-education at all stages of education, it concedes that 'exception can be made in the secondary stage until prejudice against it has been overcome'.[125] Ideas of differential educational needs and systems for men and women were at the root of sexual inequality. Hansa Mehta, one of the authors of the Charter, later presided over an influential committee on the subject of separate curricula for boys and girls which reaffirmed that there is no natural difference between the abilities of men and women, and as such their education at should be common and aimed at disabusing the social prejudices regarding gender difference at all stages of education.[126] The entire right to education was framed as a right to freedom from several disabilities that were inflicted on women, either through social practices, institutional inadequacies, and persistent insensitivities or through other factors that helped create a constituency of citizens deprived of the opportunities to develop their full potential. The Charter's demands were not merely remedial but formed important suggestions that resonated with the positive liberties that were to be enshrined in the directive principles of the Indian Constitution.

The Charter argued that 'the health of every man, woman and child is the nation's *greatest* asset'[127] and, like education, grounded the demand for the right to health in terms of women's status and the appalling figures of maternal and infant mortality. If education was to be 'free and compulsory for every boy and girl between the ages of seven and fourteen', health services too were to be free for all citizens. The Charter demanded that 'a nation-wide plan for free health services, including medical, dental and hospital treatment and provision for free medical examination be adopted'.[128] The primary thrust of the demands was towards creating conditions that would be especially protective for women – free pre-natal and infant welfare clinics, maternity hospitals and nursing services, child welfare centres, among them.

Yet the framework of the Charter's section on health was built on the wider conception of health as a closely connected system in which everybody is affected by each other and by the conditions surrounding them. Thus, the Charter stressed sanitation, general hygiene, industrial hygiene, immunization and free treatment of infectious diseases, clean water, and drainage systems. The demand for healthcare was not limited to the prevention and cure of diseases but articulated as a composite programme for the promotion of public health that would improve the lives of citizens, women in particular. Amrit Kaur, the Minister in Charge of Health at the time of the framing of the Charter, had played a pioneering role in the promotion of a holistic concept of public health. As an author of the Charter and a member of the Constituent Assembly, she envisioned the development of a more centralized system of public health administration than was finally adopted.

The most important aspect of the Women's Charter vis-à-vis health and education was the conception of them as dynamically intertwined concepts, mutually reinforcing rights. An important item in the list on the right to education was health education 'including nutrition and citizenship'[129] whereas several items in the right to health implied the right to education and training of not just doctors, nurses, and health visitors, but the overall education of the public. Clearly, in the social democracy the Women's Charter had envisaged, these two rights constituted the core values of active and constructive citizenship that would allow women to enjoy their rights and fulfil their duties towards society.

Asserting women's identity as citizens

The most remarkable aspect of the Charter is that it completely reimagines the nation in terms of a synchronic arrangement of rightful and equal citizens; it makes no references to the affective bonds between them as members of a community with shared history. Women, if they were to be citizens of a democratic society had to be reassigned the identity of equal citizens who have a legal personality with the same economic, political, social, physical, and mental potentials as men. The right to work was recognized as a fundamental right by the Charter, both for men and women, who must be treated as equals regarding 'living wage, leave, hours of work, sickness allowance, holidays with pay and free medical treatment'.[130] Women, however, were a minority with disabilities, the realization of their full rights as workers obstructed by their additional responsibilities as mothers. Hence the Charter demanded special facilities for women: crèches for their babies and children, rest rooms for expectant and nursing mothers, milk canteens, and break during work hours, to name a few. The Charter also demanded a comprehensive scheme of social insurance for women which would include maternity benefits for workers.

The most radical suggestion that the Charter made with regard to women's work was the recognition of the work of the housewife. The economic rights of the 'housewife' were already in discourse for a few years, initially contested but recognized by the National Planning Committee on Woman's Role in Planned Committee in 1939. Among the most important members of the Sub-Committee on Woman's Role in Planned Economy, were Hansa Mehta, Muthulakshmi Reddy, Begum Jahanara Shahnawaz, and Mridula Sarabhai, all of them aspirants for seats in the Constituent Assembly and two finally elected to it. The Sub-Committee felt that women's work at home 'which at present receives no recognition either by the State or society, should be recognized as having an economic value and it should not be considered inferior to the other type of work done outside the home'.[131] This recommendation, made by the select members of the National Planning Committee of 1939 but only published in 1947, had resonated in the women's movement and was even adopted by women's organizations in 1941.[132] In her presidential address at the AIWC session of 1944, Kamaladevi presented the theoretical premises for such a demand in terms that informed the moral imagination that women had imported into the discourse of international feminism, the UN Commission on Human Rights, and, of course, the Constituent Assembly of India. The correct premise to recognize women's economic worth, Kamaladevi argued, was

> the recognition of the social division of labour between the sexes, which gives the lie direct to the middle and upper-class conception of women as domestic and social parasites, living on their husbands and contributing nothing. Woman power is basic and the woman must be recognized as a social and economic factor on her own, not as an assistant to man…. To state blandly that woman produces children and rears them, cooks food, cleans, washes, is not enough. According to industrial economy she produces labour power, and labour power is basic, for without it none of the other kinds of power can be made to operate. But that too is not good enough. The housewife is as much of a working woman as a factory worker.[133]

On careful reading, one can notice an increasing discomfort in her terminology with the characterization of women's labour in essentialist terms: as reduced to reproductive labour and care of the household. She goes on to argue for an opening of the gendered division of labour, advocating women's entrance into other fields of activities that will break the

> relative segregation of women as a sex, [relax] the restrictions that otherwise narrow women's functions…. Correctly viewed and rightly interpreted, the women's movement is found resting on a scientific basis, shaped by a rational ideology and indispensable in the social scheme of things.[134]

Although the Women's Charter did not go to the extent of claiming wages for the work of the woman as a homemaker, nor did it compare it with factory work as Kamaladevi did, it did, in fact, make demands for women who are 'mothers of the race'. It sought an economic status for women by redefining the family as an economic unit. In the imagination of the Charter, women were not passive workers bound to their houses but homemakers whose work was 'as important as any other' and needed to be given its full legal and economic status. Noticeably, the Charter uses the gender-neutral word 'homemaker' instead of 'housewife' in its attempt to redefine the family:

> we believe that the present conception of the family as an institution with man as its head who looks upon his wife and his children as his property to do what he likes with them is wrong; and whereas we believe that such a conception which has affected the laws of this country must be changed and the family be regarded as a co-operative concern where every member has an equal share....[135]

This radically altered concept of the family brought equality to the core of its moral definition and made it naturally rightful that the homemaker had a share in its income.[136] Since work at home had to be treated at par with work outside it, the homemaker was entitled to the benefits of all the social insurance schemes introduced for other workers as well as other facilities that could enhance her status. The Charter clearly demanded that the woman should have 'the right to limit her family'[137] implying that she had control over her reproductive rights.

These statements challenge core ideas about the gendered divisions of the private and the public spheres. Read together with Hansa Mehta's interventions during the debates on the draft of the UDHR, these seem to be performing acts of radical redefinition, and opening up possibilities of alternative social formations, all protected within the arc of constitutionalism and human rights. During the discussions on what became article 16 of the UDHR, going against the dominant suggestion that the family has to be recognized as the fundamental unit of society, and the purpose of marriage was to be recognized as the creation of a family, Hansa Mehta had recommended that the Declaration 'should give no definition of the family'.[138] Most members, including Charles Malik had pressed for 'the retention of the words, "the natural and fundamental group unit of the society"' to describe the institution of the family deriving from marriage.[139] Mehta was not willing to agree that the family is the basic unit of society, reiterating a position she had taken on several other occasions. Ten years earlier, her young Bombay AIWC colleague Kapila Khandvala had written a note of dissent in the Report of 1939 on *Woman's Role in Planned Economy*, arguing that marriage must be seen as 'an association of equal individuals binding only so long as their desire to remain associated holds' and the individual should be 'the *only* basic unit of society irrespective of any association or "family" ties'.[140] Khandvala had argued for a radical notion of family, uncoupling it from the idea of the production of children and demanded that a woman, whether 'she is an unmarried mother or not' should be given equal 'social, economic and civic rights'.[141] In what reads like an echo of Khandvala's position on social morality, Hansa Mehta, argued that if the Commission found it 'necessary to adopt a provision for the protection of the family, the idea to be kept in view was that the family, whether deriving from marriage *or not*, was entitled to protection'.[142]

One is impressed by the enormously rich discursive shift that women framers had achieved, often manipulating the dominant tropes available to them but sometimes boldly challenging conventional paradigms. Before and during the framing of the Constitution, they had already worked to extend the notion of rights in all human life spheres which were mired in inequality between the sexes. They constituted the category of women as a minority that needed constitutional protection and articulated a compelling vision of constitutional justice that gave their radicalism a legitimacy not available earlier. It is to this unprecedented role that women played in adopting, enacting, and giving 'to ourselves' the Constitution that we may now turn.

NOTES

1. For a brief comparative account of the evolution and priorities of these three organizations, see Geraldine Forbes, *Women in Modern India* (Cambridge: Cambridge University Press, 1996), 72–83.
2. Ibid., 75.
3. Ibid., 77.
4. Ibid.
5. Kamaladevi Chattopadhyay, *Indian Women's Battle for Freedom* (New Delhi: Abhinav Publications, 1983), 7.
6. Ibid.
7. Urmila Pawar and Meenakshi Moon, *We Also Made History: Women in the Ambedkarite Movement*, trans. Wandana Sonalkar (New Delhi: Zubaan, 2008), 139.
8. K. T. Shah (ed.), *Report of the Sub-Committee on Woman's Role in Planned Economy* (Bombay: Vora & Co., 1947), 33. The Sub-Committee on Woman's Role in Planned Economy was one of the 29 sub-committees of the National Planning Committee conceived by the Indian National Congress in 1938. In many ways, the National Planning Committee anticipated the Planning Commission of India. The Sub-Committee's report was presented before the National Planning Committee on 31 August 1940. For a brief report

on its resolutions, see K. T. Shah (ed.), *National Planning Committee: Report* (Bombay: Vora & Co. Publishers Ltd., 1949), 214–222.

9. K. T. Shah's 'Preface' to the *Report of the Sub-Committee on Woman's Role in Planned Economy*, 17. Hansa Mehta and Vijayalakshmi Pandit, later to be members of the Constituent Assembly, were members of this Sub-Committee.

10. Nirmala Banerjee, 'Whatever Happened to the Dreams of Modernity? The Nehruvian Era and Woman's Position', *Economic and Political Weekly* 33, no. 17 (1998): WS2–WS7, WS4.

11. Shah, *Report of the Sub-Committee on Woman's Role in Planned Economy*, 35.

12. Ibid., 32.

13. Amrit Kaur, *Challenge to Women* (Allahabad: New Literature, 1946), 54.

14. K. M. Munshi, 'Our Objective: A Constituent Assembly', originally published in *Hindustan Times*, 21 July 1934, printed in A. K. Majumdar (ed.), *Indian Constitutional Documents: Munshi Papers*, Vol. II (Bombay: Bhartiya Vidya Bhavan, 1967), 1–5, 5.

15. Jawaharlal Nehru, Presidential Address at the Faizpur session of the Indian National Congress, 27 December 1936, in B. Shiva Rao (ed.), *The Framing of India's Constitution: Select Documents*, Vol. 1 (Delhi: Universal Law Publishing, 2004; originally The Indian Institute of Public Administration, 1967), 81.

16. Ibid.

17. Arvind Elangovan, *Norms and Politics: Sir Benegal Narsing Rau in the Making of the Indian Constitution, 1935–1950* (New Delhi: Oxford University Press, 2019), 35. For more discussion on the galvanization of the nationalist demand for a Constituent Assembly after the Government of India Act, 1935, see ibid., 84–89.

18. Congress Resolution of April 1936 on the Government of India Act, 1935, in Rao, *The Framing of India's Constitution*, Vol. 1, 80.

19. Chattopadhyay, *Indian Women's Battle for Freedom*, 98.

20. Kamaladevi Chattopadhyay, *At the Cross-roads*, ed. Yusuf Meherally (Bombay: The National Information and Publications Ltd., 1947), 21.

21. Ibid., 27.

22. Ibid.

23. Ibid.

24. Kamaladevi Chattopadhyay, *The Awakening of Indian Women* (Madras: Everyman's Press, 1939), 10.

25. Ibid.

26. Ibid., 9.

27. Ibid.

28. Ibid., 10.
29. Renuka Ray, 'Women's Movement in India', ch. 3, unpublished manuscript, 3, Renuka Ray Papers, Speeches/Writings by Her, File no. 88, NMML.
30. Chattopadhyay, *Indian Women's Battle for Freedom*, 1.
31. Ibid., 2
32. V. V. Joshi to Renuka Ray, 24 August 1943, Subject File 18/68, Renuka Ray Papers, NMML.
33. Ibid.
34. Renuka Ray to B. C. Roy, 4 June, 1943. Subject File 18/68. Renuka Ray Papers, NMML.
35. Ibid.
36. B. N. Rau to Renuka Ray, 5 June 1943. Subject File 18/68, Renuka Ray Papers, NMML.
37. Renuka Ray, 'History of Social Reform and Social Work from 1947 to 1963', File no. 59, Speeches/Writings by Her, Renuka Ray Papers, NMML, 5.
38. Partha Chatterjee, 'The Nationalist Resolution of the Women's Question', in Kumkum Sangari and Sudesh Vaid (eds), *Recasting Women: Essays in Colonial History*, 233–253 (New Delhi: Zubaan, 2006; originally Kali for Women, 1989), 249
39. Ibid., 250 (emphasis mine).
40. Amrit Kaur, speech delivered in Jullundur, 1932, in Kaur, *Challenge to Women*, 15 (emphasis mine).
41. Granville Austin, *The Indian Constitution: Cornerstone of a Nation*, 2nd ed. (New Delhi: Oxford University Press, 1999), x.
42. Kamaladevi Chattopadhyay, *Status of Women in India* (New Delhi: Indian Council of World Affairs, 1947), 16.
43. Renuka Ray, Assorted notes for presentation in the Hindu Law Committee, Renuka Ray Papers, Subject File 18/68.
44. AIWC members to President, Indian National Congress, 1937 undated, Hansa Mehta Papers, Correspondence: President of Indian National Congress, NMML.
45. AICC Papers, File no. 84, 75–77, NMML Collections.
46. Wendy Singer, *A Constituency Suitable for Ladies* (New Delhi: Oxford University Press, 2007).
47. Shah wrote only the Editor's Preface to the Report. The *Report of the Sub-Committee on Woman's Role in Planned Economy* was prepared by a group of women leaders including Hansa Mehta and Vijayalakshmi Pandit, who later became members of the Constituent Assembly. Shah, *Report of the Sub-Committee on Woman's Role in Planned Economy*, 18.
48. See Chapter 4.

49. Amrit Kaur, Memorandum on Minorities, 20 March 1947, in Rao, *The Framing of India's Constitution*, Vol. 2, 309–312, 310 (emphasis mine).

50. The team comprised Kamaladevi Chattopadhyay, Hannah Sen, Kitty Shiva Rao, and Renuka Ray.

51. Draft of AIWC Press Release for 19 March 1946, Subject File no. 106, Hansa Mehta Papers, NMML.

52. Programme of the XIV Congress, first version, Women's Library, London School of Economics and Political Science Archives, 2/IAW/1/C/9. The international trajectory of the Charter needs exclusive attention.

53. All India Congress Committee Papers, File no. 84, 75–77, NMML.

54. Ibid.

55. Ibid.

56. Reba Som, 'Jawaharlal Nehru and the Hindu Code: A Victory of Symbol over Substance', *Modern Asian Studies* 28, no. 1(1994): 165–194, 165.

57. Ibid., 168.

58. Ibid., 165.

59. Editor's footnote to the 'Resolution on Fundamental Rights', in S. Gopal (ed.), *Selected Works of Jawaharlal Nehru*, Vol. 4 (Delhi: Jawaharlal Nehru Memorial Fund, 1973), 511.

60. Kamaladevi Chattopadhyay, *Inner Recesses Outer Spaces: Memoirs* (New Delhi: India International Centre and Niyogi Books, 2014), 161–162.

61. Ibid., 162. Kamaladevi claims that both she and Sanyal 'enjoined Nehru not to divulge the source of our resolution'. Ibid., 163.

62. Ibid., 162.

63. Editorial Note, in *Selected Works of Jawaharlal Nehru*, Series 1, Vol. 5, 292n2.

64. Jawaharlal Nehru, 'On Protection of Women Workers', *The Bombay Chronicle*, 9 August 1931, in *Selected Works of Jawaharlal Nehru*, Series 1, Vol. 5, 292.

65. Ibid.

66. From a draft letter signed by 30 Gujarati and Maharashtrian women, including Hansa Mehta, addressed to the President of the Indian National Congress, 1937. Hansa Mehta Papers, Subject File no. 6, 10, NMML.

67. Ibid. (emphasis mine).

68. Half Yearly Report of the Member in Charge of the Legal Disabilities of Indian Women, AIWC, 1939, 1, AIWC Papers, IV Instalment, Subject File no. 44, NMML.

69. Chattopadhyay, *Indian Women's Battle for Freedom*, 109.

70. Half Yearly Report of the Member in Charge of the Legal Disabilities of Indian Women, 4.

71. *Report of the Hindu Law Committee* (Shimla: Government of India Press, 1941), 24.
72. Ibid., 12.
73. Ibid.
74. Ibid.
75. Draft of the Indian Woman's Charter of Rights and Duties, 1946, Hansa Mehta Papers, Subject File no. 7, NMML. For a published version of the Draft, see Maithreyi Krishnaraj (ed.), *Remaking Society for Women: Visions – Past and Present* (Background Volume for VIIth Annual IAWS Conference) (New Delhi: Indian Association for Women's Studies, 1995), 57–66.
76. Austin, *The Indian Constitution*, 53.
77. Ibid., 54.
78. Ibid., 55
79. Rohit De, 'Constitutional Antecedents', in Sujit Chaudhary, Madhav Khosla, and Pratap Bhanu Mehta (eds), *The Oxford Handbook of the Indian Constitution*, 17–37 (New Delhi: Oxford University Press, 2016).
80. Ibid., 32.
81. Ibid., 37.
82. Niraja Gopal Jayal, *Citizenship and Its Discontents: An Indian History* (Ranikhet: Permanent Black, 2013), 136–162.
83. UN Documents, E/JJR/ST/5, 1 May 1946, 4.
84. Ibid., 13.
85. Kamaladevi Chattopadhyay, 'Presidential Address at the All India Women's Conference', Bombay, 7 April 1944, printed in Chattopadhyay, *At the Crossroads*, 90–98, 97.
86. Hansa Mehta, *Civil Liberties* (Aundh: Aundh Publishing Trust on behalf of AIWC, 1945); Hansa Mehta, *The Woman under the Hindu Law of Marriage and Succession* (Bombay: Pratibha Publications, 1941).
87. UN Documents. E/CN.4/SR.50, 8.
88. Ibid.
89. Johannes Morsink, *The Universal Declaration of Human Rights: Origins, Drafting, and Intent* (Philadelphia: University of Pennsylvania Press, 1999), 33.
90. Mary Ann Glendon, *A World Made New: Eleanor Roosevelt and the Universal Declaration of Human Rights* (New York: Random House, 2002), 90.
91. Ibid.
92. UN Documents, E/CN.4/SR.34, 4.
93. Ibid.
94. Ibid.

95. Hansa Mehta Papers, II Instalment, Speeches by Her, File no. 5, 3 (my emphasis).

96. Renuka Ray, 'The Draft Hindu Code', in *Hindusthan Standard*, 31 August 1945.

97. Transcript of the Vanity Fair talk show, broadcast on 21 June 1949, Subject File no. 16, Hansa Mehta Papers, 7. The show hosted Eleanor Roosevelt, Hansa Mehta, and Margueritte Bowtez, the UK representative on the UN Commission.

98. UN Documents, Summary Record of Meeting, Commission on the Status of Women, E/CN.6/SR 26, 13 January 1948, 4.

99. Ibid. (emphasis mine).

100. Glendon, *A World Made New*, 38–39.

101. Hansa Mehta's speech in the Commission on Human Rights, 4 February 1947, reproduced in Allida M. Black (ed.), *The Eleanor Roosevelt Papers*, Vol. I, *The Human Rights Years, 1945–1948* (Detroit: Charles Scribner's Sons, 2007), 508 (emphasis mine).

102. *The More Important Speeches and Interventions of Charles Malik, Taken from the Verbatim Records of the First Session of the Human Rights Commission*, 11–12 (Papers of Charles Habib Malik, Library of Congress, Manuscript Division), 44, cited in Glendon, *A World Made New*, 41.

103. Memorandum and Questionnaire on the Theoretical Bases of The Rights of Man, circulated by UNESCO in March 1947, Hansa Mehta Papers, Subject File 14, Hansa Mehta Papers, 1.

104. Ibid., 3.

105. Mehta, *Civil Liberties*, 9.

106. UN Documents, Summary Report, Meeting of the Commission on Human Rights, 15 December 1947, E/CN.4/SR.39, 4.

107. 'India: Proposal on Implementation'. This is a separate petition that Mehta submitted on 21 June 1948 to the Commission with her recommendations on procedures for implementation of human rights. UN Documents, E/CN.4/153.

108. Hansa Mehta, speech delivered at the Commission on Human Rights while presenting the Report of the Working Group on Implementation, reproduced in Hansa Mehta, 'The International Bill of Rights', typescript of an unpublished article for *World Affairs*, 20 January 1950 issue, Hansa Mehta Papers, I instalment. Writings/Speeches by Her, File no. 7, NMML, 10–11.

109. Ibid., 11.

110. Ibid., 10–11 (emphasis mine).

111. Ibid., 7.

112. Rajkumari Amrit Kaur's Letter to B. N. Rau, 31 March 1947, written on behalf of 'Hansa Mehta and myself', in Rao, *The Framing of India's Constitution*, Vol. 2, 146.
113. Hansa Mehta, 'Human Rights: Their Significance', 1951, typescript, Hansa Mehta Papers, 1st Instalment, Speeches/Writings by Her, File no. 26, NMML, 1.
114. Ibid., 4.
115. Ibid.
116. Draft of the Indian Women's Charter of Rights and Duties, 1946, 3, Hansa Mehta Papers, Subject File no. 7, NMML.
117. Ibid.
118. Ibid., 4.
119. Ibid.
120. Ibid.
121. Ibid., 5.
122. Draft of the Indian Women's Charter of Rights and Duties, 1946, Clause IV (b).
123. Kaur, *Challenge to Women*, 140.
124. Draft of the Indian Woman's Charter of Rights and Duties, 1946.
125. Ibid., 5.
126. Report of the Committee on the Differentiation of Curricula for Boys and Girls, typescript printed at the National Council for Women's Education, New Delhi from Hansa Mehta Papers, Subject File no. 31, 27.
127. Emphasis mine.
128. Ibid., 8.
129. Draft of the Indian Woman's Charter of Rights and Duties, 1946.
130. Ibid., Article 11.
131. Shah, *Report of the Sub-Committee on Woman's Role in Planned Economy*, 104.
132. Margaret Cousins, *Indian Womanhood Today* (Allahabad: Kitabistan, 1941), 137–138. Cousins writes that 'The wife in the home has no legal status as a worker or as a person whose work has economic value. Two years ago groups of women at a Women's Conference were indignant that any suggestion should be made that women should be legally entitled to a certain proportion of the income of their husbands. In the 1941 session of the same Conference, a Resolution to this same effect was passed unanimously in the open session.'
133. Chattopadhyay, 'Presidential Address at the All India Women's Conference', Bombay, 7 April 1944, 91–92.
134. Ibid., 92.

135. Draft of the Indian Woman's Charter of Rights and Duties, 1946, Article 13.

136. Ibid., Article 11.

137. Ibid., Article 14.

138. UN Documents, Summary Record of the Meeting of the Commission on Human Rights, 3 June 1948, E/CN.4/SR.58, 14.

139. Ibid., 11.

140. 'Note of Dissent by Kapila Khandvala', in K. T. Shah (ed.), *Report of the Sub-Committee on Woman's Role in Planned Economy*, 232–243 (Bombay: Vora & Co., 1947), 241, 238. For more on Kapila Khandvala, see Heather Goodall and Devleena Ghosh, 'Reimagining Asia: Indian and Australian Women Crossing Borders', *Modern Asian Studies* 53, no. 4 (2019): 1183–1221.

141. 'Note of Dissent by Kapila Khandvala', 243.

142. UN Documents, Summary Record of the Meeting of the Commission on Human Rights, 3 June 1948, 14 (emphasis mine).

4

Patterns of Participation

Women Members in the Constituent Assembly

I remember Dr. Ambedkar remarking during the debate on the revised budget proposals, pointing at me, 'this woman has a bee in her bonnet'. He classified women into three categories – females, women, and ladies, and placed me in the category 'women'!

—Durgabai Deshmukh, *Chintamani and I*, 1981[1]

Every member has the right to be inconsistent.

—Rajendra Prasad, Chairman, Constituent Assembly, 28 August 1947[2]

EVOLVING STRATEGIES, MAKING JUDICIOUS CHOICES

The established conventions of reading the *Constituent Assembly Debates* are marked by an engagement with the exterior of the Constituent Assembly – the Library Hall of the Parliament Building which hosted more than 300 members, dozens of secretarial staff, reporters and other members of the Indian and foreign press, general visitors, and guests, while the debates were taking place. Think of the grand architecture of this space, with its 13 arc-shaped rows clasped on each other in circles of elevated wooden benches, facing an enclosed dais with an imperial elevation on which is seated the chairman, a widely respected patriarch of conservative sympathies. On either side of this dais, below him, are seated seasoned bureaucrats, providing secretarial assistance to the members among whom are Ministers of the first Cabinet of Independent India. At the centre of the hall, an enormous candelabrum is suspended, from the 80-foot high dome. For a woman member, one of 'the back-benchers of this house', to speak is to walk on the green carpet up to the front and mount the rostrum which has one of the two microphones in the Hall – the other reserved for the chairman – and speak to a crowd of argumentative men, literally taking the floor, amid the sound of 40 fans and, in prolonged Delhi winters, that of several heaters.[3]

The absence of the voice of a woman member in the annals of the debates conducted on this floor is no surprise and should be read as evidence of the inherently patriarchal architecture of the Constituent Assembly. A woman's voice, of course, is evidence of the resistance against it. We must remember this architecture when we hear of their presence or absence. There are plenty of instances of both.

On 11 December 1946, the very second day that the Constituent Assembly of India met on the floor of the Parliament Hall, the most famous and the eldest of its woman members, Sarojini Naidu, defined the task of the Constituent Assembly as the framing of 'the immortal charter of India's freedom ... a charter that restores to our Mother – our mother still in fetters – her place as torch bearer of *liberty, love and peace*'.[4] She spoke as the 'hostess' of the Indian National Congress from whose ranks the members predominantly came, and blessed the President elect of the Assembly, Dr Rajendra Prasad, as an elder 'sister' and 'comrade.'[5] Naidu had been the President of the Indian National Congress and was among the senior-most members of the House. Famous and widely addressed as 'Bulbul-i-Hind, the Nightingale of India',[6] she attended the sessions of the Assembly, speaking rarely but eloquently, from the front row.

Three years later, when the Assembly had nearly finished its task and was reflecting on the Draft Constitution it would soon ratify, one of the women framers, Purnima Banerji, began her reflections by thanking the Drafting Committee 'on behalf of the back-benchers of this House'.[7] Banerji, one of the youngest members of the Assembly, well known in her own right but by no means a veteran like Naidu emerges from the records as one of the most articulate and engaged participants in the framing process. She commended the Constitution as 'a very important and precious document' in which are 'embodied those historical words which ... have since then been making a circle round the world and will continue to circulate till [they become] a reality. These words are the call of *Equality, Liberty and Fraternity* which today find a place in our Constitution'.[8]

Between Naidu's prefatory ideals of love, peace, and liberty and Banerji's summary of the constitutional principles of equality, liberty, and fraternity had passed three years of debates and deliberations, the tragic violence of the Partition, the Universal Declaration of Human Rights (UDHR), and, of course, the fully drafted text of the Constitution with its grand Preamble. Between them was also the difference between two generations of feminist vision, politics, and aspirations. This difference represented a steady evolution of the feminist attitude towards what is known as the 'woman question' (Image 4.1).

Image 4.1 Hansa Mehta addressing the Constituent Assembly on 15 August 1947.

Source: Photos of the making of the Constitution, Department of Justice, Ministry of Law and Justice, Government of India (https://doj.gov.in/page/photos-making-constitution, accessed on 17 June 2021).

The framing of the Constitution attempted a harmonious textual accommodation of the attitudes expressed by Naidu and Banerji, respectively.

Relocating women's voice

The interventions by the women members often implied critiques of the collective male rationality throughout the framing. Unfortunately, the standard histories of constitution-making have remained blind to this fact. Instead, these histories have been dominated by gender-blind readings of debates between men in which women have been conceived of as, at best, passive observers. This has led to the failure to carry out gender-sensitive readings of the debates on the floor of the Constituent Assembly.

The *Constituent Assembly Debates* constitute the standard source about the making of the Constitution.[9] These 12 volumes, aptly named *Debates*, contain the long speeches that members made either in support or against the proposed articles prepared first by the Constitutional Adviser, the Committees and sub-committees of the Assembly, and later by the Drafting Committee chaired by B. R. Ambedkar. They also contain the hundreds of amendments to these draft articles, and speeches in support or against these amendments. Finally, the speeches made by the members on the overall Constitution expressing their satisfaction or happiness at the final shape of the Constitution find a place in the *Constituent Assembly Debates*. One important factor that contributes to the blindness among scholars of the Constitution towards the woman question (and the women members) is that scholars seldom look beyond these *Debates* for their understanding of the founding moment. The most important and effective articulation of the ideas of the women members did not take place in the public portal of Constituent Assembly, but in its inner chambers. This was the space of affective performances and strategic enunciations in the 'inner' domain of the framers' Assembly. This domain was constituted by the numerous committees of the body of framers. Women were part of nearly all the important committees and contributed to their deliberations, which became the foundation of the entire discursive frame of the discussions on the floor. It is this aspect of women's location in the framing process that must be understood for a comprehension of the framing and its gendered aspects.

A sequential representation of the framing process must notice the following stages. First, the Constitutional Adviser to the Assembly B. N. Rau prepared a tentative draft of the Constitution, based on his wide-ranging studies of constitutional texts, and political and philosophical principles of constitutionalism. His draft was then perused by members of the Assembly, and particularly, the members of the Advisory Committee. The Advisory Committee, chaired by Vallabhbhai Patel, consisted of 68 members including some from outside the house. Its two most important sub-committees were the Fundamental Rights Sub-Committee and the Minorities Sub-Committee, whose members were elected on the basis of competence and interests. The number of members was unimportant because they seldom voted except in cases of hard choices. Then, voting was the last resort. The small size of the committees facilitated discussions and it was easier for members to be heard during their intense sessions. The members of the sub-committees would circulate their private ideas, often in the form of draft proposals and memoranda, which along with the Constitutional Adviser's recommendations were used to compile a working paper. This was then debated in detail passing each clause through consensus as far as possible. In cases when consensus could not be reached, the committees resorted to voting.

The Sub-Committee on Fundamental Rights' draft chapter on fundamental rights was submitted to the Minorities Sub-Committee and the Advisory Committee. The Advisory Committee, the higher body, went through the recommendations of the Sub-Committee subjecting each clause to rigorous discussion, and when necessary, votes and amendments.

Thus, it was in these committees that the primary written text of the Constitution was prepared, as the reconciled and consolidated recommendation of the Advisory Committee. It would be appropriate to consider the work of the committees to be the home-work of the Constituent Assembly, the committees being the interior spaces which produced the templates for all the debates. Despite the long, vigorous, but often tangential speeches by the members on the floor, the decisions and proposals of the committees were not significantly changed. These proposals were then incorporated by the Drafting Committee which presented its Draft Constitution to the entire assembly on 4 November 1948, more than a year after its formation in August 1947.[10]

Barring the Drafting Committee, women were strategically placed on all other committees of the Constituent Assembly. The instance of women's membership in the Advisory Committee chaired by Vallabhbhai Patel should prove my point. This Committee was arguably, with the exception of the Drafting Committee, the most important body in the entire Constituent Assembly. There is hardly any matter of importance in the Constitution, especially in its chapters on fundamental rights and directive principles, in which the final text deviated significantly from the recommendations of the Advisory Committee. The Assembly, in case it failed to resolve an issue, would refer it back to the Advisory Committee for a reconsidered resolution. Records show that even sub-groups within the pressure groups vied for membership of the Advisory Committee.[11] Hansa Mehta was nominated to the Advisory Committee by the President, while Amrit Kaur was elected as a representative of the Christian community. The President of the Constituent Assembly, Rajendra Prasad, was aware that 'the problems with which the Advisory Committee will be concerned are of greatest importance and are of far-reaching consequence to the future of India'.[12] Hence it was agreed that its members should, as far as possible, be *men* of outstanding ability and should have influence in all communities. Women's election to the Advisory Committee was their first successful act of finding a place in the decision-making process, an act which had important implications for the destiny of the Constitutional text.

Intimate committees and public floor debates

Women were fully aware of their numerically inferior status in the constitution-making body, and of the difficulty of both getting elected to it and playing an effective role, if they did. Within one month of the Cabinet Mission Statement of 16 May 1946 urging the Constituent Assembly to include an Advisory

Committee on the rights of citizens, minorities, and other disadvantaged groups,[13] women had begun lobbying for a position on it.[14] Women's agenda was to make sure that 'no disability is attached to any citizen on the grounds of sex', and that the Constitution 'provides equal rights and equal opportunities for women in all spheres of human activities'.[15] The two women elected to the Fundamental Rights Sub-Committee of the Advisory Committee were Hansa Mehta and Amrit Kaur, with Amrit Kaur also having membership on the Minorities Sub-Committee. Women were members of other permanent and ad hoc committees on substantial affairs like finance and language, and involved in numerous issues that generated contention during the debates. Besides these, G. Durgabai occupied effective positions on two important committees on procedural affairs: the Steering Committee and the Rules Committee. She was instrumental in shaping the dynamics of the Constituent Assembly in ways that require considerable attention.

Women's voice and its impact on the Constituent Assembly can best be understood if we explore these committees and their proceedings. Women members of the committees performed with more vigour, attention, and assertion. The committees were not masculine in the way the Assembly was. They were spaces conducive for what Ranajit Guha calls 'the small voice of history'.[16] These words, used by Guha in a different context,[17] can also be applied to the conventional discourse on the founding of the Constitution, which resembles 'a commanding noise characteristically male in its "inability to hear what the women were saying"'.[18] Accounts of the framing that have privileged the *Debates* over sources like the committees, sub-committees, private meetings, and shared spaces of affect and solidarity, can be argued to have been written from a 'prefabricated statist perspective in which a hierarchized view of contradiction upholds a hierarchized view of gender relations with no acknowledgement of women's agency' in the framing process.[19] The return to the small, rational voices of the committees in which women participated, challenges the exclusive privilege of the loud voice of the parliamentary form of debates, and enables a recognition of women's agency in the framing. It rescues women from the status of being 'the beneficiaries of [Constitutional] rights'[20] and restores to them their share in the authorship of these rights.

The inter-relationship between the committees and the larger processes of the *Debates* must now be examined. As mentioned above, committees were smaller groups where an intervention was not necessarily weighed in terms of the numerical support behind the arguments. The working of the committees was intimate and suitable for women, who could also work as an effective team there. The proceedings of the Fundamental Rights Sub-Committee are replete with instances where the women members spoke on numerous issues. When Hansa Mehta was absent owing to her work on the United Nations (UN) Commission on Human Rights, Amrit Kaur sometimes spoke for both of them. That numbers were not of great procedural significance in its proceedings benefitted the women members. The operative principle behind these committees was dialogue rather than debate. Govind Ballabh Pant, in the Constituent Assembly Debates, explained the mode of their functioning in the following words:

> After all the decisions in such Committees are *not* ordinarily taken by vote. Everyone is expected to appreciate the point of view of other colleagues of his. There should be a spirit of accommodation and give and take. So we look forward to unanimity in the decisions and not to majority voting in a Committee of this type ... it is possible ... that the numbers allotted to different groups are not strictly in accordance with their population. In matters of this type you cannot have a yard-stick for measuring millions of people and their interests.... One worthy representative like Dr. Ambedkar or like Mr. Anthony can, I think, do, as much as half-a-dozen or more. It is not so much number as calibre and the spirit which inspires the members which ought to count in matters of this character.[21]

The fact that 'calibre and the spirit' were more important than votes in the committees helped women members to be heard as specialists during the meetings. As opposed to the grand floor of the Assembly, where interventions could often lose their focus, and had to be addressed in hierarchically arranged circles – most women belonging to the back benches – the committees were less stratified and made more space for individual interventions. This spirit of accommodation and sense of camaraderie were not available on the large floor of the House where members had to speak to 300-odd members over a microphone. The committee sessions were also open to select public audiences, which included journalists and other professionals. This is not to suggest that women were incapable of making public speeches but to drive home the difference between their participatory roles in the committees and the Assembly.

The committees, by virtue of being smaller, also looked less intimidatingly masculine. Renuka Ray, remembering her experience in the Central Assembly, recounted being overcome by nervousness:

> I remember how I used to be overcome by shyness and embarrassment in the lobby because, though I had been a member of several committees where most

members were men ... the very atmosphere of the legislature and its lobby was *overwhelmingly masculine.*[22]

The Constituent Assembly overlapped with the Central Assembly in its membership, and like it, was predominantly masculine and patriarchal in idiom and structures. Women members often faced disrespect and discrimination. In case of disagreements, men were not always kind. A case in point is the way some members reacted to Renuka Ray's opposition to the clause on the Right to Property which put the compensation given in lieu of property acquired by the Government within the purview of the courts. In Renuka's account, Nehru, initially determined to ensure that the laws related to compensation not be called in question in any court, was convinced by the lawyers in the Drafting Committee and 'almost overnight changed his mind'.[23] When Renuka told him that he had disappointed the socialist members of the Assembly, 'he was very angry with me, and for some time we were not on speaking terms'.[24] During the debates on the floor of the Assembly too, she was 'constantly interrupted and heckled even by a man of the eminence of Shri K. M. Munshi who tried to deride my amendment'.[25]

Such gendered inflections of the vocal space are inevitably excised out of the printed records of the *Constituent Assembly Debates*. Reading them as standalone documents leaves these signifiers inert. While the entire Assembly tacitly believed in democratic modes of discussion, and disapproved of aggressive behavior on the part of women, some male members passively perpetrated a kind of discrimination on their female counterparts. A more nuanced and gendered politics of communication was evident in the frequent practice of not uttering women's names and referring to them as a common collective with phrases like 'our sisters' or 'lady members'. Alladi Krishnaswami Ayyar, while supporting women's arguments that freedom to practice religion may invalidate certain social laws, recommended that some clause may be 'inserted on the lines suggested by the lady members of the committee'.[26]

Privileging the written word and notes of dissent

Another crucial feature of the committees' groundwork leading to the debates on the floor of the Assembly was the privileged place of the written word in their proceedings. The committees usually worked through the preparation of collated working papers comprised of memoranda, advices, letters, and notes of dissent. This was different from the vocal debating practices on the floor of the Assembly, and worked to the benefit of women members. Occasionally women would even write letters to influential members of the committee and to the Constitutional Adviser who would then circulate these letters with their endorsements to the office bearers.

The records of the Fundamental Rights Sub-Committee, the Minorities Sub-Committee, and the Advisory Committee furnish ample examples of this.[27] Women members developed sufficient boldness to make written interventions before joining the Constituent Assembly.

The most memorable exercise of written interventions by women members of these committees was through their notes of dissent. These notes of dissent, written jointly by Hansa Mehta and Amrit Kaur, but sometimes by Kaur alone, constitute a special archive of women's determined refusal to be appropriated by the dominant discourses of the Constituent Assembly. These dissents also register women's desire to remain outside the circuit of complicity in matters on which they differed from the majority of the framers. For example, Amrit Kaur and Hansa Mehta wrote notes of dissent against many decisions including those that allowed for the free practice of religion, relegated the uniform civil code to the non-justiciable rights, allowed the state to impose conscription for compulsory military service, among others, at each of the stages when the committees made their official recommendations to the higher bodies of the Assembly. Amrit Kaur wrote two long notes of dissent expressing her disagreement in principle with any kind of reservations for any community.[28]

The notes of dissent performed two crucial functions in the development of the gendered voice in the authoring of the Constitution. Instrumentally, they added individuality to the impersonality of the collective authorship of the Constitution. These notes of dissent were marked with signatures of individual women. Written at an early, foundational stage of the framing, they were meant to resist the erasing march of the collective, oral debates. Normatively, they were written expressions of the consistency of women's moral position that stood at variance with the dominant attitude of the Assembly. Read together with the demi-official letters, memoranda, and other correspondence, these notes of dissent formed a written record of women's interventions in the framing. Sometimes, instead of writing a note of dissent, women members of the committees chose to write an official letter to an influential male member who could build upon the phrases they had written. Having once germinated the idea, it was for the written word to reinvent and claim for itself a place in the final draft of the Constitution. Women's work was done. A gender-sensitive narrative of the founding moments can only be established by recognizing women's preference for the written word in the preliminary stages over the speeches of the later debates.

Planning in advance: Strategies from behind the scenes

Finally, the committees also provided women with a window to the working of the Assembly, and enabled them to plan their strategies in advance. G. Durgabai was on the Steering Committee which was meant to arrange the order in which the proposed amendments or dissents would move in the Constituent Assembly. The Steering Committee was located at the pivotal position from which all the organs of the Constituent Assembly were regulated. Its task was

> to group similar motions and amendments and secure, if possible, assent of the parties concerned to composite motions and amendments; and act as a general liaison body between the Assembly and the Sections, between the Sections inter se, between Committees inter se, and between the President and any part of the Assembly.[29]

Being a member of the Steering Committee helped Durgabai to have a grip on the procedural matters of the Assembly. She would know in advance the amendments that were to be proposed during the full sessions and have some control over the order in which they were to be moved and by whom. This meant that she could help women members strategize about moving certain amendments (Image 4.2).

Most importantly, being a lawyer, she was of great help in drafting an amendment or note, and since 'she kept a watchful eye on possible loopholes or ambiguities that could lead to different interpretations against people's interest on constitutional issues'.[30] Her work in the Steering Committee meant she would meet all its members including the Chairman, Rajendra Prasad, and other influential members like Patel, Nehru, and Syama Prasad Mookerjee 'every morning before the session and go through the business of the day'.[31] Working on the Committee brought her in close contact with the mightiest of its members, whom she might persuade.[32] As the work of the Constituent Assembly progressed and the Drafting Committee grew in stature and power, the work of the Steering Committee, too, became more important. The mechanism of the Assembly required her to work in tandem and solidarity with the Drafting Committee which she supported on numerous occasions in the course of the framing. On occasion, Ambedkar rose in defence of amendments moved by Durgabai. For example, he supported her proposals regarding the rules for the amendment and passing of the Constitution prepared by the Drafting Committee.[33]

Image 4.2 Jagjivan Ram standing behind Purnima Banerji (*left*) and Durgabai (*right*), while Dakshayani looks on.

Source: *Women at the Midnight Hour*, calendar issued by the Centre for Women's Development Studies, New Delhi, 2018, curated by Malavika Karlekar (https://www.cwds.ac.in/wp-content/uploads/2018/06/Calendar2018.pdf, accessed on 25 May 2020).

Note: The calendar acknowledges Meera Velayudhan for providing this photograph from her precious family photographs. The calendar does not identify Purnima Banerji sitting on the far left of the frame and dates it as 1953. This cannot be the case since Purnima had died in the year 1951. In all likelihood, the photograph was taken during the framing of the Constitution in the lawns of the Teenmurti House when members had gathered over tea. Jagjivan Ram and Dakshayani were both Dalit members of the Constituent Assembly and had, on occasions, locked horns during the debates.

Durgabai's position of privilege as a member of the Steering Committee suggests that women's contribution to the Constituent Assembly can only be gauged by a scrutiny of *all* the texts produced at the different levels of the framing. Moreover, these texts have to be read in relation to each other, recognizing their location in the sequence of enunciations. In contrast with the huge and loosely structured corpus of the *Constituent Assembly Debates*, the proceedings of the committees can be treated as composed of specific statements, abstract and principled, and theoretical in their orientation. These statements led to resolutions and recommendations which could be considered as embodying the thematic of the framing process. They provide structure to the *Constituent Assembly Debates*, which contain article by article discussions of the Draft in a considerably ordered manner.

The entire framing process, including the committees and the debates on the floor of the Assembly, constituted one discursive field and statements made by women in the Assembly have to be interpreted with reference to this discursive field on the one hand, and the moral imaginary discussed in the last chapter on the other. An extremely crucial component of this field is the corpus of deliberations of the Constituent Assembly when it served as the Legislative Assembly, and framed ordinary laws for the running of the newly independent state. The Constituent Assembly (Legislative) had an overlapping membership except that its members had to perform other roles there, answering questions in case they were members of the Cabinet or bringing up issues as representatives of their constituencies. As legislators, the same members of the Constituent Assembly had to debate bills like an ordinary parliament, which enabled them to shape their thoughts regarding the abstract rules they were framing in their roles as constitution-makers. Since the purpose of this work is to retrieve the voices of women – and not just their statements – it becomes imperative to recognize that members of the Constituent Assembly were inescapably involved in the task of parallel translations: from 'abstract statements' made in the Constituent Assembly to the 'quantitative' ones proposed in the Constituent Assembly (Legislative) and vice versa. The latter, since they involved discussions on everyday issues, also allow us to get a clearer glimpse of the sexism and gender bias of the founding members.

Thus, the full implications of an intervention in the Constituent Assembly can be gauged only by looking at this composite discursive field in its entire complexity. For example, women's interventions in the debates on the uniform civil code have to be understood in the light of the positions women took in the committees on fundamental rights and minority rights, on the modes of social reform, and their engagement with the Hindu Law Committee of 1941. Also one would have to consider the parallel discussions on the Hindu Code Bill in the Constituent Assembly (Legislative), their positions on secular education, and on the moral authority of the state.[34]

The project of the retrieval of women's presence in the founding moment must go beyond the debates. We have to remember the 'procedures' of women's interventions and locate them not just in the debates on the floor but also trace them in the written documents of the committees, the inner chambers of the Assembly. The committees provided women scope for new modes of arguments, allowed them to challenge received opinions, and through written modes of communication, to disrupt patriarchal biases.

In the committees, women worked as a group but in a self-effacing way so that their moves did not invite undue resistance. But the same strategy of self-effacement in the magnified field of the debates led to the invisibility of women's subjectivity, a reason why exclusive reliance on the accounts of the Debates misses the voice of women in the framing process. A close reading of the *Constituent Assembly Debates* reveals that women members did not specifically represent any ideology. Unless urgent, women had avoided any explicit reference to themselves, thereby attracting minimal attention, unlike men who never tired of reminding the house of their contribution to the national movement. The Constituent Assembly, however, was not an abstract gathering and we know that women participated in it with a certain solidarity, with those male members with whom they shared a vision of a just and progressive society.

Women and Ambedkar: Alignments for principles and progress

Women were keen on making the Constitution more than a regulating text. They sought to make the text of the Indian Constitution a source for a moral order – a constitutional morality – which was not hitherto available to the people. The concept of constitutional morality was introduced in the Constituent Assembly by B. R. Ambedkar who cited the great nineteenth-century British historian of Greece, George Grote to explain what he meant by constitutional morality. 'Constitutional morality', according to Grote, consisted in

> a paramount reverence for the forms of the Constitution enforcing obedience to authority acting under and within these forms yet combined with the habit of open speech, of action subject only to definite legal control, and unrestrained censure of those very authorities as to all their public acts combined too with a perfect confidence in the bosom of every citizen amidst the bitterness of party contest that the forms of the Constitution will not be less sacred in the eyes of his opponents than in his own.[35]

At a simple level, the idea of constitutional morality can be described as a people's conviction in a set of principles, which may be written or unwritten, in the form of a constitution which will guide, regulate, and control the practices of a state and its citizens. For women, too, the conviction in these principles went beyond merely subjecting the government to limitations defined in a text. It was an extension of their vision of law as an important agent of social transformation, something that had been expressed in the numerous battles that members of the women's movement were fighting against the legal disabilities of women.

Following Grote, Ambedkar argued that this form of reverence for a constitutional form is not a natural sentiment and is definitely not available in India which was 'essentially undemocratic'. One can see in Ambedkar's choice of Grote's definition a reference to the pedagogical role the law and the constitution could play in society. Part of the function of a written constitution was the diffusion of constitutional morality into society.

Women had taken a similar position on the indispensability of constitutional morality and the idea that it must percolate down to every level of Indian society. Given his location and acute sensitivity towards the hierarchy embedded in society, Ambedkar had refused to draw inspiration from past and prevalent Indian practices. If the Constitution had to establish a new moral social order, based on equality and human dignity, it had to look towards the future. As Andre Beteille puts it, Ambedkar saw more clearly than others the pervasive contradictions between the hierarchical social structures inherited from the past and the urge for a democratic legal and political order forcefully expressed in the Assembly. Like the other members of the Assembly, he too had expectations about the future, but unlike most of them, he had few illusions about the past.[36] While 'other members of the Constituent Assembly were *aware* of the inequality, conflict and disorder prevalent in Indian society in their time',[37] it was Ambedkar, and we *must* add, the women, who were the most directly affected by them. Their stakes in making the Constitution an instrument for a fundamental change in society were much higher than for other members who might be critics but were beneficiaries of the existing order.

Thus, we see striking parallels between Ambedkar's focus on the desirability of written codes of law as opposed to customs and women's investment in the expansion of the genre of constitutions and the codification of law. Women too had identified in law the transformative potential which Ambedkar sought to mobilize. Like Ambedkar, they also identified Manu as the figure who ushered in a legal regime of inequality, causing 'the spiritual disenfranchisement of women'.[38] In their sociological understanding they seemed to concur with Ambedkar that patriarchy became entrenched when customs became more powerful than law, and, like him, dedicated themselves to strengthening the force of law. For the women constitution-makers, the emancipatory force of law could only be reinforced through its written-ness and codification. Having participated in the reform committees established under the colonial rule, they were aware of the colonial regime's reliance on customary law and its unhealthy effects.[39]

Women framers as well as Ambedkar were well aware that giving precedence to customs was regressive and akin to giving in to the demands of the social forces which they were contesting. At each stage of constitution-making and parliamentary deliberations, the women framers had reminded the house of the disabilities attached to women through customs. Written law, in contrast, and even in its breach, could anchor the progress of people's morals, and respond to the new demands raised by such movements as they represented. Thus, while acknowledging that the Child Marriage Restraint Act of 1929 had not been very successful, Renuka Ray appreciated that 'it has acted as a guide to social behaviour'. 'The purpose of social legislation', she argued, was 'to bridge the gap between the law as it exists and the changing needs of man'.[40] This normative ideal animated woman's constitutional politics throughout the period.

THE DETOURS TO EQUALITY

Are we a minority? Class, caste, and representation

Women's moral imaginary did not treat politics as 'a representational discourse that presumes a fixed or ready-made subject, usually conceived through the category of "women"'.[41] In Amrit Kaur's conception of constructive citizenship, women were not just rights-bearing subjects but also participants in the making of the republic. For the constitutional politics of the women's movement, however, it was important to showcase the socially induced disability of women so that they could be regarded as constituting an objectively verifiable minority category; as a minority they were in urgent and rightful need of constitutional attention. Their conceptualization of minority, however, was neither based on the biological difference that informed the editors of the report on *Woman's Role in Planned Economy* nor was it based on women's numerical proportions in the nation's population.

Although Amrit Kaur did claim that women are 'technically' the 'largest single minority', the reason for her characterization was not their numerical inferiority vis-à-vis men but the unequal and differential treatment meted out to them: 'not only have custom and usage dealt harshly with us, but even the law has militated and still *continues* to militate against us'.[42] Women's identification as a minority group was based on a critique of discriminatory social institutions, primarily law and custom that had not allowed women to avail the full range of possibilities that constitutional citizenship would now grant.

The idea of minority rights was one of the most contentious and delicate issues for the Constituent Assembly. This is evident from Govind Ballabh Pant's prefatory remarks while moving the proposal for the formation of the Advisory Committee as early as January 1947:

> The question of minorities everywhere looms large in constitutional discussions. Many a constitution has foundered on this rock. A satisfactory solution of questions pertaining to minorities will ensure the health, vitality and strength of the free State of India that will come into existence as a result of our discussions here. The question of minorities cannot possibly be overrated.[43]

The minority question had a pronounced status in the Constituent Assembly with an entire sub-committee dedicated to the framing of rights and measures that would define and protect their interests. Its first mention is found in Nehru's historic speech moving the Objectives Resolution on 13 December 1946 and the debates that followed. In that famous speech Nehru, referring to 'the great past of India, to the 5,000 years of India's history, from the very dawn of that history which might be considered almost the dawn of human history, till today',[44] did not mention women and their rights. Yet he proposed the Assembly resolve to 'proclaim India as an Independent Sovereign Republic and to draw up for her future governance a Constitution ... wherein adequate safeguards shall be provided for minorities, backward and tribal areas, and depressed and other backward classes'.[45] Pant too, while moving for the appointment of the Advisory Committee, was aware that 'unless the minorities are fully satisfied, we cannot make any progress....'[46] He also reminded the house of its responsibility 'to take particular care of the Depressed Classes, the Scheduled Castes and the Backward classes':[47]

> We have to atone for our omissions – I won't use the word commissions. We must do all we can to bring them up to the general level and it is a real necessity as much in our interest as in theirs that the gap should be bridged. The strength of the chain is measured by the weakest link of it and so until every link is fully revitalised, we will not have a healthy body politic.[48]

Debate on minority status

The Assembly was sensitive to the rights of minorities and the classes it deemed weak and marginalized. There was no agreed definition or measurement of minority status among the members of the Constituent Assembly and each group, fully aware of the special position of minority groups in a democratic constitutional set up, conceptualized it to suit its own interests. Prominent expressions of such faith in constitutionalist protection of minority interests can be found in the draft articles and memoranda submitted by members of the Fundamental Rights Sub-Committee which included proposed articles by K. M. Munshi and Harnam Singh, and a comprehensive draft of fundamental rights prepared by B. R. Ambedkar. Among these only Munshi's draft regarded women as a distinct category, entitled to the right to equality as 'the equal of men citizens in all spheres of political, economic, social, and cultural life'.[49] The others made special recommendations regarding the rights of minorities and other marginalized groups conceptualized as belonging to the same family of citizens. In all these memoranda, excepting Ambedkar's, the term minority was reserved for religious and linguistic minorities – who were considered deserving subjects for constitutional safeguards.[50] Ambedkar's strategic conceptualization of minority was broader and grounded on a rational social framework. In his 'Memorandum and Draft Articles on the Rights of States and Minorities' of 24 March 1947, and later during debates in the Advisory Committee, his use of the term minority implied any social group that has systematically been subjected to discrimination.[51]

The conceptual debates that took place in the Advisory Committee veered around the issue of the mutually exclusive relation between minorities and classes, and primarily around the rationale for deciding which classes or groups of persons should be considered minorities. Does the phrase 'classes not adequately represented' mean minorities? Are the terms minorities and backward classes mutually exclusive? Members like Syama Prasad Mookerjee suggested they retain both terms, 'minorities and other classes'[52] while others like Frank Anthony suggested 'reservations in favour of minorities *or* classes'.[53] Although Ambedkar and other members eventually conceded to Patel's assertion that 'Classes include minorities. This is absolutely unnecessary. It is as clear as daylight',[54] the intense discussions in the Advisory Committee raised the significance of interpreting the meanings of the terms. Both 'minorities' and 'classes' were considered as reinforcing the idea of marginalization and discrimination that needed to be righted by the Constitution. As Rajagopalachari anticipated:

According to the ordinary interpretation if you introduce the word minority, the question whether a class is minority will become justiciable. Classes will be interpreted in the sense of minority. The use of the general term 'classes' is followed by the phrase 'not adequately represented' and the opinion of the State finally determines it.[55]

The debates around this clause continued in the Constituent Assembly in subsequent stages, and when the article was finally passed, it was settled with the addition of the term 'backward', alluding to the social discrimination which Ambedkar had argued to be the only yardstick for minority status. Thus the 'classes who, in the opinion of the State, are not adequately represented in the public services'[56] became 'any backward class of citizens which, in the opinion of the State, is not adequately represented in the services under the State'.[57] The dense discourse in the Constituent Assembly was grounded in the double principle of constitutional reassurance for minorities and a broader social definition of the latter. The Draft Constitution of February 1948 which was prepared by the Drafting Committee following 'the decisions taken by the Constituent Assembly or by the various committees appointed by the Constituent Assembly' had prepared a special section titled 'Special Provisions Relating to Minorities'. According to its classification, 'minorities' included communities based on religious, caste, and ethnic denominations: Muslims, Christians, Sikhs, Anglo-Indians, Scheduled Castes, and the Scheduled Tribes. The provisions included reservations for seats in both legislatures and the executive. At a later stage, when the Assembly revised its decision of providing reservations for religious minorities, the section was retained with the new title 'Special Provisions Relating to Certain Classes', once again evoking the semantic binary of classes and minorities. Before this final revision, during the debates it was argued that 'in fairness to the country, protection can be granted to any class, whether you call it a backward class or a minority, only on the ground that it is backward and if left to itself, would be unable to protect its interests'.[58]

These debates expose some of the most significant ideological entrapments within which the woman question, particularly special provisions for women, was negotiated in the Constituent Assembly. The liberal democratic framework that served the members of the Assembly, pulled the demands in two directions: one, defining a minority on grounds of numerical proportions of communities, and two, broadening the base of such minority by conceptualizing them as a class that had undergone social discrimination. The first, which, owing to the uncertain unfolding of events around Partition, was negotiated and renegotiated several times in the process of the framing, finally led to the retraction of reservations to religious communities. It was overshadowed by the anxieties of territorial and sub-national disintegration in the minds of the framers. The second determined the nature of the concessions and special aids that the Constitution would provide to the classes identified as backward or discriminated against.

The women framers located themselves as representing a special interest group in the Assembly, and yet articulated their interests in consonance with their moral imagination of women as competent, constructive citizens whose disabilities would be removed as soon as the Constitution granted them the fundamental right to equality. A prima facie examination of the records of the Constituent Assembly and its committees seems to suggest that women members did not participate in the discussions conceptualizing minorities and passively agreed to the predominantly patriarchal concept of communities based on religious denomination, caste, or other customary identities. A close reading of the proceedings of the Constituent Assembly, examined in the light of some of the avowed positions that women had taken before becoming its members, reveals a complex strategy on their part. During the entire discussion that specifically conceptualized the meaning of 'minority' in the Assembly, women members kept a silent watch on the proceedings without speaking on the subject. This was despite the fact that women had in fact claimed for themselves minority status, as explicitly evidenced in Amrit Kaur's statement cited above.[59]

The minutes of the Advisory Committee proceedings on 21 April 1947, when the most intense debates about the definition of 'minority' took place show that its two women members had chosen to stay quiet on the issue. The primary reason was that women did not seek any special provisions from the Constitution: unlike Ambedkar and leaders of other minorities they believed that equality in the sense of non-discrimination would be sufficient for their interests. Women members carried into the Constituent Assembly a confidence in the morality of the state and a definite non-communitarian position against reservations. In her concluding remarks on the Constitution, Hansa Mehta regretted that the Constitution had failed to define 'minority':

> The most difficult problem that we had to tackle was the problem of Minorities. Nowhere in the Constitution we have defined 'Minorities'. We accepted the definition that was given to us by the last Rulers. They created religious minorities, communal minorities in order to help their policy of divide and rule and that policy has culminated in the partition of this country. We do not want any more partitions. What do the minorities what? ... If they want privileges, that is not in the spirit of democracy. They cannot ask for privileges.[60]

'The only exception', to this rule, she stated, were the Scheduled Castes, not women.[61] Amrit Kaur, herself a devoted associate of Mahatma Gandhi, had represented the official stance of the women's movement as against separate electorates. In 1932, when she was the President of the All India Women's Conference (AIWC), the Memorandum of the AIWC clearly denounced special electorates and reservations for women, a position that was then justified in the interests of national unity. However, in 1933, during an examination by B. R. Ambedkar on behalf of the Joint Committee on Indian Constitutional Reform, Amrit Kaur had clearly said that even though women were against reservations,

> if reservations are to be *forced down on us* as so many things have been forced down on us against our wishes, then the only condition on which we would recommend the acceptance of reservation to our organizations would be definitely that they would be through a system of joint electorates and direct action.[62]

On being questioned by Ambedkar, she repeated her naïve conviction that joint electorates do not act in a communal manner.[63]

Dakshayani Velayudhan and the annihilation of caste

Before we examine Amrit Kaur's position on the issue, it would be useful to gain the crucial perspective of Dakshayani Velayudhan. As the only woman member belonging to the Scheduled Castes, she had made 'a personal appeal to Dr. Ambedkar to join the nationalist forces of the country',[64] and told 'the Harijan delegates ... that they should not harp on separatism', evoking discursive binaries prevalent since the Poona Pact of 1932.[65] In contrast with Ambedkar, she refused 'to believe that the 70 million Harijans are to be considered as a minority' and argued that reservations would not be in the best interests of the Harijans.[66] Dakshayani and Ambedkar's confrontation over the question of separate electorates at the time of the Cabinet Mission Plan of 1946 unfolded more clearly during the discussions in the Constituent Assembly (Image 4.3). Dakshayani's opposition to separate electorates and reservations was situated at an epistemological standpoint which was different from both Ambedkar's and that of the other women members of the Constituent Assembly. It was hemmed by a Gandhian framework of redemption and reconciliation within a national community, and fuelled by a socialist desire for fundamental economic change. Anti-colonial nationalist angst informed her ideas of self-respect and dignity making it difficult for her to accept 'any kind of reservation in any

Image 4.3 A close-up of the signatures of B. R. Ambedkar and Dakshayani Velayudhan, among the two most remarkable Dalit members of the Constituent Assembly.

Source: The original copy of the Constitution of India.

place whatsoever' where she saw a legacy of the patronizing (and presumably patriarchal) bias of the colonial rule.[67] While Ambedkar had appealed to Churchill to raise a voice for the untouchables in the British Parliament in the aftermath of the Cabinet Mission Plan in June 1946,[68] she chastised Churchill in her first speech in constitution-making for an independent India.[69] She asserted that

> the Harijans are Indians and they have to live in India as Indians and they will live in India as Indians. Neither Lord Pethick-Lawrence, the Secretary of State for India, nor even the Prime Minister, Mr. Attlee, nor even the Leader of the Opposition, Mr. Churchill, is going to improve the condition of the Harijans.[70]

If the caste Hindus had been oppressors, the British were no better and with a veiled reference to Rao Bahadur N. Sivaraj, with whom she had bitterly contested for a seat in the Constituent Assembly, she accused the British of creating class disparities among the Dalits. Mr Churchill, she asserted, may at best give 'protection to a few communalists who might fly to England':

> What has the British Government done to improve the social status of the Harijans? Did they ever pass any legislation to remove the social disabilities of the Harijans except producing some chaprassis and butlers?[71]

The caste question, she explained could be addressed by Indians through 'an Independent Socialist Indian Republic [that] can give freedom and equality of status to the Harijans'[72]: it alone could ensure 'the removal, immediate removal, of our social disabilities'.[73]

In his 'Memorandum and Draft Articles on the Rights of States and Minorities' submitted to the Constituent Assembly in March 1947, Ambedkar summarized his test for the definition of minorities and argued that numbers or religious separation are not a 'good and efficient test' to determine what constitutes a minority.[74] The real test, he argued, was social discrimination, and if the social relations between any two communities are 'marked by social discrimination', the community on the receiving end constitutes the real minority. Thus, for Ambedkar, 'Muslims are given separate electorates not because they are different from Hindus in the point of religion. They are given separate electorates because – and this is the fundamental fact – the social relations between the Hindus and the Musalmans are marked by social discrimination.'[75]

Further, in the same memorandum, Ambedkar described the pervasiveness of the social discrimination that marked the relationship between untouchables and caste Hindus in detail. Its main feature was the 'positive anti-social and inimical attitude to the Untouchables that the Hindus' have in all spheres.[76] Read closely, Ambedkar's discourse in the Constituent Assembly (at least until this point of time) painted a picture of an unassailable wall between two communities informed by an indissoluble mistrust of each other's intentions. Ambedkar's interest was in identifying the wall but not in fixing responsibility. While Dakshayani did not deny the fact of social discrimination of which she spoke during the debates frequently enough, she was less sceptical of the caste Hindus and, in her Gandhian commitment to the idea of transformation of the self, was willing to acknowledge the possibility of a change of heart of the caste Hindus with whom lay the responsibility of bringing social change. Her intervention in the Constituent Assembly during the discussion on article 11 of the Draft Constitution, later to become article 17 of the Constitution that abolished untouchability, bore the complexity and profundity of her thoughts. She began by acknowledging

> that there is a vast change in the outlook and attitude of the people today towards the untouchables. Nowadays what we find is that the people who are called caste Hindus dislike the very idea of, or the very term, 'untouchability' and they do not like to be chastised for that, because, they have taken a vow that they are responsible for it and that they will see that it is abolished from this land of ours.[77]

She claimed that the 'change of heart that we find in the people today is only due to the work that has been done by Mahatma Gandhi and by him alone'.[78] The emphasis was on the responsibility of the caste Hindus. Gandhi had *reminded* people of this responsibility and now the Constitution was to do the same. However, the task of removing untouchability and the attendant social injustices it is symptomatic of lay with the people of India. She recounted her college days in the course of her speech to emphasize this point:

> While I was a student in College, one of my class-mates approached me for subscribing to a fund for the abolition of untouchability. My reply was, 'you people are responsible for this and therefore it is for you to raise the money and it is not proper that you should ask me for money'.[79]

Although she did not move an official amendment to the effect, one can read an implied refusal on her part to speak in the juridico-penal language in which the article was worded:

> 'Untouchability' is abolished and its practice in any form is *forbidden*. The enforcement of any disability arising out of 'Untouchability' shall be an *offence punishable* in accordance with law.[80]

Instead of speaking of the *culpability* of the offender, she spoke of their *responsibility*, and envisaged a future when 'there will be no necessity for us to incorporate such a clause in the Constitution'.[81] This would happen with a pedagogical praxis: 'what is needed is that there should be proper propaganda done by both the Central and Provincial Governments' and not law, she argued.[82] Her speech ran counter to the arguments of the previous speaker who had 'requested Members of the House to try their best to make the law effective'.[83] According to Dakshayani, 'The working of the Constitution will depend upon how the people will conduct themselves in the future, not on the actual execution of the law'. She said that 'When this Constitution is put into practice, what we want is not to *punish* the people for *acting against the law*',[84] but for the state to take on the task of educating citizens for a transformation. One can clearly notice the distinction she made between the Constitution and the laws that it promulgates; the former refers to principles that have to be rediscovered in the soul of the people and the latter to injunctions made by the state.

It is in this larger normative, one might say, idealistic view of constitutional morality that one must locate the full force of Dakshayani's arguments during the framing. A discriminatory society can be transformed not merely by paying special attention to those discriminated against but by making those who discriminate take responsibility for their actions. It is the agents of discrimination who must imbibe the values of the Constitution before a fundamental change can be achieved. Her opposition to reservations, then, may be read as consistent with her approach of addressing the cause of a problem, rather than curing its symptoms and that, she argues, can only happen in a socialist democratic republic.

Given the nature of the Constituent Assembly Debates, where it was easier to evoke than adumbrate principles, one needs to understand what a member meant by an abstract idea like socialism. Collating Dakshayani's synchronous participation in the Legislative Debates of the Constituent Assembly with the constitution-making debates helps us reconstruct her position. The Dalits and the lower castes, who she refers to variously 'as economic slaves of other people',[85] 'underdogs of this land',[86] 'the unfortunate brethren of the neglected community',[87] and 'the so-called Scheduled Castes of India',[88] are victims of 'the fascist social structure existing in India'.[89] 'By whatever name they are called', they 'are the *economic* slaves of the other people', she emphasized during her speech objecting to the demand for fixing a minimum number of votes for a Dalit representative. Her point was that Harijans belonged to a group whose autonomous political identity for an electoral democracy could not be created in a class-society:

> The Harijans are not in a position to withstand the *attractions* that they will have to face at the time of elections. So many parties can set up candidates and they can purchase the Harijans and put up any candidate they desire, and any candidate can come up in the assembly and certainly he may not represent the community though he may get the percentage of votes that is desired by this system.[90]

Throughout her participation in the Constituent Assembly, Dakshayani never lost sight of the class position of the Dalit woman, and contested any possibility that the Dalit woman's interest might be forgotten in the course of making abstract formulations. In her interventions in the parallel sessions of the Constituent Assembly (Legislative), she opened up an entire discourse on positive discrimination by demanding special provisions for women. She repeatedly asked the Government about scholarships for Dalit students, asking specially about the gender ratio of the beneficiaries and the number of those in Government services.[91] Demanding special assistance for Dalit students' who wanted to pursue their education abroad, she reminded the Government that

> If the Government have any desire to see that Harijans should be educated and that they should be given all facilities for foreign studies, it is the *duty* of the government to renew the scheme and give full facilities for them to go abroad so that they can secure degrees of foreign Universities. I will have no quarrel if the Government have a scheme for educating all the poor people of this country but as far as the Government have they do proper Justice to those unhappy brethren of this land [*sic*].[92]

She reminded the House that the Dalits 'cannot go abroad for higher studies or even for college or school studies spending money from their own pockets'.[93] Rather than granting scholarships in proportion of the Dalit community in the population, the government should utilize its funds and give scholarships 'to at least a maximum number of students'.[94] She disagreed with – or at least put less emphasis on – the idea of 'communal ratio prescribed by the Ministry of Home Affairs for purposes of appointment to services, etc.'[95] The thrust of her demand for positive discrimination was not for representation but for education and empowerment or capability enhancement and the removal of inequalities. This is consistent with her emphasis on social class rather than the liberal vocabulary of minorities. For her, the caste question was firmly grounded in the question of class and the Constitution could address it only by ushering in an economic revolution – without which 'there is no meaning in demanding either separate electorates or joint electorates or any other kind of electorates'[96]– not by containing it within the liberal framework of identities and representation. Yet, until such time as that happened, she accepted reservations with joint electorates as 'a necessary evil'.[97]

She continued to pay attention to the class–caste connection later in life and was sceptical of the idea that deeply held caste prejudices can be abolished by measures like inter-caste marriages. In a popular article written 25 years after the enactment of the Constitution, she critiqued the policy of promoting such marriages, citing examples of upper-caste women who carried their caste prejudices into these marriages. Condemning such women, she claimed that

> there is nothing creditable in marrying a man and then refusing to bear his child because he belongs to a low caste. Such things have unhappily happened even in cases of 'love marriage'…. As it happens, the growing number of marriages between high-caste girls and Harijan boys is not an unmixed blessing. Since only the best educated Harijan boys are 'eligible' – most of them, if suitably employed, are snapped up usually by upper caste girls – the educated Harijan girls often fail to match within their castes. Nor do upper-caste boys seem anxious to marry them.[98]

She argued that 'high-caste girls are prepared to marry only those scheduled caste boys who are in the IAS [Indian Administrative Service] or are doctors, engineers, and business executives' and yet, after marriage, those girls treated the parents 'literally as untouchables in the homes of their own sons'.[99] Clearly she was sceptical about Ambedkar's hope that 'The real remedy for breaking caste is intermarriage', following which 'the separatist feeling – the feeling of being aliens – created by caste will vanish'.[100] The instances she cites run counter to the hope that 'by breaking the association of women with the reproduction of caste community, inter-caste marriage would annihilate caste distinctions'.[101] Instead she was forever mindful of the intersection of class and gender at which inter-caste bonds are formed, and their limitations in breaking caste barriers. Writing in 1975, she suggested that only when 'genuine sentiments' informed the 'feelings of the couple' that could override class-calculations, could this 'communal gulf' be bridged. This required a 'tremendous transformation' of society, in which, one may presume, constitutional morality responded to an affective ethics that Dakshayani invoked as frequently as did the other women members of the Constituent Assembly.

Equality before law and after: Affirmative action and substantive equality

Returning to the other women members, the thrust of their argument was that reservations and separate electorates would weaken the unity of the nation, an idea that had a considerable presence in the Constituent Assembly after the creation of Pakistan. However, there was a certain amount of contingency in their position due to the anxiety that joint electorates may not yet be possible. Even during the framing of the Constitution, they thought that 'there is a possibility of their not being accepted by the majority in the unfortunate atmosphere that exists in the country today'.[102] Women members' 'strong objections to the system of separate electorates' in the meetings of the Fundamental Rights Sub-Committee fitted well into accepted tropes of the unity of the nation.[103] The frequently evoked binary of national unity and the 'fissiparous tendencies' of demanding special provisions, made it easy for women to be in consonance with the dominant narrative. A month before the debate in the Advisory Committee on the notion of minorities, Amrit Kaur had already evoked the notion of fragmentation in the demand for privileges. 'We do not and we must never look upon ourselves as anything but an integral part of a whole', she submitted, 'nor must we claim any privileges'.[104] Speaking from within a liberal democratic framework of formal equality, she claimed that:

> Equality before the law and in society and equal opportunities for education and services are all we claim as human beings, and I believe that in the fulfilment of our duties as citizens – and duties must go hand in hand with rights – lies our best safeguard.[105]

The rhetoric of national interest and unity in the Constituent Assembly is easily noticeable in this position and can hardly be distinguished from the unifying projection of the nation as a seamless community. There is, however, a strong gendered dimension to women's refusal to accept reservations, which they viewed as privileges. Besides showing a belief in women's potential as citizens, this refusal contained a resistance to what the women members perceived as men's paternalistic favours granted to them. Reservations, as evident in Renuka Ray's later assertion on the floor, were almost an affront to women's self-respect:

> All along the women of India have been against reservation of seats or special electorates. Before the 1935 Act came in we were against it and put forward our views in no uncertain terms, but it was forced upon us; and today, in spite of the chivalry of the previous speaker, Indian women will not *tolerate* any such reservations in the Constitution.[106]

Reserved seats were given to women by the 1935 Act 'in direct contravention to our desires'[107] as part of the colonialist approach of exploiting 'the social backwardness of women'.[108] In continuance with Amrit Kaur's testimony before Ambedkar, Renuka Ray's statement too was couched in language of force, coercion, and toleration: reservations were 'forced' upon women and they would not 'tolerate' it anymore. In the context of the legislative stereotyping of women, these were phrases of resistance to patronizing discourses that sustained the idea of generous men granting equality to women.[109] Read in conjunction with Dakshayani Velayudhan's remarks, reservations ostracized a group, making them inferior in the eyes of those who do not claim its privileges. Moreover, women's resistance introduced a feminist notion of self-esteem and confidence in the discourse on reservation, anticipating some of the commonly stated positions against affirmative action. According to Amrit Kaur:

> Privileges and safeguards really weaken those who demand them. They are a definite bar to unity, without which there can be no peace, as also to efficiency without which the standards of good governance are lowered.[110]

It may be argued that she was speaking from the position of her class privilege, representing an elitist bias in her understanding of the consequences of reservations for social unity and the efficiency of governance. Yet one must also note the consistency of this position with moral ideas about constructive citizenship and the ideals of state to which it partly belonged. 'Society is made of men', she argued in an essay written in 1945, 'and women have to become self-reliant, fearless and enterprising if they are to contribute their full quota to the moral well-being of a State'.[111] In the Minorities Sub-Committee, Kaur submitted that only integrity and merit – she insisted in that order – could ensure maximum efficiency of the state. She placed 'integrity advisedly before merit because high standards of public morality must be maintained if the State is to be a great moral agency'.[112] Most women members agreed that asking for privileges was 'not in the spirit of democracy'[113] and believed that women could become self-reliant if the Constitution could prevent discrimination against them. Women were a minority only inasmuch as they were disabled by laws and discriminatory practices. In their conceptualization, merit was a universally available quality that could be honed and developed in the ideal circumstances of equality of opportunity and social dignity.

To cite one example, speaking of the achievements of Vijayalakshmi Pandit, Renuka Ray told the Constituent Assembly:

> Vijayalakshmi Pandit has not been selected because she is a woman nor was sex made a bar to the appointment. It is her proven worth that has been responsible for her appointment to the high office of ambassador to a land which is admittedly one of the greatest forces in the world today. This has vindicated our position and women are indeed proud of this.[114]

She was aware that Vijayalakshmi and her other colleagues could be cited as exceptional women, and thus were insufficient proof of women's overall capability. Therefore, she extended her claim by asserting that

> it will not only be women of exceptional ability who in future will be called upon to occupy positions of responsibility, but *all* women who are equally capable, equally able as men will be considered irrespective of sex.[115]

All women needed was conditions without impediments and disabilities attached to their lives through legislation or social structure. Special privileges, in the women members' argument, may 'weaken' the chances of this equality, which in turn would make the state less of a moral agency.

As a special interest group, women did not ask the state to make positive interventions on their behalf but wanted the Constitution to ensure that all discrimination be removed. With fundamental rights enshrined in the language of prohibitions, it seems tempting to argue that the Constitution they sought had syntactic affinities with what Catherine MacKinnon called 'a constitution of abstinence'.[116] The articles under the fundamental right to equality, whose syntactical arrangement was prepared in the 11-member committee on fundamental rights of which Hansa Mehta and Amrit Kaur were active members, are designed thus:

> The State *shall not deny* to *any person* equality before the law or the equal protection of the laws within the territory of India. The State *shall not discriminate* against *any citizen* on grounds only of religion, race, caste, sex, place of birth or any of them. *No citizen shall*, on grounds only of religion, race, caste, sex, place of birth or any of them, *be subject to any disability, liability, restriction or condition* with regard to access to shops, public restaurants, hotels and places of public entertainment.... *No citizen shall*, on grounds only of religion, race, caste, sex, descent, place of birth, residence or any of them, *be ineligible for, or discriminated against* in respect of, any employment or office under the State.[117]

A superficial reading of these articles by one unaware of the interventions of the feminist women members of the Assembly might lead to the conclusion that the state thus constituted adopted 'the standpoint of male power on the relation between law and society'.[118] The language of abstinence that it adopted, perpetuated the myth of neutrality and sustained status quo in society, maintaining that 'conditions that pertain among men on the basis of gender apply to women as well'.[119] A close reading of the proceedings of the Constituent Assembly, on the contrary, reveals that women used the same language of prohibition to insert a woman's perspective into the design of the Constitution.

The suggestion that the fundamental rights must be stated in the form of a prohibition of 'discrimination on such and such grounds'[120] had come from jurist Alladi Krishnaswami Ayyar. In response, the women framers worked to reconcile their positions to this syntax to ensure that the prohibitions served the interests of women as citizens. After considerable debate it was decided that rights would be enunciated in such a design that a 'positive statement about rights and obligations [would be] followed by a statement in a negative form to the effect that there shall be no discrimination on the grounds of religion, race, sex, etc.'[121] Through subsequent drafts, these operative injunctions became the constitutional statements of fundamental rights that went through several stages of scrutiny before finally being incorporated in the Constitution of India. During the textualization of the fundamental right to equality, women framers directed their authorial energy to substantiating these injunctions, ensuring thereby that the legal and social disabilities they had historically accumulated were removed. At each of the successive stages of drafting, they were alert to the possibility of expanding the formal guarantees of non-discrimination, either by adding to the list of prohibitions that should be implied in these guarantees or seeking to modify statements that adversely affected the status of women and hurt the movements fighting for women's interests. They demanded a constitutional prohibition on child marriages,[122] a clause guaranteeing 'marriages between persons professing different religious faiths, each retaining his or her own religion without abatement',[123] and insisted that the grounds mentioned in the Constitution on which access to be public places cannot be denied specifically include 'sex'.[124]

At this stage, we need to juxtapose the narrative of women members' disapproval of reserved seats or quotas with their numerous demands for special provisions that were part of the Women's Charter. Their rejection of reserved seats flows from a view of affirmative action not based on proportionate representation.

Since women were 'technically ... the largest single minority',[125] to use Amrit Kaur's phrase, the idea of proportion would have distorted the entire notion of equality in the Constitutional framework. And, as the entire trajectory of the women's movement attests, 'representation' for them was always an expanding category. Their demand for special provisions, on the other hand, derives from the concept that the full realization of citizenship had been impeded for women by social and legal handicaps. Hence they needed special Constitutional support.

The idea that law is not limited to the removal of disabilities but can enhance capability had evolved among women members by the time they time they came to the Constituent Assembly. In the process of framing the abstract principles for the Constitution, they made sure the word 'sex' was included in all provisions that sought to mark out 'categories' against which discrimination was prohibited.[126] Notably, the insertion of the word 'sex' meant that discrimination could not be exercised against either men or women or, as the word has now been semantically expanded, against any gender. During the debates in the Advisory Committee in April 1947, K. M. Panikkar commented that Amrit Kaur's zeal in getting 'sex' included in all such clauses meant that 'Discrimination for women means discrimination against men'.[127] 'Sex' must also include men, and such prohibitions must also mean that there should be no discrimination against men, he had argued. Interestingly, in the landmark *NALSA* v. *Union of India* judgment of 2014, the court declared that 'The expression "sex" used in Articles 15 and 16 is not just limited to biological sex of male or female, but intended to include people who consider themselves to be neither male or female'.[128] The Court's judgment built a radically progressive jurisprudence on the energy of women's interventions without recognizing their contribution. The full observation reads:

> Articles 15 and 16 sought to prohibit discrimination on the basis of sex, recognizing that sex discrimination is a historical fact and needs to be addressed. Constitution makers, it can be gathered, gave emphasis to the fundamental right against sex discrimination so as to prevent the direct or indirect attitude to treat people differently, for the reason of not being in conformity with stereotypical generalizations of binary genders. Both gender and biological attributes constitute distinct components of sex … gender attributes include one's self image, the deep psychological or emotional sense of sexual identity and character. The discrimination on the ground of 'sex' under Articles 15 and 16, therefore, includes discrimination on the ground of gender identity.[129]

K. M. Panikkar's remarks possibly meant as a pun, ironically, were given shape under a progressive judicial hammer! Evidently, the court's reference to the intention of the 'Constitution makers' alluded to social practices that women members had encapsulated in the term 'sex' during their intervention.

Besides focusing on the areas in which discrimination on the ground of sex needed to be constitutionally invalidated, Hansa Mehta and Amrit Kaur ensured that the state recognized women's needs to the extent that special provisions for them could be made. The debate on what was to become article 15 of the Constitution began after the Minorities Sub-Committee in its recommendations omitted sex from the list of denominations against which discrimination in access to public spaces was to be prohibited.

The original draft of article 15 had a prefatory clause (1) which had stated that 'There shall be no discrimination against any person on grounds of religion, race, caste, language or sex'.[130] It was proposed that in the following clause about particularities of access to institutions, 'sex' be dropped from the list. Amrit Kaur clearly refused to agree to the elimination of 'sex' as a ground.[131] She also demanded a provision that 'nothing in the clause shall prevent public institutions or places of recreation being set apart solely for women'.[132] Kaur and Mehta insisted that the Constitution should make space for positive discrimination for women. C. Rajagopalachari spoke on their behalf and got the Committee to agree to their demands. 'The substance of

Rajkumari's suggestion', he summed up, 'is to add the words "or sex" in clause 2 also and follow it up with a proviso "Nothing herein shall prevent separate places of public resort being exclusively reserved for women".'[133] He moved on to suggest, as a response to women's insistence, that the clause should not be confined merely to the particularities of public places but be broadened to provide that 'nothing herein contained shall prevent separate provision being made for women and children'. [134] As it turned out, this became the germ of what eventually emerged as article 15(3) of the Constitution of India that made it possible for the state to make special provisions for women.

Contrary to the perceived understanding of women's disavowal of reservations, women members demanded special treatment for women. They presented women as a category with specific interests that could not be submerged in the universalizing language of constitutional injunctions. Their interventions in the Constituent Assembly in its role as the Parliament must be read as performative acts of resistance against such undifferentiated language and its politics of erasure, inscribing the entire field with the experience of women to which the Constitution must respond. A few instances of such inscriptions will substantiate these claims and demonstrate the centrality of the social experience and situatedness of women as putative citizens with constitutional rights. Thus, the demands for special waiting rooms, compartments, and safety measures for women in the railways by Dakshayani Velayudhan, Aizaz Rasul, and Annie Mascarene must be read as activation of the constitutional articles even as they were being formulated.[135] Mascarene's interventions read like the soliloquy of a woman travelling the length and breadth of India – from Trivandrum to New Delhi – on a third class compartment, suffering and watching other women travellers suffer, many with babies at their breast, in overcrowded trains, and produced an affective context for the drafters of the Constitution.[136]

Dakshayani took special interest in scholarships for Dalit girls and protective clauses for Dalit female factory-workers.[137] Renuka Ray proposed special attention to the mental health of refugee women.[138] Durgabai demanded vocational training for refugee women who were victims of Partition violence,[139] a special budget for women's education,[140] raised questions about women's recruitment into the IAS and the IPS,[141] sought attention to the education of female students abroad,[142] and advocated women's license to drive hackney carriages.[143] Several of these women also demanded the enhancement of women's presence in the police force and provision for their necessary training.[144] Aizaz Rasul demanded special recruitment of women to defence services,[145] objected to the Armed Forces (Special Powers)

Bill,[146] demanded registration of women in Employment Exchanges,[147] and emphasized the recruitment of women in diplomatic services.[148] Ammu Swaminathan sought special assistance for female medical personnel in securing employment.[149] Annie Mascarene demanded raising the salary of and better-equipping nurses and female medical workers.[150] These and several other interventions made in the Constituent Assembly in its legislative functions contributed to the gendering of the entire framing discourse. These are evidence of the way in which women members compelled the framing body to engage with the contingencies and vulnerabilities of women.

Close readings of the Advisory Committee proceedings of April 1947 show the discussions that generated the foundational templates for article 15 and article 16 had taken place simultaneously – Ambedkar himself being an active participant in both. It was on Amrit Kaur's insistence that the word 'sex' was added to the list of categories against which discrimination was to be prohibited in the original draft of article 16. In the proceedings, it is clear that although women framers did not demand reservations directly, their interventions provided Ambedkar with supplementary logic for his own insistence on a provision for reserved quotas based on proportional – and by implication, descriptive – representation.[151] On the surface, it may appear that Ambedkar laid more emphasis on the clauses that made exceptions to the norm (those that led to articles 15(3) and 16(4) of the Constitution) and women framers only focused on the ambit of the ground of non-discrimination. But as the discussion shows, these were not mutually exclusive positions for either of them. Ambedkar and the women members found themselves in positions with overlapping interests and presented complementary paradigms which were left to the Drafting Committee to reconcile. As Ambedkar stated in the final debates on reservations, it was up to the Committee to reconcile the views of members who felt that 'there ought to be no reservations of any sort for any class or community at all, that all citizens, if they are qualified, should be placed on the same footing of equality so far as the public services are concerned' and of members who insisted that 'although theoretically it is good to have the principle that there shall be equality of opportunity, there must at the same time be a provision made for the entry of certain communities which have so far been outside the administration'.[152]

Ambedkar, however, could not place women in any of these categories. As someone who had followed women's interventions at every stage of the long framing process – from their ground-setting role in the Fundamental Rights Sub-Committee to rigorous debates on the floor of the Assembly – he could see that women had ingeniously adapted their script at every stage without losing the plot. Women's understanding of the concept of equality and the attendant constitutional provisions of affirmative action was deeply intertwined with their thoughts on representation. In making demands for special provisions, women members, too, must have noticed that their own presence in the Assembly was a performative act of what political scientists call descriptive representation, embodying 'in their own persons and lives' experiences 'typical of the larger class of persons whom they represent'.[153] The persuasive power of such representation of which the instances discussed in this chapter are only a few, led them to significant success in transforming several of the rights mentioned in the Women's Charter into constitutionally possible legislation. These successes were built on their ability to forge a distinct identity for women whose specific needs they had foregrounded in the Constituent Assembly.

Yet their experiences of constitutional politics for several years made them aware of the dangers of identity-based representation. Their own positions had been contested by women from within and outside their movement, very often under what they called the 'communal virus'. It would be only a partial reading to see in that expression a discomfort with the identity-based movements for Pakistan or Dalit rights. This must also include women's groups from within the Hindu community, which had viciously campaigned against the women's movement led by them. On numerous occasions, the women framers had expressed dismay at the fact that 'The [Hindu] Code that will benefit women most, has found some women opposing it.'[154] Having confronted the strategies of conservative parties to 'organize a women's bloc as a divisive element within the country',[155] the women framers had been suspicious of the idea of women's representation by women. These were women governed less by an autonomous will for a transformation than by what Amrit Kaur had called the 'male conscience' of communities. In a patriarchal society, women could hardly be expected to have their independent judgement and were bound by 'group prejudice', to use Hansa Mehta's term to describe such tendencies. She said these tendencies produced a 'conservatism' which was 'positively harmful if it trie[d] to preserve what is not good because of lack of judgement'.[156] Hansa Mehta's example of such women was not limited to female detractors of the Hindu Code Bill but also included Kasturba Gandhi who had obstinate caste prejudices against the untouchables before Gandhi slowly weaned her away from them.

If we agree to see the framing of articles 15 and 16 together, as this narrative shows, we can notice that women were making contingent choices between identity-based representation and interest-based representation, each impinging on the other. The former was the immediately enabling context of their own participation in the debates filled with a mistrust of the ideologically interpellated woman who would uphold patriarchal values while the latter involved a contest about what constituted the interest of women. The strategy the women framers deliberately adopted was not to push for an exclusive choice but ensure that the text of the Constitution could reconcile these two in ways that could be of maximum advantage to women. Their contribution on the question of affirmative action, thus, becomes multivalent, waiting to be discovered by contemporary political thought.

To return to the configuration of the equality code of the Constitution, it becomes evident that it was heavily dependent on women's interventions, with far-reaching implications. With regard to article 15(3), it can be argued that what reads like a 'mere' conferment of 'a discriminatory power on the state to make special provisions for women', is a gift of the collective voice of women framers unshackling the state from the bindings of the overarching abstraction of equality.[157] Following H. M. Seervai's astute reading of article 15(4) that was inserted by the first amendment, one can argue that women's strategic interventions made sure that the Constitution empowered the state, or else it 'would have no power to make special provisions' for women 'because such a provision would violate the prohibition of Article 15(1)'.[158] These enabling provisions of the Constitution lent a special legitimacy to several acts of feminist practice in which the women members were engaged since 1950.

Durgabai who was an important member of the first Planning Commission and the presiding spirit over the field of social work in India, consolidated her work around these articles of the Constitution. The landmark multi-volume *Encyclopedia of Social Work* published under her leadership in 1968 laid special emphasis on legislative and activist energy derived from the Constitution.[159] In the course of judicial evolution, the idea of special provision for women has also been understood by the Supreme Court as meaning reservations or affirmative action.[160] Attention to the aspirations of the women framers – keeping in mind their textual interweaving of clauses on non-discrimination with those demanding reverse discrimination – may further tilt judicial force towards a substantive model of equality in which 'difference need not preclude equality'.[161] Read in their entire context, one can argue that going beyond a liberal feminist demand for formal equality, the women framers laid down the outlines of a design for substantive equality. This was driven by the consideration of the articles of the Constitution in terms of their impact in ameliorating women's 'historic and systemic disadvantages'.[162]

As opposed to formal equality that focused on equal treatment, women framers were concerned with 'the actual impact of law'.[163] It was with this impact in mind that they made their interventions – verbal and written, formal and informal. In them, they argued against the inclusion or exclusion of any term in the draft articles. One instance of this meticulous attention is the objection to the term 'practise' in the phrase 'the right freely to practise and propagate religion' during the discussions on the right to freedom of religion. The term, they feared, may 'invalidate legislation against anti-social customs which have the sanction of religion'.[164] When the Fundamental Rights Sub-Committee submitted its report to the Advisory Committee, it had retained the right to the free 'practice' of religion. Amrit Kaur, who had formally recorded her dissent to this phrase, submitted a letter to B. N. Rau on behalf of Hansa Mehta and herself expressing their 'considerable hesitation' in accepting the clause:

> As we are all aware there are several customs practised in the name of religion, e.g. pardah, child marriage, polygamy, unequal laws of inheritance, prevention of inter-caste marriages, dedication of girls to temples. We are naturally anxious that no clause in any fundamental right shall make impossible future legislation for the purposes of wiping out these evils.[165]

The letter further expressed their fear that with a grant of the freedom of practice of religion, 'the validity of existing laws such as Sarda Act, and the Widow Remarriage Act may even be questioned'.[166]

I cite this here to complement my caution that women's contribution to the Indian Constitution must not be read solely in terms of the proceedings of the Constituent Assembly, nor should the evolution of the idea of women's rights be understood only in terms of their participation in the framing process. Unfortunately, cursory readings of the *Constituent Assembly Debates* have led feminist scholars to believe that women members had refused to engage with the contradictions involved in their interventions on the question of equality.[167] According to Mary John, they had 'reserved for themselves – urban, educated, modern and progressive – the right to represent Indian womanhood'[168] and abstained from recognizing the tension between '"social" issues and the abstract language of political rights "irrespective of caste, creed, race or sex"'.[169] In such readings, the founding mothers of the Constituent Assembly 'appeared *eager* to declare their opposition to any special privileges in the form of reservations'.[170] She supposes that women's choices were made in the face of an 'effective disavowal of distinct political rights to the "untouchables"'.

These conclusions seem to be eager statements themselves, unmindful of the entire discursive rationality of women's choices. They are based on a dispersed reading of a statement by one woman member taken out of context – John suggests that it was a 'spontaneous' intervention and probably the only one made by a woman member[171] – whereas the records show that women made an exception for caste minorities and for special provisions for themselves.

A further corrective to these accounts, that the discussion above offers, is the contribution of the Dalit woman member that shows that women endeavoured to make the state constitutionally responsible towards the promotion of equality and freedom in all dimensions. The following chapters reinforce this view.

In this chapter I have offered a genealogical reading of the contribution of the women members to the framing of the fundamental rights section of the Constitution. My argument is that these members were astutely aware of the centrality it would have in the future jurisprudence of the nation-state. While they paid scrupulous attention to ensure that women-as-citizens received equal protection from state action through these rights, they also endeavoured to turn these rights into affirmative exhortations for the state. By insisting that 'sex' as a category be recognized by the Constitution, they ensured that the fundamental rights became semantically versatile enough to accommodate an idea of personhood that went beyond the narrow notions of their times. The current generation must also acknowledge the debt that constitutional jurisprudence around the rights of queer and transgender communities owe to the interventions of women framers. The implications of women's intervention for constitutional struggles for social justice in all its forms are immense and will become clearer with more examples that we discuss in the next chapter.

NOTES

1. Durgabai Deshmukh, *Chintamani and I* (Delhi: Allied, 1981).
2. Rajendra Prasad, Constituent Assembly of India, 28 August 1947, *CAD*, V: 260.
3. Purnima Banerji described the women members as back-benchers. Constituent Assembly of India, 24 November 1949, *CAD*, XI: 878. The description of the Constituent Assembly is built on news reports about the setting-up of the Assembly, collected in File IOR/L/P&J/10/62, Part 1, India Office Records, British Library, London. According to some reports, the benches had the facility of internal heating and the hall was air-conditioned as well.

4. Sarojini Naidu, Constituent Assembly of India, 11 December 1946, *CAD*, I: 48 (emphasis mine).

5. Ibid., 47.

6. Ibid., 47.

7. Purnima Banerji, Constituent Assembly of India, 24 November 1949, *CAD*, XI: 878.

8. Ibid., 879 (emphasis mine).

9. *Constituent Assembly Debates: Official Reports*, 12 vols, 4th Reprint (New Delhi: Lok Sabha Secretariat, 2003; first published 1950).

10. An entire chronological account of the stages in which the drafting and the discussions took place is provided in the Appendix.

11. Syed Ali Zaheer to Rajendra Prasad, 2 January 1947. Zaheer requested Prasad to ensure that there were Shia Muslims on the Minorities Sub-Committee too. Rajendra Prasad Papers, 4-C/47, National Archives.

12. Office Note of the President on the Advisory Committee, January 1947. Rajendra Prasad Papers, 4-C/47, National Archives.

13. Cabinet Mission Plan, 1946, reproduced in Subhash C. Kashyap (ed.), *The Framing of India's Constitution: A Study*, Vol. 1 (Delhi: Universal Law Publishing Co., 2004).

14. Kitty Shiva Rao to Hansa Mehta, 19 June 1947, Hansa Mehta Papers, Subject File 06, NMML.

15. Hansa Mehta, 'The Constituent Assembly of India', probably 1947 (draft prepared for publication in the AIWC journal *Roshni*), Hansa Mehta Papers NMML.

16. Ranajit Guha, *The Small Voice of History: Collected Essays*, ed. Partha Chatterjee (Ranikhet: Permanent Black, 2010), 304–317.

17. The words were used to characterize the 'authorised view' of the Telengana uprising. The work in question is P. Sundaraiya, *Telangana People's Struggle and Its Lessons* (Calcutta: Communist Party of India–Marxist, 1972).

18. Guha, *The Small Voice of History*, 31. The words within the double quote marks are from Vasantha Kannabiaran and K. Lalitha, 'That Magic Time', in Kumkum Sangari and Sudesh Vaid (eds), *Recasting Women: Essays in Colonial History*, 180–203 (New Brunswick: Rutgers University Press, 1990), 199.

19. Guha, *The Small Voice of History*, 315.

20. Kumud Sharma and C. P. Sujaya (eds), *Towards Equality: Report of the Committee on the Status of Women in India*, 1974 (New Delhi: CWDS and Pearson, 2012; originally published in 1974 by the Department of Social Welfare, Ministry of Education and Social Welfare, Govt. of India), 5. This landmark report mentions what the Constitution gives women but makes no mention of women's contribution to the Constitution of India.

21. Govind Ballabh Pant, Constituent Assembly of India, 24 January 1947, *CAD*, II: 346 (emphasis mine).

22. Renuka Ray, *My Reminiscences: Social Development during the Gandhian Era and After* (Kolkata: Stree, 2005), 59–60.

23. Ibid., 134.

24. Ibid., 135.

25. Renuka Ray, 'Article 31 in the Constituent Assembly' (undated). She was referring to the debates on the floor of the Assembly on 12 September 1949. Renuka Ray Papers, Subject File no. 32, NMML.

26. Alladi Krishnaswami Ayyar, Note on the Draft Report of the Sub-Committee on Fundamental Rights, 14 April 1947 in B. Shiva Rao (ed.), *The Framing of India's Constitution: Select Documents*, Vol. 2 (Delhi: Universal Law Publishing, 2004; originally The Indian Institute of Public Administration, 1967), 158–161, 160.

27. Examples include Amrit Kaur's letter to B. N. Rau of 31 March 1947, in Rao, *The Framing of India's Constitution*, Vol. 2, 146–147; Amrit Kaur' letter to B. N. Rau of 10 April 1947 in which she asks for a prohibition against carrying arms, in Rao, *The Framing of India's Constitution*, Vol. 2, 146–147, 153; Amrit Kaur's letter to H. V. R. Iyengar of 10 April 1947, in Rao, *The Framing of India's Constitution*, Vol. 2, 146–147.

28. Amrit Kaur, 'Memorandum on Minorities', 20 March 1947, in Rao, *The Framing of India's Constitution*, Vol. 2, 309–312; Amrit Kaur, 'Minute of Dissent', 27 July 1947, in Rao, *The Framing of India's Constitution*, Vol. 2, 401–402.

29. Rules 40 and 41 of the Constituent Assembly Rules of Procedure, reprinted in Rao, *The Framing of India's Constitution*, Vol. 1, 483–484.

30. Ray, *My Reminiscences*, 134.

31. Durgabai Deshmukh, Oral Transcripts, Session 1, NMML.

32. Ibid.

33. B. R. Ambedkar, Constituent Assembly of India, 27 January 1948, *CAD*, VI: 25–28; Durgabai Deshmukh, Oral Transcripts, Session 1, NMML.

34. The tendency is to quote the single note of dissent that Amrit Kaur, Hansa Mehta, and M. R. Masani had written against the inclusion of the uniform civil code in the chapter on directive principles arguing that the lack of a common civil code obstructs national unity. The tendency of choosing single quotations, disconnected from the other statements made by the same people, leads to erroneous understandings of the individual framer's motives. See for example, Flavia Agnes, *Law and Gender Inequality* (New Delhi: Oxford University Press, 1999), 72–73.

35. George Grotte, cited by B.R. Ambedkar, Constituent Assembly of India, 4 November 1948, *CAD*, VII: 38.

36. Andre Beteille, 'Constitutional Morality', *Economic and Political Weekly* 43, no. 40 (4–10 October 2008): 35–42, 35.

37. Ibid. (emphasis mine).

38. Damayanti Thergeankar's notes assorted by Renuka Ray for submission to the Hindu Law Committee, Renuka Ray Papers, Subject File no. 18, NMML.

39. For colonial jurisprudence, beginning with the *Collector of Madura* v. *Mootoo Ramalinga* in 1868, the rule was that custom was to override the written text of law if its antiquity was proved. Kalpana Kannabiran, *Tools of Justice: Non-discrimination and the Indian Constitution* (London and New York: Routledge, 2012), 309.

40. Renuka Ray, 'History of Social Reform and Social Work from 1947 to 1963', Renuka Ray Papers, Speeches/Writings by Her, File no. 59, NMML, 4.

41. Judith Butler and Joan Scott, 'Introduction', in Judith Butler and Joan Scott (eds), *Feminists Theorize the Political*, xiii–xvii (New York: Routledge, 2001), xiv.

42. Kaur, 'Memorandum on Minorities', 310 (emphasis mine).

43. Govind Ballabh Pant, Constituent Assembly of India, 24 January 1947, *CAD*, II: 331.

44. Jawaharlal Nehru, Constituent Assembly of India, 13 December 1946, *CAD*, I: 60.

45. Ibid., 59.

46. Govind Ballabh Pant, Constituent Assembly of India, 24 January 1947, *CAD*, II: 331.

47. Ibid., 332–333.

48. Ibid., 333.

49. K. M. Munshi, 'Draft Articles on Fundamental Rights', 17 March 1947, in Rao, *The Framing of India's Constitution*, Vol. 2, 69–80, 74.

50. Ibid.; Harnam Singh's 'Draft on Fundamental Rights', 18 March 1947, in Rao, *The Framing of India's Constitution*, Vol. 2, 81–84.

51. B. R. Ambedkar, 'Memorandum and Draft Articles on the Rights of States and Minorities', 24 March 1947, in Rao, *The Framing of India's Constitution*, Vol. 2, 84–114.

52. Syama Prasad Mookerjee in the Proceedings of the Advisory Committee, 21 April 1947, in Rao, *The Framing of India's Constitution*, Vol. 2, 213–288, 259.

53. Frank Anthony in the Proceedings of the Advisory Committee, 21 April 1947, in Rao, *The Framing of India's Constitution*, Vol. 2, 213–288, 261 (emphasis mine).

54. Patel in the Proceedings of the Advisory Committee, in Rao, *The Framing of India's Constitution*, Vol. 2, 213–288, 262.

55. C. Rajagopalachari in the Proceedings of the Advisory Committee, 21 April 1947, in Rao, *The Framing of India's Constitution*, Vol. 2, 213–288, 262.

56. Article 5 of the Justiciable Fundamental Rights, Interim Report of the Advisory Committee on the Subject of Fundamental Rights, 23 April 1947, in Rao, *The Framing of India's Constitution*, Vol. 2, 294–299, 296.

57. Article 16(4) of the Constitution of India.

58. Hriday Nath Kunzru, Constituent Assembly of India, 30 November 1948, *CAD*, VII: 681.

59. Kaur, 'Memorandum on Minorities', 20 March 1947, 310.

60. Hansa Mehta, Constituent Assembly of India, 22 November 1949, *CAD*, XI: 796.

61. Ibid.

62. Amrit Kaur to B. R. Ambedkar, Evidence Taken before the Joint Committee on Indian Constitutional Reform, 29 July 1933, printed in *Dr Babasaheb Ambedkar: Writings and Speeches*, 2nd ed., Vol. 2 (Mumbai: Govt. of Maharashtra, 2005), 698–704, 701 (emphasis mine).

63. Ibid., 703.

64. Dakshayani Velayudhan, Constituent Assembly of India, 19 December 1946, *CAD*, I: 152.

65. Ibid.

66. Ibid.

67. Dakshayani Velayudhan, Constituent Assembly of India, 28 August 1947, *CAD*, V: 264.

68. See Chapter 2, discussions on Ambedkar's response to the Cabinet Mission Plan. Also see *Dr Babasaheb Ambedkar: Writings and Speeches*, Vol. 17(2), 210.

69. Dakshayani Velayudhan, Constituent Assembly of India, 19 December 1946 *CAD*, I: 152.

70. Ibid.

71. Ibid.

72. Ibid.

73. Ibid.

74. Ambedkar's Memorandum, in Rao, *The Framing of India's Constitution*, Vol 2, 109.

75. Ibid.

76. Ibid., 103.

77. Dakshayani Velayudhan, Constituent Assembly of India, 29 November 1948, *CAD*, VII: 667.

78. Ibid.

79. Ibid.

80. Article 11 of the Draft Constitution prepared by B. R. Ambedkar and the Drafting Committee; article 17 of the Constitution of India (emphasis mine).

81. Dakshayani Velayudhan, Constituent Assembly of India, 29 November 1948, *CAD*, VII: 667.

82. Ibid.

83. Santanu Kumar Das, Constituent Assembly of India, 29 November 1948, *CAD*, VII: 667.

84. Dakshayani Velayudhan, Constituent Assembly of India, 29 November 1948, *CAD*, VII: 667 (emphasis mine).

85. Dakshayani Velayudhan, Constituent Assembly of India, 28 August 1947, *CAD*, V: 264.

86. Dakshayani Velayudhan, Constituent Assembly of India, 1 May 1947, *CAD*, III: 480.

87. Ibid.

88. Dakshayani Velayudhan, Constituent Assembly of India, 19 December 1946, *CAD*, I: 152.

89. Dakshayani Velayudhan, Constituent Assembly of India, 1 May 1947, *CAD*, III: 480.

90. Dakshayani Velayudhan, Constituent Assembly of India, 28 August 1947, *CAD*, V: 264 (emphases mine).

91. Dakshayani Velayudhan, Constituent Assembly of India (Legislative), 19 March 1948, *CA(L)D*, IV: 2429; Constituent Assembly of India (Legislative), 23 March 1948. *CA(L)D*, IV: 2580.

92. Dakshayani Velayudhan, Constituent Assembly Debates (Legislative), 29 March 1948, *CA(L)D*, IV: 2700 (emphasis mine).

93. Ibid.

94. Ibid.

95. Ibid.

96. Dakshayani Velayudhan, Constituent Assembly of India, 28 August 1947, *CAD*, V: 264.

97. Ibid.

98. Dakshayani Velayudhan, 'Limited Lure of Cash-awards: Inter-caste Marriages', *The Times of India*, 4 November 1975, 8.

99. Ibid.

100. B. R. Ambedkar, *Annihilation of Caste: The Annotated Critical Edition*, ed. S Anand. (New Delhi: Navayana, 2014; originally published 1936), 285.

101. Anupama Rao, *The Caste Question: Dalits and the Politics of Modern India* (Berkeley: University of California Press, 2009), 233.

102. Amrit Kaur to H. V. R. Iyengar, 10 April 1947, in Rao, *The Framing of India's Constitution*, Vol. 2, 153.

103. Minutes of the Fundamental Rights Sub-Committee, 29 March 1947, in Rao, *The Framing of India's Constitution*, Vol. 2, 130.
104. Kaur, 'Memorandum on Minorities', 20 March 1947, 310.
105. Ibid.
106. Renuka Ray, Constituent Assembly of India, 9 November 1948, *CAD*, VII: 357. She was responding to Rohini Kumar Chaudhury's statement that women need separate electorates (emphasis mine).
107. Renuka Ray, Constituent Assembly of India, 18 July 1947, *CAD*, IV: 668.
108. Ibid.
109. Munshi's speech of 23 November 1948 is a good instance of such patronizing attitudes of men, *CAD*, VII: 548.
110. Kaur, 'Memorandum on Minorities', 310.
111. Amrit Kaur, *Challenge to Women* (Allahabad: New Literature, 1946), 148.
112. Kaur, 'Memorandum on Minorities', 310.
113. Hansa Mehta, Constituent Assembly of India, 22 November 1949, *CAD*, XI: 796.
114. Renuka Ray, Constituent Assembly of India, 18 July 1947, *CAD*, IV: 669.
115. Ibid. (emphasis mine).
116. Catherine A. MacKinnon, *Toward a Feminist Theory of the State* (Cambridge, MA: Harvard University Press, 1989), 163.
117. Constitution of India, articles 14, 15(1), 15(2), 16(2) (emphasis mine).
118. MacKinnon, *Toward a Feminist Theory of the State*, 163.
119. Ibid.
120. Rao, *The Framing of India's Constitution*, Vol 2, 117.
121. Ibid., 117.
122. Hansa Mehta, Proceedings of the Sub-Committee on Fundamental Rights, 28 March 1947, in Rao, *The Framing of India's Constitution*, Vol. 2, 127–129, 129.
123. Amrit Kaur, Hansa Mehta, M. R. Masani, Minutes of Dissent to the Draft Report of the Sub-Committee on Fundamental Rights, 14 April 1947, in Rao, *The Framing of India's Constitution*, Vol. 2, 162–163, 162.
124. Amrit Kaur, Proceedings of the Advisory Committee, 21 April 1947, in Rao, *The Framing of India's Constitution*, Vol. 2, 213–289, 219.
125. Kaur, 'Memorandum on Minorities', 310.
126. See interventions by Amrit Kaur and Hansa Mehta during the proceedings of the Advisory Committee, 21–22 April 1947, in Rao, *The Framing of India's Constitution*, Vol. 2, 219–222, 256–258.
127. K. M. Panikkar's response to Amrit Kaur during the proceedings of the Advisory Committee, 21–22 April 1947, in Rao, *The Framing of India's Constitution*, Vol. 2, 257.

128. *National Legal Services Authority* v. *Union of India*, Writ Petition No. 400 of 2012, Decided 15 April 2014, para 59, 41411.pdf (sci.gov.in) (accessed 1 December 2020).
129. Ibid.
130. Annexure to the Draft Report of the Sub-Committee on Fundamental Rights, 3 April 1947, in Rao, *The Framing of India's Constitution*, Vol. 2, 138–143, 138.
131. Proceedings of the Advisory Committee, 21–22 April 1947, in Rao, *The Framing of India's Constitution*, Vol. 2, 213–289, 256.
132. Ibid., 257.
133. Ibid.
134. Ibid., 258.
135. Constituent Assembly Debates (Legislative), 18 February 1949, *CA(L)D*, 668, 670–671.
136. Ibid.
137. Dakshayani Velayudhan, Constituent Assembly Debates (Legislative), 19 March 1948, *CA(L)D*. IV: 2429; Constituent Assembly Debates (Legislative), 26 August 1948, *CA(L)D*. VI(II): 684.
138. Renuka Ray, Constituent Assembly Debates (Legislative), 12 March 1948, *CA(L)D*, III: 2009.
139. Durgabai Deshmukh, Constituent Assembly Debates (Legislative), 2 April 1948, *CA(L)D*. IV: 3041–3042.
140. Durgabai Deshmukh, Constituent Assembly Debates (Legislative), 18 March 1949, *CA(L)D*, III: 1530.
141. Durgabai Deshmukh, Constituent Assembly Debates (Legislative), 7 March 1949, *CA(L)D*, III: 1307.
142. Durgabai Deshmukh, Constituent Assembly Debates (Legislative), 8 March 1948, *CA(L)D*, III: 1716.
143. Durgabai Deshmukh, Constituent Assembly Debates (Legislative), 8 April 1948, *CA(L)D*, V: 3458.
144. Durgabai Deshmukh, Constituent Assembly Debates (Legislative), 12 December 1949, *CA(L)D*, IV(I): 350; Dakshayani Velayudhan, Constituent Assembly Debates (Legislative), 24 March 1949, *CA(L)D*, III(I): 1827.
145. Begum Aizaz Rasul, Constituent Assembly Debates (Legislative), 1 September 1948, *CA(L)D*, VII(II): 834–835.
146. Aizaz Rasul, Constituent Assembly Debates (Legislative), 11 December 1947, *CA(L)D*, III: 1746.
147. Aizaz Rasul, Constituent Assembly Debates (Legislative), 11 February 1949, *CA(L)D*, I (I): 520.

148. Aizaz Rasul, Constituent Assembly Debates (Legislative), 21 November 1947, *CA(L)D*, I: 433; Constituent Assembly Debates (Legislative), 17 August 1948, *CA(L)D*, VI (I): 317.

149. Ammu Swaminathan, Constituent Assembly Debates (Legislative), 7 March 1949, *CA(L)D*, II (Part I): 1295.

150. Annie Mascerene, Constituent Assembly Debates (Legislative), 18 March 1949, *CA(L)D*, III: 1515.

151. Proceedings of the Advisory Committee Meetings, 21–22 April 1947, in Rao, *The* Framing of India's Constitution, Vol. 2, 259.

152. B. R. Ambedkar, Constituent Assembly of India, 30 November 1948, *CAD*, VII: 702.

153. Jane Masbridge, "'Should Blacks Represent Blacks and Women Represent Women?' A Contingent 'Yes'", *The Journal of Politics* 61, no. 3 (August 1999): 628–657, 629.

154. Hansa Mehta, 'Women and Group Prejudice in India', undated, Hansa Mehta Papers, Writings by Her, File no. 104.

155. Renuka Ray, 'The Background of the Hindu Code Bill', *Pacific Affairs* 25, no. 3 (September 1952):268–277, 273.

156. Mehta, 'Women and Group Prejudice in India'.

157. H. M. Seervai, *Constitutional Law of India*, Vol. 1 (Delhi: Universal Book Traders, 1991), 556.

158. Ibid., 558.

159. *Encyclopaedia of Social Work*, 3 vols (Delhi: Publications Division on behalf of the Planning Commission, 1968). See particularly P. B. Gajendragadkar, 'Constitution and Social Work', *Encyclopaedia of Social Work*, Vol. 1, 153–160. See also articles on the welfare of the Scheduled Castes and Scheduled Tribes, mid-day meals, the relationship between social reform and social work, workers and their participation, drug addiction, and education.

160. For a specific discussion of the progressive judicial implications of article 15(3) see Flavia Agnes, *Family Law: Family Laws and Constitutional Claims* (New Delhi: Oxford University Press, 2011), 137–138. See also the Supreme Court judgment in *Government of Andhra Pradesh* v. *PB Vijay Kumar*, AIR 1995 SC 1648, paras 8, 14.

161. Ratna Kapur and Brenda Cossman, 'On Women, Equality and the Constitution: Looking Glass of Feminism', in Nivedita Menon (ed.), *Gender and Politics in India*, 197–261 (New Delhi: Oxford University Press, 1999), 207.

162. Ibid., 745.

163. Ibid., 744.

164. Amrit Kaur, Minutes of the Sub-Committee on Fundamental Rights, 26 March 1947, in Rao, *The Framing of India's Constitution*, Vol. 2, 121–124, 122.

165. Amrit Kaur to B. N. Rau, 31 March 1947, in Rao, *The Framing of India's Constitution*, Vol. 2, 146.

166. Ibid.

167. Mary John, 'Alternate Modernities? Reservations and Women's Movement in 20th Century India', *Economic and Political Weekly* 35, no. 43 (2000): 3822–3829.

168. Ibid., 3827.

169. Ibid.

170. Ibid. (emphasis mine).

171. Ibid., 3828.

5

Writing the Rights

Inscribing Constitutional Morality

Man must be greater than the institutions he creates. The success of government does not depend so much on the perfection of constitutions as on conditions in the environment which again are dependent on the quality of the citizens.

—Amrit Kaur, 1945[1]

Women members of the Constituent Assembly were profoundly aware of the foundational role the Constitution would play in shaping the destiny of the nation. Almost every aspect of the framing, from the complex textual process to its political creativity, was marked and influenced by their participation. The Constitution was meant to prepare the blueprint of the political programme of the state, envisaged by the women members as a moral agency whose contours they were eager to shape. The women framers wanted the Constitution to be more than a regulating text. No article of the Constitution was considered irrelevant by them for each article affected the other, and together shaped the entire structure of the democratic state.

Their level of intensity and overall attention were matched only by that of the Chairman of the Drafting Committee. For them, as for Ambedkar, the new, ethical distribution of political power had to flow from a text that would create conditions for the diffusion of the principles of the Constitution. They shared with Ambedkar a sceptical attitude towards the romantic celebration of Indian heritage and culture. His remark that 'democracy is only a top-dressing on Indian soil',[2] in connection with the need for cultivating constitutional morality was echoed by the women in the Assembly who knew that the Indian 'people have been used to centuries of autocratic rule and, therefore, to carry on more or less on the lines they have been accustomed for some time'.[3]

The main features of their interventions, therefore, included attention to the processes and form of constitutional practices. Women were aware that 'constitutional morality is not a natural sentiment'[4] and realized that each institution of the polity would contribute to its diffusion. In Ambedkar's words, it was important to recognize that 'the form of administration has a close connection with the form of the Constitution' and that 'it is perfectly possible to pervert the Constitution, without changing its form by merely changing the form of the administration and to make it inconsistent and opposed to the spirit of the Constitution'.[5] Women members were careful at every stage of the drafting to make sure that the form of the Constitution is coordinated with their overall constitutional vision and enough precautions are taken to prevent the perversion of the vision. They contributed significantly to the framing of both justiciable and non-justiciable rights: the right to property, secular and compulsory education, precaution against the state's right of preventive detention, and several other aspects of the Indian Constitution. These were framed following debates in which women members participated with vigour and commitment. The character of the legislative bodies, both upper and the lower houses, was profoundly affected by women's judicious interventions.

Women also intervened prominently in conceptualizing the judiciary since they knew that it was to be the most significant formal instrument for the infusion and circulation of constitutional morality in the state, and a central site for constitutional politics.[6] While supporting the right to constitutional remedies which gave the Supreme Court the power of judicial review[7] – now considered part of the basic structure of the Constitution – Durgabai argued that 'this is a right which is fundamental to all the fundamental rights guaranteed under this Constitution'.[8] She was echoing the convictions of her women colleagues when she said that 'a right without an expeditious and effective remedy serves no purpose at all, nor is it worth the paper on which it is written'.[9] The wider ramifications of this conviction and the struggle to get it translated into the words of the Constitution become clearer when we look at women's tactful interventions during the framing of the fundamental rights and directive principles.

FUNDAMENTAL RIGHTS AS GUARANTEES OF SELF-EXPRESSION

The most important aspect of women's participation in the framing was their conviction that the Constitution was a document of rights. The moral imaginary of the women's movement had culminated in a comprehensive

Charter of Rights that had pervaded their entire political consciousness, and spread beyond the walls of the Indian Parliament to the United Nations (UN). The shape of these rights was supra-national and was meant to make fundamental changes in society. These were correctives to the long history of colonial and patriarchal social frameworks and promised to make the country a better place. In the Constitution, these rights were placed under two chapters, one entitled Fundamental Rights and the other Directive Principles of State Policy. Both were carved out of the list of justiciable and non-justiciable rights prepared by the Constitutional Advisor and the Sub-Committee on Fundamental Rights of which women were important members. When the Constitution was finally placed for general evaluation, women argued that 'the Constitution actually rests on two pillars – Fundamental Rights and the Directive Principles of State Policy'.[10] Responding to the 'wild disappointment' of 'some unkind critics' who had 'described this Constitution as no better than the Motor Vehicles Taxation Act', Durgabai had asserted that 'this Constitution which for the first time gives adult franchise, for the first time guarantees the Fundamental Rights, and which has amazingly succeeded in blotting out the hundreds of patches of this country and made it a strong and united country' is 'a people's Constitution'.[11]

The rationale of the fundamental rights, for women, was that they would lead to full freedom for and create conditions through which women could achieve substantial equality with men and develop into creative and self-reliant citizens. As Aizaz Rasul hoped, 'Even though these Fundamental Rights are hedged in by various conditions and provisos, yet to my mind, Sir, they guarantee to the citizen that measure of liberty which is necessary for a free and full development of his total personality'.[12] As I argued in Chapter 4, the fundamental rights in the Indian Constitution are rendered in syntactically negative provisions beginning, almost invariably, with terms like 'the state shall not' or 'no person shall be denied/deprived' meant to put restraints on the state's actions vis-à-vis the individual's liberties. Although they sound like injunctions, women framers saw them as positive constructs, enabling instruments conferred upon individuals for their full development. These rights were expected to 'give free scope to the individual for progress' and opportunities 'of developing his or her faculties'.[13] Women members agreed that fundamental rights were not absolute and invited necessary limitations and yet were fundamental in the sense that they were constitutive of 'constructive citizenship'. This was Amrit Kaur's term for the 'sense of being an integral part of the state', insofar as the citizen helps to 'make it and maintain it as a great civilized and civilizing group'.[14] It was only a constructive citizen, with fundamental rights (and duties), who could 'contribute to the well-being of that society'.[15]

Noticeable in these views is the interchangeable use of the terms state and society. The distinction between 'state' and 'society' does not appear pertinent in the discourse of the women members. Fundamental rights, to them, were not just guarantees against the government but also restored their 'inherent' freedoms that were curtailed by social institutions of the 'private sphere' – religion and the family, for example – which enjoyed privileged insulation from political interventions. In the formalized settings of the Constituent Assembly, these women performed an early rehearsal of the feminist refusal to distinguish between the personal and the political. They aspired for a complete transformation of the social system and 'make up the leeway of centuries in almost every field as rapidly as possible',[16] while remaining assured that the Constitution would preserve the 'inherent right of every citizen to self-expression'.[17]

Preventive detention and individual liberty

Two examples of women's commitment to constitutional assurance of individual liberty may be cited from two major debates on the question of personal liberty and the issue of compulsory labour and conscription. Life and personal liberty are guaranteed by the Indian Constitution in article 21 which reads: 'No person shall be deprived of his life and personal liberty except according to procedure established by law'. In its embryonic form in the Sub-Committee on Fundamental Rights, the article repeated the American Constitution's guarantee that no person shall 'be deprived of life, liberty, or property without due process of law'.[18]

There was considerable debate on the article at the earliest stages in the Advisory Committee which made two articles out of the one recommended by the Fundamental Rights Sub-Committee. One of these guaranteed the fundamental right to life and liberty, while the second guaranteed the fundamental right to property.[19] Life and liberty, it was ensured could only be taken by due process of law, whereas property could be taken if the 'law provides for the payment of compensation'.[20] This made the right to life and personal liberty the subject of intense theoretical debate. At the level of legal technicalities, the contention was whether the state could deprive a person of life and liberty only by due process of law or by any procedure established by law. For those who believed in the former, 'due process' was important to 'prevent legislative extravagance and executive excesses', while for the latter due process may 'provide excessive powers to the court'.[21] But at the more fundamental level the choice was between substantive and procedural forms of state action, a choice that was difficult for the Constituent Assembly to make in the backdrop of memories of coercive colonial government and the communal violence that surrounded its working.

According to Granville Austin, one of the reasons the Drafting Committee, after a majority vote of four against three, preferred the procedural over the substantive enunciation of process was 'an increasing conviction that preventive detention provided the best weapon against the communal violence that had ransacked North India during the past year'.[22] The Drafting Committee, however, had to face considerable opposition and voting before its choice was accepted by the Assembly. As Ambedkar confessed, he found it a difficult choice between 'two sharp points of view'.[23] He summed up the arguments on both sides by reducing them to the question of 'the relationship between the legislature and the judiciary....'[24] If the text included the term 'due process', then

> the judiciary would be endowed with the authority to question the law ... also on the ground whether the law was *good* law, apart from the question of the powers of the legislature making the law.... The question now raised by the introduction of the phrase 'due process' is whether the judiciary should be given the additional power to question the laws made by the State on the ground that they violate certain fundamental principles.[25]

He explained his moral dilemmas:

> I cannot altogether omit the possibility of a Legislature packed by party men making laws which may abrogate or violate what we regard as certain fundamental principles affecting the life and liberty of an individual. At the same time, I do not see how five or six gentlemen sitting in the Federal or Supreme Court examining laws made by the Legislature and by dint of their own individual conscience or their bias or their prejudices be trusted to determine which law is good and which law is bad. It is rather a case where a man has to sail between Charybdis and Scylla and I therefore would not say anything. I would leave it to the House to decide in any way it likes.[26]

While these extracts indicate his troubled conscience over the issue, Ambedkar's summarization was a lawyer's brief that condensed the entire debate to the question of institutional jurisdiction and credibility. His own belief in the need for a strong state and his suspicion that the state may become a tool of prejudiced forces brought him to a temporary standstill. On the one hand, there was the deeply felt need for individual liberty and on the other, anxieties about judicial exaggeration. Eventually in September 1949, at the final stage of the Assembly's work, he had settled with his conscience by incorporating a new set of clauses which became article 22 of the Constitution. These, he hoped, would 'satisfy the enthusiasts of individual liberty'.[27] These enthusiasts included the women members of the Constituent Assembly, most notably Purnima Banerji and, to some extent, Durgabai. Members like Thakur Das Bhargava, H. V. Kamath, and Bakshi Tek Chand were also part of the group.

In this case, too, we see women members finding ingenious ways out of the quandaries at which the Assembly would occasionally arrive. Once the debate was settled in favour of procedural due process as opposed to substantive due process, women members focused their energy on making these procedural provisions more robust and detailed. Ambedkar's recapitulation of the debates fairly summed up the position of these enthusiasts who believed that protection of personal liberty was the paramount expression of justice in the Constitution. Yet, unlike people like Thakur Das Bhargava, who made emphatic claims that the removal of 'due process' would be a 'blot on the Constitution'[28] and argued that 'the first casualty in this Constitution is justice',[29] women members sought to find alternative ways of compensating for the loss of individual liberty that was incurred by the defeat of substantive due process in the debates.

Purnima Banerji brought in amendments to Ambedkar's proposed articles that laid the procedural guidelines in cases of preventive detention. Her amendment sought to specify the time frames within which a person detained should be informed of the reasons of his/her detention and within which he/she must be released.[30] She argued on behalf of 'most of my colleagues here that any form of detention of persons without trial is obnoxious to the whole idea of democracy and to our whole way of thinking'.[31] Based on what she described as 'our own experiences in our own short political lives and careers of what it is to be detained and on what laws one is detained', she felt that the protections against the arbitrariness of preventive action must come with specified periods. So far, her arguments were well within the discourse of setting restrictions on executive action. These were in consonance with and grounded in the experience of leaders of the colonial period when several members of the Constituent Assembly had been imprisoned. These included women members like Hansa Mehta and Durgabai who had been detained by the British government for participating in anti-colonial movements.

It was her last amendment, however, that brought in a demand raised by the women's movement. Her proposal was to include a clause providing that 'if the earning member of a family is so detained his direct dependents shall be paid maintenance allowance'.[32] In this, she was echoing a demand of the All India Women's Conference (AIWC). Two years earlier, in her tract on civil liberties that had severely chastised the British government for having exorbitantly 'armed the Executive with very wide powers', Hansa Mehta had raised several questions on the implications of preventive detention for democratic justice.[33] Mehta's questions were taken up by Purnima Banerji. Mehta had written:

An important question that arises in connection with persons detained without trial is their treatment in jail. The question is, are they to be treated as ordinary criminals? Are persons who are not charged with any offence but are denied at the sweet will of the Government on par with those who are convicted for an anti-social act and are therefore criminals? Another question that arises is what happens to families whose earning members are thus detained by Government? Is not the Government bound to compensate the family for depriving them of their income, their livelihood?[34]

Mehta had demanded an 'allowance to be made to the families of the detenue' and claimed that 'it is the responsibility of the government to support the families of those whom they have detained without trial'.[35] Speaking in the context of the making of the Constitution, Purnima extended Hansa Mehta's arguments but also grounded them in the same doubts about the efficacy and moral purposefulness of institutions that Ambedkar had expressed in the statement cited above. If Ambedkar doubted the legislature and the judiciary, Banerji extended this doubt to the entire process of justice that the Constitution would set up. In demanding a maintenance allowance for the family of a detained person, she was asking the state to compensate for its failure to deliver justice and be responsible towards citizens whose lives would be affected by its action:

whereas in our Constitution many provisions have been made as to how much salary one should draw, what allowance members of the House shall get, what shall be each one's position and status, if a person is detained in prison and if he is an earning member of the family I do earnestly plead that he should be given a maintenance allowance. It should not be left to the arbitrary will of any one to deprive anybody of his liberty and then later on to decide, by leaving it to their sweet will, as to how his dependents shall live and maintain themselves.[36]

These arguments may be read as extremely idealistic and even impractical, and were summarily dismissed by Ambedkar:

> I think the argument in favour of maintenance is very weak. If a man is really digging into the foundations of the State and if he is arrested for that, he may have the right to be fed when he is in prison; but he has very little right to ask for maintenance.[37]

Yet these arguments were arguments against the arbitrary nature of the state, not just its practical manifestations. Banerji was alluding to the eloquent defence of substantive due process by the previous speaker who had reminded the house that 'at least in fifty percent of the criminal cases brought before the courts the accused are either discharged or acquitted'.[38] The anxieties about the state were grounded in the understanding of the climate in which the Constitution would operate. It was a country, her ally in these debates Thakur Das Bhargava noted, 'not trained to the restraints and discipline which mark out a country in which democracy has worked for a long time'.[39] Locating these positions in the consistent discursive pattern of women's engagement in the framing, Banerji's zeal to protect personal liberty could be read as an endeavour to inscribe constitutional morality in the very Constitution of the state.

Durgabai expressed solidarity with Purnima's amendments, with which she was in 'very much sympathy'.[40] She agreed that

> if the person detained is a bread-winner, then his dependents, his immediate dependents have got to be provided [for]. It would be better to give some sort of guarantee about this, instead of leaving it to Executive Power and to their sweet will.[41]

In spite of being in moral agreement with her friend's argument, Durgabai could not recommend such a provision for maintenance allowance. She found such an allowance impracticable:

> But how is it practicable? That is the question. There are many people who are poor in our country. Her point is that about fifty per cent of the cases would result in releases or discharges. And she also says that the benefit of doubt might be given to the accused in these cases.[42]

If Purnima had approached the question of constitutional morality from the side of the state, Durgabai saw it from the side of the citizens. For Durgabai, lack of constitutional morality on the part of citizens might lead to the drying up of the state coffers. Her acute insight into human behaviour developed through legal practice compelled her to reason that a maintenance allowance will only put 'a premium on delinquency'.[43] A maintenance allowance could work as an incentive for more crimes; someone 'assured of provision for his family...might go on committing crimes and challenging the foundations of the State'.[44] She disagreed with 'the enthusiastic champions of individual freedom and individual liberty' who she thought had wrongly placed 'the exigencies of individual liberty above the exigencies of the State'. She said:

> When it comes to a question of shaking the very foundations of the State, which stands not for the freedom of one individual but of several individuals, I yield the first place to the State. I say this because I know that in my love and enthusiasm for individual freedom, I only stand for myself, and my interests; and the State is far superior, because it stands for the freedom and liberty of several individuals like myself.[45]

Compulsory labour and military conscription

Women first faced the question of the conflict of the interest of the state and that of individuals during the debates on conscription that took place in the Sub-Committee on Fundamental Rights. Later, they faced it on the floor of the Assembly.

The case for military conscription as essential for nation building was made during the framing of the Karachi Resolution of 1931. In the original draft of the Resolution, Harbilas Sarda's recommended 'compulsory military training for all boys above 16 years of age attending schools and colleges'. Others advocated 'free military education'.[46] In 1939, the National Planning Committee established by the Congress under Nehru recommended

> the establishment of a system of compulsory social service, so as to make every young man and woman contribute one year of his or her life, between the ages of eighteen and twenty-two, to national utility, including agriculture, industry, public utilities, and public works of all kinds. No exception was to be allowed except for physical or mental disability.[47]

After the Second World War, there was need for larger manpower for reconstruction, and anxieties regarding the security of the state were strong. The earliest mention of the need for conscription in documents related to the framing of the Constitution is found in K. T. Shah's note on fundamental rights of December 1946. Shah recognized that the right of the State to provide for the defence and security of the country may actually result in conscription of all adult citizens to be trained and available in times of need for national defence, or part of the ordinary normal provision against possible emergency.[48]

However, Shah made a distinction between compulsory military service and social service. He hoped 'the social demands for building a healthy, just and progressive civilization would command the aid of conscription much more freely and willingly than the destructive purposes of war have hitherto done'.[49] However his draft of the fundamental rights included both purposes for the state's right to conscript citizens: 'for organizing properly the defence of the Union', 'for any social service, or to meet a sudden emergency, or natural calamity or for maintaining peace and tranquility'.[50] The idea of conscription for social service was always part of the nation-building discourse and women supported it. Social conscription was already a part of the National Education Plan of the National Planning Committee in 1940. It recommended compulsory social service for the young in rather stringent terms:

> A system of Compulsory Social or Labour Service should be established, so as to make every young man and woman contribute his or her life, between the ages of 18 and 22, to disciplined service in such form and place, and under such conditions, as the State may prescribe in that behalf…. No exemption should be allowed from the service except on certified grounds of physical or mental disability. Under no circumstance should the privilege of buying oneself out of this *universal obligation* be permitted.[51]

When the issue of conscription entered the framing process, through K. M. Munshi's draft proposal on fundamental rights, it was in the form of an exception to the fundamental rights of individuals rather than an obligation on them. Munshi's draft had an injunction on any form of forced labour, of which military conscription was made an exception. Clause 2 of his article XIV read thus:

> The requisition of the services of a citizen to meet the needs of national defence shall not be construed as a limitation on any of the fundamental rights.[52]

Another clause in Munshi's Draft referred to the notion of conscription for purposes other than military, but again in terms of an exception to a rule. According to clause 2 of his article XIV,

> Every form of slavery or traffic in human beings or compulsory labour other than public service equally incumbent upon all or as part of punishment pronounced by a court of law is abolished and if such form of traffic or labour is enforced it shall be punishable by the law of the Union.[53]

These two clauses were subjected to rigorous debates in the Sub-Committee on Fundamental Rights on 27 March 1947 after which a new, brief clause was drafted which stated that 'Every form of slavery or traffic in human beings is abolished and contravention of this prohibition shall be an offence'.[54] This was followed by a discussion regarding whether or not certain forms of labour should be made exceptions to this clause, a discussion that called for a vote. After two rounds of the 'Committee agreed by majority to add a clause exempting compulsory service under any general scheme of education'.[55]

It was largely due to the efforts of Amrit Kaur, Hansa Mehta, M. R. Masani, and Jairamdas Daulatram that a revised clause was mooted. It stated 'Conscription for military service or training is hereby prohibited'.[56] This was challenged the next day by B. R. Ambedkar and K. M. Munshi, at whose request the clause was put to vote. The Sub-Committee on Fundamental Rights decided in favour of prohibition of compulsory military service. When the Report of the Sub-Committee on Fundamental Rights was submitted to the Advisory Committee, it recommended conscription for the purposes of education but prohibited the same for military purposes.[57] However, among the many accompanying notes of dissent was Ambedkar's on military conscription emphatically recommending it in terms of national security. B. R. Ambedkar's draft articles on fundamental rights had initially provided that 'Subjecting a person to forced labour or to involuntary servitude shall be an offence'.[58] Yet, like Munshi, he too made an exception for military conscription. To ban military conscription, for Ambedkar, was an act of 'willful self-immolation'. In his dissenting note Ambedkar said:

> No country however peaceful and non-violent in its intention or philosophy can escape the necessity for compulsory military service for defending itself and its liberty when attacked by another nation. The fact must be faced that there are so many nations which are neither peaceful nor non-violent. Ban on Compulsory Military Service by a nation living in the midst of hostile nations free to impose compulsory Military Service is nothing but willful self-immolation which is contrary to wisdom and morally quite heinous.[59]

In Ambedkar's note, India was granted a 'peaceful and non-violent character', conceding to Gandhi's overwhelming presence in the popular imagination.

Yet he sought an exception to that character in moral terms that evoked the protection of the liberty of the nation. Military conscription in the post-War period was the norm, rather than the exception as he and other pro-conscription members pointed out. The debate was carried out in a period of expansion of the Indian army, both as a result of imperial policies as well as of the rise of a particular kind of national spirit. More than 2 million Indian soldiers had participated in the Second World War following the massive expansion of the Indian army from a size of 200,000 to 2.5 million in the inter-War period alone.[60] The memory of the Red Fort trial of the Indian National Army was fresh in public memory and a powerful narrative about the defence needs of the country was active in the minds of the members of the Constituent Assembly. Had the clause been put to vote in the entire floor of the Assembly, military conscription would have been approved with significant majority. It would have merely been an endorsement of a norm. But the opposition of the two women members to any idea of forced labour in the Sub-Committee on Fundamental Rights and their resistance to the extravagant stress on military rule produced a counter-discourse against it from the earliest stage of the framing.

Amrit Kaur, due to her association with Mahatma Gandhi and her advocacy of international peace, could not have agreed to the proposition of compulsory military service. A significant backdrop to the women members' objection to conscription was their recent attempts to get the Women's Auxiliary Corps of the Indian Army dismantled which made them sensitive to the plight of military training. The All India Conference in its 18th conference in 1945 had unanimously resolved to ask for the 'immediate dissolution' of the Women's Auxiliary Corps owing to the 'treatment accorded to the Indian rank and file involved and in many instances the loss of national and personal self'.[61] As authors of the Indian Women's Charter of Rights and participants in the post-war dialogue on international peace on numerous international platforms, both Kaur and Mehta had reservations against such compulsions. In contrast with a nationalist spirit that advocated protection by a national army, Hansa Mehta promoted UN organizations as 'alternatives to war' and imagined a world in which states were willing to 'sacrifice(e) part of their national sovereignty' to establish peace.[62]

An avowed principle of the AIWC was to replace 'militarism and other aggressive means' with 'peaceful co-operation' at all levels.[63] Conscription for purposes of public services was an important item in their strategy for developing social work. While speaking in the Constituent Assembly (Legislative) on the Union Budget presented by John Mathai, Renuka Ray criticized the exorbitant allocation for defence, and recommended spending part of the amount on social conscription:

> I can understand a huge army of occupation in a country under occupation, to subjugate the people, but what right or justice is there in keeping a huge land army in a country which is free? ... Should we not have instead voluntary or auxiliary forces and National Cadet Corps and such things?[64]

Soon after the Constitution of India was passed with provisions for 'compulsory service for public purposes',[65] she recommended social work modelled on military conscription for students 'who may be asked to give at least one year's compulsory social service for the nation's needs'.[66]

Conscription found a place in the Indian Constitution in article 23, not as a main clause but as an exception:

> *Article 23:* Prohibition of traffic in human beings and forced labour
> 1. Traffic in human beings and *begar* and other similar forms of forced labour are prohibited and any contravention of this provision shall be an offence punishable in accordance with law
> 2. Nothing in this article shall prevent the State from imposing compulsory service for public purposes, and in imposing such service the State shall not make any discrimination on grounds only of religion, race, caste or class or any of them.

Although the title of this section of the chapter on fundamental rights is 'Rights against Exploitation', the second clause seems to be more about the rights of the state. In the sequence described above, this confrontation was staged with the women members refusing to grant this right to the state. Their refusal did not merely limit the constituency of citizens to be affected by the provision as in the case of K. M. Munshi who proposed that 'No person who has any conscientious objection should be compelled to join the armed forces or military training'.[67] They also did not agree to exceptions in case of an educational scheme or public service. Indeed, before they finally got military conscription prohibited through vote, they had nearly succeeded in doing so through arguments and persuasion.

The terms of their interventions are very pertinent for our understanding of women's strategies to argue in constitutional terms. Mehta and Kaur exercised a relentless and sustained dissent, writing against the idea of compulsion at every stage of the Committee's proceedings. In her letter to B. N. Rau, Kaur reminded him that the women members had voted 'against compulsory service in any form during the discussions and adhere to this position'.[68] In their Minute of Dissent, submitted to the Advisory Committee along with the Report of the Sub-Committee on Fundamental Rights, the women members explained their objections in detail:

> We look upon compulsion as against all tenets of democracy and would point to the danger of giving to the State the powers of compulsion in any sphere of life. We would instead suggest the creation of paid social service in both the Centre and the units for the spread of education and other nation-building activities. In a country where there is no lack of manpower compulsion is particularly out of place.[69]

Finally, Amrit Kaur recorded her dissent against 'compulsion in any form' in the Advisory Committee.[70] Later during the debates on the floor of the Constituent Assembly, women stood by their position. They also demanded that in clause 1 of the article a prohibition of devdasi may be specifically mentioned.[71] They simultaneously enjoined the state to impose parallel restrictions on trafficking of women and refused to grant it the right to make conscription compulsory.

Read together, women's position on the two separate clauses of article 23 reveals that in their constitutional vision, the state could use force to prevent exploitation of citizens by other citizens but could not compel citizens to work for it. Military conscription was, H. V. Kamath told the Assembly, akin to 'unqualified enforcement of the duty to bear arms', 'an outward expression of the idea of dying for the state', and thus in its conceptualization represented an enormously powerful and totalitarian state.[72] In the historic circumstances following the War and the precarious state in which the Constituent Assembly had taken the mantle of framing the Constitution, most influential members believed in the necessity of compulsory military service and training. Women, acutely sensitive to the damage caused by the war of which they were 'the greatest sufferers' and conscious of their role as 'custodians of peace and social stability' were sceptical of introducing militarist education in a country that had been ravaged by violence. Conscription itself, would be an act of violence by the state. The women members' interventions were marked with a deep conviction in the morality of a non-coercive state and the need to protect individual liberty from its exigencies.

DIRECTIVE PRINCIPLES AND THE MORAL VISION OF WOMEN

Women members of the Constituent Assembly were among the first group of astute readers who recognized the pivotal role the directive principles would play in the implementation of the constitutional vision.

Pious directives but nonetheless fundamental

Women played a momentous role in determining the prelude to the chapter on directive principles which are provisions not enforceable by any court, but 'nevertheless fundamental in the governance of the country' and which the state has a duty to apply in making laws.[73] The evidence from the Sub-Committee on Fundamental Rights makes it clear that Amrit Kaur and Hansa Mehta played a significant role in bringing these words into the Constitution. When some of their demands for example, for a uniform civil code, were relegated to the non-justiciable rights, they pushed for the strengthening of these rights so that they would not remain ineffectual once the Constitution became operative. Apart from participating in the debates on the necessity of the distinction between the fundamental rights and directive principles and making substantial contributions to their content, women contributed to the very legal status of these rights and their relationship with each other.

Amrit Kaur's letter to the Constitutional Adviser, written on behalf of the two women members of the Sub-Committee, formed the textual basis of article 37 of the Constitution. She wrote:

> While the non-justiciable rights shall not be cognizable by any court, we would respectfully urge that they are nonetheless fundamental. We would therefore like this to be stressed either in the foreword or at the end of clause 35 so that it shall be the duty of the State to take, as soon as possible, the necessary action in fulfilment of the directives.... Indeed all the non-justiciable rights are fundamental to the well-being and ordered progress of the society.[74]

The original text of what was to become article 37 of the Constitution, actually a literal adaptation of article 45 of the Irish Constitution, was amended according to the suggestions in this letter. The original text had restricted the directives as 'intended for the general guidance' of the state. It had settled that they 'shall not be cognizable' by any court, and that 'the application of these principles' shall be 'the care of the State'.[75] It was at the women's suggestion that a new article was added to the Draft Constitution, that though 'these principles shall not be cognizable by any court', they were 'nevertheless fundamental in the governance of the country and their application shall be the duty of the State'.[76] This article, initially incorporated by the Sub-Committee on Fundamental Rights and approved by the Advisory Committee went through subsequent stages of the Assembly with only one minor change when the Drafting Committee replaced the word 'cognizable' with 'enforceable'.[77]

An amendment was suggested by K. T. Shah during the discussions on the Draft Constitution. He thought that by making the principles non-enforceable and still calling them fundamental, the article becomes contradictory and confused. An article that 'exempts', 'exonerates', and 'excuses' the courts from giving effect to 'one of the most cardinal, important and creative Chapters of this Constitution', Shah argued, was 'an insult to the entire Constitution'.[78] His amendment was lost and the article was passed in its current form. Women had thus ensured the phrase 'was intended for general guidance' became 'nevertheless fundamental' and the application of the principles did not remain 'the mere care' but became 'the duty of the State'. Shah's anxieties proved justified in the initial decades of the implementation of the Constitution but the changed expressions – two due to the firm contentions of Amrit Kaur and Hansa Mehta – eventually led the same courts to produce the most compelling constitutional interpretation of the value of the directive principles.

Thus, worded according to the women's suggestions, article 37 is central to the ascendancy of the directive principles in the constitutional jurisprudence of India. It constituted the justification for a radical shift from the avowed position of the primacy of the fundamental rights over the directive principles to the judgment that both – the directive principles and the fundamental rights – were equally important. Especially after the *Kesavananda Bharati* judgment[79] that established the basic structure doctrine in Indian constitutional jurisprudence, introducing the idea that the basic features of the Constitution are inviolable and beyond the amending powers of the Parliament, the directive principles became especially relevant.[80] The court declared in a subsequent judgment that the 'harmony and balance between Fundamental Rights and Directive Principles is an essential feature of the Basic Structure of the Constitution'.[81] The terms in which these principles are described by the Constitution are among the women members' most far-reaching contributions. The above mentioned changes to the original article were later understood by the court as crucial for the judicial construction of the framers' intention. Justice P. N. Bhagwati remarked in a landmark judgment of the Supreme Court:

> The changes made by the framers of the Constitution are vital and they have the effect of bringing about a total transformation or metamorphosis of this provision, fundamentally altering its significance and efficacy.[82]

This judgment, a milestone in the evolution of the directive principles as one the most important features of constitutional law in India, went on to make the following remarks that warrant full reproduction here:

merely because the directive principles are not enforceable in a court of law, it does not mean that they cannot create obligations or duties binding on the State.... There could not have been more explicit language used by the Constitution makers to make the Directive Principles binding on the State and there can be no doubt that the State is under a constitutional obligation carry out this mandate contained in Article 37. In fact, non-compliance with the Directive Principles would be unconstitutional on the part of the State and it would not only constitute a breach of faith with the people who imposed this constitutional obligation but it would also render a vital part of the Constitution meaningless and futile.[83]

Building partly upon the expression 'nevertheless fundamental', the judgment upheld the practice of 'importing the Directive Principles in the construction of Fundamental Rights'[84] concluding that both were, in fact, 'equally fundamental'.[85]

Thus, we see, that in the debate on the effectuality of the directive principles which occupied the mind of the Constituent Assembly, women had taken a stand by contributing the operative terms to article 37. Yet the fact that these directives were expressly made 'non-enforceable' by the court generated much debate regarding their incorporation by the Constituent Assembly.

A section of the members who believed that 'rights were no rights unless enforceable' argued that the directive principles were a 'useless appendix' and nothing more than 'pious platitudes'.[86] For them, these directives contained 'more verbal promise, than holds out any hope for actual performance'.[87] Their unenforceability meant that there was no guarantee that 'they will be made real, actual, living possession and enjoyment of the people'.[88] Women members expressed the opposite view, arguing that there was no reason to think that 'there is anything to despair because it is possible for the parliament and the Government of the future to bring these rights which are now directives as economic rights, and as fundamental rights'.[89] Their hope was built around the mechanisms of democracy which Ambedkar had cited in defence of the directive principles while introducing the Draft Constitution a year earlier. To say that the directive principles were mere pious declarations without any binding force, according to Ambedkar, was a misplaced and '"superfluous" criticism'.[90] They may have 'no legal force behind them' but were binding still because they formed the moral yardstick with which the people would judge the government.[91] In Ambedkar's words:

whoever captures power will not be free to do what he likes with it. In the exercise of it, he will have to respect these instruments of instructions which are

called Directive Principles. He cannot ignore them. He may not have to answer
for their breach in a Court of Law. But he will certainly have to answer for them
before the electorate at election time. What great value these directive principles
possess will be realized better when the forces of right contrive to capture power.[92]

Thus, for Ambedkar, the force behind the directive principles was the
democratic will of the people the exercise of which will make them stronger
with the further entrenchment of democracy.

Even Durgabai, who could not initially repose enough trust in the
effectuality of the directive principles was convinced. There was a living legal
structure inherent in them. Her anxiety that these articles would remain a mere
'pious declaration of our intention'[93] gave way to a belief that they were in the
tradition of economic policies of the state which were morally binding on it.
She traced their antecedents far beyond the Irish Constitution to injunctions
prescribed by the great Indian text of political science, Kautilya's *Artha Shastra*.
In particular, she cited the verses

The king shall provide the orphan, the dying, the infirm, the afflicted, the
helpless with maintenance. He shall also provide subsistence to the helpless and
the expectant mothers and to the children they give birth to.[94]

For her these 'basic injunctions of the Artha Shastra, which the King has no
option but to obey' were ideals for the modern state too and were reflected in
the directive principles.[95] Durgabai, who was one of independent India's most
eminent thinkers and champions of social welfare and social work, clearly saw
in these constitutional principles the foundation of a welfare state.[96]

This leads us to the most important debate on the directive principles.
The debate was centred on the very substance of the principles, their nature,
ideological slant, and theoretical basis. These debates at whose heart was the
relationship and perceived conflict between the directive principles and the
fundamental rights anticipated the most sustained and productive tension
in the constitutional democracy of India. This tension, which brought the
Parliament and the Judiciary in confrontation with each other, came to
the fore when certain fundamental rights, most notably that of property,
obstructed the pursuit of the social order envisioned by the directive principles.
The judiciary, which was 'indeed cold in the beginning' towards the directive
principles attributed a transcendental and unique status to the fundamental
rights making them legally and morally superior to the directives.[97] In an early
judgment, it had concluded that 'the Directive Principles of State Policy have
to conform to and run as subsidiary to the Chapter on Fundamental Rights'.[98]

The conflict intensified when certain amendments to the fundamental rights made in order to gain prominence for the directive principles were struck down by the Supreme Court under the logic of the superiority and transcendence of the fundamental rights. The process of restricting amendments to the Constitution, begun in the *Golaknath* case,[99] soon led to the introduction of the doctrine of the basic structure of the Constitution, according to which the directive principles and fundamental rights together formed the inviolable spirit of the Constitution that was beyond the powers of amendment.

A detailed discussion of the entire doctrine and the relationship between the fundamental rights and the directive principles is beyond the scope of this work. It has been argued that the constitutional demotion of the directive principles belongs to 'a story of political compromises' in India – between Gandhi and Nehru during the framing of the Karachi Resolution, and between Ambedkar and the Congress and the Gandhians in the Constituent Assembly.[100] Christophe Jaffrelot argues that relegating the directive principles to an effectively lesser position helped Ambedkar 'diffuse' Gandhian elements in the Constitution.[101]

An examination of women's contribution to these debates, vis-à-vis this narrative of compromise and contract reveals that they took positions with major theoretical and practical implications. Granville Austin characterizes the distinction between the fundamental rights and the directive principles in the Indian Constitution within Isaiah Berlin's framework of positive and negative liberties. The fundamental rights, according to Austin, are 'those negative obligations of the State not to encroach on individual liberty, that have become well-known since the late eighteenth century and since the drafting of the Bill of Rights of the American Constitution'.[102] The fundamental rights within this scheme correspond with Berlin's negative liberties conceived as freedom from interference, while the directive principles are analogous to positive liberties which are described as the freedom to 'lead one's prescribed form of life.' 'The "positive" sense of the word "liberty",' Berlin argues, 'derives from the wish on the part of the individual to be his own master'.[103] It is rooted in the wish of the individual 'to be a subject, not an object; to be moved by reasons, by conscious purposes, which are my own, not by causes which affect me, as it were, from outside'.[104] This characterization of the directive principles as positive rather than negative, active rather than passive, runs deep in the discourse on constitutionalism and democracy in India. Jawaharlal Nehru, while moving the Constitution (First Amendment Bill), argued:

> The Directive Principles of State Policy represent a dynamic move towards a certain objective. The Fundamental Rights represent something static, to preserve certain rights which exist.[105]

Women members, while eager to protect the fundamental rights of the citizens, considered the Constitution a tool of emancipation, capable of creating, in the words of Amrit Kaur, 'constructive citizenship'. It is only as subjects – 'self-reliant, fearless and enterprising' – as opposed to passive objects that citizens could 'contribute their full quota to the moral well-being of the state'.[106] The directive principles provided a comprehensive moral code that had to be actively pursued for the fulfilment of such aspirations. In the landmark *Kesavananda Bharati* case, that resurrected this code to a high judicial status, they were described as 'moral rights' that translated the moral claims into duties.[107]

The moral content of the directive principles

What, ultimately, was the content of the moral well-being of society? Women framers looked at economic and social rights as forming the basis of the moral prosperity of the nation. While some members opposed the directive principles, women framers like Purnima Banerji looked at the socialist spirit embodied in the directive principles as 'absolutely essential and in fact our guiding star in the future'.[108] If the fundamental rights, which included the right to property, were on the axis of passive citizenship, involuntarily accruing to women and men, the directive principles had transformational potential and required consistent application.

The first two directives, articles 38 and 39, which enjoined the state to secure a social order in which justice, social, economic, and political – in that order – shall inform all the institutions of national life, and ensure, among other things, that the ownership and control of the material resources of the community are so distributed as best to serve the common good 'provided us with the means for changing the structure of the society'.[109] These two articles, Purnima Banerji concluded, were the 'cornerstone of this Constitution'.[110] Without these means the Constitution could only have laid the foundations of a limited, 'negative democracy'[111] granting us nothing more than the 'hollow benefit of registering the status quo'.[112] The directive principles, she implied, created the conditions for a positive democracy that encouraged the active citizenship of the country. Democracy, as shaped by the Constitution, would 'fashion and remould and change the whole structure of society'[113] and would not merely be content with a preservation of the formal rights of individuals.

Austin paraphrases these interpretive sentiments behind the directive principles thus:

> In the Directive Principles, however, one finds an even clearer statement of the social revolution. They aim at making the Indian masses free in the positive sense, free from the passivity engendered by centuries of coercion by society and nature, free from abject physical conditions that had prevented them from fulfilling their best selves.[114]

The intertextual overlap of Purnima Banerji's arguments with those of Austin and the following remarks of Justices K. S. Hegde and A. K. Mukherjea in the monumental *Kesavananda Bharati* judgment reveal the vital entrenchment of the wisdom of the founding mothers in the constitutional discourse of the nation. 'The purpose of the Directive Principles' remarked the judges

> is to fix certain social and economic goals for immediate attainment by bringing about a non-violent social revolution. Through such a social revolution the Constitution seeks to fulfil the basic needs of the common man and to change the structure of our society. It aims at making the Indian masses free in the positive sense.[115]

Women, whose constitutional vision leaned towards a socialist reconfiguration of society, were anxious that the directive principles were given their due in the future. B. R. Ambedkar explained the inclusion of the directive principles in the Constitution by arguing that they provided directions 'as to what our economic ideals, as to what our social order ought to be'. Having initially argued that the Constitution was not a document for embodying such principles, he had, in the words of a member, a rapid conversion, in agreeing these principles were fundamental. The directive principles, Ambedkar went on to admit, laid down 'the ideals of economic democracy', without which political democracy would hardly make any sense. In his often quoted valedictory speech addressed to the Constituent Assembly, Ambedkar reminded the house of the contradiction between political democracy and economic democracy:

> On the 26th of January 1950 we are going to enter into a life of contradiction. In politics, we will have equality and in social and economic life we will have inequality. In politics we will recognize the principle of one man one vote and one vote one value. In our social and economic life, we shall, by reason of our social and economic structure, continue to deny the principle of one man one value.... If we continue to deny it for long, we will do so only by putting our political democracy in peril.[116]

Ambedkar's juxtaposition of political democracy with social and economic democracy, which he felt was envisioned in the directive principles, defined one of the most vital debates in the constitutional vision. Many members considered the directive principles as embodying those socialist values that could bring about the principle of 'one man one value' Ambedkar mentioned. M. Ananthasayanam Ayyangar, who initially thought 'the word socialism was reprehensible', was later convinced that 'by various clauses in the Directive Principles we have remedied the rigours of capitalism'.[117] Yet others argued that by granting the right to property the status of a fundamental right we have incapacitated these principles. Shibban Lal Saksena regarded the right to property as framed by the Constitution as 'the charter of capitalism in India'.[118] Arguing that 'the Directive Principles of State Policy which have been so beautifully described in Part IV cannot be realised so long as Article 31 forms part of this Constitution', he regretted that these principles were not incorporated in the chapter on fundamental rights.[119]

Women, we have seen, had engaged in designing and enumerating the fundamental rights and directive principles with distinct energy and focus. When an article was relegated to the category of non-justiciable rights (subsequently, the directive principles), for example, the common civil code, they considered it a loss. Their strategy was, first, to design ways in which their demands could obliquely find a place in the fundamental rights, and second, to mobilize more constitutional force for the directive principles. Even towards the end of the framing discourse, women endeavoured to make certain shifts between these two chapters. Renuka Ray, the leading member who sought to make the Constitution a document of economic democracy, complained that it was 'very unfortunate that although the political rights are in these fundamental principles, the economic rights of citizens have not been able to be put in as justiciable rights today'.[120] In her last speech in the Constituent Assembly, she lamented that 'among these directives of State policy are some of the most vital rights of citizens and along with them are lumped many matters of much lesser moment'.[121]

Renuka Ray hoped that at some future time, this 'most unfortunate' anomaly would be rectified and the economic rights that existed as directives would be turned into fundamental rights. Purnima Banerji, during the final debate on the right to property (which was the last article among the fundamental rights and directive principles taken up by the Assembly), proposed such an amendment. She proposed it to the effect that the clause from the directive principles securing 'adequate means of livelihood'[122] was implanted into the fundamental right to property. Her stated object was 'to give effect to some of the principles and clauses which we have already passed when laying down the Directive Principles of State Policy'.[123] These, of course, were the principles of social and economic justice. She claimed that 'if provisions are not made in this article dealing with Property Rights and the economic policy of the future State is in any way fettered and made rigid, we feel that we shall not be able to succeed in these articles which we have already passed'.[124] Banerji built her argument upon the moral consensus around a principle that was already ratified by the Assembly.

As argued earlier, the framing of the Constitution was not a linear process that culminated at once on 24 January 1950 when the members of the Assembly put their signatures on the handwritten copies of the text. It was a meandering operation in which certain sections that were ratified before others were in a dialectic relationship with sections that were yet to be finalized. Women were keenly alert to this dialectic between the written and the yet-to-be-written text and made the maximum possible interventions throughout the framing. However, after the final enumeration of the directive principles – labelled fundamental but still non-enforceable – women strove to enhance their effectuality. Banerji's strategy was to extend the logic of the directive principles to the enforceable section of rights, that is, the fundamental rights and seek to extend what we call positive democracy. Though it failed, we can see in her attempt an early performance of the creative method of judicial hermeneutics that imports a directive principle into a fundamental right. The right to livelihood, formally a part of the directive principles (articles 39 (a) and 41), has since been construed by the Supreme Court as implicit in the fundamental right to life (article 21). The court's judgment makes the application of the logic very clear:

> Article 39 (a) of the Constitution, which is a Directive Principle of State Policy, provides that the State shall, in particular, direct its policy towards securing that the citizens, men and women equally, have the right to an adequate means of livelihood. Article 41, which is another Directive Principle, provides inter alia, that the State shall, within the limits of its economic capacity and development, make effective provisions for securing the right to work in cases of unemployment and undeserved want.… The principles contained in Articles 39 (a) and 41 must be regarded as equally fundamental in the understanding and interpretation of the meaning and content of fundamental rights. If there is an obligation upon the State to secure to the citizens an adequate means of livelihood and the right to work, it would be sheer pedantry to exclude the right to livelihood from the content of the right to life.[125]

Though the court has not yet gone so far as to imply the right to work or the right to employment arises out of the fundamental right to life, in *Olga Tellis*, the case cited above, it reached the conclusion that 'the right to life which is conferred by Article 21 includes the right to livelihood',[126] thereby fulfilling Purnima Banerji's objective by applying her own strategy. The court's pronouncement can be seen as an exemplary juridical moment permeated by authorial spirit of the founding mothers. Indeed, this method of textual construction which has infused life into many a dead letter of the Constitution has emerged as a hallmark of judicial creativity in India. Given the stress women laid on the directive principles, it is fortuitous that one of their own framing strategies played such a significant role in the evolution of the directive principles into the most important apparatus of constitutional justice.

At the heart of the evolution of the directive principles of state policy lies women's strategy of emphasizing the social and economic aspects of democracy and constructive citizenship, and to a great extent their strategy of reading the directive principles into subsequent articles. The directive principles have gained a centrality in 'all the institutions of the national life'.[127] Regarding the extension of the directive principles into the 'eventful journey' of article 21 (Right to Life and Liberty), a standard textbook on Indian constitutional law says:

> From non-deprivation of life to its preservation, from negative to positive content, Art. 21 has been fundamentally transformed as a result of judicial creativity. A most remarkable feature of the expansion of Article 21 has been that many of the non-justiciable Directive Principles have been converted into enforceable Fundamental Rights by the magical wand of judicial creativity. In the process of expanding the ambit of Art 21, the Supreme Court has integrated many Directive Principles with Art 21. The result of this judicial activism has been that not only many directive principles have been activated but also many new Fundamental rights have been implied by the Supreme Court from Art 21.[128]

This strategy has not merely expanded the ambit of the fundamental rights, transforming them from mere articles of negative liberty into a dynamic arsenal of positive rights, but ensured that 'the values underlying the Directive Principles have also become enforceable by riding on the back of the Fundamental Rights'.[129] Renuka Ray lamented in the late 1970s that 'the most important of these directives have not been implemented'[130] – these values have now come to occupy a preeminent position in the constitutional discourse of

India, bringing to life some of the authorial concerns of the founding mothers of the Constitution. It would be helpful to recall the trajectory that Hansa Mehta had hoped the social and economic rights would follow during her participation in the Commission on Human Rights – in several senses, they have followed the same trajectory. The women framers' hopes that the state would implement these directives and give life to the clauses they helped to be termed *fundamental* were finally attended to through judicial creativity, which, as noticed in the *Olga Tellis* judgment, followed the same principle of interpretation as that the founding mothers had followed during the framing of the text.

THE SECULARISM DEBATE

The other vital feature of the Constitution which women members saw as central was secularism. Other than Aizaz Rasul who believed that the purely secular character of the state was 'the most outstanding feature of the Constitution' and argued that in its affirmation of secularity essentially lies 'the sanctity of the Constitution', no other woman used the term during her reflections in the Constituent Assembly.[131] Women members were engaged in a parallel battle around the reforms of Hindu Law where the term 'secularism' was subjected to rigorous analysis and even hostile criticism. Renuka Ray who was at the forefront of the Hindu Code Bill struggle did not touch upon the issue in her reflections. This was quite in tune with women's strategy of conserving their verbal energy for the right authorial opportunities.

In the Sub-Committee on Fundamental Rights, to recall, women had tried to prevent the right to freedom of religion because they believed it would curtail the right to equality and impact the validity of statutes doing away with social practices like child marriage. For the women framers, the principal problematic of the secularism debates was clear. Secularism was to be established as a modern value, situated within the constitutional guarantees of the fundamental rights and the directive principles. It was an extension of the freedom of the self to grow to its full potential, an essential condition for active citizenship within the social versus political frame. This entailed the initiation of a process of secularization with its own machineries of expansion of choices and entrenchment of a rational, moral education. It also necessarily meant an entrammelling of religion as a force and being alert to any unwarranted sanction it gained from the Constitution. Women framers were aware of these crucial demands on them, and straddled between their own notions of secularism and secularization throughout the process.

Secularizing the religious

In the early stages of the drafting, Amrit Kaur and Hansa Mehta demanded that the term 'free practice of religion' be replaced by 'freedom of religious worship.' Religions, they believed, sanctioned certain practices which went against the basic rights of equality, and granting them a constitutional guarantee of freedom would impede social reforms, especially those related to women's issues.

Women opposed the inclusion of the free 'practice' of religion at several stages during the framing of the fundamental rights. In her first dissenting letter, submitted to B. N. Rau on 31 March 1947, Amrit Kaur proposed on behalf of Hansa Mehta and herself, that the words 'freedom of religious worship' should be used instead of 'free practice of religion'.[132] The range of the term 'practice', the letter argued, was very large and might result in giving constitutional sanction to several social practices that were discriminatory towards women. Records of the proceedings show that the term 'practice' was debated in the Sub-Committee on Fundamental Rights with considerable vigour, and following the women's suggestion, the term was omitted in its preliminary report.[133] Women members had achieved this with the support of the legendary lawyer Alladi Krishnaswami Ayyar who shared the apprehension that this may indeed lead the court to construe the clause related to religion in a very wide sense, thereby causing impediments to gender-related social reforms.[134]

That choice was contested by the Minorities Sub-Committee where it was subjected to a vote on 18 April 1947.[135] The decision, as a result of the vote, was to retain the 'right to practise' religion in the fundamental rights. Among the dissenting votes were those of Amrit Kaur, B. R. Ambedkar, and Jagjivan Ram, a woman member and the two Dalit members, a remarkable fact for it shows a pattern of collaboration between Ambedkar and the women members. In this case, their theoretical predilections privileged the same set of concerns and were framed in the same order. Ambedkar's much-cited remarks about the pervasive presence of religion in Indian social life, made on the floor of the Constituent Assembly on 2 December 1948 were strongly reminiscent of this early contest in the Advisory Committee. He feared that since religious conceptions covered 'every aspect of life, from birth to death', giving them absolute protection would 'disable the legislatures in India from enacting any social measures whatsoever'.[136] In her second note of dissent, submitted after her proposal lost the vote, Amrit Kaur expressed an even stronger caution − that the constitutional guarantee of the 'free practice' of religion:

would not only be a bar to future social legislation but would even invalidate past legislation such as the Widow Remarriage Act, the Sarda Act or even the law abolishing *sati*. Everyone is aware how many evil practices which one would like to abolish, are carried on in the name of religion, e.g., pardah, polygamy, caste disabilities, animal sacrifice, dedication of girls to temples, to mention a few.[137]

In the same vein, she also argued that the right to 'propagation of religion' did not require an extra provision, since that was 'amply assured' by the clause on 'freedom of speech and expression'.[138]

Although neither Ambedkar nor the women's dissenting voices counted when the Constitution finally granted the right to freedom of religion under a sub-section titled 'Freedom of conscience and free profession, practise and propagation of religion', their dissent points to crucial debates on Indian secularism. Moreover, these dissents are part of a project to secularize law in which women participated with considerable zeal. In the final reading of the Constitution, Hansa Mehta lamented that the while the Constitution did manage to restrict the interference of the state in religion, it could not reign in the interference of religion in matters of social life. She regretted that in order to avoid hurting 'the religious susceptibilities of some people', the Constitution could not abolish evils like purdah.[139] Evoking her own defeated argument in the Fundamental Rights Sub-Committee over the incorporation of the word 'practise' in the text, she repeated that 'Any evil *practised* in the name of religion could not be guaranteed by the Constitution'.[140]

One cannot fail to notice how women members anticipated the centrality of the term 'practise' to the judicial discourse around defining the essential and integral parts of a religion. The most recent instance is the *Sabarimala* judgment on the question of women's entry to a temple.[141] In this judgment, the sole dissenting voice was of a female judge who argued that 'The religious practise of restricting the entry of women between the ages of 10 to 50 years [to the Sabarimala Temple], is in pursuance of an "essential religious practise"' and, to put it ironically, upheld the right of a celibate God not to be worshipped by women in a certain age group.[142]

Other dimensions of women's involvement with the question of secularism, too, become clear through a reading of their interventions and statements in the Constituent Assembly. For instance, in the same note of dissent, Kaur (and Mehta) argued that constitutionally protected religious practices might also include such acts, like 'religious meetings or processions', that can generate hostilities between religious communities and lead to communal clashes.[143] In her final speech, Ammu Swaminathan spoke of the fundamental right to 'freedom of worship' as 'very vital' for the citizens of the country. While the word 'worship' does not appear in the above-mentioned article,[144] Swaminathan who confessed she knew 'very little about constitution-making' was still haunted by it. Her own congratulatory note on the Constitution was steeped in secularism-as-tolerance, particularly Hindu tolerance:

> The Hindus have always been known to be tolerant towards all religions and we have put that down in our Constitution so that there will be no mistake about it and nobody can say that our Constitution did not include freedom of worship to every citizen of this country.[145]

Although the women framers knew that secularism in the polity could only be sustained by the secularization of society, they did not advocate a complete rejection of religion per se. The percolation of a rational modernity which would respond to the needs of gender justice in a multi-religious society was possible through an emphasis on widespread education that draws upon the rational and the ethical in all religious traditions. The central insight – or the driving hope – of their vision was that a democratic and informed education would lead increasingly to a general acceptance of a constitutional morality. Education remained vital for the vision of the founding mothers. Once the Constitution was adopted, they applied rigorous constitutional logic to develop policies for Indian education at all levels. After 1950, they continued to imagine education as an expression of the rationality of justice embodied in the Constitution, and substantially reworked its framework at all levels, making education one of most significant sites for the exercise of the reaffirmation of the ideas they had proposed during the framing of the Constitution.[146]

Education so conceived – as a force that would reshape social conscience to bring it in conformity with the moral vision of the Constitution – was part of women's larger project from the very beginning. As early as in 1937, Amrit Kaur hoped that a rational code of personal laws would gradually become popular and supersede all other legal regimes,[147] presumably, because she thought that right education will wean men and women away from the restrictive legal regimes of their particular cultures. Women members, however, did not employ such reasoning in the Constituent Assembly: instead, during constitution-making, they relied upon the Gandhian insistence on tolerance as morally desirable because of the common ethical core of all religions, and advocated educating young citizens in these common values. Most of them were close associates of Mahatma Gandhi and demanded a constitutional guarantee for spiritual education during the framing. Purnima Banerji moved an amendment (rejected by the Assembly) to what became article 28(3) of the Constitution:

> All religious education given in educational institutions receiving State-aid will be in the nature of elementary philosophy of comparative religions calculated to broaden the pupils' mind rather than such as will foster sectarian exclusiveness.[148]

Such education, spiritual as well as secular, would have the effect of developing a child into 'a healthy citizen of India capable of appreciating each other's point of view'.[149] In a typically Gandhian spirit, the education envisaged by the women framers was meant to deepen the grounds of tolerance and lead to stronger civility. For Gandhi, as Raghavan N. Iyer notes,

> The more deeply founded tolerance is, the more meaningful and profound civility becomes. The stronger the roots of civility, the richer the fruits of tolerance. Thus tolerance and civility constitute the minimal foundations of a liberal society as well as the mature graces of a good society.[150]

In the same spirit, the secularism of the women framers was not incompatible with religion. Citing Gandhi, they even argued for a clause granting a constitutional guarantee to 'marriages between persons professing different religious faiths, each retaining his or her own religion without abatement'.[151] Their secularism was not oriented towards a militant confrontation with religion but to a respect for what Gandhi called the 'ordered moral government of the universe'.[152] The resistance was not to religion or religious education but to anything that promoted a particular denominational prejudice.[153] Religion in itself was a noble value that had to be harmonized with social values. 'The rejection of religion', Amrit Kaur affirmed, was 'the root cause of all the ills of the world'.[154] 'Institutional religion', 'the religion of dogma and ritual' however tended 'to divide rather than bind people together'.[155] In this, Kaur and other women members followed Gandhi, in whose utopian imagination of India 'religious, that is ethical, education will occupy the first place'.[156] Such an education was only possible if religion was purified, and its misappropriation was stopped. Renuka Ray reminded the house of the abuse of religion:

> In this country we have seen the exploitation, and the prostitution of what we call religion and we have seen to our bitter cost what is done in the name of

denominational religion. It has not only led to the dismemberment and division of our country, but it has also led to the worst horrors that could be perpetrated in the name of religion.[157]

She recommended education for the next generation which would make them believe that 'the religion of humanity is much greater to them than religious dissensions on a denominational religious basis'.[158] Women's mobilization of the secularist discourse was based on these concepts. Religion, taken in its organizational, social form caused friction and disintegration which secular values built on anti-denominational principles would counteract.

Secularism was an intermediate principle for these women with which they negotiated throughout their struggle to re-define the relationship between the state and the citizen on the axis of gender. In their negotiations with the Assembly on the question of personal laws, women recognized the difficulty that a vast jurisdiction of denominational religion posed before attempts at social legislation. Ambedkar summed up their problem and explained the choice of delimiting religious jurisdiction. According to his arguments, partly cited earlier:

> The religious conceptions in this country are so vast that they cover every aspect of life, from birth to death. There is nothing which is not religion and if personal law is to be saved, I am sure about it that in social matters we will come to a standstill. I do not think it is possible to accept a position of that sort. There is nothing extraordinary in saying that we ought to strive hereafter to limit the definition of religion in such a manner that we shall not extend beyond beliefs and such rituals as may be connected with ceremonials which are essentially religious.[159]

Reducing the hegemony of denominational religion was a primary strategy in the women framers' constitutional politics. The demand for a common, rational civil code for all citizens, which took shape as the 'Uniform Civil Code', was part of the same larger project.[160] This project was informed by women's experience of the tension between the various affiliations of their gendered identities. The category of religious minorities, Hansa Mehta argued in her concluding remarks on the Constitution, was created by the colonial regime to complement the policy of divide and rule that 'culminated in the partition of this country'.[161] These communal identities were not formed on what Amrit Kaur called 'the essence of religion' which generates an 'inner bonding of affection'.[162] Mehta lamented that the Constitution seemed to have accepted the notion of religious minorities handed down by the British without defining the term minority.

Caught in a struggle of competing loyalties, women members rejected privileging religious affiliations as sources of identities in their constitutional politics before the inception of the Constituent Assembly. Citizenship, as they defined it, was the 'right ordering of our several loyalties' and involved distinguishing between religion as a source of love and 'dissensions and such perversions of religion as stress what is "an fond" [*sic*] immaterial and bring into jeopardy what is definitely vital to the spiritual and moral development of life'.[163] Generating a civic sense was only possible by wiping out separatism, 'the abstraction of a negation, the shadow of a shadow, which divides man from fellow-man'.[164] Thus secularism and national integrity are not two mutually exclusive chapters of women's moral vision, but part of one unified project that has at its centre a certain notion of progressive justice.

Between community and secularity: The case of Aizaz Rasul

Aizaz Rasul claimed that the secularity of the nation was fundamental to its unity. 'This secularity will always be kept guarded and unsullied', she hoped, 'as upon it depends that complete unity of the peoples of India without which all hopes of progress would be in vain'.[165] The terms of emphasis included secularity, progress, and the unity of the nation. The last of these aspects, one of the three strands identified by Granville Austin as weaving the seamless web of the Constitution (the other two being social revolution and democracy), served these women as the rhetorical frame within which their demands were presented. Aizaz Rasul, the sole Muslim woman member in the Constituent Assembly perhaps privileged it as a position against the charge of separatism that was brought against her fellow Muslim colleagues.

Rasul's position against reservations for minorities has been read in numerous ways. Historians have assumed that 'a recent defector from the Muslim League', she was the 'only' Muslim member who was 'persuaded' by the Congress to speak in favour of the abolition of minority seats in the Constituent Assembly.[166] They argue that she was cajoled and prodded by Patel to take such a position.[167] Once again, this is based on a reading of only one of the many speeches she made in the Assembly. Rasul's subjective interests in the Assembly lay at the interstices of her identity as a Muslim woman with roots in Pakistan married to a major landlord in the United Provinces, and as a member of a faction of a secular women's movement that had opposed the two-nation theory. It is imperative to read her location in the discursive field of the Constituent Assembly before one can arrive at any conclusion about her interventions.

It may be recalled that from the very beginning, Amrit Kaur, the sole woman member on the Minorities Sub-Committee, had taken a position against any political safeguard for minorities. In doing so, she was initially herself in a minority. Thus, when the Sub-Committee submitted its report to the Advisory Committee, it came with her note of dissent while most minority members sought reserved seats in the legislatures. Between August 1947, when the Advisory Committee had agreed to include these safeguards and October 1949, when they were revoked, circumstances within and beyond the Constituent Assembly had changed. Patel told the Assembly that these changes had led many minority communities to revise their positions and give up their demands. In her detailed account of the framing of minority rights in the Constituent Assembly, Rochana Bajpai attributes this change to 'deals, disarray, and direct and indirect pressure from Congress leadership', that forced to Rasul to speak for the Muslim Community.[168] It seems however, that although Rasul's position did help Patel and the Congress leadership to convince the Assembly that minority communities had given up on their demand for political safeguards, it is by no means clear that she was speaking under any pressure.

As a member of the women's movement and former vice-president of the AIWC, she stood for a united India and always took a position against reservations for minorities. She reminded the Assembly of her 'conviction that it was absolutely suicidal for a religious minority to keep alive the spirit of separatism by demanding reservation on communal lines'.[169] Like Hansa Mehta who lamented the persistence of identities like religious minorities, Rasul too claimed that she looked forward to a day 'when individuals will cease to regard themselves as members of religious minorities'.[170] Yet she was not willing to leave the entire responsibility to members of any one group. The Constitution would provide safeguards to minorities, but eventually create a condition when the binary of majority and minority would disappear. This ideal could be achieved, Rasul argued, 'only if and when the majority also cease to be conscious of their majority and members of all communities, big or small, sincerely and simultaneously begin to consider themselves and one another as full and equal citizens of a Secular State'.[171] A secular Constitution would give protection to minorities but, as women members argued, would not allow them to perpetuate through such privileges and protections.

While introducing the Draft Constitution, B. R. Ambedkar made similar remarks, exhorting both the communities for having 'followed the wrong path'.[172] While it was wrong for the majority to deny the existence of minorities, Ambedkar said, it was 'equally wrong for the minorities to perpetuate themselves. A solution must be found which will serve a double purpose.'[173] Like Rasul, Ambedkar too hoped that once the majority changes its habit, the binary would dissolve:

> It is for the majority to realize its duty not to discriminate against minorities. Whether the minorities will continue or will vanish must depend upon this habit of the majority. The moment the majority loses the habit of discriminating against the minority, the minorities can have no ground to exist. They will vanish.[174]

Both Ambedkar and Rasul, representatives of minorities in their own right, seemed to be driven, rather naively, by the values of reciprocity and symmetry inherent in constitutional morality (Image 5.1). The 'diffusion' of this morality 'not merely among the majority but throughout the whole'[175] was also an ethical task of citizens if this binary had to 'vanish'. It was her performance of this task that Aizaz Rasul remembered till the end of her life, reiterating with pride the position she had taken in the Constituent Assembly.[176] Her attempts at integrating Muslims with mainstream political life in India

Image 5.1 Aizaz Rasul with B. R. Ambedkar in the Constituent Assembly.

Source: Album hosted by Nehru Memorial Museum and Library, originally from *BR Ambedkar: Man and Vision*, by V. Chandra Mawli, 1990, p. 53, accessed at Making of the Indian Constitution (1946–1950) – Google Arts & Culture (https://artsandculture.google.com/asset/making-of-the-indian-constitution-1946-1950/hgHlw2sTRfho_w, accessed 1 January 2022).

were part of this performance and rooted in an understanding of religion as a weak and transient source of identity. The value that religion acquires as a source of identity and politics is contingent upon time, a fact that must not be forgotten while judging the historical actors involved in negotiating with it. In her reminiscences, Rasul admonished the later generation for their de-historicized understanding the choices made by the founders at the complex historical moment of the framing of the Constitution. 'It is most unfair and unjust of Muslims of the post-independence generation', she said, 'to pass judgements on our actions of those times':

> Are they in a position to visualise the suffering and anguish of the millions of Muslims living in India during those times? Even a broken knife found in a Muslim house could send the family to jail. It is not possible for Muslims of today to visualize the conditions of those days. What difference would a few seats more or less in the legislatures have made if reservation had been retained?[177]

These remarks provide us with an important insight into women's subjective recollection of their authorship of the Constitution, opening several windows to the historicity of the founding moments. They also provide us with a counter-narrative to Sunil Khilnani's claims that 'the Constituent Assembly was an island of calm deliberations amidst the historical currents that swirled through the country'.[178]

These accounts serve as a reminder that for the women founders, secularism was not one reified political position but a set of contingent political positions regarding the multiple spaces that religion occupied between the state and citizenry. Rasul's later remarks help to further historicize women's assertions regarding affirmative action and other positions that involved their identities as embedded patriarchal subjects. Their identities as privileged subjects in the larger structure of caste-hierarchy and concordant position with Ambedkar in the Constituent Assembly made it possible and even necessary for them to make exceptions for the Scheduled Castes. The Scheduled Castes, in Hansa Mehta's words 'had suffered and suffered long at the hands of the Hindu society and any exception in their case would be making amends to what they have suffered'.[179]

Women members were Ambedkar's allies in the framing process. Like him, they earned displeasure for upsetting or attempting to upset the social order. Speaking towards the end of the debates a male member of the Assembly had warned the house that the fundamental rights guaranteed by the Constitution – liberty and equality – 'whatever they may be professing in practice they will not give the desired result'.[180] He feared that these rights will 'unfortunately' empower the new woman, whose emergence he saw as a threat to the very civilization of India. He imagined a future when

> women claim freedom and equality in all respects with men and thereby become competitors and rivals to men, I am sure there will be an end of our civilisation on which we have been living all these years.[181]

His reference was to his women colleagues in the Assembly, members like Hansa Mehta (who had spoken just before him with her calm eloquence) and Renuka Ray, who were at the forefront of the movement for reforms in religious and personal laws. These women knew their feminism was perceived as divisive and dangerous within some sections of the Assembly. They were disparaged at various points in public and private life for attacking the 'foundations of Indian culture', and chastised for what the eminent jurist Kailash Nath Katju, in a personal letter to Renuka Ray, mockingly called their 'consuming passion ... to revolutionize our society in our own lifetimes'.[182] Their attempts to introduce the notion of constitutional rights in the family were perceived as threats to the social fabric of India, in particular, to the Hindu social structure. The guarantees of positive freedoms that aimed at producing constructive citizenship were threatening to the hegemony of religion.

Hansa Mehta was compelled to complain against Islam's approval of purdah. She complained that the Constitution failed to put an end to the 'inhuman custom', exhorting Islam to 'better get rid of this evil'.[183] In women's vocabulary, the word 'custom' had the same connotations as in Ambedkar's reading of the historical–jurisprudential status of certain Indian practices of injustice. In a contemporary analysis, Renuka Ray argued that Purdah had no scriptural sanction. Its earlier legitimacy was derived from 'gross misinterpretation of the Quoranic [sic] edicts',[184] and was later reified as colonial India began 'clinging to outworn customs and rites as the last remnants of a golden age'.[185] The pivotal moment that radically worsened the condition of women was 'when custom became stronger than law'.[186] Women's constitutional sense was in agreement with Ambedkar who, defending the Hindu Code Bill, argued that it is a 'fundamental proposition' that 'a code is inconsistent with customary laws' 'because a custom could always eat into the code and make the code null and void'.[187] The religious force behind customs like purdah, in Renuka Ray's reading, was produced by the entrenchment of wrong interpretive practices, a process common to both Hindu and Muslim societies.[188] It was the burden of customs – misinterpreted religion thriving in 'practice' rather than in the authority of sacred scriptures – that women sought the Constitution to delimit. The Constitution would lay down the framework of a code, and only a code could arrest the aggrandizing movement of social–patriarchal power. The test of the secularity of the Constitution was its willingness to impartially circumscribe the reach of religion-in-practice, replacing the varied customs with the uniformity of rational codes in the interest of women.

B. R. Ambedkar and the women members were collaborators in this project of secularization. In some statements, Ambedkar spoke in the women's voice:

> I personally do not understand why religion should be given this vast, expansive jurisdiction so as to cover the whole of life and to prevent the legislature from encroaching upon that field. After all what are we having this liberty for?[189]

This liberty, according to Ambedkar, was to 'reform our social system which is so full of inequities, so full of inequalities, discriminations and other things, which conflict with our fundamental rights'.[190] Ambedkar thought it natural for the Constitution to strive hereafter to limit the definition of religion to the essentially religious.

In the sanctioned history of the framing, Ambedkar's remarks about the jurisdiction of religion constitute the authorial intention of 'the founding fathers'. This version is oblivious to the fact that these remarks belonged to a political discourse first initiated in the Constituent Assembly by its women framers who were the keenest to seek restriction of religion to private rituals of worship. Ambedkar's remarks were an extension of what women had said in the Fundamental Rights Sub-Committee. The women said that the free practice of religion 'might invalidate legislation against anti-social customs which have the sanction of religion'.[191] Kaur and Mehta were the first members of the Constituent Assembly who objected, both verbally and in written notes of dissent, to a comprehensive guarantee of the freedom of religion. Allowing religions to have an unrestricted domain, Ambedkar argued, would 'disable the legislatures in India from enacting any social measures whatsoever'.[192] He was echoing, if not building upon an insight about the mutual incompatibility of social laws and fundamental rights that was originally introduced in the framing process by the women members.[193]

This authorial partnership and discursive enterprise, which is at the heart of the foundational moment is consumed within the historiographical space dominated by the overarching figure of the founding father. Ambedkar's key presence in the drafting and moving of the Hindu Code Bill is well documented and rightly so, but in discussions on the question of personal law and delimiting of religion in the Constituent Assembly, he seems to have become the sole agent, subsuming the performance of women members. In his biography of Ambedkar, Christophe Jaffrelot mentions Ambedkar's 'determination to reform Indian society' and regrets that Ambedkar 'obtained nothing more than an article of the Directive Principles'.[194] Such a reading forecloses the possibility of inscribing a joint authorship and collaboration between women and men in the framing of the Constitution. It reinforces the assimilating trope of men as founders and misses the entire narrative of women's contribution.

The anxieties over the 'feminist denial'[195] of Ambedkar's contribution and the recently felt need to reclaim 'the significance of Ambedkar's writings for the feminist discourse'[196] must be complemented with an open-hearted acknowledgement of the interrelationship of Ambedkar's emancipatory politics and women's project of social justice. The nuances of the framing process and its gender politics do not allow for any blanket separation of women's issues and women's voices from men's interventions and other general issues. Retrieving women's voices in the heterogeneous space of the Constituent Assembly, returns us to a moment of foundation also marked by episodes of strategic collaboration, mutual nurturing, and intersectional alliances. This, not surprisingly, is the moment when the 'woman question' is pushed to its most radical implications, as will be discussed in the following chapter.

NOTES

1. Speech delivered by Amrit Kaur in Shimla in 1945, in Amrit Kaur, *Challenge to Women* (Allahabad: New Literature, 1946), 148.
2. B. R. Ambedkar, while presenting the Draft Constitution on the floor of the Constituent Assembly, 4 November 1948, *CAD*, VII: 38.
3. Aizaz Rasul, Constituent Assembly of India, 8 November 1948, *CAD*, VII: 105.
4. B. R. Ambedkar, Constituent Assembly of India, 4 November 1948, *CAD*, VII: 38.
5. Ibid.
6. Durgabai, herself a prominent lawyer, took great interest in and contributed significantly to the debates on what became articles 133 and 134 of the Constitution. These articles define the appellate jurisdiction of the Supreme Court. *CAD*, VIII: 619–634.

7. Article 32 of the Constitution of India.
8. G. Durgabai, Constituent Assembly of India, 9 December 1948, *CAD*, VII: 937.
9. Ibid.
10. Ammu Swaminathan, Constituent Assembly of India, 24 November 1949, *CAD*, XI: 914.
11. G. Durgabai, Constituent Assembly of India, 24 November 1949, *CAD*, XI: 886–888.
12. Aizaz Rasul, Constituent Assembly of India, 22 November 1949, *CAD*, XI: 774.
13. Amrit Kaur, 'Women's Civic Responsibilities', in *Challenge to Women* (New Literature: Allahabad, 1946), 53–54.
14. Ibid., 52.
15. Ibid., 53.
16. Renuka Ray, 'Report of the Leader of the Team of Social Work', Planning Commission, Renuka Ray Papers, Subject File no. 13, NMML.
17. Ibid.
18. Fifth Amendment, the United States Constitution. The Fundamental Rights Sub-Committee used the same words in the same order in its Draft Reports of 3 April 1947 and 16 April 1947. Draft Report of the Sub-Committee on Fundamental Rights, 3 April 1947, in B. Shiva Rao (ed.), *The Framing of India's Constitution: Select Documents*, Vol. 2 (Delhi: Universal Law Publishing, 2004; originally The Indian Institute of Public Administration, 1967), 137–143, 139; Report of the Sub-Committee on Fundamental Rights, 16 April 1947, in Rao, *The Framing of India's Constitution*, Vol. 2, 169–176, 173.
19. Clauses on Fundamental Rights as Adopted by the Constituent Assembly on the basis of the Report of the Advisory Committee, April–May 1947, in Rao, *The Framing of India's Constitution*, Vol. 2, 300–303.
20. Ibid., 303.
21. T. R. Andhyarujina, 'The Evolution of Due Process of Law by the Supreme Court', in B. N. Kirpal, Ashok H. Desai, Gopal Subramanium, Rajeev Dhavan, and Raju Ramchandran (eds), *Supreme but Not Infallible: Essays in Honour of the Supreme Court of India*, 193–213 (New Delhi: Oxford University Press, 2000), 196.
22. Granville Austin, *The Indian Constitution: Cornerstone of a Nation*, 2nd ed. (New Delhi: Oxford University Press, 1999), 104.
23. B. R. Ambedkar, 13 December 1948, *CAD*, VII: 999.
24. Ibid.,1000.
25. Ibid. (emphasis mine).

26. Ibid., 1000–1001.

27. B. R. Ambedkar, Constituent Assembly of India, 15 September 1949, *CAD*, IX: 1499.

28. Thakur Das Bhargava, Constituent Assembly of India, 15 September 1949, *CAD*, IX: 1506.

29. Ibid., 1503.

30. Purnima Banerji, Constituent Assembly of India, 15 September 1949, *CAD*, IX: 1512.

31. Ibid., 1513.

32. Ibid., 1512.

33. Hansa Mehta, *Civil Liberties* (Aundh: Aundh Publishing Trust for All India Women's Conference, 1945), 11.

34. Ibid., 15.

35. Ibid.

36. Purnima Banerji, Constituent Assembly of India, 15 September 1949, *CAD*, IX: 1512.

37. B. R. Ambedkar, Constituent Assembly of India, 16 September 1949, *CAD*, IX: 1565.

38. Thakur Das Bhargava, Constituent Assembly of India, 15 September 1949, *CAD*, IX: 1508.

39. Ibid., 1502.

40. G. Durgabai, Constituent Assembly of India. 16 September 1949, *CAD*, IX: 1557.

41. Ibid.

42. Ibid.

43. Ibid., 1558.

44. Ibid.

45. Ibid., 1556.

46. Copy of the Original Resolution of the Karachi Congress on Fundamental Rights and Economic Changes with suggestions on individual clauses. All India Congress Committee Papers, File 84/1931. The recommendations for free military education had come from the Provincial Congress Committee, Ajmer and a few individuals.

47. Jawaharlal Nehru, *The Discovery of India* (New Delhi: Penguin, 2010; originally 1946). 442–443.

48. K. T. Shah, 'Preliminary Notes on Fundamental Rights', 23 December 1946, in Rao, *The Framing of India's Constitution*, Vol. 2: 36–55, 45–46.

49. Ibid.

50. Ibid., 52.

51. K. T. Shah (ed.), *Report of the Sub-Committee on General Education and Technical Education and Development Research* (Bombay: Vora & Company, 1948), 87 (emphasis mine). The Sub-Committee, headed by S. Radhakrishnan, had submitted its resolutions in June 1940.

52. K. M. Munshi, 'Note and Draft Articles on Fundamental Rights', 17 March, 1947, in Rao, *The Framing of India's Constitution*, Vol. 2, 69–80, 80.

53. Ibid., 77.

54. Proceedings of the Sub-Committee on Fundamental Rights, 27 March, 1947, in Rao, *The Framing of India's Constitution*, Vol. 2, 124–127, 125.

55. Minutes of the Meeting of the Sub-Committee on Fundamental Rights, 28 March 1947, in Rao, *The Framing of India's Constitution*, Vol. 2, 128.

56. Ibid., 126–127.

57. Article 15, Draft Report of the Sub-Committee on Fundamental Rights, 3 April 1947, in Rao, *The Framing of India's Constitution*, Vol. 2, 137–143, 140; Report of the Sub-Committee on Fundamental Rights, 16 April 1947, 173.

58. B. R. Ambedkar, 'Memorandum and Draft Articles on the Rights of States and Minorities', 24 March 1947, in Rao, *The Framing of India's Constitution*, Vol. 2, 84–114, 87.

59. B. R. Ambedkar, Note of Dissent to the Report of the Sub-Committee on Fundamental Rights, Rajendra Prasad Papers, 1-F/47, National Archives of India, also printed in Rao, *The Framing of India's Constitution*, Vol. 2, 183.

60. Rita J. Simon and Mohamed Alaa Abdel-Moneim, *A Handbook of Military Conscription and Composition the World Over* (New York: Lexington Books, 2011), 174.

61. Hansa Mehta to His Excellency the Commander-in-Chief, 11 January 1946, Hansa Mehta Papers, Subject File no. 7, NMML.

62. Hansa Mehta's handwritten report on the Commonwealth Parliamentary Conference on 15 October 1948, Hansa Mehta Papers, II Instalment, Writings/Speeches by Her, File no. 22, NMML.

63. Kulsum Sayani, General Secretary, AIWC to Mrs Pethick Lawrence, 5 November 1946, AIWC Papers, File no. 1566, 23, NMML.

64. Renuka Ray, 4 March 1949, Constituent Assembly (Legislative) of India, *CA(L)D*, II (II): 1081.

65. This was based on the report of a seven-member ad hoc committee comprising Ambedkar, Munshi, Alladi Krishnaswami Iyer, and other legal luminaries in the Advisory Committee. Report of the ad hoc Committee, Annexure to the Interim Report of the Advisory Committee, 1 May 1947, in Rao, *The Framing of India's Constitution*, Vol. 2, 299.

66. Renuka Ray, 'Planning and the Congress Election Manifesto', *The People*, 11 August 1951, Renuka Ray Papers, Speeches/Writings by Her, File no. 15, NMML.

67. Proceedings of the Sub-Committee on Fundamental Rights, 28 March 1947, in Rao, *The Framing of India's Constitution*, Vol. 2, 127–129, 128.

68. Amrit Kaur to B. N. Rau, 31 March 1947, in Rao, *The Framing of India's Constitution*, Vol. 2, 147.

69. Amrit Kaur and Hansa Mehta, Minute of Dissent to the Report of the Sub-Committee on Fundamental Rights, 17–20 April 1947, in Rao, *The Framing of India's Constitution*, Vol. 2, 178.

70. Amrit Kaur, Proceedings of the Advisory Committee, 21 April 1947, in Rao, *The Framing of India's Constitution*, Vol. 2, 213–289, 256.

71. Interventions by Renuka Ray, Constituent Assembly Debates, 3 December 1948, *CAD*, VII: 810. Also the speech by Durgabai on the same day, 3 December 1948, *CAD*, VII: 808.

72. H. V. Kamath, 3 December 1948, *CAD*, VII: 807.

73. Article 37, Constitution of India.

74. Amrit Kaur to B. N. Rau, 31 March 1947, 147.

75. Draft Report of the Sub-Committee on Fundamental Rights, 3 April 1947, 142.

76. Report of the Sub-Committee on Fundamental Rights, 16 April 1947, 175.

77. Draft Constitution Prepared by the Drafting Committee, 21 February 1948, in Rao, *The Framing of India's Constitution*, Vol. 3, 509–677, 527.

78. K. T. Shah, Constituent Assembly of India, 19 November 1948, *CAD*, VII: 479.

79. *His Holiness Kesavananda Bharati Sripadagalavaru v. State of Kerala*, (1973) Supp. 1 SCR.

80. S. P. Sathe, 'India: From Positivism to Structuralism', in Jeffrey Goldsworthy (ed.), *Interpreting Constitutions: A Comparative Study*, 215–265 (New Delhi: Oxford University Press, 2006), 252–253.

81. *Minerva Mills Ltd. v. Union of India*, (1981) 1 SCR 255 B-D.

82. Ibid., 325.

83. Ibid., 327–328.

84. Ibid.

85. Ibid., 220.

86. Sardar Hukam Singh, Constituent Assembly of India, 21 November 1949, *CAD*, XI: 751.

87. K. T. Shah, Constituent Assembly of India, 17 November 1949, *CAD*, XI: 620.

88. Ibid.

89. Renuka Ray, Constituent Assembly of India, 19 November 1949, *CAD*, XI: 716.

90. B. R. Ambedkar, Constituent Assembly of India, 4 November 1948, *CAD*, VII: 41.

91. Ibid.

92. Ibid.

93. G. Durgabai, Constituent Assembly of India, 3 September 1949, *CAD*, IX: 934.

94. G. Durgabai, Constituent Assembly of India, 24 November 1949, citing Kautilya's *Artha Shastra*, II: 1: 26, *CAD*, XI: 888.

95. Ibid.

96. In his acclaimed commentary on the *Artha Shastra*, R. P. Kangle reads these verses as invoking the 'idea of a "welfare state"' but with a rider that 'the idea of a welfare state of today is evidently bound up with industrialism and its attendant evils'. R. P. Kangle, *The Kautiliya Arthasastra*, 3 vols (New Delhi: Motilal Banarasidas, 1969), Vol. 3, 119.

97. O. Chinnappa Reddy, *The Court and the Constitution of India: Summits and Shallows* (New Delhi: Oxford University Press, 2008), 76.

98. *State of Madras* v. *Champakam Dorairajan*, (1951) SCR 525.

99. *I. C. Golaknath* v. *State of Punjab*, (1967) 2 SCR 762.

100. Niraja Gopal Jayal, *Citizenship and Its Discontents: An Indian History* (Ranikhet: Permanent Black, 2013), 153.

101. Christophe Jaffrelot, *Dr Ambedkar and Untouchability: Analysing and Fighting Caste* (Ranikhet: Permanent Black, 2005), 112.

102. Austin, *The Indian Constitution*, 50–51.

103. Isaiah Berlin, 'Two Concepts of Liberty', in Isaiah Berlin, *Liberty: Incorporating Four Essays on Liberty*, ed. Henry Hardy, 166–217 (Oxford: Oxford University Press, 2002; originally 1958), 178.

104. Ibid.

105. Jawaharlal Nehru, cited by Chinnappa Reddy, *The Court and the Constitution of India*, 74–75.

106. Kaur, *Challenge to Women*, 148.

107. *Kesavananda Bharati*, 828–829.

108. Purnima Banerji, Constituent Assembly of India, 10 September 1949, *CAD*, IX: 1240.

109. Purnima Banerji, Constituent Assembly of India, 24 November 1949, *CAD*, XI: 880.

110. Ibid.

111. Ibid., 879.

112. Ibid., 880.

113. Ibid., 879.

114. Austin, *The Indian Constitution*, 51.

115. *Kesavananda Bharati*, 343.

116. B. R. Ambedkar, Constituent Assembly of India. 25 November 1949, *CAD*, XI: 979.

117. M. Ananthasayanam Ayyangar, Constituent Assembly of India, 18 November 1949, *CAD*, XI: 661.
118. Shibban Lal Saxena, Constituent Assembly of India, 19 November 1949, *CAD*, XI: 706.
119. Ibid.
120. Renuka Ray, Constituent Assembly of India, 19 November 1949, *CAD*, XI: 716.
121. Ibid.
122. Purnima Banerji, Constituent Assembly of India, 10 September 1949, *CAD*, XI: 1240.
123. Ibid.
124. Ibid.
125. *Olga Tellis & Others* v. *Bombay Municipal Corporation & Others*, (1985) Supp. 2 SCR 80.
126. Ibid., 83.
127. Article 38 (1) of the Constitution of India reads: 'The State shall strive to promote the welfare of the people by securing and protecting as effectively as it may a social order in which justice, social, economic and political, shall inform *all the institutions of the national life*' (emphasis mine).
128. M. P. Jain, *Constitutional Law of India*, 6th ed. (Nagpur: LexisNexis Butterworths Wadhwa, 2010), 1225.
129. Ibid., 1492.
130. Renuka Ray, *My Reminiscences: Social Development during Gandhian Era and After* (Kolkata: Stree, 2005), 138.
131. Aizaz Rasul, Constituent Assembly of India, 22 November 1949, *CAD*, XI: 774.
132. Amrit Kaur to B. N. Rau, 31 March 1947, in Rao, *The Framing of India's Constitution*, Vol. 2, 146–147.
133. Amrit Kaur's Note of Dissent regarding the 'Freedom of Religion' clause, 20 April 1947, Rao, *The Framing of India's Constitution*, Vol 2, 212–213.
134. Ayyar, 'Note to the Constitutional Advisor', 4 April 1947, in Rao, *The Framing of India's Constitution*, Vol. 2, 143
135. Proceedings of the Minorities Sub-Committee, 18 April 1947, in Rao, *The Framing of India's Constitution*, Vol 2, 205.
136. B. R. Ambedkar, Constituent Assembly of India, 2 December 1948, *CAD*, VII: 781.
137. Amrit Kaur's Note of Dissent regarding the 'Freedom of Religion' clause, 213.
138. Ibid.

139. Hansa Mehta, Constituent Assembly of India, 22 November 1949, *CAD*, XI: 796.

140. Ibid. (emphasis mine).

141. *Indian Young Lawyers Association* v. *The State of Kerala*, Writ Petition (Civil) no. 373 of 2006.

142. Ibid., para 13.11.

143. Amrit Kaur's Note of Dissent regarding the 'Freedom of Religion' clause, 213.

144. Article 25 (1) of the Constitution states: '... all persons are equally entitled to freedom of conscience and the right to freely profess, practice and propagate religion'. The Preamble talks about securing the liberty of 'thought, expression, belief, faith and worship'.

145. Ammu Swaminathan, Constituent Assembly of India, 24 November 1949, *CAD*, XI: 914.

146. See, for example, *Report of the Committee on the Differentiation of Curricula for Boys and Girls*, 1954, and the *Report of the National Committee on Women's Education*, 1959, committees chaired by Hansa Mehta and G. Durgabai, respectively.

147. Kaur, *Challenge to Women*, 27. Kaur believed that a rational and fair code would gradually wean people away from the restrictive regimes of their religious or customary law. I discuss the implications of this insight in the section on Hindu Law and the uniform civil code in Chapter 6.

148. Purnima Banerji, Constituent Assembly of India, 30 August 1947, *CAD*, V: 350.

149. Ibid.

150. Raghavan N. Iyer, *The Moral and Political Thought of Mahatma Gandhi* (New Delhi: Oxford University Press, 2000), 245.

151. Minute of Dissent by Amrit Kaur, Hansa Mehta, and M. R. Masani, 17 April 1947 in Rao, *The Framing of India's Constitution*, Vol. 2, 178.

152. Mahatma Gandhi, *Harijan*, February 1940, cited in Iyer, *The Moral and Political Thought of Mahatma Gandhi*, 42.

153. Renuka Ray, Constituent Assembly of India, 30 August 1947, *CAD*, V: 351.

154. Kaur, *Challenge to Women*, 152.

155. Ibid., 152–153.

156. Mahatma Gandhi, *Hind Swaraj and Other Writings,* ed. Anthony J. Parel (New Delhi: Cambridge University Press, 1997), 105.

157. Renuka Ray, Constituent Assembly of India, 7 December 1948, *CAD*, VII: 878.

158. Ibid.

159. B. R. Ambedkar, Constituent Assembly of India, 2 December 1948, *CAD*, VII: 781.

160. The phrase in the Constitution is 'a uniform civil code', all in small letters. It has been reified in public discourse as the 'UCC' creating an impression that the original phrase is 'Uniform Civil Code'. I discuss this in Chapter 6.

161. Hansa Mehta, Constituent Assembly of India, 22 November 1946, *CAD*, XI: 796

162. Kaur, *Challenge to Women*, 152.

163. Ibid., 109.

164. Ibid., 141.

165. Aizaz Rasul, Constituent Assembly of India. 22 November 1948, *CAD*, XI: 774.

166. Steven Ian Wilkinson, 'India, Consociational Theory, and Ethnic Violence', in Sanjib Baruah (ed.), *Ethnonationalism in India: A Reader*, 431–457 (New Delhi: Oxford University Press, 2010), 441.

167. Ibid., 442.

168. Rochana Bajpai, *Debating Difference: Group Rights and Liberal Democracy in India* (New Delhi: Oxford University Press, 2011), 54.

169. Aizaz Rasul, Constituent Assembly of India, 22 November 1948, *CAD*, XI: 774.

170. Ibid., 775.

171. Ibid.

172. B. R. Ambedkar, Constituent Assembly of India, 4 November 1948, *CAD*, II: 39.

173. Ibid.

174. Ibid.

175. Ibid.

176. Aizaz Rasul, *From Purdah to Parliament* (New Delhi: Ajanta, 2001), 129–135, 223–224.

177. Ibid., 132.

178. Sunil Khilnani, *The Idea of India* (New Delhi: Penguin, 1997), 33.

179. Hansa Mehta, Constituent Assembly of India, 22 November 1949, *CAD*, XI: 796.

180. Lokenath Mishra, Constituent Assembly of India, 22 November 1949, *CAD*, XI: 797.

181. Ibid. 798.

182. Kailash Nath Katju to Renuka Ray, 7 June 1949. Renuka Ray Papers, Correspondence, NMML.

183. Hansa Mehta, Constituent Assembly of India, 22 November 1949, *CAD*, XI: 796.

184. Renuka Ray, 'Women's Movement in India', unpublished manuscript, Renuka Ray Papers, *Speeches/Writings by Her*, Subject File no. 88, NMML.

185. Ibid., 5.
186. Ibid.
187. B. R. Ambedkar, Speech in the Constituent Assembly (Legislative), 24 February 1949, reprinted in *Dr. Babasaheb Ambedkar: Writings and Speeches* (Mumbai: Govt. of Maharashtra, 1982–2003), Vol. 14, part 1, 272.
188. Ray, 'Women's Movement in India', 3.
189. B. R. Ambedkar, Constituent Assembly of India, 2 December 1948, *CAD*, VII: 781.
190. Ibid.
191. Amrit Kaur's record of intervention during the proceedings of the Sub-Committee on Fundamental Rights, 26 March 1947, in Rao, *The Framing of India's Constitution*, Vol. 2, 121–124, 122.
192. B. R. Ambedkar, Constituent Assembly of India, 2 December 1948, *CAD*, VII: 781.
193. Amrit Kaur's remarks in the proceedings of the Fundamental Rights Sub-Committee, in Rao, *The Framing of India's Constitution*, Vol. 2, 122; Amrit Kaur's letter to B. N. Rau, Rao, *The Framing of India's Constitution*, Vol. 2, 146–147; Advisory Committee Proceedings of 21–22 April 1947, in Rao, *The Framing of India's Constitution*, Vol. 2, 210–292.
194. Jaffrelot, *Dr Ambedkar and Untouchability*, 115 (emphasis mine).
195. Sharmila, Rege, 'Introduction: Towards a Feminist Reclamation of Dr. B. R. Ramji Ambedkar', in Sharmila Rege (ed.), *Against the Madness of Manu: B. R. Ambedkar's Writings on Brahmanical Patriarchy* (New Delhi: Navayana, 2013), 13–56, 24.
196. Ibid., 53.

6

Reformulating the 'Woman Question'

Challenging Customs and Traditions

To be without a code is, in my opinion, to be without justice.
—Durgabai Deshmukh, *Constituent Assembly* (*Legislative*)
Debates, 1 March 1949

At the moment of its emergence in colonial India, the woman question 'was identified with a reified notion of culture that cast it narrowly as a "social problem", and hence as the object of "social reform"'.[1] Imperialist reformers used the woman question to counteract the force of 'indigenous demands for political reform' – pitting home against the public sphere. The nationalist patriarchal solution, which, according to Partha Chatterjee, emerged sometime around the end of the nineteenth century, resolved it by separating the two spheres of the home and the world.[2] It was in the 'home', intimately contiguous with the 'inner' or 'spiritual' spheres of the nation that women were deigned to be located.[3] It is evident that in both these approaches, the imperialist and the nationalist, the woman question was of subsidiary and instrumental interest to the agents of the discourse. At best it was an effect, a by-product of a larger re-imagining of the social world undergoing a transition towards modernity. These were representational discourses in which women had no significant roles to play, but were already constituted as fixed subjects, attributed with a given identity.

With the emergence of the women's movement in the twentieth century and the constitutional politics associated with it, these discourses were transformed into conflicts over the representation of women. Rather than remaining passive recipients of the identity imposed on them, women, among them our constitutional framers, staked claims to their self-definition, and determined the terms in which the woman question was raised. They did 'unusual things': 'banding together, writing and petitioning for better health and childcare facilities, female education and maternal benefits, improved marriage and inheritance laws, suffrage'.[4] They campaigned nationally and internationally for equal labour rights, for recognition of the economic value of domestic work, extended their demands to constitutional rights, envisioned a central role for women in a planned economy, and created a constituency of their own. In other words, women radicalized the content of the woman question. They defined it in their own terms.

To return to Chatterjee's template:

> A renewal of the struggle for equality and freedom of women must, as with all democratic issues in countries like India, imply a struggle against the humanistic construct of 'rights' set up in Europe in the post-Enlightenment era and include within it a struggle against the false essentialisms of home/world, spiritual/ material, feminine/masculine propagated by the nationalist ideology.[5]

The question that the historian of the Indian Constitution must ask is whether these binaries were deconstructed or reinforced in the framing process, and what role women played in either of the cases. These binaries provide us with a template for a gendered reading of the debates and the other interventions in the Assembly. Rather than delimiting the discourse to rigid binaries, the formulation of this dichotomous series opens up the dialogic, textual world of the Constituent Assembly to more nuanced investigation. The hegemonic pattern of the nationalist discourse that Chatterjee characterizes in the series of binaries does not reduce the discursive field of framing into two planes. Instead, it opens up for investigation all gestures, speeches, interventions, advocacies, and dissents in the Assembly as moving between the two ends of the pairs. The force and the implications of these acts can thus be exposed as not merely historical but textual and gendered.

Apparently innocent acts like the dedication of the national flag by the women of India in the Constituent Assembly or singing of the national anthem by a chorus of women framers, therefore, cease to be innocent or neutral. These signs are not to be read as positive evidence of women playing into a resolved equation of gendered function but as steps towards the political normalization of their performance as mothers of the Constitution. Or was it, on the part of women, a collective strategy to conform to some norms so that others could be challenged? Within the wider play of meanings, they assumed a singularly political role that shrewdly subverted the gendered assumptions operating behind the framing. On the surface, women portrayed themselves as performing the outer function assigned to them by the nationalist patriarchy, staging – externally, of course – a conservative programme, but at the level of the actual framing, this staging created a condition for women to trespass into the 'masculine' territory of constitutional framing.

Women's audacious presence in the Constituent Assembly, framing the ultimate law of the nation, can be read as a powerful counter to any attempt at designating separate spheres, relegating them to the 'inner' private domain. Several instances of women members' dedicated efforts to extend the fundamental propositions of the Constitution emerged during the framing process. The most important of these instances, whose implications still reverberate in our social and political lives, was their direct engagement with the reforms in personal laws. The issue has gained perplexing complexity, with the 'Uniform Civil Code' or UCC producing a heavy discursive chapter in modern Indian history.

The Constitution seldom uses block letters anywhere in its text, including the chapters on the fundamental rights and directive principles. Article 44 of the Constitution says, 'The State shall endeavour to secure for the citizens a uniform civil code throughout the territory of India'.[6] Women framers, as we have seen, insisted that this article be placed in the chapter on fundamental rights which were justiciable. In her final speech in the Constituent Assembly, Hansa Mehta reminded the house of the civil code, claiming that it was more important than the national language. The most crucial, but completely overlooked dimension of women's demand for reforms in personal law was their persistent use of the term common or national for the proposed code. Mehta's speech cited above referred to a common civil code which had to be so progressive that it could be acceptable to all. For the code to be national it needed an acceptability that flowed not from the authority of the laws but from a common rationale, whose foundations were laid down in the Constitution. I would like to argue that this rationale was best expressed in the constitutional ideals of equality and non-discrimination.

ARGUING FOR A COMMON CODE: A PLEA FOR GENDER JUSTICE

Ten years before the Constituent Assembly met, Amrit Kaur had spoken of the demand for a common, though optional, code of civil laws in terms of 'an Act embodying equitable laws of marriage, inheritance, property'.[7]

She hoped that the ideal, by which she evidently meant the ideal of equitability, 'if successful in its working, is certain to be universally accepted'. This code of law, 'if it worked *fairly* for both men and women' she asserted in a later comment, 'would become increasingly popular and would in time supersede all codes'.[8] These references correct the inaccurate perception that 'the idea of a UCC was introduced into the national political debate in 1940 when a demand for such a code was made by the National Planning Committee appointed by the Congress'.[9] It is also clear that the demand for the common code was initiated by the founding mothers in pursuit of equality between men and women.

The superiority of the proposed code was guaranteed by its fundamental principle of fairness, which women thought would lead to its acceptability. This was the point Mehta made during her final speech: 'It must, however, be remembered that the Civil Code that *we* wish to have must be on a par with, or in advance of, the most progressive of the personal laws in the country. Otherwise, it will be a retrograde step and it will *not* be acceptable to *all*.'[10] In saying so, she affirmed her long-standing conviction that personal laws had to framed on rational principles built on a recognition of equality. In 1928, 10 years before Amrit Kaur made her demand for an equitable code of personal laws, Mehta was already thinking of a rational basis for such a code. Responding to the proposed Child Marriage Restraint Bill of the Government of Bombay, she cautioned that

> a complete legal definition of marriage from a rational social standpoint could not fittingly be inserted in a casual manner in a section on Definition… The nature, incidents and consequences of marriage at law must be defined on the basis and ideal of a strictly monogamous, but mutually equal contract.[11]

Read together, the demand for a 'rational social standpoint' that informs a 'mutually equal contract' and the hope that a fair code would eventually be acceptable to all, point to a conviction in an eventual secularization of society.

That there was no coercion involved in such a conviction is also evident from the willingness to let such a code be optional until it becomes possible for it to supersede other systems in *popularity*, as Amrit Kaur said in 1937. Amrit Kaur was possibly referring to the mode in which the Shariat Act of 1937 had been implemented. The Muslim Personal Law (Shariat) Application Act, 1937 provided that any person may by declaration state that 'he desires to obtain the benefit of this Act….'[12] A decade later during the debates on the uniform civil code on the floor of the Constituent Assembly, Ambedkar made a similar point:

It is perfectly possible that the future Parliament may make a provision by way of making a beginning that the Code shall apply only to those who make a declaration that they are prepared to be bound by it, so that in the initial stage the application of the Code may be purely voluntary. Parliament may feel the ground by some such method.... It would be perfectly possible for Parliament to introduce a provision of that sort; so that the fear which my friends have expressed here will be altogether nullified.[13]

Ambedkar, of course, was referring to the fears expressed by the minority Muslim members of the Assembly in a post-Partition state and was proposing the need to test the ground, that is, the willingness of members of religious communities to adopt the code. For the women members, however, this willingness was to be created by convincing the citizens of the justness and rationality of the code, its core element being equality between men and women. The fine point of political rationality that is missed under the burden of the stress on the term Uniform with a capital U (which is not the case anywhere in the Constitution or the debates around its framing), is the full import of the phrase 'acceptable to all'. This stress misleads us into thinking that the constituency of the 'uniformity' is all religious communities governed by their respective personal laws. A historicized reading instead would stress on the uniformity of principles which could be codified for rational individuals and not just members of communities.

This elision has produced a gross imbalance in the discourse around the uniform civil code which could be corrected by attending to the historicity of the framing of the Constitution. I would like to argue that when Mehta speaks on behalf of women – 'the civil code that we wish to have' – she refers to women's long-cherished demand for a fair code of laws that govern marriage and inheritance, and any law that fails to meet that criteria of constitutionally guaranteed fairness will not be acceptable to *all* men and *women*. One of the most precisely worded articles of the Constitution,[14] it affirms as much: 'the State shall endeavour to secure for the citizens a uniform civil code throughout the territory of India.' Article 44 of the Indian Constitution was worded not as a compromise between patriarchal religious communities but as the enunciation of women's own voice as citizens securing justice for themselves. Women's negotiation with religious communities took place in the debates on the Hindu Code Bill, to which we shall now turn.

WOMEN MEMBERS AND THE HINDU CODE BILL

On 9 and 10 October 1943, Hansa Mehta delivered two lectures at the Vanasthali Vidyapith on the question of women's rights in the Hindu laws of marriage and succession to property. These lectures contained her response to the Report of the Hindu Law Committee submitted four months earlier, on 19 June. But, addressed as they were to young female students, they were also meant to educate the audience about the motivations of the women's movement of which the speaker was a leading light. A year later, when they were published, Hansa Mehta added the following remarks as a preface to her lectures:

> Do we wish to continue with the rigidity of the caste system? *Do we wish to trace our ancestry to remote Rishis and continue the Gotra myth?* It would require persons with larger vision, persons who are students of sociology and not mere students of law to solve these and similar questions. Law must help and not hinder the social progress. This we can do by taking into consideration the needs of the changing times. It is on the understanding of the principles that we can improve, and not only the Hindu law but even evolve a common code that will bring all the communities of India into one fold.[15]

Her call was clearly for a redefinition of society and an invitation to look at it from the perspective of a rational individual – a sociologist, more interested in understanding the changing the dynamics of a society, not a conservative law-maker who bases his ideas on regressive myths that imagine the nation as a conglomerate of patriarchal kinships. She was generally supportive of the Hindu Law Committee which aspired to create a Code basing its law of succession on

> the ideas of Jaimini rather than of Baudhayana and its law of marriage on the best parts of the Code of Manu rather than those that fall short of the best; a Code that shall recognize that men and women are equal in status with appropriate obligations as well as rights; a Code, which, generally speaking, shall be a blend of the finest elements in the various Schools of Hindu Law....[16]

However, she minced no words in criticizing the Committee for not representing what she represented – 'the organized opinion of women'.[17] The Committee, she believed, 'merely patch(ed) up the Hindu Law here and there', and tried to 'reconcile the orthodox and the heterodox views'.[18] The common code that Hansa Mehta envisioned was not merely a synthesis of existing codes and customs but an invitation to subordinate the instrumentalities of law to the fundamental changes in society. For her young audience, she identified the women's movement as both, a symptom and an agent of these changes. It was born out of 'a keen desire to remove the social evils and free woman from her disabilities'.[19] Read in conjunction with her preface and later remarks, this desire seems to be one of the clearest articulations by her and her feminist comrades to contest Brahmanical patriarchy.

These articulations, grounded in the idea of the evolution of a common code, have often led scholars to miss the radical direction they had taken. The current discourse on the 'Uniform' civil code with its excessive communal and nationalist overtones has made the implications of the earlier engagement with a common code inaccessible to the present times. Yet I would like to argue that a careful reading of the archives of women's voice at the founding moment reveals that their thrust for the codification of Hindu law was driven by a strong desire to inscribe a sovereign female subject in the heart of a patriarchal discourse. Between 1945 and 1949, this female subject was projected as a gendered citizen whose agency, if denied, would be a failure of the Constitution. The feminist energy invested in this projection has seldom been recognized by scholars who have only seen the operation of the dominant tropes of levelling, compromises, and balancing acts during the Hindu Law controversies of the period. While it may be true that the reforms that were achieved at the end of this 15-year long legislative drive for codification were meagre and in many ways failed to bring in the female citizen imagined by the women framers, it is no less urgent to acknowledge the full force of subversion that this imagination contained. If there ever was a concentrated full-scale confrontation in modern Indian history between the fundamental principles of patriarchy and considered feminist attack on them, it was in the spectacle – intellectual and argumentative – of the founding mothers taking on powerful conservative men.

In her lectures, Mehta referred to the ongoing work of the Sub-Committee on Woman's Role in Planned Economy, of which she was an important member, and cited its resolution that in a planned economy:

(a) … woman's place should be equal to that of man. Equal status, equal opportunities, and equal responsibilities shall be the guiding principles to regulate the status of woman *whatever the basis of society* in the Plan; (b) Woman shall not be excluded from any sphere of work merely on the ground of her sex; (c) Marriage shall not be a condition precedent to the enjoyment of full and equal civic status and social and economic rights by woman; (d) The State shall consider *the Individual as the basic social unit* and plan accordingly.[20]

Mehta's lectures drew attention to the 'bills after bills' introduced by men and women who worked 'hard to bring about the social changes through legislation' in the face of hostile opposition by conservative forces and an indifferent colonial government.[21] She cited these bills as evidence of the vigour and intensity of a legislative politics of reform, whose radical agenda was set by the women's movement.

This agenda found its most succinct expression in Kamaladevi Chattopadhyay's written statement submitted before the Hindu Law Committee, as President of the All India Women's Conference (AIWC) in 1945. Reminding the Committee that the AIWC had been agitating for 'the last fifteen years' for 'the codification and reform of Hindu Law', Kamaladevi spoke of the same relationship between law and society as Hansa Mehta.[22] The 'modern conditions of life require *radical modification* of a law', she insisted, 'that was made to suit a different structure of society'.[23] The uniformity of law was not meant merely to create a single legal jurisdiction for the entire Hindu population or to blend the diverse schools of law but as 'a practical measure to suit the requirements of our times'.[24] The times required a radical reconfiguration of the economic structure of Indian society, keeping the individual woman at the centre, a woman whose economic independence and autonomy must begin with a recognition of her rights in the family. The 'uniform' code was a 'vital necessity' for all Hindus and could be complete only if it restructured women's inheritance rights and agricultural land rights with the same ideals.

STILL HARPING ON DAUGHTERS: THE QUESTION OF SUCCESSION

By keeping 'succession to agricultural property' out of their purview, Kamaladevi implied, the reforms were keeping intact the patriarchal structure of society.[25] In supporting 'the principle of the daughter's right to a share in the father's property and the same right to be given to the mother's "streedhan"' and 'the restoration of an absolute right of inheritance to women',[26] she envisaged society not very different from that imagined by the Sub-Committee on Woman's Role in Planned Economy. This Sub-Committee of the National Planning Committee set up in 1938 by the Indian National Congress, recommended in its report that in a planned economy 'every Hindu, man or woman, will be deemed to be the absolute owner of his or her property, *whatever be the nature* thereof, including any property he or she may inherit'.[27] The Sub-Committee's report and AIWC's demands for the uniform code aimed at a reconceptualization of women's status in the family – the demand for making the daughter a coparcener in agricultural property leading to a radical change in the entire kinship structure of the patriarchal Hindu family and its definition of property and ownership. This demand, not surprisingly, was too radical even for the socialist elements in the Congress who, while they called for nationalization of agricultural property and a system of land-ownership that promised land to the tiller, could not imagine giving agricultural land to the daughter.

The National Planning Committee's Sub-Committee on 'Land Policy, Agricultural Labour, and Insurance' whose terms of reference included 'the use and ownership of land, and their effects on cultivation and social stratification' and 'measures ... for agrarian reform, a view to bring about an equitable distribution of land resources, and their effective utilization for the maximum benefit of the country' did not even consider the question of women's inheritance to agricultural land.[28] The complete separation of the reforms in the personal law of inheritance and reforms in agricultural policy and land-redistribution presents a gendered and hierarchical binary at the very founding of the nation.

Further, as Eleanor Newbigin argues, the report of the Sub-Committee on Agriculture 'seemed to differentiate between women's work as necessary for agricultural development and men's "labour" which generated property rights in land'.[29] The resistance to women's demands for property rights was built on the zeal to protect the Hindu family as a natural site where this gendered hierarchy could be maintained and by extension, projected on the national self. Women's unpaid and unacknowledged labour on agricultural land and in the domestic sphere strengthened the justification for the refusal to grant women an absolute right in ancestral property.

The feminist project of reconstituting the nation, however, ran against the grain of such ideas by inserting the constitutional ideal of equality in the discourse on the one hand, and by presenting the woman as a citizen whose identity is not dependent on her marriage or belonging to a family, on the other. The former took the shape of demands for equality in property rights and the latter led to demands for making marriage laws more rational and flexible. In both cases, the woman was introduced as a gendered citizen towards whom the obligations of the state were to be redefined. The women's movement had made slow progress towards the recognition of women's absolute estate in property, from the concession given by the Rau Committee in 1943 when a daughter's absolute right was first granted though the share was limited to one-fourth that of the son, to the Bill presented by Ambedkar in April 1948 increasing this share to half that of the son. This was not enough, Hansa Mehta told Ambedkar during her speech following his introduction of the Bill since it did not abolish sex discrimination completely and did not agree with the principles of the Constitution:

... we feel that it does not go far enough. A daughter who is recognized an heir inherits the property, but she inherits half the share of the son. This violates the principle of equality on which we have again and again said that our new Constitution is going to be based – a Constitution which aims to secure for the people of this country justice social, political and economic. We therefore feel that the daughter should get an equal share in the property of her father with the son, and the son should also get an equal share in the property of his mother with the daughter. It is also argued that a daughter gets her share from her father as well as from her husband, while the man does not get anything from his wife.[30]

The reference to the Constitution was remarkable – it was yet not ratified by the Constituent Assembly – but its principles were evoked as a guide for a piece of legislation which had generated the most profound debates on the norms being set for the family. More importantly, the constitutional principles cited here may also be read as expanding the feminist concerns with the right of the daughter to dissolving the difference between the son and the daughter that was at the heart of the entire discussion. The celebrated affective bonds of the family were critiqued and employed for feminist purposes by all the women members of the Constituent Assembly. Replying to the suggestion that a daughter getting an equal share with the son may damage the bonds between brothers and sisters, Durgabai pointed to the material prejudices inherent in such relationships:

Also it is said that if the daughter takes away a share, the love of her brothers is lost. It is also said that sons in many families would simply be ruined under the double burden of marriage expenses and also a share to the daughter. May I ask what sort of affection it is of brothers if only it would involve putting a little more strain on their self-interest? *May I also ask if no share is given to the daughter the sons' love will be greater?* ... The daughter being of the same flesh and blood should there be so much uproar, I ask, if a share is sought to be given to her?[31]

The staggering opposition to women's share in property was also premised on the fear that this might lead to fragmentation of property and diminish it to a point where it becomes useless for property-holders. This, Durgabai indicated, should not be of much concern, for the Bill was already restricted to urban property and did not affect agricultural property for which, she suggested, separate laws could be made. Remarkably, while in Durgabai's understanding, a reformist code must apply the principles of equality of distribution among gendered constituencies for it to be 'uniform' and just, she was willing to make exceptions for agricultural property. She recommended that

In the interest of agriculture itself, if not for anything else, separate laws and special laws will be enacted by appropriate legislatures which may include a special law of succession which is quite different from the law of succession applying to other forms of property.[32]

Durgabai was no socialist, yet she commented on the need for a special law of succession for agricultural land, something that was eschewed by the National Planning Committee. As for the fragmentation of property, she suggested that it could be solved in several ways but could not be used as an argument against women's inheritance.

Hansa Mehta, however, took the more socialist route and recommended that 'there should be law against fragmentation and the property should be sold if it goes below the prescribed limit' or alternatively the state could take the route of 'collectivization of [such] property'.[33] What is important to remember about these debates is the level of consistency with which the women members of the Constituent Assembly confronted the prejudices of other members, questioning the patriarchal premises of their arguments on every occasion even at the risk of being subjected to sexist comments. They conceived the rights of the woman as non-negotiable and inserted a female citizen as an 'exemplary reader' of the Constitution, a recipient of its emancipatory benefits in the future to come. Social justice for this citizen was not to be subservient to any grand narrative of the nation. It required a larger, more comprehensive change brought in with the purpose of addressing the injustice Indian women had been suffering.

CHALLENGING PATRIARCHAL PRINCIPLES OF ADOPTION

Ambedkar presented the Hindu Code as Law Minister on 9 April 1948. He introduced two new provisions. The first made it imperative that 'the husband, if he wants to make an adoption [must] obtain the consent of his wife and if there are more than one, at least the consent of one of them'.[34] The second provision concerned adoption by a widow. According to the new Code, she could 'only adopt if there [we]re positive instructions left by the husband authorising her to adopt in order to prevent litigation.... The Code also provide[d] that the adoption may also be evidenced by registration.'[35]

After Ambedkar's speech, Hansa Mehta criticized the provisions regarding adoption and asked them to be scrapped:

With regard to adoption, 1 think the whole chapter should be scrapped. We are a secular State. We want to be a secular State. *Adoption in Hindu law is for religious purposes. Why should a secular State have anything to do with a religious custom?* What we are concerned with is whether adoption which is for religious purposes should be recognized by the State for purposes of inheritance. We say that it should not. If a child is adopted – whether it is a boy or a girl – *we would like a daughter also to be adopted* – if a child is adopted not for religious purpose but for real purpose, i.e., that the parents want a child, then that child should have the same rights as the natural child. *But if there is adoption for religious purposes, only then I think that adoption should not be recognized for purposes of inheritance.*[36]

What Hansa Mehta was disputing was the centrality of the son in the Hindu family structure.[37] The inequality in the positions of the daughter and the son in this context was a result of the role of the adopted son as a substitute for the natural son. 'As with all substitutes for the natural son', to refer to a contemporary authority on Hindu Law, 'the twin motives of having both a legal heir and a person to perform the ancestral rites prompted the practice of adoption'.[38] Hansa Mehta's objection was built on her recognition of this religious principle. The adoption of the male child was concerned with spiritual benefits in an after-life and hence discriminated against daughters. The moot point was that India was to be a secular state and could not have anything to do with adoption in Hindu Law, which was for religious purposes. In arguing that women would support the adoption of both boy and girl only if it was for a 'real purpose, i.e., that the parents want a child'[39] she was making two parallel moves: challenging the implied misogyny of Hindu Law that considered only the son as having spiritual worth, and arguing for the secularization of any practices related to the adoption of a successor.

While a detailed discussion of Ambedkar's Amended Bill presented in the Constituent Assembly (Legislative) on 12 August 1948 is not within the purview of this work, it may be noted that it did not address any of Hansa Mehta's concerns. Ambedkar's code clearly stated, 'No females shall be adopted by or to any male or female Hindu' (Image 6.1).[40] Mehta had asked for a radical redefinition of the Hindu family and demanded the abolition of its androcentric principles. The custom of adoption, she clearly saw, was built on the principle of transfer of spiritual benefits from the son to the father in the next life (afterlife) and of material benefits from the father to the son in this life. The entire exchange was informed by a narrative that allegorized the nation as a kinship whose citizens are related to each other as agnate, that is, 'related by blood or adoption wholly through males'.[41] Thus, while exceptions were made for sons of daughters, sisters' female children were kept

Image 6.1 Protecting the daughter. This much-discussed cartoon published in the
11 December 1949 issue of the *Shankar's Weekly* showing Ambedkar steering
the Hindu Code Bill under his anxious but paternal care through the hostile
corridors of history hardly gets the history right.

out of it entirely. Though some concession was made to the AIWC's demands
by introducing the figure of the consenting wife of the adoptive father, no
fundamental change was made to the androcentric religious principles
governing adoption laws. These were the concessions to religion that Hansa

Mehta and Amrit Kaur had expressed anxiety about during the discussion on the right the freedom of religion in the Fundamental Rights Sub-Committee. The feminist project of reform of Hindu Law was simultaneously a project of its secularization.

It is worth remembering that while the entire conservative section of the Constituent Assembly was anxious about the double burden that will fall on a family if its daughter were to get a share in the property of her natal family as well as in that of her husband, the provisions on adoption made it possible for the adoptive son to inherit shares in the property of both his natal and adoptive families.[42] Mehta's anxiety about a secular state endorsing a gender-unjust religious method of inheritance was not paid heed to. Women members had to wage a relentless battle against seasoned male political leaders and other male members of the Constituent Assembly who were at best paternalistic and at worst openly misogynist. However, following the nearly decade-long battle for reforms in Hindu Law, women leaders became more assertive and uncompromising. The Renuka Ray of 1943 was flexible, not so anymore.

TURNING THE GAZE TO THE FUTURE: WOMEN MEMBERS ARGUE AGAINST PATRIARCHAL CUSTOM

When Thakur Das Bhargava presented his bills proposing amendments to the Child Marriage Restraint Act, 1929, and termed these as measures to achieve a 'kind of social justice' that we should 'concede' to our 'girls', Renuka Ray was quick to notice the import of his terms.[43] Bhargava presented his arguments in masculinist–nationalist terms, speaking of girls not as citizens but as mothers of citizens:

> It is said that our labourer does not stand in comparison with the labourer of other countries. And our labourer is not paid well. Our professors, our legislators and all persons living in India are regarded as, in a measure, inferior to the nationals of other countries. Why? *Because many of us are children of child mothers.* When a girl gives birth to a child at the age of fifteen, certainly the child will not be so healthy as when the mother is, say, eighteen years of age.[44]

Renuka Ray supported Bhargava for having brought the amendments and spoke with congratulatory zeal about the new nation that members of the Constituent Assembly shared:

> It is quite true that if we can make the operation of the Child Marriage Restraint Act effective it will protect girls, and prevent many grievous abuses but at the

same time, the greatest measure of reform that it will bring about is that it will help towards bringing in a healthy, virile and a strong nation. Now that we are a free country we cannot afford any longer to ignore these basic factors which have gone against the health of the nation. It is from that angle that we have to primarily support this measure.[45]

Yet she did not restrain herself from telling him that the aspiration for having a 'virile and healthy nation', presumably of strong male citizens, is not the same thing as seeking social justice. She admonished him for being 'over-ambitious in using the words "social justice"' and clearly told him that although it can 'help to bring in a better and a healthier nation by not allowing women to become mothers at an age when they are not fit to be mothers, and prevent the maluse of young girls', it is not a Bill 'by which you can bring social justice to women'.[46] Social justice, for Renuka, had 'a wider context' and could be achieved by all 'measures of social reform which will bring in equality', the Hindu Code being one of them.[47] One can read in Renuka's admonition, advocacy for the Hindu Code as well as a desire to prevent feminist motives from being appropriated by other forces. This is a crucial feminist dimension of women's interventions that we must remember even when they seem to have agreed with a particular proposal, though for a different reason. The discursive space of the Constituent Assembly was rife with numerous matrices of speaking about women, and women members were often compelled to wrest their own ideas away from such interpretive situations that could potentially erase their feminist motives. Given the passion and political meaning with which the metaphor of the nation as family was invested, it was inevitable that the most dramatic of such battles took place during debates on property rights, inheritance, and marriage.

An important matrix of such debates was woven around the celebration of the past. During the debates on the Hindu Code Bill in the Constituent Assembly (Legislative), after a long speech by Pattabhi Sitaramaiyya extolling the virtues of the classical Hindu system of marriages and family, Hansa Mehta rebuked him for being obsessed with a past that had had its day. The two speeches provide us with a good illustration of how these positions were pitted against each other. Pattavi Sitaramaiyya defended child marriage as a pristine, pure, and glorious tradition:

I look upon child marriage as a splendid institution as our ancients conceived it because they conceived it good for the average man and the average woman to be married. And this marriage is a good thing because the child has to be grafted into another family and grafting should take place while the plant is young and not when the plant has become old.[48]

Responding to these sexist views of a seasoned patriarch, Hansa Mehta retorted that Indians had looked to the past for long and it was time that one looked to the future:

> It is for the future generation that we are making this law. It is not for us, but for the future generation that is coming after us that this law will be applied. We have to look to the future conditions. After all, it is the conditions that determine the law. The law reflects the society. The law reflects the conditions in which the people live. We have to see that the future generation is not fettered by our own prejudices with regard to marriage or divorce or with regard to any other ideas that we may have today.[49]

In this parallel performance in the Constituent Assembly (Legislative), these women were debating the Hindu Code Bill, etching in the annals of India's parliamentary records, the enduring voice of women every time they spoke in the first person collective pronoun. The unuttered 'the women of India' echoed in every single 'we' that they pronounced. This speech, for instance, teemed with sentences beginning with 'We' qualified occasionally to clarify that Mehta is speaking in the name of the women of India. Regarding the daughter's inheritance in the father's property, her statement began: '*We*, therefore feel, that the daughter should get an equal share....' On the husband's right to inherit his wife's property, she said, '*We* have already proposed, that is the Women's organizations have said that the husband can also inherit the property of his wife in the same way as the wife inherits the property of her husband'. Further, on monogamy, she stated, '*I* am gratified, and the women of India will be very happy to know, that the principle of monogamy is recognized ...', and on the age of marriage, '*we* would like the age of marriage also to be a valid condition of marriage'.[50]

Similar speeches by other women, most notably Renuka Ray and G. Durgabai, in the legislative sessions that took place parallel to those of the Constituent Assembly, represent Indian women's embodied voice in the founding moments of the republic. B. R. Ambedkar, always a sensitive listener to the critical voices in a debate, was among the first to hear Mehta speak for the women of India. He understood her to be saying that 'the women and particularly herself [Mehta] were not satisfied with some of the provisions ... relating to the rights of women'.[51] In his response to Mehta, Ambedkar stressed that the women of India 'must remember that the Hindu society is an inert society. The Hindu Society has always believed that law-making is the function either of God or the "Smriti" ... it has never accepted its own power and responsibility in moulding its social, economic and legal life.'[52] In a tone expressing solidarity with the women founders, he congratulated them for pushing Hindu society towards a radical shift and making it agree to let people frame their own laws:

> It is for the first time that we are persuading Hindu Society to take this big step and I have not the slightest doubt in my mind that a society which has bucked up courage enough to tolerate the large step that we are asking it to take by reason of this Bill, will not hesitate to march on the path that remains to be trodden and reach the goal that she has in mind.[53]

This was the clearest expression of how Ambedkar and the women members formed one legislative constituency, breaking into the long-preserved dominion of authorship, in order to produce radically unconventional texts presented as being 'in perfect consonance with the conscience of the community'.[54] The community, however, was not willing to allow these women and Ambedkar to trespass into the sacred territory of such law making.

REFUTATION AND RESISTANCE BY WOMEN ON GROUNDS OF EQUALITY

Women adhered to their own notion of equality, deriving from the Constitution, and, in the case of Sucheta Kripalani, referring even to the pledges of non-discrimination between the sexes, made in the Karachi Resolution.[55] If there were differences between men and women, between sons and daughters, women argued, it was not because of any natural law but because of the social structure. In what may be read as one of the first feminist arguments about the social construction of gender difference in Indian parliamentary discourse, Renuka Ray framed the difference between men and women as 'difference of status'.[56] A social structure that kept women uneducated and colonized their consciousness ensured that women remained inferior to men. Drawing an analogy between patriarchy (without naming it) as an ideological shackle that stunts the growth of consciousness, and colonialism that creates a pathological contentment in the colonized, she wrought an argument that calls for serious attention:

> ... it is well-known that slaves have resisted when shackles of their slavery were removed. It is a fact serfs have objected to freedom ... it was held by the British that it was only the wretched Congress agitators who wanted freedom but that

the mass of the people were quite willing to remain in the pathetic contentment of thraldom. If you speak today of pathetic contentment amongst the women, it is true, it is *perfectly* true that many women are not yet conscious.[57]

There are multiple implications of her argument. One, women were not naturally different or given to accept their roles and 'difference of status'. Considering that at the time she was speaking, 'the women who [we]re educated [we]re only about 3 to 4 percent',[58] it stands to reason that they were not conscious of their rights and true equality. Implicit in the dichotomy between educated and uneducated women was a conception of education that generated feminist consciousness, without which these women remained complicit in patriarchy. Two, she located herself and the other founding mothers in the same league as the Congress, as those men who claimed to be the legitimate law-givers, the constitution-makers, having broken the ideological chain in which colonial rule had bound the masses.

This strategic comparison between nationalism and feminism can be read as an exhortation to nationalist men to collaborate in their project of securing freedom for women at the founding moment. The demand for social freedom vis-à-vis caste, Sudipta Kaviraj has argued, was in conflict with the demand for national freedom. 'These two meanings of freedom' according to him, 'social freedom from caste domination and political freedom from colonial rule – remained in a state of potential conflict in Indian thinking of the twentieth century'.[59] Regarding gender, Renuka Ray's argument seemed to be imploring the framers to fuse these two struggles as one, emanating from the same desire for justice and equality. By evoking the master–slave dichotomy and locating it within the realm of the construction of consciousness, she raised the status of law-making to a higher level. Law, in this sense, had to break out of the hold of the 'Hindu' jurisprudential conceptualization of sexual difference that opponents were championing, and work towards the 'awakening' of a consciousness, the activating of a conception of equality that had hitherto been forgotten.

The constitutional principles were most effectively mobilized on behalf of women by Durgabai, whose uncompromising support to the daughter's share in the father's property, women's absolute estate in property, and monogamy was clearly articulated in terms of equality of the sexes. Any instance of compromise circumscribing the reach of equality was 'not or will not be acceptable to women'.[60] Durgabai argued that there could be no double standards on equality. It formed the basis of the freedom movement, and now that 'India has been pleading for human rights and also for equal treatment of

Indians in foreign countries', it would be 'a great misfortune' if it failed to apply the principle of equality of the sexes in the field of personal laws and did not enact the Hindu Code.[61] Having accepted the chapter on fundamental rights with its recognition of the principle of equality, there was an obligation to make an equitable code of personal laws for men and women. She concluded her speech by reminding the house of the constitutional provision 'enabling ourselves to have a uniform civil code'.[62]

The uniform civil code remained an important demand of these founding mothers after the Constitution was implemented, most of them regretting at various points in their later lives that the objective had not been achieved. At this point, however, it must be mentioned that for the women framers, the uniform civil code contained within its ambit two important dimensions of their moral imaginary: a common, national character, and the cardinal virtue of rationality. The code, Renuka Ray recollected, had two sources of origin: one, 'the diversity of the legal system prevailing in India and the disunity that arose from such diversity'[63] by which the framers of the Constitution were 'haunted', and two, the search for a 'rational system of common laws'.[64] The uniform code was offered as an answer to both these pursuits, as a kind of culmination of the series of social–legal reforms beginning with the Special Marriage Act of 1892, aimed at *inter alia* removing the legal disabilities of women and progressively giving legal articulation to the principle of equality that had been at the centre of the women's movement.

In Renuka Ray's recounting, the question of a national code was taken up as early as 1920–1921, but after the Indian Succession Act, when 'women's organizations grew stronger, the demand for a national code of social laws gathered momentum'.[65] As early as in 1928, Hansa Mehta demanded a legislative definition of marriage from a 'rational social standpoint' based on the 'ideal of a strictly monogamous, but mutually equal contract'.[66] The project of the uniform civil code was that of achieving a universalization of rationality in the field of social laws by merging the diversity of laws into conformity with each other. It was motivated, as evident from women's persistent interventions in the Hindu Law reforms, by 'a justifiable demand of women that legal disabilities in social laws be removed'.[67] The women founders' entire discourse on the common civil code was pervaded by the demand for equality. This common code, it was later remarked, was conditional upon an overall acceptance of equality between men and women: 'it is only when the personal laws of Christians and Muslims are changed to give equal position to men and women that we shall be able to finally enact a common code'.[68]

The nucleus of the common code existed not in any specific school or tradition but in the Indian Succession Act and the Special Marriage Act.[69] The project had to be truncated to the project of codifying Hindu Law in the face of such fierce opposition that, in the words of Renuka Ray, 'even so great a social reformer as Sir B. N. Rau advised us [the women's movement] that it would be better to enact legislation for the large majority of citizens, namely, the Hindus first'.[70] It was at B. N. Rau's advice that a bill for a national code was not introduced (presumably in the Central Assembly) and the emphasis was directed towards Hindu Law. The Hindu Law Bills were conceived as 'the fore-runner of a national code of social laws'.[71] The strategic order was formulated thus:

> it would be best to first reform the laws of each community bringing them into conformity with each other and seeing to it that the disabilities from which women under these laws suffered were removed, and as the Hindu community embraced the largest majority it would be better to deal with the Hindu Law first.[72]

While it is beyond the scope of this work to comment on the merits of the strategy and the successes and failures it met with, we can still arrive at some vital conclusions, which are quite different from the received understanding of the genesis and content of the 'UCC' debate. It is obvious from the discussions so far that the demand for universalization of social laws was brought up by the women's movement. It had a strong feminist motive and strove towards a rational code, which could accommodate all communities. This contradicts the conclusion that gender concerns were absent from the discourse of the Constituent Assembly.[73] Moreover, it was not a particular community's legal reform with any Brahmanical or upper-caste or North-Indian bias that grew into women's demand for a larger, national reform; it was a general project of reason and reform that took into account all contingencies of community life in India in order to achieve gender justice in the private sphere. In contrast with the codified Hindu laws of 1955 and 1956 that were arguably based on 'inegalitarian Victorian English patterns of marriage and inheritance and on the customary practices of some of the dominant communities in North-West India, among whom women's rights have been seriously eroded',[74] women's method of codification privileged gender equality at every step, borrowing from as many sources as necessary. For instance, Hansa Mehta, in agreement with the conceptualization of marriage as a mutual contract, presented examples of 'certain Shudra castes and even some Vaishya castes' that gave their members 'the right to divorce'.[75] Her caution to the Hindu Law Committee of 1941, to ensure that the rights of these communities must not be eroded may be read as an act of reverse Sanskritization, where practices of lower-caste communities were showcased as exemplary for a uniform code. Similarly, the two women members of the Select Committee of the Constituent Assembly (Legislative) on the Hindu Code 1948, Renuka Ray and Ammu Swaminathan, put a note of dissent to prevent the nullification of the matrilineal '*Marumakkattayam, Aliyasanatana*, and *Namboodiri* law of inheritance'.[76]

Moreover, although the founding women supported the Hindu Code Bill, they were not completely satisfied with all its provisions, and knew that it was a compromise project, a half-way measure that served to defer their ultimate programme. The founding mothers of the Constitution were driven by the larger feminist spirit of freedom from social and legal disabilities, and equality between the sexes. This was the rationality from which the idea of a quasi-national civil code emanated, which took the shape of a uniform civil code. This was also later transposed on Hindu Law as a tentative, strategic, contingent, and intermediate reform. The '"collective" political agency of women', which has rather hastily been characterized 'as an ideological cover for a unitary nationalist imagination that was implicitly a reconstituted male, Hindu, and upper-caste conception'[77] resulted in the authorship of an accommodating and liberal Constitution, that has remained an effective deterrent to such a conception of the nation.

ANXIETIES AND FEARS ABOUT THE HINDU CODE BILL

Speaking less than a month after the Constitution of India was ratified by the Constituent Assembly, the Congress stalwart Dr B. Pattabhi Sitaramayya refused to believe that the Hindu Bill was in agreement with the collective conscience of society. He referred to Ambedkar sarcastically as 'the doctor' who was 'out of tune with society' and said he felt 'very sorry that it should have fallen to Dr Ambedkar's lot to pilot this Bill'.[78] He was no less contemptuous of women's audacity to try to bring down the personal laws from the sacred sphere to the secular, human act of legislation: 'If half a dozen lady members of this House can drag us by heels and make us take up this Bill, I wonder what our position will be when there are two hundred and fifty of them here'.[79] The entire opposition to the Hindu Code Bill was suffused with misogyny, directed expectedly at members trying to secure for women the constitutional promises of equality under the proposed Hindu Law.

Women mobilized their argument around the principles of equality and fairness, which were the driving force behind their movement for social reform.

In her speech in the Constituent Assembly functioning as the legislature, Hansa Mehta proposed to the Select Committee that the problems of inheritance and marriage must now be approached from the point of view of 'equality of individuals'.[80] The debates that followed resulted in a rather bitter conflict around the very concept of equality, dragging women into further misogynist and stereotypical discursive terrain. The thrust of the opposition was to show that men and women were different and therefore unsuitable for equal treatment. To claim equality with men, in their argument, was to lose their difference, their distinction. Seeking equality was an androcentric enterprise. H. V. Kamath cited Radhakrishnan, 'our great savant and philosopher', 'an authority on Hindu *dharma* and [the] Hindu way of life':

> The modern woman, if I may say so, is losing her self-respect. She does not respect her own individuality and uniqueness, but is paying an unconscious tribute to man by trying to imitate him. She is fast becoming masculine and mechanical.[81]

This essentializing of the sexes was a central trope in the argument against the Hindu Code Bill. O. V. Alagesan, who was repeatedly objected to by Durgabai and the Deputy Speaker for his misogynistic remarks during his speech against the Bill, argued that the Hindu conception of equality of man and woman is based on the recognition of their fundamental differences. His comment is worth citing for its illustrative and figurative potential:

> [The basic conception of Hinduism] is not one of inequality, but it is one of dissimilarity. If man represents strength woman represents endurance; if man represents intellect woman represents enlightenment; if man represents grammar, woman represents poetry. The great poet Kalidasa has described Parvati and Parmeshwara as word and meaning and that is the basic approach. You do a basic wrong when you approach this question from the point of inequality between man and woman.[82]

Hindu jurisprudence, in the arguments of these speakers, was also based on the idea of equality but it was not equality in the sense supporters of the bill were advocating. In their framework, the Constitution's notion of equality was to be read in light of this conception of difference. To be sure, the difference that was made in reference to tradition was a veiled synonym for inferiority and a series of attributes that disqualified women from the various applications of the constitutional right to equality. Women were categorized as imbeciles, incapable of making rational choices, lacking in determination, fickle, and selfish, most attributes cited under the authority of some or the other classical text.[83]

This essentialization was extended to the notion of separate spheres, arguing that women's destiny lay in the home. In this sphere, in the words of Lakshmi Kant Maitra, 'The Law Minister or his honourable colleague will have to crouch before her however much he may thunder here' and where she rules with 'a whip, a soft, silken cord made up of filaments of love which takes off all harshness and roughness ... menfolk have submitted to her rule'.[84] Even such men as J. B. Kripalani, who supported the Bill, spoke from the same discursive position. He told an open house that his wife, the eminent leader Sucheta, herself a member of the Constituent Assembly, 'is as good a housewife as any ancient woman'.[85] He went on to report details proving her willing subservience: 'she does everything for me, including the brushing of my chappals and washing of my clothes'.[86]

Expectedly, the strongest resistance to the proposed reform in Hindu Law came from the members of the conservative Hindu parties. Their anxieties and fears were that the proposed Hindu Code Bill would strike at the very roots of traditional Hindu society, namely, its strictly controlled marriage rules and succession laws. Their sense of revulsion was brought out in the virulent, deeply communal, and misogynist reaction of Janakibai Joshi of Poona, the President of the All-India Hindu Women's Conference, the women's wing of the Hindu Mahasabha.[87] Perplexed that the committee is not interested in protecting the Hindus, she created a hypothetical scenario expected to strike terror in the hearts of her audience: A daughter of a Hindu gentleman (referred to as A) is kidnapped by a Mohammedan who marries the woman after her conversion into Islam; thereafter, because

> with the Code as it is proposed the daughter will claim the property of 'A' and will be a neighbour with her Mohammedan husband of 'A's on the bungalow and in the landed property, I ask whether he would like the situation created in his family.[88]

The terms of Janakibai's objections – and she went on to make sarcastic comments about the expectation that Hindus have *viswabandhutwa* (generosity towards all communities) – are worth pondering upon.

For my purpose I wish to isolate only one aspect of her speech: the couching of the relationship between a Hindu woman and Muslim man solely in terms of the latter's 'abduction' of the former. The idea of the virile Mohammedan male eyeing with lust the demure, young Hindu woman and

then finding the opportunity of abducting her against her will was a narrative
that had gained legitimacy over a long period of time. This assumed special
urgency with the impending partition of the nation. If the Mussalman
abductor had cast a shadow on the deliberations of the Hindu Code Bill in
the period between 1941 and 1945, his presence would gradually overwhelm
the majority Hindus – both men and women. Though arson, looting, killing
by Hindus and Muslims became normalized during the Bengal riots and later,
in the Partition in Bengal and Partition of the country, it was the figure of the
abducted Hindu woman that emerged as a central to the discourse. Linked
to this discussion was the question of 'recovery' and 'restoration' of Hindu
women from Muslim territory. Scholars, indeed, have noticed that in claiming
the abducted woman-as-property, 'The provision of the Abducted Person's
Restoration Act presented state authority and power in a manner strongly
reminiscent of a wider family collective such as the male coparcenary unit
that lay at the heart of Mitakshara law'.[89] What has not been noticed is that
in the Constituent Assembly, it was only women members who privileged the
question of the 'consent' of the abducted woman, irrespective of whether she
was Muslim or Hindu.

ON WOMEN'S ABDUCTION AND RECOVERY AFTER PARTITION: GIVING VOICE TO WOMEN'S WILL

Two weeks after B. R. Ambedkar made his final speech in the Constituent
Assembly, and the house voted to turn the Draft Constitution into the
Constitution of India, the Assembly met in its legislative capacity to discuss
one of the most important issues concerning women: an amendment to the
Abducted Persons (Recovery and Restoration) Bill. The amendment sought
the recovery of women abducted during the turmoil in the aftermath of the
Partition (it is crucial to remember that the other Bill they were discussing
on that day was the Hindu Code Bill). These debates, concerned as they were
with women who had been victims of the riots, and were abducted on both
sides of the two-year-old border between India and Pakistan – Hindu and
Sikh women by Muslim men and Muslim women by Hindu and Sikh men –
raised fierce storms within the Assembly. Scholars have read these debates as
containing a foundational script that conceives the nation as a social and sexual
contract between men divided as guardians of rival nations-as-community.
Veena Das argues that during these debates the figure of the 'abducted woman
was transfigured to institute a social contract that created the nation as a
masculine nation'.[90] According to her:

The circulation of the figure of the abducted woman, with its associated imagery of social disorder as sexual disorder, created the conditions of possibility in which the state could be instituted as essentially a social contract between men charged with keeping male violence against women in abeyance. Thus, the story about abduction and recovery acts as a foundational story that authorizes a particular relation between social contract and sexual contract – the former being a contract between men to institute the political and the latter the agreement to place women within the home under the authority of the husband/father figure.[91]

For Das, such an occasion was turned into a moment of exception which the state usurped to consolidate this idea of the nation. Underpinning such readings is the idea of a contract between men in which women were either absent or entirely passive figures. In an act of what I would call a partial reading, Veena Das goes to the extent of attributing to the women of the Constituent Assembly a certain complicity in this script of unjust social–sexual contract.

Durgabai asked several questions of moral and psychological import during the discussion on the difficult question about Muslim women who had married their abductors in India and refused to return to their families in Pakistan (and by implication Hindu or Sikh women who refused to come to India). By inviting the house to probe the minds of such women caught in the battles of nation-making, she made a rhetorical move and offered some answers without necessarily presenting them as final and unambiguous. Subsequently, Durgabai's female colleagues, Purnima Banerji, Renuka Ray, and Ammu Swaminathan disagreed with but built upon her arguments. Durgabai asked:

Are they really happy? Is the reconciliation true? Can there be a permanent reconciliation in such cases? Is it not out of helplessness, there being no alternative, that 'the woman', consents or is forced to enter into that sort of alliance with a person who is the murderer of her very husband, her very father, her very brother?[92]

Having argued that social workers involved in the recovery 'know the psychology of these abducted recovered women very well', she conceded later in her speech that the truth of the recovered woman's mind, her real desire, is difficult to ascertain, not least because a woman traumatized by her experience and uncertain of how she would be treated at home does not know what she wants:

The abducted and recovered woman is such, her psychology is such that she behaves in a semi-mad condition. So some time must lapse before she is restored to her normal senses. Sometimes she makes conflicting statements. Sometimes she changes her opinion constantly.[93]

She thus pleaded that the government must be patient and wait until an understanding of the recued women's intentions could be reached. The Act should, therefore, not fix a time before which the nationality of such women would be decided. Before Durgabai even spoke, the figure of the abducted woman had been turned into a site for a contest of honour between two nations. Members like Thakur Das Bhargava treated the abducted women in terms of prisoners of war:

> Nations agree to exchange prisoners. A prisoner in this country cannot be held in any manner as a hostage of another country. If I don't send away a prisoner away from here are they justified in not sending one from there? Yet we know there is an exchange of prisoners. May I know why we entered into agreements on exchange of property? If a refugee does not get property here, is it any reason that a refugee should not get property there?[94]

The Hindu nation was evoked and a rhetoric of revenge and retaliation planted in the discourse:

> … when one Ellis was kidnapped by some Pathans the whole of Britain shook with anger and indignation and until she was returned, Englishmen did not come to their senses. And we all know of own history, of what happened in the time of Shri Ram when Sita was abducted. Here, where thousands of girls are concerned, we cannot forget this. We might forget all the properties, we can forget every other thing, but this cannot be forgotten.[95]

Even the official position of the Minister-in-charge was presented within the trope of masculine honour that was completely blind to women's subjectivity:

> It is very important to remember that it is a matter of conscience, it is a duty, which we owe to human society that we should continue to make recoveries in our own Dominion. *It is a duty which we owe to the fathers, mothers and husbands of large numbers of non-Muslim women who are still to be recovered from Pakistan,* that we should continue this arrangement with that Dominion with a view to get as many more of them recovered as possible....[96]

It was to an inflamed audience and in such vitriolic circumstances that Durgabai turned the focal point of the discussion to the mind of the abducted women. Her own reading of the situation was presented in terms that stirred the feminist impulses of her female colleagues who either built upon or responded to her arguments. Durgabai initiated a discussion that made it possible for other women members like Purnima Banerji, Renuka Ray, and Ammu Swaminathan to speak of issues like affective relationships that effectively contested the binary of Hindu and Muslim nations at the very moment of their construction. Each of these women challenged the dominant tropes of the arguments made. Collectively they argued that women should not be counted as items in a nationalist bargain and emphasized that every woman has to be treated as an individual irrespective of what slot of the narrative her story falls in. 'There is no question of retaliation', Purnima Banerji said, 'there is no question of how many women has Pakistan recovered and how many people India has recovered'.[97] Ammu Swaminathan insisted that if the 'Pakistan government is not carrying out the moral obligations that they are supposed to, it is not the fault of the girls and we must not victimize them more than they have already been victimized'.[98]

Most importantly, these women members cited examples of marriages that may have taken place in the cruel circumstances of the communal frenzy but had grown into affective bonds between an inter-religious couple. In opposition to the state which became 'the father–patriarch' and 'found itself reinforcing the official kinship relations by discrediting and in fact declaring illegal, those practical arrangements that had in the meantime come into being, and were functional and accepted',[99] the women members pleaded for the grant of legitimacy to such arrangements and marriages. 'After a lapse of two years', Purnima reminded the house,

> there may be cases – and there have been cases when girls of the tender age have been abducted or rescued by young men of the same age. Time had passed and in between they have lived in association with one another and developed mutual attachment as young couples. They deserve sympathetic consideration and such girls should not be made to go back to countries to which they originally belonged merely because they happen to be Muslims or Hindus and merely because the circumstances and conditions under which they had been moved from their original homes could be described as abduction.[100]

While Purnima suggested that recovering such women would be another act of coercion, Renuka Ray argued that such marriages should be treated as 'marriages of honour and dignity'.[101] Ammu Swaminathan also urged that such cases be treated with great care and understanding.[102] All three women recommended that someone like Rameshwari Nehru be given the responsibility of deciding on the delicate issue of such marriages and the consent of these women. Rameshwari Nehru had been their colleague in the AIWC and took a keen interest in women's role in constitution-making. By this time, 'strong differences between Rameshwari Nehru (who opposed forcible recovery) and

Mridula Sarabhai (who wished to press on) began to surface; Mridula Sarabhai believed that no woman could be happy with her abductor, Rameshwari Nehru, not so.'[103] By supporting Rameshwari, the women members of the Constituent Assembly did not merely reaffirm their old alliance but also took an ideological stance on the question of women's consent and nationality. They opposed the very idea of imposing official kinship (masquerading as nationality) on the newly formed contingent but emotional marriage. Forced recovery, they implied, was also a kind of nationalist coercion. Earlier in the Sub-Committee on Fundamental Rights, Hansa Mehta and Amrit Kaur had demanded, though unsuccessfully, the inclusion of inter-community marriage in the fundamental rights. In fact, in their note of dissent, they lamented that their proposal was turned down, leaving such 'primitive restrictions' intact.[104]

A close reading of women's interventions invites us to challenge the idea that these debates enacted a passive redefinition of women as 'semiotic objects on which the actions of the state are to be inscribed'.[105] In order to do so, the voices of the women framers need to be recovered not just empirically but hermeneutically as well. Though women members occasionally resorted to the logic of the moral superiority of India, their main argument was that we must *listen* to women who were the real victims. It is strange that Das has concluded that Durgabai, speaking 'on behalf of both social workers and the women's movement, defended her social workers on the grounds that they knew women's true preferences *best*.'[106] In her reading of Durgabai's speech, 'the authority of the woman social worker is here being deployed to silence the voice of the victim; it is putting upon her an obligation to remember that her abductor, to whom she is now married, is the murderer of her husband or her father.'[107] She accuses Durgabai of attributing a false consciousness to the victim women, and effectively silencing them. Das's conclusion is deeply troubling and hasty:

> We witness here an alliance, between the state and social work as a profession, which silences the voice of victims by an application of the 'best interest' doctrine. This voice is silenced by *an abstract concern* with justice, the punishment of the guilty, and protection of the honour of the nation. This concern, lucidly articulated within the Constituent Assembly as well as outside the Assembly by national leaders, comprises a discourse of abstract, heroic and flatulent nationalism which takes no cognizance of the feelings of the women themselves.[108]

As the subsequent interventions by other women members show, they opposed the very framework of the debate that was making women empty signs to be filled by patriarchal nationalist sentiments. Read in its full context, it becomes clear that Durgabai spoke against the idea that abducted women should be used for retaliation and as weapons of blackmail by the two warring 'masculine' sides. In so doing, she was heckled twice in that parliament of men which lamented the death of civilizational values.[109] She had to face sarcasm because she was fighting misogyny in the course of her 10-minute speech. Rohini Kumar Chaudhury made deeply misogynistic remarks about women being incapable of telling the truth.

Above all, Durgabai spoke about the complexity of women's experience and the impossibility to understand it. She urged the nation-state to go slow, cautioning them against setting any time limit to the project of recovery, thereby allowing the abducted women to reach a self-willed understanding of what they wanted. She talked about the undecidability of the question of consent. Contrary to erasing women's voice, she spoke about the impossibility of having a stable, certain voice in the circumstances in which these women found themselves.

She demanded that some special powers be given to the police for the recovery process but certainly did not support making this the norm, serving the patriarchal cause. For her the most important juristic feature of the Bill was that although it was morally motivated as a response to the crime committed by these men, it had not provided any punishment for acts of rape. The reasons she cited are similar to the feminist arguments against death penalty for rapists:

> The crime of abduction of women and children is a serious one and as such should be punished severely. From that point of view this Bill is very harmless. It does not try to punish even the criminal abductor, the reason being that thereby we would be defeating the very objects we have, namely, rescuing the abducted women. The abductor adopts all sorts of tricks to hide the women; he tries to see that the woman is not sent back.[110]

Interestingly, in most discussions around these abducted women, in their zeal to establish that women were stripped of all voice and agency and made tools in the semiotics of national honour, feminist scholars forget that these abductions were a combination of several acts of criminal violation of the woman's body including rape.

However, Durgabai classified the abductor as a criminal, a murderer, and a rapist though she did not refer to the crime of rape directly. She mentioned the selling of the woman, the domestic quarrel to which she is daily subjected, and the hiding of these women. Most importantly her argument revolved around the consent of the woman. Is not 'to consent or to be forced to enter into that sort of alliance' when one has no alternative, synonymous with being raped? Durgabai's arguments, I would like to believe, are in line with arguments that are being made in favour of recognition of marital rape, and yet she suggested that these crimes not be punished in the interest of these women. Strangely, Veena Das chooses to forget this part of Durgabai's speech and its relationship with the speeches of her female colleagues, thus ignoring their full import on questions of women's consent and violence and accuses Durgabai of forcing women to remember something that they should forget: the same acts whose memories are much in need of retrieval for any feminist ethics.

While this reading puts an exceptional, I would even say perverse, emphasis on Durgabai's registering that these women had not forgotten the series of crimes that had landed them in that state of having no alternatives, it also completely erases the question of consent of women. Menon and Bhasin, too, cite the same passage and emphasize the same 'obligation to remember', reaching similar conclusions.[111] I am not arguing that the programme of recovery of abducted women did not constitute an act of coercion, but trying to correct this misplaced accusation of complicity of women members in this programme. This misreading, once again, is a result of our inability to hear all women's voices at the founding moment. It is evident that women, both Durgabai and Purnima, even in their divergence, were concerned with women's consent and the circumstances in which the consent was given. For Durgabai, the concern was with a consent that was forcefully produced in abducted women, and for Purnima, it was the consent of women who had fallen in love and had developed consent in an atmosphere of care devoid of nationalist hostility.

The women members of the Constituent Assembly worked against tremendous odds to reclaim the 'woman question' which in India was shaped in the early-nineteenth century by male social reformers and had been apparently 'resolved' by male nationalists towards the end of that century. When the women members began to demand changes in the Hindu Law in matters of marriage and succession, they stirred up, as we saw, a hornet's nest. Their task was doubly difficult because not only were they challenging age-old custom and tradition which were considered sacrosanct but they also had to face the hostility of men whose misogyny was sometimes couched in paternalism, but often overt.

Undaunted by this, the women members managed to bring on the floor of the Constituent Assembly, the voices of the women who had so far been passive recipients of the structural violence endemic to patriarchy.

By speaking for these women – wives who had to suffer the humiliation of competing for sexual and other favours of the husband who could have many wives, of widows and daughters who had been denied property rights – they made public what Hindu patriarchy had kept within the dark recesses of its being. Though they did not speak of the woman's rights of sexual choices and sexuality, the women members did not forget those who had dared to fall in love with men outside their community and caste, and sought to determine the consent of the women who had been abducted and had agreed to love and live with their abductors, before bringing them back forcefully. They allowed the language of affect to permeate the dry, withering rationality of the condescending explanations of their male colleagues. Their roles in reformulating the 'woman question' in the act of writing the Constitution vindicated their role as founding mothers; if the metaphor of mothering were to be extended, then one could see the duration of the Constituent Assembly as the necessary protracted gestation which would ensure the safe birth of a republic – a republic of both men and women as rights-bearing citizens.

NOTES

1. Mrinalini Sinha, *Spectres of Mother India: The Global Restructuring of an Empire* (Durham and London: Duke University Press, 2006), 43.
2. Partha Chatterjee, 'The Nationalist Resolution of the Women's Question', in Kumkum Sangari and Sudesh Vaid (eds), *Recasting Women: Essays in Colonial History*, 233–253 (New Delhi: Zubaan, 2006; first published Kali for Women, 1989).
3. Sinha, *Spectres of Mother India*, 44.
4. Tanika Sarkar and Sumit Sarkar, 'Introduction' in Sumit Sarkar and Tanika Sarkar (eds), *Women and Social Reform in Modern India: A Reader*, 2 vols (Ranikhet: Permanent Black, 2007), Vol. 1, 1–18, 6–7.
5. Chatterjee, 'The Nationalist Resolution of the Women's Question', 252.
6. Article 44, *The Constitution of India*, Part IV Directive Principles of State Policy. The article is titled 'Uniform civil code for the citizens'.
7. Amrit Kaur, *Challenge to Women* (Allahabad: New Literature, 1946), 27. This is from a speech delivered at the Lady Irwin College, at the annual conference of the AIWC, 1937.
8. Ibid., 103 (emphasis mine).
9. Archana Parashar, *Women and Family Law Reform in India* (New Delhi: Sage Publications, 1992), 231.
10. Hansa Mehta, Constituent Assembly of India, 22 November 1949, *CAD*, XI: 797–798 (emphasis mine).

11. Hansa Mehta's reply to Secretary, Home Department, Government of Bombay, 18 May 1928, Hansa Mehta Papers, Subject File 32, NMML.
12. Section 3 (c) of the Muslim Personal Law (Shariat) Application Act, 1937.
13. B. R. Ambedkar, Constituent Assembly of India, 23 November 1948, *CAD*, VII: 550–552.
14. The only shorter one that comes to my mind is article 52, which says: 'There shall be a President of India'.
15. Hansa Mehta, *The Woman under the Hindu Law of Marriage and Succession* (Bombay: Pratibha Publications, 1941), i–ii (emphasis mine).
16. *Report of the Hindu Law Committee* (Shimla: Government of India Press, 1941), 24.
17. Mehta, *The Woman and the Hindu Law of Marriage and Succession*, 4.
18. Ibid., i.
19. Ibid., 4.
20. Ibid., 7 (emphasis mine).
21. Ibid., 5.
22. Kamaladevi Chattopadhyay, *Written Statement Submitted to the Hindu Law Committee: 1945*, Vol. 1, India Office Records, V/26/100/17, 29 (emphasis mine).
23. Ibid.
24. Ibid.
25. Ibid.
26. Ibid.
27. K. T. Shah (ed.), *Report of the Sub-Committee on Woman's Role in Planned Economy* (Bombay: Vora & Co., 1947), 124 (emphasis mine).
28. K. T. Shah (ed.), *Report of the Sub-Committee: Land Policy, Agricultural Labour and Insurance* (Bombay: Vora & Co. Publishers Ltd, 1948), 2.
29. Eleanor Newbigin, *The Hindu Family and the Emergence of Modern India* (Cambridge: Cambridge University Press, 2013), 209.
30. Hansa Mehta, Constituent Assembly (Legislative) of India, 9 April 1948, *CA(L)D*, V: 3643.
31. Durgabai Deshmukh, Constituent Assembly (Legislative) of India, 1 March 1949, *CA(L)D*, I: 992 (emphasis mine).
32. Ibid.
33. Hansa Mehta, Constituent Assembly (Legislative) of India, 9 April 1948, *CA(L)D*, V: 3643.
34. B. R. Ambedkar, Constituent Assembly (Legislative) of India, 9 April 1948, *CA(L)D*, V: 3632.
35. Ibid.

36. Hansa Mehta, Constituent Assembly (Legislative) of India, 9 April 1948, *CA(L)D*, V: 3644 (emphasis mine).

37. For an incisive overview of the centrality of the figure of the 'son' in Hindu Law, see Donald R. Davis, Jr., 'Children: *Putra, Duhitra*', in Patrick Olivelle and Donald R. Davis, Jr. (eds), *Hindu Law: A New History of Dharmashastra*, 151–163 (New Delhi: Oxford University Press, 2018).

38. Ibid., 158.

39. Hansa Mehta, Constituent Assembly (Legislative) of India, 9 April 1948, *CA(L)D*, V: 3644.

40. *The Hindu Code, 1948: As Amended by the Select Committee*, Clause 63, printed in the Report of the Select Committee on the Hindu Code, presented to the Constituent Assembly (Legislative) on 12 August 1948, British Library, V/26/100/19.

41. Hindu Succession Act, Act No. 30 of 1956, Section 3 (1) (a).

42. *The Hindu Code, 1948: As Amended by the Select Committee*, Clause 67 (b). The Hindu Adoptions and Maintenance Act, 1956 continued with the same provisions, mentioned in sections 12 (b) and 12 (c). See *Mayne's Treatise on Hindu Law and Usage*, 14th ed. (New Delhi: Bharat Law House, 1996), 521–522.

43. Thakur Das Bhargava, Constituent Assembly (Legislative) of India, 25 August 1948, *CA(L)D*, VI: 586.

44. Ibid., 586 (emphasis mine).

45. Renuka Ray, Constituent Assembly (Legislative) of India, 25 August 1948, *CA(L)D*, VI: 596.

46. Ibid.

47. Ibid.

48. Pattabhi Sitaramayya, Constituent Assembly (Legislative) of India, 9 April 1948, *CA(L)D*, V: 3635.

49. Hansa Mehta, Constituent Assembly (Legislative) of India, 9 April 1948, *CA(L)D*, V: 3644.

50. Ibid., 3643 (emphasis mine).

51. B. R. Ambedkar, Constituent Assembly (Legislative) of India, 9 April 1948, *CA(L)D*, V: 3652.

52. Ibid.

53. Ibid., 3652–3653.

54. Ibid., 3653.

55. Sucheta Kripalani, Constituent Assembly (Legislative) of India, 24 February 1949, *CA(L)D*, II (II): 868.

56. Renuka Ray, speech in the Constituent Assembly (Legislative) of India, 25 February 1949, *CA(L)D*, II (II): 928.

57. Ibid. (emphasis mine).

58. Ibid.

59. Sudipta Kaviraj, *The Enchantment of Democracy and India: Politics and Ideas* (Ranikhet: Permanent Black, 2011), 55.

60. Durgabai Deshmukh, Constituent Assembly (Legislative) of India, 1 March 1949, *CA(L)D*, II(II): 992.

61. Ibid., 994.

62. Ibid., 994–995.

63. Renuka Ray, 'A National Code', undated article (probably from the early 1960s), AIWC Files, IV Instalment. File no. 965, NMML.

64. Ibid., 2.

65. Ibid., 1.

66. Hansa Mehta to Secretary of the Government of Bombay, Home Dept., Bombay, 18 May 1928. Hansa Mehta Papers, Subject File no. 32, NMML.

67. Renuka Ray, 'Uniform Code of Social Laws', undated article (probably from the early 1970s), Renuka Ray Papers, Writings/Speeches by Her, File no. 86, 3, NMML.

68. Renuka Ray, 'History of Social Reform and Social Work from 1947 to 1963', unpublished article, 1963. Renuka Ray Papers, Writings/Speeches by Her, File no. 59, 7, NMML.

69. Ibid., 7.

70. Ray, 'Uniform Code of Social Laws', 1.

71. Ibid., 3.

72. Ibid., 2.

73. Flavia Agnes, *Law and Gender Inequality: The Politics of Women's Rights in India* (New Delhi: Oxford University Press, 1999), 72.

74. Nivedita Menon, 'Embodying the Self: Feminism, Sexual Violence and Law', in Partha Chatterjee and Pradeep Jeganathan (eds.) *Subaltern Studies XI: Community, Gender and Violence*, 66–105 (Delhi: Permanent Black, 2000), 80n35.

75. Hansa Mehta, Handwritten note to be submitted on the proposed Hindu Code Bill, 1941, Hansa Mehta Papers, Subject File no. 32, NMML.

76. Note of Dissent by Ammu Swaminathan, Renuka Ray, and B. Shiva Rao, Extracts of the Report of the Select Committee on the Hindu Code presented to the CAL, 12 August 1948, British Library, V/26/100/19, 12–13.

77. Sinha, *Specters of Mother India*, 247.

78. Pattabhi Sitaramayya, Constituent Assembly (Legislative) of India, 13 December 1949, *CA(L)D*, IV(II): 548.

79. Ibid., 546.

80. Hansa Mehta, Constituent Assembly (Legislative) of India, 9 April 1948, *CA(L)D*, V: 3643.

81. H. V. Kamath, Constituent Assembly (Legislative) of India, 28 February 1948, *CA(L)D*, I(II): 942.

82. O. V. Alagesan, Constituent Assembly (Legislative) of India, 14 December 1949, *CA(L)D*, IV(II): 617.

83. A summary of these remarks can be found in Ambedkar's response to the argument that women cannot be trusted with absolute property rights. B. R. Ambedkar, Constituent Assembly (Legislative) of India, 24 February 1949, *CA(L)D*, II(II): 839. Other straightforward instances can be found in the speeches of O. V. Alagesan and Pattabhi Sitaramayya cited earlier. A notorious example is also available in Lakshmi Kanta Maitra's purportedly *naiyyayik* arguments made on 1 March 1949 during the same debates, *CA(L)D*, II(II): 996–1018.

84. Lakshmi Kant Maitra, Constituent Assembly (Legislative) of India, 1 March 1949, *CA(L)D*, II(II): 1007.

85. J. B. Kripalani, Constituent Assembly (Legislative) of India, 14 December 1949. *CA(L)D*, IV(II): 561.

86. Ibid.

87. Janakibai Joshi, President, All India Hindu Women's Conference, Written Statement Submitted to the Hindu Law Committee: 1945, Vol 1 (Madras: Government Press, 1947), 22–25. Previously, Janakibai Joshi had also objected to the appointment of Renuka Ray to the Hindu Law Committee on grounds that, given her Brahmo Samaj background and her reformist ideas, she was 'ill-conversant with Hindu Law' and her participation would lead to the destruction of Hindu values. Janakibai Joshi to Lord Wavell, 20 March 1944, File C-67, Hindu Mahasabha Papers, NMML.

88. Ibid., 24.

89. Newbigin, *The Hindu Family and the Emergence of Modern India*, 156.

90. Veena Das, *Life and Words: Violence and the Descent into the Ordinary* (Berkeley: University of California Press, 2007), 20.

91. Ibid., 21

92. Durgabai Deshmukh, Constituent Assembly (Legislative) of India, 15 December 1949, *CA(L)D*, VII(II): 662.

93. Ibid., 664.

94. Thakur Das Bhargava, Constituent Assembly (Legislative) of India, 15 December 1949, *CA(L)D*, VII(II): 643.

95. Ibid.

96. N. Gopalaswami Aiyyangar, Constituent Assembly (Legislative) of India, 15 December 1949, *CA(L)D*, VII(II): 641 (emphasis mine).

97. Purnima Banerji, Constituent Assembly (Legislative) of India, 15 December 1949, *CA(L)D*, VII(II): 665.

98. Ammu Swaminathan, Constituent Assembly (Legislative) of India, 16 December 1949, *CA(L)D*, VI(II): 713.

99. Ritu Menon and Kamla Bhasin, *Border and Boundaries: Women in India's Partition* (New Jersey: Rutgers University Press, 1998), 124–125.

100. Purnima Banerji, Constituent Assembly (Legislative) of India, 15 December 1949, *CA(L)D*, VII(II): 665.

101. Renuka Ray, Constituent Assembly (Legislative) of India, 16 December 1949, *CA(L)D*, VI(II): 716.

102. Ammu Swaminathan, Constituent Assembly (Legislative) of India, 16 December 1949, *CA(L)D*, VI(II): 712–713.

103. Ritu Menon and Kamla Bhasin, 'Recovery, Rupture, Resistance: Indian State and Abduction of Women during Partition', *Economic and Political Weekly* 28, no. 17 (24 April 1993), WS2–WS11, WS8.

104. Note of Dissent by Amrit Kaur, Hansa Mehta, and M. R. Masani, Submitted to the Advisory Committee, 16 April 1947, in B. Shiva Rao (ed.), *The Framing of India's Constitution: Select Documents*, Vol. 2 (Delhi: Universal Law Publishing, 2004; originally The Indian Institute of Public Administration, 1967), 177–178, 178.

105. Veena Das, *Critical Events: An Anthropological Perspective on Contemporary India* (New Delhi: Oxford University Press, 1997), 70.

106. Ibid., 72 (emphasis mine).

107. Ibid.

108. Ibid., 73 (emphasis mine).

109. Sardar Bhopinder Singh Man and Rohini Kumar Chaudhary, Constituent Assembly (Legislative) of India, 15 December 1949, *CA(L)D*, VII(II): 663–665.

110. Durgabai Deshmukh, Constituent Assembly (Legislative) of India, 15 December 1949, *CA(L)D*, VII(II): 662

111. Menon and Bhasin, *Border and Boundaries*, 104.

7

After the Framing

I hope that some of us will live to see that the Constitution becomes a real stronghold for human rights and it will be worked towards establishing a real democracy, so that there will be happiness and prosperity for everyone in India.

—Ammu Swaminathan, *Constituent Assembly Debates*, 24 November 1949[1]

On Thursday, 17 November 1949, B. R. Ambedkar moved the last resolution of the Constituent Assembly. He asked 'that the Constitution as settled by the Assembly be passed'.[2] The terms of reference had changed. It was no more the first or the second draft that the Assembly was asked to consider. There were no amendments left to be moved. It was the Constitution itself, as it was to be signed by all the founding mothers and fathers, which he was moving before the house. The President, Dr Rajendra Prasad, thought a general discussion about the Constitution would be a fitting end to the work of the Assembly and must take place before the Assembly could be adjourned *sine die*. The discussions began on that day and continued for 10 days, ending with Ambedkar's valedictory speech on 26 November 1949 which was cheered by 'a resounding applause by the entire house for more than three minutes'.[3]

Many members spoke on the Constitution, about their experience of participating in these great moments of the framing, and the hopes they had of the future. Five women members, namely, Renuka Ray, Aizaz Rasul, Purnima Banerji, Hansa Mehta, and G. Durgabai participated in these general debates. These readings can be considered the first act of constitutional interpretation by these women. The Constitution emerged in their reading as a living document, which needs to be read as a whole, and not just as list of governmental purposes and processes.

First, the Constitution became a source of a national identity based on the principles and aspirations that would bind the citizens. The will of the people was the will of a people who were tied to each other not by inherited, common cultural and social capital, but by shared principles and aspirations. We must not 'look backwards and dissect this Constitution',[4] said Durgabai, because as an expression of the will of the people, it was a forward-looking document. The Constitution could be judged against the standards of democracy that it had itself established. There was 'only one standard' by which 'this Constitution' could be judged.[5] Durgabai emphasized that the Constitution was meant to 'find a device and to establish a machinery to find out the general will of the people and also to give scope for the general will to prevail'.[6] The people, she argued 'should be left alone, and they should be the masters to shape the destiny of this country and also to mould their machinery as they like, as long as they hold the field'.[7]

The will of the people, consolidated by principles and aspirations, was the *only* thing that should be read in the words of the Constitution. The Constitution was living evidence that the people had taken their destiny in their own hands, and an embodiment of the idea of the nation that India constituted. Remembering the 'stages through which India has passed', particularly the 'recent periods in the history of our political subjection, when we were told that we were hardly a nation', Purnima Banerji interpreted the Constitution as the voice of the nation.[8] The language that the Constitution spoke arranged the aspirations of the people. In her words, the Constitution gave us the 'idea of how the great people of a country fashion their institutions, how they want to live, what are the political arrangements under which they exercise their judgment and what are the hopes and aspirations which they entertain for the future'.[9] Her argument described the Constitution as the most eloquent response to the charge that we cannot govern ourselves and our rightful place is in 'an imaginary waiting room of history', to use a phrase Dipesh Chakrabarty uses to describe the logic of inferiority evoked by the colonialists.[10]

Second, the Constitution was seen as providing a discursive basis for the unity of the nation. Purnima Banerji saw it as an ethical corrective to the perceived division 'among ourselves in mutually hostile groups', a sound historical response to the allegation that 'democratic institutions were congenitally not suited to Indian conditions'.[11] The unity of the nation, Granville Austin shows, was one of the three strands of the seamless web the Constitution wove, the other two being social revolution and democracy.

According to Austin, national unity inhered in the very structure of the polity framed by the Constitution. He argues:

> National unity and integrity were to be served by the Constitution's highly centralised federalism, characterised, among other elements, by central government distribution of revenue, national development planning, continuation of the inherited central civil services, state governors who were presidential appointees, the well-known Emergency provisions, and a wide variety of state–centre coordinating mechanisms.[12]

Thus, for Austin the unity of the nation seemed to be rooted in the structure of the state. It was through the mechanisms of the government and the distribution of power through institutional channels that the unity of the state was ensured by the Constitution.

THE MOMENT OF ARRIVAL: A CAUTIOUS JUBILATION

When the Constitution was being adopted by the Assembly, speaking on its final draft, women expressed a cautious jubilation. Their speeches conveyed a sense of achievement and arrival, a newly shaped hope and a sense of responsibility. The first signs of the rearrangement of the discursive terrain were visible as soon as the framing process was complete, and women members saw their generation of women and men in new roles assigned by the Constitution they had made. In spite of reservations about specific features and individual clauses on part of some members, the overall reception of the Constitution within the Assembly was marked by a note of self-congratulation. Most members remarked on the Constitution and the polity of the nation whose foundations were laid down by it. As Ambedkar put it during his concluding speech, barring a solitary member, Naziruddin Ahmad, 'there is a general consensus of appreciation from members of the Constituent Assembly'.

Women members, however, had a long-term view of the Constitution. Like Ambedkar, who claimed that he came to the Constituent Assembly 'with no greater aspiration than to safeguard the interests of the Scheduled Castes',[13] women too, had the declared purpose of ensuring that no 'inequality attaches to women' when they began their work in the Assembly. By the end of the work, however, they displayed a comprehensive interest in the framing of the Constitution belying their narrowly stated purposes. They believed that the Constitution was only as good or as bad as the future generation would make it. Ambedkar refused to speak on 'the merits of the Constitution' because he felt that 'however good a Constitution may be, it is sure to turn out bad because those who are called to work it, happen to be a bad lot. The working of the Constitution does not depend wholly on the nature of the Constitution.'[14] Unlike a majority of the members, Renuka Ray, for example, did not congratulate the Assembly for creating a Constitution of which they should be proud. 'It is not for us to say', she reminded the Constituent Assembly, 'whether we have done our job well or badly. It is only posterity that can really judge of us.'[15] In the same vein as Ambedkar, she spoke of the dialogic, dynamic nature of the Constitution which, far from being a static text with inert, innate qualities, was an organism whose life depended on the nourishment its future custodians would provide:

> it is the architects who will actually implement this Constitution, who will give it life and breath, who will really determine what manner it will be worked. It will be to them to make of it something worthy and worthwhile and also it may be that they can mar it, distort it, maim it and make those very fundamental principles and rights which for the security of citizens be used in such a way as to bring about the detriment of the citizen.[16]

Hansa Mehta echoed Ray and argued that the test of the Constitution was in its ability to work for the people, which, in turn, would depend on the people who would work on it:

> If it works in the interests of the people, it will be a good Constitution; if it works otherwise, it will be a bad Constitution. It is for the future electors to elect *the right kind of persons*, who will work the Constitution in the interests of the people.[17]

The responsibility, therefore, lay with the people. Women framers' realist assessment of the future of the Constitution also assigned a greater responsibility to the framers themselves.

Although Dakshayani Velayudhan did not speak on the occasion of the final reading of the Constitution, it would be appropriate to remember her remarks on the Draft Constitution when it was presented for the first reading before the Constituent Assembly. She complained against the excessive centralization of power of which she found two instances in the Constitution: the unelected figure of the governor and the provisions for centrally administered areas, the union territories. Not convinced by Ambedkar's defence of the Draft Constitution, she was one of the few members of the Constituent Assembly who offered a Gandhian objection to the centralization:

There are two ways of making India a strong unit. One is by the method of centralisation of power and the other is by decentralisation; but centralisation is possible only through parliamentary system which now goes under the safe words 'democratic methods', but in this draft we can't find anything that is democratic and decentralisation is totally absent. It is a great tragedy that in making the constitution of a great country with thirty crores of people, with a great culture behind it and the great principles and teachings of the greatest man of the world on the surface, we were only able to produce a constitution that is totally foreign to us.[18]

In the provisions for centrally controlled union territories, she read a vestige of the imperious tendencies of the colonial government, a desire to create a military state:

I cannot understand why there should be Centrally Administered areas under the new Constitution. The British kept these areas simply to have the [sic] military rule in the country. But I do not understand why we should have such areas under the present Constitution. It is better that these provinces are merged with the adjoining provinces and thus we will not be losing anything.[19]

Finally, she made the surprising proposal of putting the Constitution itself before the people of India, to be evaluated, accepted, or discarded.

The present Constitution, when it comes into force, will be put before the public by way of the General Elections. Then this Constitution can be made an election issue either for its acceptance or rejection. If the majority of the electorates accept the Constitution, then we can take it that the whole country has accepted it. If the majority of the electorates reject it then we must take it that the whole country has rejected it, and the party that comes into power, and the Legislature that will be formed thereafter, can take up the Constitution and make the amendments that are necessary. I think, Sir, the Congress Party that is in power today will accept such a policy and see that we are not blamed for being undemocratic in our approach to Constitution making.[20]

Taken symbolically, rather than literally, and in the light of her other remarks, her reading invited the people of India to take the responsibility of the Constitution. In this, she seemed to be expressing the same sense of anxiety about the future as her female colleagues. One can read this anxiety, for instance in Renuka Ray's exhortation, when she put the responsibility on 'the architects of this generation and the next who are going to put this Constitution into working, on whom will depend a great deal, its success or its failure'.[21] Indeed, between Ambedkar, Dakshayani, Renuka Ray, and Hansa Mehta, a very important aspect of constitutional theory and interpretation was raised. Constitutional legitimacy and effectiveness were left to generational interpretation. Ambedkar, citing Thomas Jefferson, argued that 'the principles embodied in the Constitution are the views of the present generation', 'the views of the Constituent Assembly'.[22] The succeeding generation is as free from the previous generation as two sovereign nations and it is the will of the succeeding generations that eventually will give the Constitution its lives. *The Constitution for the framers, one can argue, was not a once-for-all text but a perpetually reproduced set of political–legal principles that emerged through an active reading by the generations that worked on it.*

As a founder of the Constitution, Renuka Ray did not exclude herself from membership of the succeeding generation and envisaged the task ahead as that of generating an effective readership for the Constitution, in the words of Mehta, 'the right kind of persons'.[23] Women members would not put readership to the exclusive service of women but to address the issues that would arise under the changed circumstances created by the new constitutional guarantee of equality of the sexes. The Constitution, therefore, was not meant just to aid the women's movement but to expand its curriculum and make it more inclusive. This became evident with the change of the character of the All India Women's Conference (AIWC) after the adoption of the Constitution, of which we shall see examples in the subsequent discussion.

Women leaders like Kamaladevi Chattopadhyay, who played an indirect but significant role in shaping women's constitutional vision, thought that the Constitution heralded a new beginning for women and their relationship with society:

> The new Constitution of India marks *a turning point in the history of women in India*. It guarantees them equal status with men. The new situation has shifted the old emphasis from equality of status to common economic and social objectives and *common problems that are now shared by men and women alike*. Appropriately, the All-India Women's Conference at its last session in 1950, changed its previous aims of gaining equal rights of women, to acquiring equal opportunities for all and establishing a society based on equity and social justice.[24]

Kamaladevi's optimism was not limited to the guarantees of equality of the sexes in the Constitution. She looked forward to the enhanced quality of social justice after the Constitution rectified the gendered inequalities inherited from the past. Later, however, she was to express her disillusionment with the Constitution in strong terms. Commenting on the poor state of social justice in India, she complained that 'we were trapped in a Constitution, which, for all its grandiose garb, to me seems ill suited to this country'.[25] She complained that the Indian state had acquired 'the garb of a bogus socialism'[26] which could have been prevented had the socialist voice been strengthened by direct participation of 'the original Socialists'.[27] She pointed to the founding moment, complaining about the Constitution's inadequate socialist tendencies, a perception which was shared and commented upon by Renuka Ray during the final discussions on the soon-to-be-ratified Constitution. Renuka condemned the fundamental right to property as the 'one great flaw, one great transgression', 'a blot on this very Constitution'. To her relief, there was 'one compensation, one consolation that we can by amendment of the Constitution change this'.[28] Though Renuka Ray and Purnima Banerji shared this socialist grudge against the way the Constitution had dealt with the right to property, they were satisfied to have been able to achieve a level of common agreement.

Durgabai, who was considered 'conservative on economic issues and [who] had held herself aloof from our fight against Article 31',[29] did not share these grievances. She clearly said that it was possible for

> a socialist to complain that the principles of his own party do not find a place in this Constitution. But ours is a Constitution which is *neither a socialist Constitution, [nor] a communist Constitution*, or even for the matter of that, a Panchayat Raj Constitution. It is a people's Constitution and a Constitution which gives *free and ample scope to the people of India to make experiments in socialism or any other ism in which they believe* would make this country prosperous and happy. It would have been wrong on the part of the makers of the Constitution to have introduced their own political philosophy, and they have done well in making this Constitution, as I say, a cent per cent people's Constitution, and leaving it at that.[30]

This apparent conflict between the conservative (with regard to the economic restructuring of society) and the radical, socialist founding mothers could be resolved by paying close attention to the characterization of the Constitution as an open text. Ambedkar, Renuka Ray, and Durgabai remarked on the nature of the Constitution as a text with endless possibilities of meaning. While Ambedkar believed that there was something called 'a good constitution' which may be abused by 'a bad lot' of readers, Renuka Ray envisaged a greater role and agency for the future reader who, in turn, could make it 'worthy and worthwhile' or 'mar, maim and distort' it.

Renuka Ray recounted that Durgabai as a lawyer, during the framing process, had kept 'a watchful eye on possible loopholes or ambiguities that would lead to different interpretations against people's interest on constitutional issues'.[31] In her final evaluation of the Constitution, Durgabai gave a specific political dimension to the richness of interpretive possibilities of the text, claiming that the text had enough flexibility to suit future readers with conviction in any ideology that they 'believe would make this country prosperous and happy'.[32]

What emerges from this discussion is that the framers of the Constitution, including the women authors, envisaged a role for its future readers. As evident from Durgabai's defence of the political neutrality of the Constitution, they took considerable pride in having drafted a Constitution which was not just dynamic and elastic but rich enough to serve a spectrum of ideological groups 'working' towards the ideals of justice embodied in the text. The task of the future reader was frequently described as work. The framers invited the future generation to work upon the Constitution. The Constitution itself invited to be worked upon. Women framers would have agreed with Granville Austin's introductory remarks in his history of the Indian experience with the Constitution:

> It is about those who acted upon the Constitution, how and why they did so, and about those the Constitution acted upon, or neglected. It is about Indians working their Constitution, for constitutions, however 'living' are inert. They do not work. They are worked.[33]

Rethinking the role of the All India Women's Conference

The historical evidence of 'motherhood' of the Constitution that one can assign to the women members of the Constituent Assembly can be complemented by recognizing the centrality they gave to the Constitution once it was adopted, enacted, and given to ourselves. The Constitution soon became the focal point of their discourse, gradually replacing the sentimental and rhetorical figures of culture and nation. The women's politics became oriented towards securing what was definite and written, the words of the promises embedded in the Constitution they had made. References to their own role in making the Constitution abound in the memoirs and speeches of these women members, all of whom spoke of that glorious moment as a turning point in their lives. As pointed out throughout this work, these founding women were members of the AIWC, the organization under whose umbrella they conducted their constitutional politics, and which they continued to be associated with. The AIWC took special pride in having contributed to the framing of the Constitution, whose ideals became important signposts for its vision of the future.

The reframing of the Constitution of the AIWC, a small event in comparison with the subject of this work, provides interesting insights into how the contribution of the women members of the Constituent Assembly fundamentally shaped the objectives of the organization. The AIWC which was originally conceived of and had first met as the All India Women's Conference on Educational Reform in January 1927 in Poona, in order to work towards 'educational reform' for 'the good of their children and the general welfare of the nation' emerged as the most important women's organization at the inception of the Constituent Assembly.[34]

In the transitional period of Independence and Partition, the AIWC deliberated on changing its own constitution. The Partition forced it to rethink its federal structure. The organization was becoming conscious of its own fissures and biases, and was directly involved in issues like comprehensive reforms in Hindu law. The Objectives Resolution of the Constituent Assembly also compelled the organization to officially expand its aims and objectives. Simultaneous with the framing of the Indian Constitution, the AIWC also reconsidered its own constitutional setup. 'In view of the great political changes that are our country is facing', the AIWC President told its members within weeks of the formulation of the fundamental rights for discussion in the Constituent Assembly, in June 1947, 'it is fortunate' that the organization's constitution was being considered for amendments.[35] She thought it fortunate because the drafting of the Constitution gave an opportunity to the Conference to legitimately expand its aspirations in terms of social and political rights. The proposed constitution, prepared by Hannah Sen in the same month, listed 'the general progress and welfare of women and children' as the first goal of the Conference, followed by the aims of promoting the value of 'citizenship' and 'education', working towards 'social reform', and securing 'equal rights and opportunity' in that order.[36]

Next in the list was the task of working towards the 'unity of India', an aspiration that became more urgent at the moment of Partition. A suggestion, made before the draft of the constitution could be circulated, amended this last objective in these words: to work for a free democratic India based on the unity of its people. The draft went through several rounds of modifications, changing the order of the objectives and often their content in the two following years.

The general drive towards these changes suggests that the proposed AIWC constitution was being inflected by the Indian Constitution (then still under preparation) and the gender neutrality of its language to such an extent that the Conference was losing its constitutional expression as a women's organization. This was not, however, under the influence of the women members of the Constituent Assembly. It was, presumably, the liberal humanist tone of the Constitutional text and its promise of a universal and equal citizenship to men and women alike that was driving the restructuring process of the AIWC. The Constitutional guarantees appeared to some sections of the Conference as heralding a future when a women's organization would become redundant. With 'a Constitution which not only guarantees fundamental rights but also abolishes discrimination based on sex' making it compulsory that 'all laws will be brought in conformity with ideals laid down in the directive principles', the need for a women's conference was itself questioned.[37] The justification for the organization, however, in the words of Lakshmi Menon, a close associate of the women framers, was this:

> Those men and women who have any knowledge of the country, and the vast disparity between the ideals laid down in the Constitution and the conditions under which the people especially our women live know that Herculean efforts are needed to stir up the unfortunate and settled ways of life which pay scant respect to women.[38]

The founding mothers, Amrit Kaur, Ammu Swaminathan, Renuka Ray, Purnima Banerji, and Hansa Mehta, also did not doubt the AIWC's relevance. They argued that the AIWC need not change any of its primary aims and objectives or add any new ones. If anything, the Constitution of India made the AIWC more relevant and ethically bound to its fundamental goal of service to the women and children of India. Under its regime, 'the specific goal has assumed tremendous possibilities' argued these women, and their responsibilities would only increase.[39] Without these responsibilities at the heart of its foundational structure, the Conference would become 'a colourless body working as an appendage to any political organization'.[40] Allowing the Indian Constitution's grand principles to completely subsume the Conference's specific character, they seemed to be arguing, would make it an organization 'without any status or *raison d'etre*'.[41]

For the founder women of India, the Constitution could be written into the AIWC's policy so as to make it more attentive and responsible towards its own vision. It has been argued earlier in this work that an intellectual and programmatic history of the AIWC needs to be written in order to gain a complete perspective on the complex trajectory of feminist thought in India. At this point it will suffice to notice that the revised AIWC constitution reconciled these two tendencies by drawing heavily upon the Indian Constitution in its list of aims and objectives, while mentioning explicitly that it would actively help women 'to utilize to the fullest the Fundamental Rights conferred on them by the Constitution'.[42]

Dismantling the binary of the personal and the secular: re-reading 'Shahbano'[43]

The summary procedures of historiography have not merely erased the voices of the women framers but have also led to serious misreadings of constitutional ethics. The ignorance of women's presence in the founding body has led to feminist loss of faith in the Constitution. An intriguing and ironical instance is the misreading of the famous case of Shah Bano[44] and the problematics of secularism in the Constitution.

The irony becomes sharp when such misreading occurs in important feminist works on the Indian Constitution. Zakia Pathak and Rajeshwari Sunder Rajan in an influential essay on Shah Bano, the Muslim woman whose fight for maintenance from her divorced husband created a furore comparable only to 'the great upheaval of 1857'[45] and brought feminists in confrontation with the state, religious leaders, and among themselves that was unprecedented in the history of Indian constitutional discourse, use the term in ways that allow us to open our inquiry further.[46] The essay situates the narrative of Shah Bano in the larger constitutional and legal discourse of India to 'describe the formation of a discontinuous female subjectivity in response to the displacement of the Muslim woman question onto several discourses'.[47] Several discourses objectify her as an 'other', stripping her off all the characteristic features of a 'subject', leaving her without 'sensibility and/or volition'.[48] At the level of each discourse, she is assigned a new subject position, which she resists with a temporalizing self, thus generating multiple identities that must be read in relation with each other.[49] As a litigant in the lower courts it is her sex attributes, as an awardee of a paltry sum of INR 25 a month as maintenance it is her class attributes, and as a subject in need of protection from 'Muslim men' by Hindu fundamentalists it is her religious attributes that are violently moved to the foreground of her identity. Shah Bano, in other words, is the subject of 'a process of writing and erasing that cannot construct that unified and freely choosing individual who is the normative male subject of Western bourgeois liberalism'.[50]

So far, there is little to contradict in these readings. The incongruity begins to surface when the Indian Constitution is evoked as having envisaged 'the unity of the Indian subject within the legal system'.[51] This unity is not envisaged by a dynamic text of impersonal attributes but in 1949, when 'the founding fathers saw the necessity of continuing to recognize personal laws at the same time that, moved by unifying secular impulse, they also declared as an objective of the state the adoption of a uniform civil code'.[52] The 'desired coexistence of the secular and the personal' in the Constitution, in their reading, is 'a temporary accommodation of contemporary reality (the partition of the country attended by large-scale communal riots)'.[53] Who desired this accommodation? Were they the founding fathers?

The flagrant contradiction in this reading becomes obvious if we compare the pains taken to understand the several discursive shifts which the multiple subjectivities of Shah Bano undergo, with the impossibly reduced will of the constitution-makers to a temporary compromise made by the 'founding fathers'. The agency and volition given to this collective of men (within a larger collective of men and women) completely erases the historical truth that women founders in the Constituent Assembly took a firm position against the coexistence of the secular and the personal in the constitutional precincts, occasionally using similar tactics of resistance as Shah Bano is described to have staged. Further, it erases the contemporary reality that women fought for a restructuring of the personal laws of the Hindus, arguing with the founding fathers at the same discursive level on which the temporary accommodation was staged.

The directive principles which grant textual status to the 'UCC', Pathak and Sunder Rajan argue, operate within the binary of the secular and the personal like the Derridean 'supplement – the marginal, extraneous, gratuitous, temporary, or subsidiary element'.[54] They explode out of their '[textual] space and deconstruc[t] the uneasy hierarchy of the governing terms of and the metaphysic of the unified legal discourse that [they support]'.[55] The exemplary supplement, in Derrida's formulation, is writing itself. A written constitution is a dangerous supplement. It contains within itself, as shown in this work, an archive of the struggle by women against a delimited subject position.

The privileged status of 'speech' collected in the 12 printed volumes of the *Constituent Assembly Debates* has contributed to the erasure of the figure of the woman who, indeed, performed all available acts to prevent herself from being inscribed as 'the normative male subject' of constitutional democracy.[56] Writing, 'that dangerous supplement', not just as evidenced in the form of written notes of dissent or amendments moved by these women members but also as the repository of justice, is available in these archives unsettling the accepted binary of the unified subject of the founding fathers and the decentred female subject of law. The sole woman lawyer in the Constituent Assembly knew that to be without a code is to be without justice.[57]

It is hardly coincidental that women framers were in the closest ideological collaboration with Ambedkar, the chairman of the Drafting Committee. The deconstruction of the binary of 'the categories of the secular and the personal' did not take place through any compromise by the founding fathers but was done by women's simultaneous participation in the framing of the Constitution and its reformation. Jacques Derrida's description of the movement of deconstruction, in this context, has immense evocative value:

> The movements of deconstruction do not destroy structures from the outside. They are not possible and effective, nor can they take active aim, except by inhabiting those structures. Inhabiting them in a certain way, because one always inhabits, and all the more when one does not suspect it. Operating necessarily from the inside, borrowing all the strategic economic resources of subversion from the old structure, borrowing from them structurally, that is to say without being able to isolate their elements and atoms, the enterprise of deconstruction always in a certain way, falls prey to its own work.[58]

Whether women fell prey to their own work or not is a question that can only be asked after we have recognized and appreciated their work.

Reimagining the nation

Standard histories of feminism in India describe the period following the enactment of the Constitution as a period of inactivity. Ironically, part of the reason cited is the Constitution itself:

> 'Equality of the sexes' was guaranteed by the Constitution of India, and there was a comparative lull in feminist activities until the nineteen seventies, when the Constitutional promise of equality was denounced as sham.[59]

'The movement which started in the seventies and eighties', the narrative continues, 'was a very different one, growing out of a number of radical movements of the time'.[60] Nivedita Menon argues that after the 1980s, the women's movement could break out of 'the dominant perceptions of women's issues as mainly social, not political or economic'.[61] She believes that feminist politics in India, at least before the second wave of the 1980s, was largely restricted to areas of family and sexuality. Its focus was hardly on 'issues related to the public sphere, such as for the enforcement of the Equal Remuneration Act of 1976 or for crèche facilities in the workplace and so on'.[62] While her complaint may be true regarding the campaigns taken up by the women's movements of the times she describes, it fails to acknowledge that several such specific demands were already foregrounded by the women authors of the Constitution, who also succeeded in laying the ground for enabling legislation in the future. Following the foundation, most women found places in state organizations to activate the Constitution. The major figures among them had lost in the elections to the first Lok Sabha revealing an interesting pattern – the socialist Kamaladevi to a Congresswoman, Renuka Ray to N. C. Chatterjee of the Hindu Mahasabha, and Durgabai to a Communist leader – each to a candidate from an ideology she had opposed. Hansa Mehta, being the Vice Chancellor of a public university could not contest elections. And yet, all of them contributed to the planning processes of the new state.

Labour and economic rights formed a central part of women's moral imaginary and led them to collaborate several times with the International Labour Organization. Non-discrimination in employment and equal pay for equal work were important items in their Charter of Rights and Duties of 1946. The Charter listed a comprehensive set of demands for women workers including not just crèches for their babies, and nursery schools but also 'maternity benefits which should form part of a comprehensive scheme of social insurance'.[63] In the Constituent Assembly, women laid a great deal of stress on the economic rights of men and women, particularly during the framing of the directive principles, which they considered the most important part of the Constitution. In their later writings too, articles 38 and 39, that constitute the core socialist principles of economic democracy, were repeatedly mentioned as the cornerstone of their future politics.[64] Their arguments on the Hindu Code Bill were also framed in terms of economic rights and the status of women. The family was at the centre of their legislative activities but it was not the economic model of a conventional family with the husband as the breadwinner and the owner of property but a family conceived as 'a co-operative concern where every member has an equal place'.[65] The most radically socialist of these women founders, Renuka Ray envisaged a future when the notion of private property would be abolished. 'A time must come when inherited property must go out', but till such time as this happens, constitutional equality should be extended to all spheres of life.[66]

The binary of the 'private' and the 'public' spheres was, however, not completely deconstructed. Instead, the nation, now morphed into a republic, guaranteeing all citizens the right to contribute to it, was reimagined as an extension of the 'private' sphere: the home, Renuka Ray, argued was 'the nucleus of the nation'.[67] It was not distinct or separate from the nation but the core where the structural principles of the nation, the constitutional ideas were to be activated in their purest form. The metaphor carried significant implications. The nation was to be worked for, 'developed' to use a word of recent parlance, and women had to play their role as active citizens. 'Women's activities cannot be confined to the home alone', Renuka Ray argued, since 'the nation is but the larger home'.[68] Therefore just as women (and men) who work for the nation outside the home have constitutionally guaranteed economic rights, the housewife too has economic rights. For, even when confined to the activities of the home, they are ultimately contributing to the nation, as 'economic units in the domestic sphere'.[69] 'The housewife', Renuka Ray argued immediately after the Constitution came into force, 'is as much a working woman as the men and women who earn their livelihood outside'.[70] The fusing of the nation and the home was an example of the strategic extension of the constitutional principle of equality. Further, it ensured that the Constitution is embedded in the new figure of the nation.

The rights of the housewife were integral to the women's movement. As seen in Chapter 3, the earliest evidence of the demand for recognizing the economic status of the housewife and her labour in India came from the 1930s. After the Constitution came into being, women (Renuka Ray in this case) articulated the demand that the economic value of the housewife's work be recognized in terms of constitutional equality. Continuing her argument from the Hindu Code Bill debates, Ray said, 'one of the basic factors which goes against women is her economic dependence'.[71] Therefore, she urged, 'it must be one of the primary duties of the women's movement and in fact of the society itself ... to give full recognition to the economic value of the housewife'.[72] The full import of her argument lay in her re-imagining the nation as a larger home to which a woman could contribute equally with men, but only when she was fully equipped and paid wages for her domestic labour.[73] Ray's stance also demolished the binary between the home and the nation, thereby superimposing the consecrated space of the home on the nation.

Having already championed the idea of equal pay for equal work, fought for an expansion of the range of women's work, and demanded a radical redefinition of the family, this act of locating women's worth in their labour and property posited women at the centre of a gendered constitutional vision of the nation.

RE-EDUCATION TOWARDS EQUALITY

Women founders saw the Constitution as setting the most important target of establishing gender justice. The value of justice enshrined in the Constitution, for them, revolved around the notion of gender equality. They spent an astonishing amount of intellectual and political energy on enriching the constitutional notion of justice. Their contribution in shaping the central problematics of the development state demands a separate study. In its initial years, the Constitution became a standard icon of reference for these women, whose expressed ideals were nothing short of finding 'the full right to self-expression' for every citizen.[74] While most of them laid special emphasis on the social welfare projects of the state, it would be reductive to imagine that they were driven by the idea of 'social service' in a narrow sense of the term. As Renuka Ray formulated it:

> In the broader sense, social services include the subjects of education, health, housing, labour welfare, rehabilitation of displaced persons, welfare of the backward classes, and social welfare: of these the last two together constitute the common field of Social Welfare Services. While social services constitute an investment in the betterment of the human resources in general, the welfare services are designed to enable the underprivileged or handicapped section to be integrated into the normal community.[75]

The reference to the 'integration' of the handicapped section of society into the 'normal' community, seems to be an extension of the investment these women had made in configuring an ideal nation-state, and an expression of their conviction in the pedagogical function of the Constitution. Social welfare was part of the constitutional project of social transformation in India. Its evolution, according to Renuka Ray, took place in three stages:

> In the pioneering phase, the main work that was done was to create public opinion and to arouse the social conscience to the need for change. Then came the second phase in which reform was sought to be brought about by legislation. Side by side we saw the growth of many voluntary organisations which took the lead in the setting up of a variety of social services and welfare activities initiated throughout the country. This was done against the greatest odds by enthusiastic and devoted social workers.... [In 1947, it] entered into the third phase wherein a comprehensive attempt is being made to convert ideas and provisions of social reforms legislation into action.[76]

Taken as a template, these three phases with their different emphases formed a sort of overlapping programme of action for the women members.

Situating themselves in the third phase, women framers attended to the implementation of these reforms, bringing them in accordance with the principles enshrined in the Constitution. After joining the Planning Commission of India, one of the first publications that Durgabai presided over was a 1956 volume that sought to identify the enabling potential of law, 'define its approach to social problems, provide the tools wherewith to tackle them and lay the duty in the appropriate quarter'.[77] The task ahead, as Durgabai's preface seemed to suggest, was two pronged: remembering the law's intimate bearing on the problems of social welfare which was 'the primary duty of the Modern State' on the one hand, and correcting 'the average citizen's notions and prejudices' against the institutions set up by the state for social welfare, on the other.[78] The first was to be achieved by 'examining all our laws' especially those concerning 'women, children, the physically, mentally and socially handicapped groups' in the light of the constitutional principles, which, in Durgabai's words,

> proclaimed the dignity of the individual, declared the equality of the sexes and is pledged to the establishment of social justice. Existing laws must conform to certain prescribed standards, and law must respect the fundamental rights guaranteed to every citizen. The Directive Principles of State Policy flow from one basic principle that concern for the human problems of its citizens is one of the great purposes of Government.[79]

A major project for this purpose with regard to the Scheduled Castes and the Scheduled Tribes was undertaken by Renuka Ray as leader of the Planning Commission's Study Team on Social Welfare in 1959.[80] Her team realized the need for differential solutions to the social problems faced by the Scheduled Castes and the Scheduled Tribes, with each community facing 'complex problems which require varied services to meet them'.[81] After rigorous surveys and studies that included discussions with experts like the eminent tribal leader Jaipal Singh and anthropologists like N. K. Bose, B. H. Mehta, and Verrier Elwin, the Committee came to the conclusion that there is no aspect of development that does not require specific consideration for these communities.[82] Its suggestions regarding economic development, education, and public health for these minority communities show unmistakable commitment to the constitutional ethics that was articulated by Renuka Ray and other female members during the framing. For example, it recommended the development of mixed habitation for Dalits and non-Dalits with provisions for houses specially reserved for the former, and suggested policies to encourage marriage between Dalits and non-Dalits.[83] The recommendations included clearing slums, making loans available at all levels for Scheduled Caste communities, making scavenger-free latrines, emphasis on schemes for the removal of untouchability, emphasis on schools that would pay attention to the education of Dalit girls, and specially empowering Scheduled Caste observers who could ensure that caste-discrimination at all levels is challenged.[84]

The report of Renuka Ray's committee laid special emphasis on strengthening the Office of the Scheduled Castes and Scheduled Tribes.[85] Radical suggestions were made for the Scheduled Tribes that included the creation of a Central Institute for Tribal Welfare.[86] The Committee made several suggestions for the protection of the land rights of the tribals and recommended the allotment of land to landless tribals.[87] In its suggestions for the development of the tribal economy based on agriculture, forestry, handicrafts, and village industries, the Committee recognized the need for appreciating different vocational abilities of the numerous groups. Interestingly, it also recommended remoulding the school curriculum for tribal children to suit the special cultural values of the communities.

Although one can see a hint of state patronization in these reports – a sign of co-option by the state of feminist impulses – they can also be read as evidence of the contrary pulls faced in the pursuit of constitutional justice between the limited demands of social welfare and the greater aspiration of social transformation that animated women's participation in the framing process. Whenever women framers led a programme of social welfare, they tried to go beyond merely providing support to marginalized communities and instead sought to restructure their relationship with society, recommending inter-community mixing and marriages for example, as in this report. This dilemma was best expressed in Durgabai's monumental project, the *Encyclopaedia of Social Work*. As the jurist P. B. Gajendragadkar put it in his article on 'Constitution and Social Work' in the *Encyclopaedia*:

> The activities undertaken by a social reformer may sometimes border on the activities of social work, and the social worker may, whilst he is doing some work, as an item of social work, seek to modify or change the social structure. This is particularly so in our country at present because since the Constitution came into existence, the country is engaged in the mighty task of bringing about socio-economic revolution. Thus social welfare activities are likely to merge in or supplement activities of social reform and vice versa.[88]

He was echoing Durgabai's conviction that the social and the economic are inseparable, and no programme of economic development can be implemented in a vacuum of social interests. Durgabai warned against the 'conceptual error' of 'the arbitrary labelling of a group of fields as social development and of others as economic development'.[89] In a lecture delivered at Bangkok at the United Nations (UN) Asian Institute for Economic Development in February 1964, she held that the 'single-minded devotion to economic development' may lead to a loss of 'other valuable objectives'.[90] She emphasized the necessity to return to the values of the Constitution, coded in its Preamble and enshrined, especially, in articles 32 and 46 of the directive principles.[91] The integration of social, political, and economic justice cannot be achieved by 'merely rechanneling economic activity within the existing socio-economic framework. That framework has itself to be remoulded so as to enable it to accommodate progressively those fundamental urges.'[92]

These examples may suffice to show that after the foundation of the republic, the Constitution was central to the transformative project in the imagination of the founding mothers. It is also evident that these women kept reading and activating the Constitution in the same spirit with which they had framed it. In my last instance, I will show how they inserted some of the most radical feminist theories of gender construction in the official discourse of the nation-state. Since they always engaged the Constitution in a pedagogical project of 'awakening consciousness', it was natural that these ideas were introduced through the field of education. The Constitution was now available to them granting 'a de-jure equality' to women but, above all, making available for them a set of conceptual resources that could be very legitimately employed in the name of the people.

Thus, a committee appointed 'to suggest special measures to make up the leeway in women's education at the primary and secondary levels' took the responsibility of providing a radical framework of society based on the constitutional notions of justice.[93] The Committee was chaired by Durgabai Deshmukh, who was already working as the Chairman of the Central Social Welfare Board towards the 'active fulfilment' of 'the programme of action drawn up' in the directive principles.[94] Speaking as if to the same men who had evoked classical Indian literature to restrict women to their perennial 'feminine' prisons, Durgabai's Committee spoke on behalf of the Indian Constitution:

> But how distressing and how degrading and how unfortunate it has been that such a simple proposition as this that man and woman are not different essentially has gone down in history unrecognized, if not in thought or word, certainly in action![95]

The emphasis of the Constitution was 'equality rather than identity'.[96] It underlined 'this equality between man and woman'[97] and 'fully expresse[d] the best and the highest aspirations of modern progressive social thought'[98] which recognized this equality. If this was not sufficiently radical, in 1961, three years later, another committee, this time under the leadership of Hansa Mehta, pushed the constitutional ideal of justice and equality further to recommend a social reconstruction so as to 'abolish the sex-dichotomy in favour of unlimited diversity'.[99] The purpose of such a reconstruction would be to translate the juridical equality inscribed in the Constitution into de facto equality[100] and create 'a democratic and socialistic society',[101] in which 'men would have to share the responsibility of parenthood and home-making with women; and women, in their turn, will have to share the social and economic responsibilities'.[102] In this society, women would have 'perfect equality' with men, 'not only de jure but de facto as well' and individuals would 'not be cramped by arbitrary stereotypes of "masculine" and "feminine" traits'.[103]

In search of its rationale, the Committee, which consisted of nine men and two women, under the leadership of Hansa Mehta to whom I ascribe the authorship of its report, studied a range of social scientists and thinkers including Havelock Ellis, Viola Klein, Otto Weininger, Sigmund Freud, Alfred Adler, C. C. Miles, Mathilde and Mathias Verting, and Margaret Mead. Up-to-date literature, though mostly Western, of the most varied kind (though there was no mention of Simone de Beauvoir) was marshalled for evidence, and it was recommended that such works be undertaken at a national level in India and sponsored by the government.[104] The committee's recommendations must be read as an outstanding example of these women's mode of working in small, quasi-academic groups to make crucial interventions. Given Hansa Mehta's role in the inter-textual production of the Constitution, this recommendation for a social transformation may be read not as its interpretation but as the broadening of the already embedded intentionality and rationality of the founding mothers.

This social transformation could take place through a rigorous programme of 're-education of men and women' designed to inculcate a rational attitude of equality and respect informed by three fundamental, we must say feminist, propositions:

> The first is to disabuse the public mind of all the traditional concepts of the physical or intellectual inferiority of women. There was no scientific foundation for such an assumption. Secondly, the public in general and the teachers in particular would have to be made to realize that it was unscientific to divide

tasks and subjects on the basis of sex and regard some of them as 'masculine' and others as 'feminine'. Thirdly, [that] the so-called psychological differences between the two sexes arise not out of sex, but out of social conditioning will have to be widely publicised and people will have to be made to realise that stereo-types of 'masculine' and 'feminine' personalities do more harm than good.[105]

The year was 1961. Thirty years earlier, in 1932, when pioneers of the same women's movement, leaders of the AIWC, had founded the Lady Irwin College of Home Sciences, they had started with an opposite position. By the 1960s, they affected an incredible shift in paradigm. The optimism in the admonition was unmistakable. The question is how far we have belied the hopes of the founding mothers of the republic:

It is in the minds of men and women that the seeds of the social inequality of the sexes have been traditionally sown; and it is, therefore, only in the minds of men and women that the true and solid foundations of the future equality of the sexes will have to be built.[106]

NOTES

1. Ammu Swaminathan, Constituent Assembly of India, 24 November 1949, *CAD*, XI: 915.
2. B. R. Ambedkar, Constituent Assembly of India, 17 November 1949, *CAD*, XI: 607.
3. *Amrit Bazaar Patrika*, 27 November 1949, 1.
4. G. Durgabai, Constituent Assembly of India, 24 November 1949, *CAD*, XI: 886.
5. Renuka Ray, Constituent Assembly of India, 19 November 1949, *CAD*, XI: 717.
6. Ibid.
7. Ibid.
8. Purnima Banerji, Constituent Assembly of India, 24 November 1949, *CAD*, XI: 878.
9. Ibid.
10. Dipesh Chakrabarty, *Provincializing Europe: Postcolonial Thought and Historical Difference* (Princeton, NJ: Princeton University Press, 2000), 8.
11. Purnima Banerji, Constituent Assembly of India, 24 November 1949, *CAD*, XI: 878.
12. Granville Austin, *The Indian Constitution: Cornerstone of a Nation*, 2nd ed. (New Delhi: Oxford University Press, 1999), x.

13. B. R. Ambedkar, Constituent Assembly of India, 25 November 1949, *CAD*, XI: 973.
14. Ibid., 975.
15. Renuka Ray, Constituent Assembly of India, 19 November 1949, *CAD*, XI: 717.
16. Ibid.
17. Hansa Mehta, Constituent Assembly of India, 22 November 1949, *CAD*, XI: 795 (emphasis mine).
18. Dakshayani Velayudhan, Constituent Assembly of India, 8 November 1948, *CAD*, VII: 308.
19. Ibid., 308.
20. Ibid.
21. Renuka Ray, Constituent Assembly of India, 19 November 1946, *CAD*, XI: 717.
22. B. R. Ambedkar, Constituent Assembly of India, 25 November 1949, *CAD*, XI: 975.
23. Hansa Mehta, Constituent Assembly of India, 22 November 1949, *CAD*, XI: 795.
24. Kamaladevi Chattopadhyay, 'Women and Food Problem', *The Free Press Journal*, 26 January 1953, 12 (from Renuka Ray Papers, Speeches/Writings by Her, File no. 23, NMML) (emphasis mine).
25. Kamaladevi Chattopadhyay, *Inner Recesses, Outer Spaces: Memoirs* (New Delhi: India International Centre and Niyogi Books, 2014), 329.
26. Ibid.
27. Ibid.
28. Renuka Ray, Constituent Assembly of India, 19 November 1946, *CAD*, XI: 717.
29. Renuka Ray, *My Reminiscences: Social Development during the Gandhian Era and After* (New Delhi: AIWC and Stree, 2005), 134.
30. G. Durgabai, Constituent Assembly of India, 24 November 1950, *CAD*, XI: 887 (emphasis mine).
31. Ray, *My Reminiscences*, 134.
32. G. Durgabai, Constituent Assembly of India, 24 November 1950, *CAD*, XI: 887.
33. Granville Austin, *Working a Democratic Constitution: A History of the Indian Experience* (New Delhi: Oxford University Press, 1999), 1.
34. AIWC's 'Memorandum on Educational Reform, 1927', in Aparna Basu and Bharati Ray, *Women's Struggle: A History of the All India Women's Conference 1927–2002* (New Delhi: Manohar, 2003), 176–179, 177.

35. President AIWC to Members of the Standing Committee, 25 June 1947, AIWC Papers, IV Inst. File no. 132, NMML.

36. Draft Constitution of the AIWC, prepared and proposed by Hannah Sen, Member-in-Charge, Constitution, June 1947 and Amendments to the Proposed Constitution, AIWC Papers, IV Inst. File no. 132, NMML.

37. Lakshmi Menon, 'Why the All-India Women's Conference?', Lakshmi Menon Papers; Subject Files Sl. no. 2; Papers relating to AIWC (1955–1995), NMML.

38. Ibid.

39. Amrit Kaur to Urmila Mehta, 17 October 1949, AIWC Papers IV Instalment File no. 39, NMML.

40. Ibid.

41. Ibid.

42. *The All Indian Women's Conference: Constitution*, article II (2). (Sarojini House: New Delhi, 1973), 1.

43. Several insightful works on the question of women's agency within Muslim personal law hemmed within the secular framework of the Indian Constitution have appeared since the publication of the essay discussed here. With the criminalization of triple *talaq*, the Citizenship Amendment Act and Muslim women's protests against it, and several new pieces of legislation brought in by the Hindu majoritarian regime, the question of the minority woman and her relationship with constitutionalism has become ever more urgent. I limit my reading to 'Shahbano' by Pathak and Sunder Rajan only as an instance of how the question of women's consent can be rethought once the voice of women in the Constituent Assembly is recognized.

44. *Mohd. Ahmad Khan* v. *Shah Bano Begum*, (1985) 3 SCR 844.

45. Zakia Pathak and Rajeshwari Sunder Rajan, 'Shahbano', in Joan Scott and Judith Butler (eds), *Feminists Theorize the Political*, 257–279 (New York: Routledge, 2001; originally published in *Signs: Journal of Women in Culture and Society* 14, 3 [1989]: 558–582), 258.

46. Ibid.

47. Ibid., 260.

48. Ibid.

49. Ibid., 268.

50. Ibid., 267–268.

51. Ibid., 268.

52. Ibid., 258.

53. Ibid., 268–269.

54. Ibid., 269.

55. Ibid., 270.

56. Ibid., 268.

57. G. Durgabai, Constituent Assembly (Legislative) Debates, 1 March 1949, in *Dr Babasaheb Ambedkar Writings and Speeches*, Vol. 14, part 2, 398–405, 399.

58. Jacques Derrida, *Of Grammatology* trans. Gayatri Chakravorty Spivak (Delhi: Motilal Banarasidas, 1994; originally 1976), 24.

59. Radha Kumar, *The History of Doing: An Illustrated Account of Movements for Women's Rights and Feminism in India, 1800–1990* (New Delhi: Kali for Women, 1993), 1.

60. Ibid., 97.

61. Nivedita Menon, *Recovering Subversion: Feminist Politics beyond the Law* (Ranikhet: Permanent Black, 2004), 7.

62. Ibid., 12.

63. Draft of the Indian Woman's Charter of Rights and Duties, 1946, Hansa Mehta Papers, Subject File no. 7, NMML.

64. See, for instance, Renuka Ray, 'Socialism', unpublished article, Renuka Ray Papers Subject File no. 93, NMML; and Renuka Ray, 'History of Social Reform and Social Work from 1947 to 1963', manuscript of an unpublished article, 1963, Renuka Ray Papers, Writings/Speeches by Her, File no. 59, NMML, 3–4.

65. Indian Women's Charter of Rights and Duties, Hansa Mehta Papers, Subject File no, 7, NMML.

66. Ray, 'Socialism'.

67. Renuka Ray, 'Women as Citizens of Free India', sent for publication in *The People*, 6 July 1951, Renuka Ray Papers, Speeches/Writings by Her, File no. 14, 5, NMML.

68. Ibid.

69. Ibid.

70. Ibid.

71. Ibid.

72. Ibid.

73. Renuka Ray, 'Women in the Republic of India', for the Republic Number of *The Free Press Journal* (published from Bombay), 8–9. Renuka Ray Papers, Speeches/Writings by Her, File no. 24, NMML.

74. Renuka Ray's report as leader of the Team of Social Work, Planning Commission, 1958, Renuka Ray Papers, Subject File no. 13, NMML, 15–19.

75. Ray, 'History of Social Reform and Social Work from 1947 to 1963', 12.

76. Ibid., 9.

77. Durgabai Deshmukh, 'Preface', in Durgabai Deshmukh (ed.), *Social Legislation: Its Role in Social Welfare* (New Delhi: Planning Commission, 1956), ix.

78. Ibid.

79. Ibid, vii.

80. *Report of the Study Team on Social Welfare and Welfare of Backward Classes*, Vol. 1 (New Delhi: Committee on Planned Projects, 1959).

81. Ibid., 3.

82. Ibid.

83. For a summary list of the recommendations of Renuka Ray's Committee for the Scheduled Castes, see ibid., 342–345.

84. Ibid.

85. Ibid., 181–185.

86. For a summary list of the recommendations of Renuka Ray's Committee for the Scheduled Tribes, see ibid., 330–337.

87. Ibid., 133.

88. P. B. Gajendragadkar, 'The Constitution and Social Work', in *Encyclopaedia of Social Work*, Vol. 1, 152–159 (New Delhi: Publications Division on Behalf of the Planning Commission, 1968), 155,

89. Durgabai Deshmukh, *Social Welfare and Economic Development* (Bangkok: United Nations Asian Institute for Economic Development and Planning, 1966), 4.

90. Ibid.

91. Ibid., 6–7.

92. Ibid. 7.

93. The National Committee on Women's Education (NCWE) was appointed in May 1958, under the chairmanship of Durgabai, at the recommendation of the Planning Commission, of which she was herself a member. Cited from extracts from its report published in Vina Mazumdar (ed.), *Education, Equality and Development: Persistent Paradoxes in Indian Women's History* (New Delhi: CWDS and Pearson, 2012), 21–60, 22.

94. Durgabai Deshmukh (ed.), *Social Legislation: Its Role in Social Welfare* (New Delhi: The Planning Commission of India, 1956), 6.

95. The report of the NCWE (1958), cited in Mazumdar, *Education, Equality and Development*, 23.

96. Ibid., 24

97. Ibid., 25.

98. Ibid.

99. Report of the Committee on the Differentiation of Curricula for Boys and Girls, typescript printed at the National Council for Women's Education, New Delhi, from Hansa Mehta Papers, Subject File no. 31, NMML, 27.
100. Ibid., 31–32.
101. Ibid., 34.
102. Ibid.
103. Ibid., 39.
104. See Annexure IV of the Report of the Committee on the Differentiation of Curricula for Boys and Girls.
105. Ibid., 33–34.
106. Ibid., 34.

Conclusion

Remembering the Founding Mothers

[In the estimation of the current generation] they were not radical, not revolutionary. They are defined sneeringly as reformists, that they only bothered about middle class problems, marriage laws, widows, inheritance.

—Kamaladevi Chattopadhyay, 1983[1]

I

In 1974, a report titled *Towards Equality* was published by the Government of India.[2] This report acquired the status of a foundational text for feminist research and practice. It was widely considered to have heralded the Second Wave of the women's movement in India.[3] Prepared by the Committee on the Status of Women in India (CSWI), comprising 10 women, the report unsettled confidence in the constitutional promises with its revealing findings about 'the further lowering of the status of women' and 'the process of regression developed during the Freedom Movement'[4]:

> *Towards Equality* was a severe indictment of the first twenty-five years of independent India's achievements to ensure Indian women's rights to equality, justice, freedom and dignity as promised to them by the Constitution.[5]

As evident from its title, at the core of the Committee's ethical and social concerns was the notion of equality, which it recognized as 'an article of faith in our Constitution'.[6] This equality, the Committee concluded, had not been achieved even after two decades of the promise made in the Preamble. What made this conclusion so extraordinarily impactful and convincing was the way it was arrived at:

In coming to this conclusion, the Committee depended on data, information and hard evidence to make its point rather than an impassioned rhetoric. Its dependence on facts, figures, testimonies, details and record rather than value making judgements, has made the report a multidimensional chronicle – a benchmark, an advocacy document, a reference book and an archive of the period.[7]

Its detailed statistical account of women's status 'in the total context of a society',[8] saw women in professional, legal, economic, cultural, and social positions. It identified 'areas and problems that required careful, scientific, and expert investigations'[9] and 'sought the assistance of scholars and experts in different fields'.[10]

Three reasons are commonly cited for the foundational status of *Towards Equality*.[11] It was the 'first' comprehensive and scientific study of women at all levels of national life, and initiated the genre of status reports of women that has become an 'acknowledged strategy of learning, policy making, political signalling and advocacy on important issues'.[12] *Towards Equality* was credited with making women 'truly visible' in print.[13] Second, it did not look at women in compartmentalized constituencies. The report saw women in the interdependencies of their various roles. It recognized 'the radicalism of the Constitution' whose implicit assumption is that 'every adult woman, whatever her social position or accomplishments, will function as a citizen and as an individual partner in the task of nation building'.[14] Finally, the report turned to the Constitution and its provisions for 'reversing the situation of women that the Committee had documented in such detail'.[15]

The authors of this landmark document claimed they 'had no model or material to use as a frame of reference'.[16] The only frame of reference they had was the 'constitutional provisions that have a bearing on the status of women' and the goal of 'enabling women to play their full and proper role in building up the nation'.[17] The Constitution for them was that ideal which had receded from the horizon of women's lives in the 20 odd years of its being. The report cited the Constitution frequently, and built its case on the articles granting the fundamental right to equality, namely, articles 14, 15, and 16 and also on articles 38, 39, 44, and 45 of the directive principles – articles that had intensely engaged women during the framing process. For the authors of *Towards Equality*, the directive principles 'concretize, together with the Fundamental Rights, the constitutional vision of a new Indian socio-political order'.[18] Through its recommendations, they sought to make women the beneficiaries of this new order.

The Committee's achievement was in its description of Indian women, transforming them from tropes of victimhood and handicaps to embedded categories of social realities. Women of India, in terms of the Committee's report, were masses with differential realities that influenced each other in a vast network of institutional and social applications. As a corollary, they were objects of knowledge that could supplement the rationality of the state and intensify its ethical compulsions. This newly created knowledge of women's status also included women's consciousness of their own status.[19] While acknowledging the historical significance of *Towards Equality*, I would like to pose certain questions regarding the assertions made by the CSWI which are linked to its status in contemporary feminist discourse.

The first question is: how new was this knowledge about women? Was not women's self-awareness, women's self-consciousness already inscribed in the Constitution? Was not this knowledge of women's status already a part of the moral imaginary that the founding mothers had framed into the Constitution? Was not equality already defined in relative, measurable terms? Was not empiricism already at work in the epistemological performance of the women framers?

This work argues that women framers' conviction in constitutionalism was based on their claim that they constituted a well-defined minority with experiences of overlapping and entrenched discrimination in the Indian social structure. A democracy which was yet to take root in this society needed a written and firmly prescribed constitutional morality. It was only as an acknowledged minority that women could do both: develop a collective self-consciousness and make specific demands in the homogenizing space of the Constituent Assembly. This led women to draw differential maps of their status that could comprise the layers of the written-ness of their constitutional politics. In a speech delivered in Jullundur in 1932, Amrit Kaur foregrounded a central idea of the process of re-imagining and re-constituting the nation: 'The proper status of women in modern societies', she claimed, 'must, therefore, be discussed and settled in the light *not of history, but of ethics*. It must accord, not with any particular phase of the past, but with the general moral ideal which is current at the present time'.[20]

Contemporary Indian feminists have applauded *Towards Equality* as the first document to introduce the political–epistemological category of 'status of women'. Yet Amrit Kaur's speech is clear evidence that as early as the 1930s, women had recognized the significance of women's 'status' especially in the context of their programme of constitutional citizenship. A definition of the term 'status of women' was the indispensable first step towards occupying a specific constituency of women. In order to gain a constitutional subjecthood, women were to be ascribed an empirically measurable 'status', which could generate an epistemological framework from which they could design their future demands. The criterion against which this status has to be measured was: 'the general moral ideal which is current at the present time'. Much intellectual labour of the women's endeavour of expressing their moral ideals to address a modern, constitutional discourse was devoted to creating a measure of their status in society. Within this discourse, women became a special category, an object of knowledge, with neatly defined social indicators, and who could set specified goals for the state. These were documents produced based on field research and statistical data.

The National Planning Committee's Sub-Committee on Woman's Role in Planned Economy (1939), for instance, studied women's status under two broad categories, namely, individual status and social status. The individual status of women was measured in terms of their civic and economic rights. This involved extremely detailed and sophisticated analyses of data pertaining to women's health, education, employment, wages, property, labour, and legal status. The Committee's report produced a diversity of knowledge about the women of India who were presented as a category comprised of many sub-categories. No aspect of the entire constituency of Indian women – urban, rural, propertied, industrial workers, and agricultural labour, among others – was left undescribed.

Kamaladevi Chattopadhyay's report on the status of Indian women, at the Asian Women's Conference in 1947, presented women's status in all these fields with a host of cross-comparative data and followed the same model as that of the National Planning Committee. The tenor of her analysis can be understood from this excerpt:

> One curious and disheartening fact about women's education is that, while the figures show a slight increase in the number of institutions from 1941 to 1942, actually there is a drop in literacy percentage from 2.73 to 2.51, which means that educational facilities do not keep pace with the increasing population, due mainly to the niggardly sums spent on education by the administration. The total amount spent on education is about 308.5 million rupees, out of which the Government spends 135 million. Even these figures are misleading, for they *throw no light on equality*.[21]

Her compilation, prepared at the time of the inception of the Constituent Assembly, contained scrupulous details of women's educational, health, and employment status. This data, collected over a decade, was a sign of women's commitment towards creating empirical evidence about the condition of women which could then become a valuable source for formulating their constitutional demands. Women's interventions during the framing of the directive principles could be cited as one example of how this knowledge of women as an empirical category helped them give specific shape to their demands.

Women recognized that the first step towards equality was a measurement of their status. Thus, with respect to women's employment and earning, the All India Women's Conference (AIWC) representative urged before the International Labour Organization (ILO) that the conditions of women's employment must be brought at par with that of men and stressed on the need for finding out the conditions of women's employment. Shanta Mukherjee, the Indian woman representative to the ILO, contributed significantly to the insertion of the word 'sex' into the section of ILO resolution on 'non-discrimination'. 'Such an invidious distinction of omitting women from non-discrimination', she argued, 'would have continued unabated the exploitation arising from a cheap supply of women's labour'.[22] The AIWC played a crucial role in getting the general clause for non-discrimination in the Draft Convention for Non-metropolitan Territories of the ILO amended. Interestingly, even after the ILO amended its clause to prohibit any kind of discrimination on the basis of sex, the representative of the Government of India 'going out of his way, expressed disapproval of the introduction of the principle of equal wages for equal work'.[23]

In all these contests for women's constitutional and human rights, the status of women became the most effective ground for rational debates giving the woman question a concrete design for action. Equality was no more just a political value; it was an achievable state of the social system. In pamphlets, advocacy reports, pleas to the public, and petitions to the government and international organizations, thanks to figures on women's conditions, equality became a tangible principle of discourse. Statistics on death rate, child mortality rate, maternity deaths, education, and average wage-earning created the new, material category of women.

Women were shifted from abstract, amorphous class-membership which embodied the spiritualized essence of the nation to the constituency of a diverse, discrete community with a measurable and hence comparable status. Accelerating towards the Constituent Assembly, this was a brief, intensive process of transformation. During the framing process, the imagined community of women became a real, 'enumerated community', to use a phrase Sudipta Kaviraj uses to describe the process of the identification of a community as a nation.[24] Women's emergence as an enumerated community in the 1930s and 1940s, circumscribed the nationalist discourse as evident in the many debates in the Constituent Assembly and the Central Legislative Assembly.

Interestingly, the CSWI was aware of the historical presence of women in the constitution-making process[25] but failed to comprehend the complex processes through which the 'mothers' conceptualized their demand for equality:

> The history of the discussion on women's rights, both in the Constituent Assembly and in the Central Legislature over the Hindu Code Bill in the period immediately after Independence, indicates that attitudes towards women's equality vary sharply. As long as the discussion was on abstract principles, as was the case during the debate on Fundamental Rights in the Constituent Assembly, there was no dissentient voice to challenge or even to provoke a discussion on this historic decision. When it came to applying the same principles on established preserves of traditional male privileges such as the right to property and the unchallenged dominance of the husband in family life the reactions of the same body was [sic] very different. One group accepted both, the concept of equality and its implications for society. The second group accepted the concept in theory, but was not prepared to practice or follow up its implications. The third group rejected the concept outright – as totally inapplicable and undesirable for Indian society.[26]

For the authors of *Towards Equality*, the founding moment was riddled with these contradictions and a pervasive binary of a theory of equality and its practice. In spite of their awareness of the presence of women in both these Assemblies, they failed to (or were unwilling to) identify the various groups divided by their level of acceptance of the constitutional guarantee of equality between the sexes. This is not surprising given the fact that the Committee was not aware of the textuality of the framing process and the internal consistency among the women in terms of their conceptualization of equality. As seen throughout this work, the artificial distinction between the theory and the practice of equality wrongly assumes that the discussions in the Constituent Assembly were on abstract principles alone. It also suggests an erroneous understanding of the very nature of constitutional equality as a homogenous abstraction whose content must be supplied from outside the text.

As the performative practices of the founding mothers show, the principle of equality was as an abstraction only inasmuch as we forget the words of experience that were distilled to give it a form in the text of the Constitution. All abstract nouns ('right') and all adjectives ('fundamental') in the text of the Constitution encapsulate meanings imbibed with practical possibilities and historical experiences. The Constitution is an intersection of moral imagination and social politics, both of which feed into each other. It is written in a language of a two-way translation between ideas and practice, a language in which the founding mothers of the republic inscribed their lives in an ever-renewing text.

Thus, I would argue that long before the CSWI, the stress had shifted from the attributes of women to the condition of women. During the framing process, the two mutually reinforcing concepts of women's status – the scale of their achievements and deprivation, and their location vis-à-vis men – gave women a subtly muted but theoretically robust claim to be protected by the Constitution. Autonomous standards to measure and improve women's 'status', encompassed various facets of the constitutional vision regarding women's lives in the legal, social, and cultural domain, articulated by women during the framing process. These standards prevented the essentializing of women with the spiritual attributes of the nation, and gave claim to their real social existence, something that *Towards Equality* rediscovered and reiterated.

The status of women, for the authors of *Towards Equality*, served as a tool for empirical measurement, record, and comparison; it was projected as the demand of situational justice that the Constitution was framed to dispense. The authors' claims to be the first in this domain appear to be accurate till we return to the *Report of the Sub-Committee on Woman's Role in Planned Economy* prepared in 1940. This was evidence of how meticulously women were engaged in finding statistical information on discrimination against women.

> To facilitate collection of data regarding the present condition of woman in India, a comprehensive questionnaire in English was issued by the sub-committee and widely circulated all over India through a) provincial worker's groups b) the central, provincial and state governments c) various existing women's institutions and other institutions interested in women's problems d) prominent workers in the social, economic, legal, educational and political fields. The questionnaire was also translated into Hindustani (Urdu and Devanagari scripts), Gujarati, Bengali, Kannada, Marathi and Oriya.[27]

In the course of their work, members had realized that there was a serious lack of statistics, investigation, and research, especially with regard to women's condition and position. And this is only one example, albeit an early one. Even 35 years later, when Vina Mazumdar and her colleagues undertook the mammoth task of gathering statistical data about the condition and status of women, they were faced with a similar hurdle.

It would appear then, that the contemporary feminist understanding of *Towards Equality* as the first document to make an assessment of women's status and demands for improving it is incorrect. Indeed, as my work has shown, it is lamentable that the considerable achievement of the women who participated in the women's movement since the 1920s, had been part of important women's organizations, and members of the Constituent Assembly, is seldom acknowledged in contemporary feminist discourse.

Looking back at the period of women's organized efforts to bring about a change in the condition of their sex, Kamaladevi Chattopadhyay, one of the founders of the AIWC and a member of the socialist party, made an assessment of the hindrances and hostilities against which her comrades had fought. She also noted with some regret how these women and their efforts had been forgotten by posterity, how they had been erased from history. Her observations are worth quoting in full:

> A grievous injustice has been done to the heroic efforts of countless women who strove against unimaginable deterrents to serve the cause of their betterment. Women did valiant service not only pushing forward their own progress but acting as levers to help other oppressed sections, while facing fierce hostility. In the Indian scene today where social work has become just a profession or at the most a leisure hour pastime for affluent class women, it is difficult to visualize the crusaders of long ago, working with passion, pursuing a goal laboriously, seeking nothing for themselves. There were no grants to feed such activities; no awards, titles, national recognition, no press publicity – instead, a lot of abuse.... The present day young women are totally unaware of the past social struggle or its nature. The past is regarded with rather a withering contempt for the leadership of the time. If conditions were so bad, why did the women not revolt they ask. They have never cared to dig up the past and get at the real history of the social changes and the many benefits they brought to the youth of today ... comparatively far more freedom, notwithstanding the many limitations that constrained them.[28]

Decades before this, during her presidential address to the 1946 session of the AIWC, she reminded her colleagues that

> The women's movement is essentially a social movement ... it operates as an integral part of the progressive social structure in the broadest sense ... it is therefore a comrade to the struggle of the backward castes and the long oppressed classes alike ... to give it any other interpretation or sheer it off to isolate it from the main current, is socially injurious.[29]

I hope my work will create a resurgence of interest in the work of the women I call the 'founding mothers of the republic' and also recognize the feminist movement they led for what it was. To turn away from these founding mothers, judging them a priori as passive and docile women who were pawns in the hands of the powerful men in the Constituent Assembly is a grave intellectual and ethical fallacy.

II

'For we think back through our mothers if we are women', Virginia Woolf asserted in *A Room of One's Own*.[30] It would, of course, be erroneous to read Woolf's comment either as a glorification of motherhood or as extolling the essentialist bond between women. In this essay which explored the complex relationship between women and writing, Woolf examined the material, ideological constraints on women as authors of fiction. The context of this particular comment was Woolf's understanding of the predicament of nineteenth-century women writers of fiction who would invariably find themselves in the shadow of the great male writers. This location in the patriarchal territory, she argued, was deeply debilitating for women who would have nothing to gain from a typically male mode of thinking and writing which had hardened into a tradition. Though she did not use the phrase 'female literary tradition', Woolf clearly indicated that an alternative, enabling condition for nineteenth-century women writers would be to establish a connection with the 'mother', a figuration which would also guarantee a freedom from that of the father and his laws.

Indeed, so evocative and influential was the trope of thinking back through mothers, that Alice Walker, who openly challenged the white European elitist bias of Virginia Woolf's essay, nevertheless chose to make women artists' relationship with their mothers the central concern of her own essay, 'In Search of Our Mothers' Gardens'.[31] Locating herself firmly within a Black 'Womanist' tradition, Walker foregrounded the necessity of connecting to the *collective* identity of Black women artists, those mothers and grandmothers who were doubly exploited within colonialism and patriarchy.

Walker's engagement with Woolf could only take place more than 50 years after the latter's death, and only through a textual intervention. The Black womanist writer could address the pitfalls of White liberal feminism only indirectly. But during the turbulent times of the 1940s in India, a time when the nascent nation was gradually taking firm steps towards becoming a republic, a public platform was available for women belonging to the upper-castes and to the Dalit community. Dakshayani Velayudhan, a Dalit woman could critique the positions arrived at by prominent liberal feminists of the AIWC like Renuka Ray on questions of women and labour rights on the floor of the Constituent Assembly. In the Factories Bill, proposed in 1948, Ray argued that working-class women ought to be able to do night shifts. This argument was based on the ground of equal rights and opportunities for the genders. While this appeared to be a progressive position, the specific needs of women workers were not factored in. They were rendered 'sexless' labour. In responding to the proposal, Dakshayani Velayudhan was firm in her opinion that:

> I think these night-shifts can be avoided. The management can very well give work for the women by taking them in the general shift and in the first shift. Even if we suppose that a large number of women are coming to work in the factories at night, it will be advisable on the part of the management to give them work during day time and I don't think that any sensible management will give women work in the factories at night.[32]

Her objection to Ray's proposal concerned the safety of working-class women, many of who were from the Harijan community. Though she did not spell out the dangers that might befall the Dalit working-class woman working night shifts, the issue of her being preyed upon by men, the possibility of being sexually assaulted was surely foremost in her mind. She firmly asserted:

> I cannot approve of the provisions of the Bill which provide not a charter of rights but a *charter of slavery* to many women.[33]

Earlier she was also vociferous in demanding restrooms for women workers in factories and also the provision of mid-day meals. During her interventions, she had persistently questioned the Dalit Labour Minister, Babu Jagjivan Ram, regarding provisions for women workers and had even asked him if he was willing to pay more wages to the women than the men. Dakshayani Velayudhan challenged both privileged upper-caste women like Renuka Ray (one who had worked extensively in mining locations, ensuring safety for miners) as well as a Dalit male leader, a stalwart, in positing the question of the safety of the woman labourer, who was more often than not a Dalit/Harijan and a soft target for factory owners or managers. Her presence and her very pertinent question return us to the image of the female subject of the new nation-state, its citizen in an avatar that is seldom discussed.

Could this intelligent, independent, and courageous Dalit mother be erased in an attempt to discount the efforts of the women members of the Constituent Assembly? Would that not be a double erasure? On the other hand, blanket attempts to isolate her from her upper-caste 'sisters' would also perhaps be an act of historical injustice. Clearly, she had not been co-opted by any of these forces as contemporary feminists might want to suspect. She could speak her mind, articulate her sensitive opinion on matters of sex and sexual exploitation, communities and communalism, capitalism and labour: in collaboration and in opposition as well.

Exploring the relationship with 'mothers' is not to suggest a seamless continuity between the past and the present but to *recognize* the concerns of the present in the light of what has been. In their assertion that they had no past models, in their confidence that *Towards Equality* had broken new ground in terms of methodological approach to the issue of the 'status' of women, the members of the CSWI nullified this very important feminist premise. By failing to understand and acknowledge that the ground for their own work had been laid by women in their preparations for the framing of the Constitution in their imagination of the nation, the authors of *Towards Equality* chose to put a veil on the memory of the founding mothers. To think back though our mothers is not a choice but an imperative. This book is an invitation is to unforget them.

NOTES

1. Kamaladevi Chattopadhyay, *Indian Women's Battle for Freedom* (New Delhi: Abhinav Publications, 1983), 2.

2. Kumud Sharma and C. P. Sujaya (eds), *Towards Equality: Report of the Committee on the Status of Women in India* (New Delhi: Centre for Women's Development Studies & Pearson, 2012; originally Department of Social Welfare, Ministry of Education and Social Welfare, Government of India, 1974).

3. Vina Mazumdar, 'Women, Equality and the Republic: Landmarks in Indian History', in Kumud Sharma and C. P. Sujaya (eds), *Towards Equality: Report of the Committee on the Status of Women in India*, xv–xxii (New Delhi: Centre for Women's Development Studies & Pearson, 2012, xviii.

4. Sharma and Sujaya, *Towards Equality*, 76.

5. Ibid., xxiii.

6. Ibid., 11.

7. Ibid., xxiii.

8. Ibid., 11.

9. Ibid., 4.
10. Ibid.
11. Ibid., xxxiv.
12. Ibid.
13. Ibid.
14. Ibid., 10.
15. Ibid., xxxiv.
16. Letter by the members of the CSWI to the Education Minister, 31 December 1974, in ibid., 1.
17. Ibid., 5.
18. Ibid., 6.
19. Ibid., 10.
20. Amrit Kaur, 'Birth of the Indian Women's Movement', speech delivered in Jullundur, 1932, in Amrit Kaur, *Challenge to Women* (Allahabad: New Literature, 1946), 15 (emphasis mine).
21. Kamaladevi Chattopadhyay, *Status of Women in India* (New Delhi: Indian Council of World Affairs, 1947), 4 (emphasis mine).
22. Shanta Mukherjee's speech at the 30th session of the International Labour Organization, Geneva, 18 June to 12 July 1947, AIWC Files IV Instalment, File no. 95, NMML.
23. Shanta Mukherjee's Report to the President, AIWC, AIWC File no. 95, NMML.
24. Sudipta Kaviraj, *The Imaginary Institution of India: Politics and Ideas* (Ranikhet: Permanent Black, 2010), 197.
25. Sharma and Sujaya, *Towards Equality*, 219.
26. Ibid., 11.
27. K. T. Shah (ed.), *Report of the Sub-Committee on Woman's Role in Planned Economy* (Bombay: Vora & Co., 1947), 30.
28. Kamaladevi Chattopadhyay, *Women's Battle for Freedom* (New Delhi: Abhinav Publications, 1983), 1.
29. Kamaladevi Chattopadhyay, Presidential Address to the AIWC, 7 April 1944, in Kamaladevi Chattopadhyay, *At the Cross-roads*, ed. Yusuf Meherally (Bombay: National Information and Publications Ltd., 1947), 90–91.
30. Virginia Woolf, *A Room of One's Own* (London: Penguin Books, 1945), 76.
31. Alice Walker, 'In Search of Our Mothers' Gardens', in Angelyn Mitchell (ed.), *Within the Circle: An Anthology of African American Literary Criticism from the Harlem Renaissance to the Present*, 401–409 (Durham and London: Duke University Press, 1994).
32. Dakshayani Velayudhan, Constituent Assembly (Legislative) of India, 26 August 1948, *CA(L)D*: 654.
33. Ibid. (emphasis mine).

Appendix
Texts and Contexts of the Framing – A Timeline

1906	Dadabhai Naoroji demands self-government
1909	Morley–Minto Reforms establish a parliamentary system in India
1914–1918	World War I
1917	The Montagu–Chelmsford Report visualizes India as a self-governing sisterhood of states presided over by a Central Government
1919	Massacre at Amritsar
December 1920	Congress resolution on the Non-coperation Movement in the Nagpur session
1919	The Government of India Act
1925	The Commonwealth of India Bill
1927	Foundation of the All India Women's Conference (AIWC)
1929	The Child Marriage Restraint Act
1930–1932	Round Table Conferences
26–31 March 1931	Resolution on Fundamental Rights passed by the Congress in its Karachi session
1932	Poona Pact between Gandhi and Ambedkar
24 November 1934	Legal Disabilities Day announced by the AIWC
1935	The Government of India Act
1937	First General Election in British India

1937	The Irish Constitution makes a distinction between justiciable and non-justiciable rights
1938	National Planning Committee established by the Indian National Congress
1939	Sub-Committee on Woman's Role in Planned Economy appointed
1939–1945	World War II
1942	Visit of Sir Stafford Cripps; Cripps' proposal that a constitution-making body be set up in India fails. This is the first recognition by the British of the need for a Constituent Assembly.
1943	Renuka Ray nominated to the Central Assembly (Legislative)
1944	Renuka Ray invited as special member of the Hindu Law Committee
1945	General Elections in Britain; Labour Government formed with Clement Attlee as Prime Minister
December 1945	Draft of the Indian Women's Charter of Rights and Duties
16–18 February 1946	16 February: Two commissions formed: a Commission on Human Rights and a Sub-Commission on the Status of Women. 18 February: Amrit Kaur elected as a member of the Sub-Commission on Human Rights. However, Amrit Kaur was replaced by Hansa Mehta who attened the inaugural sessions of the Sub-Commission on Human Rights in New York from 29 April 1946 to 13 May 1946. When Mehta, later, moved to the Commission on Human Rights that drafted the UDHR, she was replaced by Hamid Ali on the Sub-Commission on the Status of Women.
1 May 1946	Hansa Mehta submits the Indian Woman's Charter of Rights and Duties to the UN Sub-Commission on the Status of Women
16 May 1946	The Cabinet Mission Plan lays down the composition and structure of the Constituent Assembly
July 1946	Completion of elections to the Constituent Assembly; 296 members from British India (undivided) and 93 members from 20 independent Indian states elected
11 July 1946	B. N. Rau appointed as Constitutional Advisor to the Constituent Assembly
August 1946	Hansa Mehta elected Vice President of the International Alliance of Women at Interlaken

20 November 1946	Viceroy invites all members of the Constituent Assembly to attend its first meeting on 9 December 1946; Jinnah and the Muslim League refuse to be part of the Constituent Assembly
9 December 1946	Inaugural meeting of the Constituent Assembly held in which 207 members take part
10 December 1946	G. Durgabai appointed to Committee on the Rules of Procedure
13 December 1946	Objectives Resolution of the Constituent Assembly moved by Jawaharlal Nehru; the Resolution is meant to be the Assembly's solemn pledge to be redeemed in the Constitution that it is to frame – this forms the basis of the Preamble to the Constitution
21 January 1947	Election of the Steering Committee of the Constituent Assembly. G. Durgabai elected as a member
23 January 1947	Objectives Resolution adopted by the Constituent Assembly; it is clear by this time that the Muslim League will not be part of the Constituent Assembly
24 January 1947	Election of the Advisory Committee on Fundamental Rights, Minorities and Tribal and Excluded Areas
27 January 1947	Hansa Mehta begins participating in the meetings of the UN Commission on Human Rights which is to prepare the Universal Declaration of Human Rights (UDHR); in the first meeting she made the formal proposal that Eleanor Roosevelt be made the chairperson on the Commission, a proposal which was unanimously accepted. She misses some meetings of the Sub-Committee on Fundamental Rights of the Constituent Assembly as a result, and divides her time between the two bodies until December 1948.
27 February 1947	First meeting of the Sub-Committee on Fundamental Rights. This sub-committee has 12 members of which two are women – Hansa Mehta and Amrit Kaur. The Sub-Committee on Minorities is formed. Amrit Kaur is a member of this sub-committee as well.
4 April 1947	The Sub-Committee on Fundamental Rights prepares its draft report with notes of dissent from members including Amrit Kaur and Hansa Mehta
16 April 1947	Report of the Sub-Committee on Fundamental Rights submitted to the Advisory Committee

16–19April 1947   The Sub-Committee on Minorities examines the Report on Fundamental Rights and gives its recommendations

21–22 April 1947   Vigorous debates in the Advisory Committee on the reports of the two sub-committees

23 April 1947   The Advisory Committee submits its report; directive principles not yet finalized

15 July 1947   The Union Constitution Committee chaired by Jawaharlal Nehru submits its report on the model constitution of the Union of India

21 July 1947   The Provincial Constitution Committee chaired by Vallabhbhai Patel submits its report on the model constitution of the states; together these committees lay the federal structure of India

8 August 1947   Advisory Committee submits its report on minority rights

15 August 1947   India and Pakistan become independent states

27–28 August 1947   The Constituent Assembly discusses the Report on Minority Rights submitted by the Advisory Committee

29 August 1947   Seven-member Drafting Committee formed after reports from the various committees are submitted

30 August 1947   B. R. Ambedkar unanimously elected Chairperson of the Drafting Committee

27 October 1947   Draft Constitution prepared by B. N. Rau submitted to the Drafting Committee. This becomes a working paper for Ambedkar.

27 October 1947–
13 February 1948   Drafting Committee considers Draft Constitution prepared by B. N. Rau and all other materials submitted to it

30 January 1948   Assassination of M. K. Gandhi in Birla House, New Delhi, by Nathuram Godse

21 February 1948   B. R. Ambedkar submits the first draft of the Constitution prepared by the Drafting Committee to the President of the Constituent Assembly

26 February 1948–
22 March 1948   First draft printed and circulated among members of the Constituent Assembly; Draft Constitution also circulated in the public domain – between March and September 1948, Drafting Committee receives comments, suggestions, and recommendations from

	members of the Constituent Assembly, government officials, international experts, and members of the public.
18–20 October 1948	Drafting Committee examines all the documents received from official and non-official sources
4 November 1948	The revised Draft Constitution of India is presented by Ambedkar on the floor of the Constituent Assembly. Ambedkar makes an introductory speech laying out its basic structure and plan, and defends the Draft Constitution. Detailed discussion of the Draft Constitution takes place between 4 November 1948 and 8 January 1949. This is the first reading and examination of the Draft Constitution on the floor of the Assembly.
15 November 1948– 17 October 1949	Clause by clause consideration of the Draft Constitution
10 December 1948	Universal Declaration of Human Rights adopted
May 1949	Constituent Assembly reconvenes discussion on Advisory Committee's report. Scraps reservations for religious communities.
16 May 1949	Constituent Assembly reconvenes for a second reading of the Draft Constitution and examines the amendments moved by members. This continues until 17 October 1949. On 15 October 1949, Steering Committee member G. Durgabai moves a proposal for the formal closing of the drafting process; the third reading scheduled for November 1949 is to be the final one.
16–26 November 1949	The third and final reading of the Draft Constitution by the members of the Constituent Assembly takes place. Ambedkar makes his concluding speech summing up the work of the Constituent Assembly and its 11 sessions in which 114 days have been devoted to the consideration of the Draft Constitution.
24 January 1950	The members of the Constituent Assembly affix their signatures on the Constitution, each page of which is adorned by paintings from the course of Indian history by artist Nandalal Bose and his students from Kala Bhavana, Visva Bharati, Santiniketan; the calligraphy is by artists from Delhi
26 January 1950	The Constitution of India comes into force

Bibliography

PRIMARY SOURCES

British Library, European Manuscripts, Geraldine Forbes Collection

Aizaz Rasul Files.
Amrit Kaur Files.
Durgabai Deshmukh Files.
Renuka Ray Files.

British Library, India Office Records

Constituent Assembly of India, Elections and Procedures (L/PJ/10/62).
Constituent Assembly of India, Committee Reports (IOR/V/26/100/13 to IOR/V/26/14).
Constituent Assembly of India, Committee Reports (OMF/IOR/NEG 9280) Microfilm.
Constituent Assembly of India (Legislative), Committee Reports (V/26/100/19: 1948).
Hindu Code Bill of India (L/PJ/7/15739).
Hindu Law Committee Reports (V/26/100/17 and V/26/100/18).

National Archives of India, New Delhi

K. M. Munshi Papers.

K. Santhanam Papers.
Rajendra Prasad Papers.

Nehru Memorial Museum and Library (Manuscript Division), New Delhi

Individual collections

Amrit Kaur Papers.
B. N. Rau Papers.
B. R. Ambedkar Papers.
B. Shiva Rao Papers.
Durgabai Deshmukh Papers.
Hansa Mehta Papers.
Kamaladevi Chattopadhyay Papers.
Lakshmi Menon Papers.
N. Gopalaswamy Ayyangar Papers.
Renuka Ray Papers.
Sucheta Kripalani Papers.
Vijaya Lakshmi Pandit Papers.

Institutional collections

All India Congress Committee Papers.
All India Hindu Mahasabha Papers.
All India Women's Conference Papers.
National Council of Women in India Papers.

Oral history archives

Ammu Swaminathan Oral Transcripts.
C. D. Deshmukh Oral Transcripts.
Durgabai Deshmukh Oral Transcripts.
Hansa Mehta Oral Transcripts.
Renuka Ray Oral Transcripts.

Other published sources

Choudhary, Valmiki, ed. *Dr. Rajendra Prasad: Correspondence and Select Documents*. 12 vols. Delhi: Allied Publishers, 1984.
Dr Babasaheb Ambedkar Writings and Speeches. 17 vols. Mumbai: Government of Maharashtra, 1982–2003.
Durgadas, ed. *Sardar Patel's Correspondence*. 10 vols. Ahmedabad: Navajivan, 1971.

Reports and memoranda

All India Women's Conference Memorandum Regarding Preparatory Asian Regional Conference of the I.L.O. 1947. AIWC Papers, File no. 95. NMML.

Constitution of the All India Women's Conference. New Delhi: Sarojini House, 1979.

Half Yearly Report of the Member-in-charge of the Legal Disabilities of Women. AIWC, 1939. AIWC Papers, Subject File no. 44. NMML.

Report of National Committee on Women's Education, 1959. In *Education, Equality and Development: Persistent Paradoxes in Indian Women's History,* edited by Vina Mazumdar, 21–60. New Delhi: CWDS and Pearson, 2012.

Report of the Committee on the Differentiation of Curricula for Boys and Girls at the Different Levels of Education. 1963. National Council for Women's Education, New Delhi. Hansa Mehta Papers, Subject File no. 31. NMML.

Report of the Hindu Law Committee. 1941. Shimla: Government of India Press, 1941.

Report of the Hindu Law Committee. Unpublished, 1947. B. N. Rau Papers, 1st Instalment. File no. 15. B N Rau Paper. NMML.

'Report of the Leader of the Team of Social Work'. Planning Commission, Renuka Ray Papers, Subject File no. 13. NMML.

Report of the Study Team on Social Welfare and Welfare of Backward Classes, Vol. 1. New Delhi: Committee on Planned Projects, 1959.

Shah. K. T., ed. *National Planning Committee: Report.* Bombay: Vora & Co. Publishers Ltd., 1949.

——, ed. *Report of the Sub-Committee: Land Policy, Agricultural Labour and Insurance.* Bombay: Vora & Co. Publishers Ltd., 1948.

——, ed. *Report of the Sub-Committee on General Education and Technical Education and Development Research.* Bombay: Vora & Company, 1948.

——, ed. *Report of the Sub-Committee on Woman's Role in Planned Economy.* Bombay: Vora & Co., 1947.

Written Statement Submitted to the Hindu Law Committee, 1945. 2 Vols. Madras: Government Press, 1947.

Resources of the Constituent Assembly

Constituent Assembly Debates: Official Reports. 12 vols. 4th Reprint. New Delhi: Lok Sabha Secretariat, 2003; first published 1950.

Constituent Assembly of India (Legislative) Debates: Official Reports.

Kashyap, Subhash C., ed. *The Framing of India's Constitution: A Study.* 2nd ed. Delhi: Universal Law Publishing, 2004.

Majumdar, A. K., ed. *Indian Constitutional Documents: Munshi Papers.* Vol II. Bombay: Bhartiya Vidya Bhavan, 1967.

Rao, B. Shiva, ed. *The Framing of India's Constitution: Select Documents*. 4 vols. Reprint, Delhi: Universal Law Publishing, 2004; first published Delhi: The Indian Institute of Public Administration, 1967.

Rau, B. N. *India's Constitution in the Making*. Edited by B. Shiva Rao. Delhi: Allied Publishers, 1960.

Women's Library and Archives, London School of Economics

Papers of Hilda Seligman.

Papers of Women's International League for Peace and Freedom, British Section.

Records of the International Alliance of Women.

Writings by women

Ali, Aruna Asaf. *The Resurgence of Indian Women*. New Delhi: Radiant Publishers, 1991.

Begum, Hajrah. *Why Should Women Vote for Communists?* Communist Party Publication, 1962.

Chattopadhyay, Kamaladevi. *At the Cross-roads*. Edited by Yusuf Meherally. Bombay: The National Information and Publications Ltd., 1947.

———. *Indian Women's Battle for Freedom*. New Delhi: Abhinav Publications, 1983.

———. *Inner Recesses Outer Spaces: Memoirs*. New Delhi: India International Centre and Niyogi Books, 2014.

———. 'Introduction'. In *Woman in Modern India*, edited by Neera Desai, 1–4. Bombay: Vora & Co., 1957.

———. *Status of Women in India*. New Delhi: Indian Council of World Affairs, 1947.

———. *The Awakening of Indian Women*. Madras: Everyman's Press, 1939.

Cousins, Margaret E. *Indian Womanhood Today*. Allahabad: Kitabistan, 1941.

Deshmukh, Durgabai. *Chintamani and I*. Delhi: Allied, 1981.

———, ed. *Social Legislation: Its Role in Social Welfare*. New Delhi: The Planning Commission of India, 1956.

———. *Social Welfare and Economic Development*. Bangkok: United Nations Asian Institute for Economic Development and Planning, 1966.

Draft of the Indian Woman's Charter of Rights and Duties, 1946. Hansa Mehta Papers, Subject File no. 7. NMML.

Ikramullah, Shaista. *From Purdah to Parliament*. Karachi: Oxford University Press, 1998; first published London: Cresset Press, 1963.

Kaur, Amrit. *Challenge to Women*. Allahabad: New Literature, 1946.

Mehta, Hansa. *Civil Liberties*. Aundh: Aundh Publishing Trust for All India Women's Conference, 1945.

———. 'Human Rights: Their Significance'. 1951. Typescript. Hansa Mehta Papers, 1st Instalment, Speeches/Writings by Her, File no. 26. NMML.

———. 'The Constituent Assembly of India'. Hansa Mehta Papers, 1st Instalment. Writings by Her, Subject File no. 8. NMML.

———. 'The International Bill of Rights'. Hansa Mehta Papers, 1st Instalment, Speeches/Writings by Her, File no. 7. NMML.

———. *The Woman under the Hindu Law of Marriage and Succession*. Bombay: Pratibha Publications, 1941.

———. 'Women and Group Prejudice in India'. Undated. Hansa Mehta Papers, Writings by Her, File no. 104. NMML.

Menon, Lakshmi N. *Political Rights of Women in India*. New Delhi: UNESCO Seminar on the Status of Women in South Asia, 1952.

———. 'Why the All-India Women's Conference?' Lakshmi Menon Papers, Subject File no. 2. Papers relating to AIWC (1955–1995). NMML.

———. 'Women and the National Movement'. In *Indian Women*, edited by Devaki Jain, 17–37. New Delhi: Publications Division, 1975.

Rasul, Begam Aizaz. *From Purdah to Parliament*. New Delhi: Ajanta Publications, 2001.

Ray, Renuka. 'A National Code'. Manuscript of undated article (probably from the early 1960s). AIWC Files, IV Instalment. File no. 965. NMML.

———. 'Article 31 in the Constituent Assembly'. Undated. Renuka Ray Papers, Subject File no. 32. NMML.

———. 'History of Social Reform and Social Work from 1947 to 1963'. Renuka Ray Papers, Speeches/Writings by Her, File no. 59. NMML.

———. *My Reminiscences: Social Development during Gandhian Era and After*. Kolkata: Stree, 2005.

———. 'Socialism'. Unpublished article. Renuka Ray Papers, Subject File no. 93. NMML.

———. 'The Background of the Hindu Code Bill'. *Pacific Affairs* 25, no. 3 (September 1952): 268–277.

———. 'Uniform Code of Social Laws'. Manuscript of undated article (probably from the early 1970s). Renuka Ray Papers, Writings/Speeches by Her. File no. 86. NMML.

———. 'What Are Democracy's Best Answers to Communism?' Renuka Ray Papers, Writings/Speeches by Her, 1946–1949. NMML.

———. 'Women as Citizens of Free India'. Renuka Ray Papers, Speeches/ Writings by Her, File no. 14. NMML.

———. 'Women's Movement in India'. Unpublished manuscript. Renuka Ray Papers, Speeches/Writings by Her. S. no. 88. NMML.

Sen, Manikuntala. *In Search of Freedom: An Unfinished Journey*. Calcutta: Stree, 2001.

Shahnawaz, Jahan Ara. *Father and Daughter: A Political Autobiography*. Lahore: Nigarishat, 1971.

Shiva Rao, Kitty. *The Draft Hindu Code*, Aundh: All India Women's Conference, 1945.

Velayudhan, Dakshayani. 'Limited Lure of Cash Awards: Intercaste Marriages', *The Times of India*, 4 November 1975.

———. 'The Task Ahead: Organize Federation in Every Village', *Jai Bheem* 1, no. 1 (31 January 1946): 1.

SECONDARY SOURCES

Ackerman, Bruce. 'A Generation of Betrayal?'. *Fordham Law Review* 65, no. 4 (March 1997): 1519–1536.

———. 'The Storrs Lectures: Discovering the Constitution'. *The Yale Law Journal* 93, no. 6 (1984): 1013–1072.

———. *We the People: The Foundations*. Cambridge, MA: The Belknap Press of Harvard University Press, 1993.

Agnes, Flavia. *Family Law: Family Laws and Constitutional Claims*. New Delhi: Oxford University Press, 2011.

———. *Law and Gender Inequality: The Politics of Women's Rights in India*. New Delhi: Oxford University Press, 1999.

Alexander, Larry, ed. *Constitutionalism: Philosophical Foundations*. Cambridge: Cambridge University Press, 1999.

Ambedkar, B. R. *Annihilation of Caste: The Annotated Critical Edition*. Edited by S. Anand. New Delhi: Navayana, 2014.

———. 'Castes in India: Their Mechanism, Genesis and Development'. In *Essential Writings of B.R. Ambedkar*, edited by Valerian Rodrigues, 241–262. New Delhi: Oxford University Press, 2003.

Anderson, Benedict. *Imagined Communities: Reflections on the Origin and Spread of Nationalism*. London & New York: Verso, 1983.

Andhyarujina, T. R. 'The Evolution of Due Process of Law by the Supreme Court'. In *Supreme But Not Infallible: Essays in Honour of the Supreme Court of India*, edited by B. N. Kirpal, Ashok H. Desai, Gopal Subramanium, Rajeev Dhavan, and Raju Ramchandran, 193–213. New Delhi: Oxford University Press, 2000.

Ashgar Ali, Azra. *The Emergence of Feminism among Indian Muslim Women: 1920–1947*. Karachi: Oxford University Press, 2000.

Austin, Granville. *The Indian Constitution: Cornerstone of a Nation*. 2nd ed. New Delhi: Oxford University Press, 1999.

———. *Working a Democratic Constitution: A History of the Indian Experience*. New Delhi: Oxford University Press, 1999.

Bajpai, Rochana. *Debating Difference: Group Rights and Liberal Democracy in India*. New Delhi: Oxford University Press, 2011.

Banerjee, Nirmala. 'Whatever Happened to the Dreams of Modernity? The Nehruvian Era and Woman's Position'. *Economic and Political Weekly* 33, no. 17 (1998): WS2–WS7

Barthes, Roland. 'The Death of the Author'. In *The Norton Anthology of Theory and Criticism*, edited by Vincent B. Leitch, 1466–1470. New York: W. W. Norton & Company, 2001.

Basu, Aparna and Bharati Ray. *Women's Struggle: A History of the All India Women's Conference, 1927–2002*. New Delhi: Manohar, 2003.

Basu, Durga Das. *Commentary on the Constitution of India*. Edited by Y. V. Chandrachud, S. S. Subramani, and B. P. Banerjee. 10 vols. 8th ed. New Delhi: LexisNexis Butterworths, Wadhwa, 2007–2012.

Baxi, Upendra. 'Emancipation as Justice: Babasaheb Ambedkar's Legacy and Vision'. In *Crisis and Change in Contemporary India*, edited by Upendra Baxi and Bhikhu Parekh, 122–149. New Delhi: Sage Publications, 1995.

———. 'Siting Secularism in the Uniform Civil Code'. In *The Crisis of Secularism in India*, edited by Anuradha Dingwaney Needham and Rajeshwari Sunder Rajan, 267–293. Ranikhet: Permanent Black, 2007.

———. 'The (Im)possibility of Constitutional Justice'. In *India's Living Constitution: Ideas, Practices, Controversies*, edited by Zoya Hasan, E. Sridharan, and R. Sudarshan, 31–63. New Delhi: Permanent Black, 2002.

———. 'The Little Done, the Vast Undone: Some Reflections on Reading Granville Austin's *The Indian Constitution*'. *Journal of the Indian Law Institute* 9, no. 3 (1967): 323–430.

Beard, Charles A. *An Economic Interpretation of the Constitution of the United States*. New York: The Free Press, 1935; first published the Macmillan Company, 1913.

Beauvoir, Simone De. *The Second Sex*. Translated by Constance Border and Sheila Malovany-Chevallier. London: Vintage Books, 2011; first published 1949.

Beeman, Richard, ed. *Penguin Guide to the United States Constitution*. New York: Penguin, 2010.

Berlin, Isaiah. *Liberty: Incorporating Four Essays on Liberty*. Edited by Henry Hardy. Oxford: Oxford University Press, 2002.

Beteille, Andre. 'Constitutional Morality'. *Economic and Political Weekly* 43, no. 40 (2008): 35–42.

Beverley, Baines, Daphne Barak-Erez, and Tsvi Kahana, eds. *Feminist Constitutionalism: Global Perspectives*. Cambridge: Cambridge University Press, 2012.

Bhagavan, Manu. *The Peacemakers: India and the Quest for One World*. New Delhi: Harper Collins, 2012.

Bhargava, Rajeev. 'Introduction: Outline of a Political Theory of the Indian Constitution'. In *The Politics and Ethics of the Indian* Constitution, edited by Rajeev Bhargava, 1–41. New Delhi: Oxford University Press, 2008.

———, ed. *The Politics and Ethics of the Indian Constitution*. New Delhi: Oxford University Press, 2008.

Bhatia, Gautam. *The Transformative Constitution: A Radical Biography in Nine Acts*. New Delhi: Harper Collins, 2019.

Bhatia, Udit, ed. *The Indian Constituent Assembly: Deliberations on Democracy*. New Delhi: Routledge, 2018.

Black. Allida M., ed. *The Eleanor Roosevelt Papers*, Vol. 1: *The Human Rights Years, 1945–1948*. Detroit: Charles Scribner's Sons, 2007.

Bourdieu, Pierre. *Distinctions: A Social Critique of the Judgement of Taste*. Translated by Richard Nice. London and New York: Routledge, 2010.

Butler, Judith, and Joan W. Scott, eds. *Feminists Theorize the Political*. New York: Routledge, 2001.

———. 'Introduction'. In *Feminists Theorize the Political*, edited by Judith Butler and Joan Scott, xiii–xvii. New York: Routledge, 2001.

Chakrabarty, Dipesh. *Provincializing Europe: Postcolonial Thought and Historical Difference*. Princeton, NJ: Princeton University Press, 2000.

Chakravorty Spivak, Gayatri. 'Constitutions and Culture Studies'. *Yale Journal of Law and the Humanities* 2, no. 1 (1990): 133–147.

———. *Outside in the Teaching Machine*. New York and London: Routledge, 1993.

Chatterjee, Partha. *Nationalist Thought and the Colonial World: A Derivative Discourse*. London: Zed Books, 1986.

———. 'The Nationalist Resolution of the Women's Question'. In *Recasting Women: Essays in Colonial History*, edited by Kumkum Sangari and Sudesh Vaid, 233–253. New Delhi: Zubaan, 2006; first published Kali for Women, 1989.

Chaudhuri, Maitrayee, ed. *Feminism in India*. New Delhi: Kali for Women and Women Unlimited, 2004.

Chitnis, Suma. 'Feminism: Indian Ethos and Indian Convictions'. In *Feminism in India*, edited by Maitrayee Chaudhuri, 8–25. New Delhi: Kali for Women & Women Unlimited, 2004.

———. 'The Institutionalisation of Social Purpose'. In *Towards Just and Equitable Development: Durgabai Deshmukh Memorial Lectures*, edited by Rajiv Balakrishnan, 1–21. New Delhi; Seattle: Konark, 2012.

Choudhry, Sujit, Madhav Khosla, and Pratap Bhanu Mehta, eds. *The Oxford Handbook of the Indian Constitution*. New Delhi: Oxford University Press, 2016.

Culler, Jonathan. *On Deconstruction: Theory and Criticism after Deconstruction*. 25th Anniversary Edition. London and New York: Routledge, 2008.

Das, Veena. *Critical Events: An Anthropological Perspective on Contemporary India.* New Delhi: Oxford University Press, 1997.

———. *Life and Words: Violence and the Descent into the Ordinary.* Berkeley: University of California Press, 2007.

Dasgupta, Sandipto. 'Conflict, not Consensus: Towards a Political Economy of the Making of the Indian Constitution'. In *The Indian Constituent Assembly: Deliberations on Democracy*, edited by Udit Bhatia, 38–57. New Delhi: Routledge, 2018.

Datta Gupta, Sarmistha. *Identities and Histories: Women's Writings and Politics in Bengal.* Kolkata: Stree, 2010.

Davis, Donald R. Jr. 'Children: *Putra, Duhitra*'. In *Hindu Law: A New History of Dharmashastra*, edited by Patrick Olivelle and Donald R. Davis, Jr., 151–163. New Delhi: Oxford University Press, 2018.

De, Rohit. *A People's Constitution: The Everyday Life of Law in the Indian Republic.* Princeton: Princeton University Press, 2018.

———. 'Constitutional Antecedents'. In *The Oxford Handbook of the Indian Constitution*, edited by Sujit Chaudhary, Madhav Khosla and Pratap Bhanu Mehta, 17–37. New Delhi: Oxford University Press, 2016.

Derrida, Jacques. 'Declarations of Independence'. In *Negotiations: Interventions and Interviews, 1971–2001*, edited by Elizabeth Rottenberg, 46–54. Stanford: Stanford University Press, 2002.

———. *Of Grammatology.* Translated by Gayatri Chakravorty Spivak. Delhi: Motilal Banarasidas, 1994; first published 1976.

———. 'The Law of Genre'. Translated by Avita Ronell. *Critical Inquiry* 7, no. 1 (1980): 55–81.

Deshmukh, C. D. *The Course of My Life.* New Delhi: Orient Longman, 1974.

de Tocqueville, Alexis. *Democracy in America and Two Essays on America.* Translated by Gerald E. Bevan. London: Penguin, 2003; first published 1835 and 1840.

Dingwaney Needham, Anuradha and Rajeshwari Sundar Rajan, eds. *The Crisis of Secularism in India.* Ranikhet: Permanent Black, 2007.

Dobrowolsky, Alexandra, and Vivien Hart, eds. *Women Making Constitutions: New Politics and Comparative Perspectives.* New York: Palgrave Macmillan, 2003.

Elangovan, Arvind. *Norms and Politics: Sir Benegal Narsing Rau in the Making of the Indian Constitution, 1935–1950.* New Delhi: Oxford University Press, 2019.

Elster, Jon and Rune Slagstad, eds. *Constitutionalism and Democracy.* Cambridge: Cambridge University Press, 1988.

Encyclopaedia of Social Work. 3 vols. Delhi: Publications Division on behalf of the Planning Commission, 1968.

Fish, Stanley. *Doing What Comes Naturally: Change, Rhetoric, and the Practice of Theory in Literary and Legal Studies.* Durham and London: Duke University Press, 1989.

Forbes, Geraldine. *Women in Modern India*. Cambridge: Cambridge University Press, 1996.

Foucault, Michel. *The Archaeology of Knowledge*. Translated by A. M. Sheridan Smith. London and New York: Routledge, 2002.

———.'The Discourse on Language'. In *The Archaeology of Knowledge and the Discourse on Language*. Translated by A. M. Sheridan Smith, 215–237. New York: Pantheon Books, 1972.

———. 'What Is an Author?' In *Essential Works of Michel Foucault: Aesthetics, Method, and Epistemology*, edited by James Faubion, 205–222. London: Penguin, 2000.

Frow, John. *Genre*. London and New York: Routledge, 2006.

Gajendragadkar, P. B. 'Constitution and Social Work'. In *Encyclopaedia of Social Work*, Vol 1, 153–160. Delhi: Publications Division on behalf of the Planning Commission, 1968.

Gallop, Jane. *The Deaths of the Author: Reading and Writing in Time*. Durham and London: Duke University Press, 2011.

Ganguli, B. N., ed. *Social Development: Essays in Honour of Smt Durgabai Deshmukh*. New Delhi: Sterling Publishers, 1977.

Gauba, Kanika. 'Forgetting Partition: Constitutional Amnesia and Nationalism'. *Economic and Political Weekly* 51, no. 39 (2016): 41–47.

Geetha, V. and S. V. Rajadurai. *Towards a Non-Brahmin Millennium: From Iyothee Thass to Periyar*. Calcutta: Samya, 2008.

Ghosh, Anjan, Tapati Guha-Thakurta, and Janaki Nair, eds. *Theorizing the Present: Essays for Partha Chatterjee*. New Delhi: Oxford University Press, 2011.

Glendon, Mary Ann. *A World Made New: Eleanor Roosevelt and the Universal Declaration of Human Rights*. New York: Random House, 2002.

Goodall, Heather and Devleena Ghosh. 'Reimagining Asia: Indian and Australian Women Crossing Borders'. *Modern Asian Studies* 53, no. 4 (2019): 1183–1221.

Gopal, S, ed. *Selected Works of Jawaharlal Nehru*. Vol. 4. Delhi: Jawaharlal Nehru Memorial Fund, 1973.

Guha, Ranajit, *The Small Voice of History: Collected Essays*. Edited by Partha Chatterjee. Ranikhet: Permanent Black, 2010.

Hasan, Zoya, E. Sridharan, and R. Sudharshan, eds. *India's Living Constitution: Ideas, Practices, Controversies*. New Delhi: Permanent Black, 2002.

Iyer, Raghavan N. *The Moral and Political Thought of Mahatma Gandhi*. New Delhi: Oxford University Press, 2000.

Jaffrelot, Christophe. *Dr Ambedkar and Untouchability: Analysing and Fighting Caste*. Ranikhet: Permanent Black, 2005.

Jain, M.P. *Indian Constitutional Law*. 6th ed. Revised by Ruma Pal and Samaraditya Pal. Nagpur: LexisNexis Butterworths Wadhwa, 2010.

Jayal, Niraja Gopal. *Citizenship and Its Discontents: An Indian History*. Ranikhet: Permanent Black, 2013.

Jayal, Niraja Gopal. and Pratap Bhanu Mehta, eds. *The Oxford Companion to Politics in India*. New Delhi: Oxford University Press, 2011.

John, Mary. 'Alternate Modernities? Reservations and Women's Movement in 20th Century India'. *Economic and Political Weekly* 35, no. 43 (2000): 3822–3829.

Kafka, Franz. 'A Report to an Academy'. In *Metamorphosis and Other Stories*, edited by Michael Hofmann, 195–204. London: Penguin Books, 2015.

Kangle, R. P. *The Kautiliya Arthasastra*. 3 vols. 2nd ed. New Delhi: Motilal Banarasidas, 1969.

Kannabiran, Kalpana. *Tools of Justice: Non-Discrimination and the Indian Constitution*. New Delhi: Routledge, 2012.

Kannabiran, Vasantha, and K. Lalitha. 'That Magic Time'. In *Recasting Women: Essays in Colonial History*, edited by Kumkum Sangari and Sudesh Vaid, 180–203. New Delhi: Zubaan, 2006; first published Kali for Women, 1989.

Kapur, Ratna. 'Gender Equality'. In *The Oxford Handbook of the Indian Constitution* edited by Sujit Choudhry, Madhav Khosla, and Pratap Bhanu Mehta, 742–755. New Delhi: Oxford University Press, 2016.

Kapur, Ratna and Brenda Cossman. 'On Women, Equality and the Constitution: Looking Glass of Feminism'. In *Gender and Politics in India*, edited by Nivedita Menon, 197–261. New Delhi: Oxford University Press, 1999.

———. *Subversive Sites: Feminist Engagements with Law in India*. New Delhi: Sage, 1996.

Kashyap, Subhash C. *Constitution Making since 1950: An Overview*. Delhi: Universal Law Publishing, 2004.

———. *Indian Constitution: Conflicts and Controversies*. New Delhi: Vitasta, 2010.

Kaviraj, Sudipta. *The Enchantment of Democracy and India: Politics and Ideas*. Ranikhet: Permanent Black, 2011.

———. *The Imaginary Institution of India*. Ranikhet: Permanent Black, 2010.

Keating, Christine. *Decolonizing Democracy: Transforming the Social Contract in India*. Pennsylvania: Pennsylvania State University Press, 2011.

———. 'Framing the Postcolonial Sexual Contract: Democracy, Fraternalism, and State Authority in India'. *Hypatia* 2, no. 4. (2007): 130–145.

Keith, A. B. *Constitutional History of India*. London: Methuen & Co Ltd, 1936.

Khilnani, Sunil. *The Idea of India*. New Delhi: Penguin, 2004.

———. 'The Indian Constitution and Governance'. In *India's Living Constitution: Ideas, Practices, Controversies*, edited by Zoya Hasan, E. Sridharan, and R. Sudarshan, 64–82. New Delhi: Permanent Black, 2002.

Khosla, Madhav. *India's Founding Moment: The Constitution of a Most Surprising Democracy*. Cambridge, MA: Harvard University Press, 2020.

———. *The Indian Constitution.* New Delhi: Oxford University Press, 2012.

Kinkar Chaubey, Shibani. *Constituent Assembly of India: Springboard of Revolution.* 2nd ed. New Delhi: Manohar, 2000; first published 1973.

Kirpal, B. N., Ashok H. Desai, Gopal Subramanium, Rajeev Dhavan, and Raju Ramchandran, eds. *Supreme but Not Infallible: Essays in Honour of the Supreme Court of India.* New Delhi: Oxford University Press, 2000.

Kohli, Atul, ed. *The Success of India's Democracy.* New Delhi: Cambridge University Press, 2001.

Kolodny, Annette. 'Dancing through the Minefield: Some Observations in the Theory, Practice, and Politics of Feminist Literary Criticism'. In *The Norton Anthology of Theory and Criticism*, edited by Vincent B. Leitch, 2146–2165. New York: W. W. Norton & Company, 2001.

Krishnaraj, Maithreyi, ed. *Remaking Society for Women: Visions – Past and Present* (Background Volume for VIIth Annual IAWS Conference). New Delhi: Indian Association for Women's Studies, 1995.

Krishnaswamy, Sudhir. *Democracy and Constitutionalism in India: A Study of the Basic Structure Doctrine.* New Delhi: Oxford University Press, 2009.

Kumar, Radha. *The History of Doing: An Illustrated Account of Movements for Women's Rights and Feminism in India, 1800–1990.* New Delhi: Zubaan, 1993.

Leitch, Vincent B., ed. *The Norton Anthology of Theory and Criticism.* New York: W. W. Norton & Company, 2001.

Love, Harold. *Attributing Authorship: An Introduction.* New York: Cambridge University Press, 2002.

MacKinnon, Catherine A. *Toward a Feminist Theory of State.* Cambridge, MA: Harvard University Press, 1989.

Mankekar, Kamala. 'Durgabai Deshmukh'. In *Women Pioneers in India's Renaissance*, edited by Sushila Nayar and Kamla Mankekar, 380–388. New Delhi: National Book Trust, 2002.

Masbridge, Jane. 'Should Blacks Represent Blacks and Women Represent Women? A Contingent "Yes"'. *The Journal of Politics* 61, no. 3 (August 1999): 628–657.

Mayne's Treatise on Hindu Law and Usage, 14th ed. New Delhi: Bharat Law House, 1996.

Mazumdar, Vina, ed. *Education, Equality and Development: Persistent Paradoxes in Indian Women's History.* New Delhi: CWDS and Pearson, 2012.

———. *Memories of a Rolling Stone.* New Delhi: Zubaan, 2010.

———. 'Women, Equality and the Republic: Landmarks in Indian History', In *Towards Equality: Report of the Committee on the Status of Women in India*, edited by Kumud Sharma and C. P. Sujaya, xv–xxii. New Delhi: Centre for Women's Development Studies & Pearson, 2012; first published by the Department of

Social Welfare, Ministry of Education and Social Welfare, Government of India, 1974.

Mehta, Uday S. 'Constitutionalism'. In *The Oxford Companion to Politics in India*, edited by Niraja Gopal Jayal and Pratap Bhanu Mehta, 15–27. New Delhi: Oxford University Press, 2011.

Menon, Nivedita. 'Citizenship and the Passive Revolution: Interpreting the First Amendment'. In *The Politics and Ethics of the Indian Constitution*, edited by Rajeev Bhargava, 189–210. New Delhi: Oxford University Press, 2008.

———. 'Embodying the Self: Feminism, Sexual Violence and Law'. In *Subaltern Studies XI: Community, Gender and Violence*, edited by Partha Chatterjee and Pradeep Jeganathan, 66–105. Delhi: Permanent Black, 2000.

———. 'Living with Secularism'. In *The Crisis of Secularism in India*, edited by Anuradha Dingwaney Needham and Rajeshwari Sunder Rajan, 118–140. Ranikhet: Permanent Black, 2009.

———. *Recovering Subversion: Feminist Politics beyond the Law*. Ranikhet: Permanent Black, 2004.

———. 'State/Gender/Community: Citizenship in Contemporary India'. *Economic and Political Weekly* 33, no. 5 (1998): PE3–PE10.

Menon, Ritu and Kamla Bhasin, *Border and Boundaries: Women in India's Partition*. New Jersey: Rutgers University Press, 1998.

———. 'Recovery, Rupture, Resistance: Indian State and Abduction of Women during Partition'. *Economic and Political Weekly*, 28, no. 17 (24 April 1993): WS2–WS11.

Mensky, Werner. F. *Modern Indian Family Law*. Richmond: Curzon Press, 2001.

Michelman, Frank I. 'Constitutional Authorship'. In *Constitutionalism: Philosophical Foundations*, edited by Larry Alexander, 64–98. Cambridge: Cambridge University Press, 1998.

Morsink, Johannes. *The Universal Declaration of Human Rights: Origins, Drafting, and Intent*. Philadelphia: University of Pennsylvania Press, 1999.

Mukherjee, Mithi. *India in the Shadow of Empire: A Legal and Political History 1774–1950*. New Delhi: Oxford University Press, 2010.

Murphy, Walter. *Constitutional Democracy: Maintaining a Political Order*. Princeton: Princeton University Press, 2005.

Nair, Janaki. 'Indian Historiography and its "Resolution" of Feminists' Questions'. In *Theorizing the Present: Essays for Partha Chatterjee*, edited by Anjan Ghosh, Tapati Guha-Thakurta, and Janaki Nair, 35–61. New Delhi: Oxford University Press, 2011.

Nariman, Fali S. *India's Legal System: Can It Be Saved?* New Delhi: Penguin, 2008.

Nayar, Sushila and Kamla Mankekar, eds. *Women Pioneers in India's Renaissance*. New Delhi: National Book Trust, 2002.

Nehru, Jawaharlal. *The Discovery of India.* New Delhi: Penguin, 2010; first published 1946.

Newbigin, Eleanor. *The Hindu Family and the Emergence of Modern India: Law, Citizenship, and Community.* Cambridge: Cambridge University Press, 2013.

Nigam, Aditya. 'A Text without Author: Locating the Constituent Assembly as Event'. In *The Politics and Ethics of the Indian Constitution*, edited by Rajeev Bhargava, 119–139. New Delhi: Oxford University Press, 2008.

Pal, Samaraditya and Deepan Kumar Sarkar. *India's Constitution: Origins and Evolution*, 10 vols. Gurgaon: LexisNexis, 2014–2016.

Parashar, Archana. *Women and Family Law Reform in India: Uniform Civil Code and Gender Equality.* New Delhi: Sage Publications, 1992.

Parel, Anthony J., ed. *Mahatma Gandhi: Hind Swaraj and Other Writings.* New Delhi: Cambridge University Press, 1997.

Pateman, Carole. *The Sexual Contract.* Stanford: Stanford University Press, 1988.

Pathak, Zakia and Rajeshwari Sunder Rajan. 'Shahbano'. In *Feminists Theorize the Political*, edited by Judith Butler and Joan Scott, 257–279. New York: Routledge, 2001.

Pawar, Urmila and Meenakshi Moon. *We Also Made History: Women in the Ambedkarite Movement.* Translated by Wandana Sonalkar. New Delhi: Zubaan, 2008.

Punter, David. *Metaphor.* London and New York: Routledge, 2007.

Rao, Anupama. *The Caste Question: Dalits and the Politics of Modern India.* Berkeley: University of California Press, 2009.

Reddy, O. Chinnappa. *The Court and the Constitution of India: Summits and Shallows.* New Delhi: Oxford University Press, 2008.

Rege, Sharmila, ed. *Against the Madness of Manu: B. R. Ambedkar's Writings on Brahmanical Patriarchy.* New Delhi: Navayana, 2013.

———. 'Introduction: Towards a Feminist Reclamation of Dr. B. R. Ramji Ambedkar'. In *Against the Madness of Manu: B. R. Ambedkar's Writings on Brahmanical Patriarchy*, edited by Sharmila Rege, 13–56. New Delhi: Navayana, 2013.

———. *Writing Caste/Writing Gender: Reading Dalit Women's Testimonies.* New Delhi: Zubaan, 2006.

Rodrigues, Valerian, ed. *The Essential Writings of B. R. Ambedkar.* New Delhi: Oxford University Press, 2002.

Roy, Anupama. *Gendered Citizenship: Historical and Conceptual Explanations.* New Delhi: Orient Longman, 2005.

Roy, Arundhati. 'The Doctor and the Saint'. In *Annihilation of Caste: The Annotated Critical Edition*, by B. R. Ambedkar. Edited by S. Anand, 17–179. New Delhi: Navayana, 2014.

Rushdie, Salman. *Midnight's Children*. New York: Random House, 2011.

Salmond, John W. *Salmond on Jurisprudence*. Edited by P. J. Fitzgerald. 12th ed. New Delhi: Universal, 2003.

Sangari, Kumkum and Sudesh Vaid, eds. *Recasting Women: Essays in Colonial History*. New Delhi: Zubaan, 2006; first published Kali for Women, 1989.

Sankaranarayanan, Gopal. ed. *The Constitution of India*. Lucknow: Eastern Book Company, 2016.

Sapiro, Virginia. 'When Are Women's Interests Interesting? The Problem of Political Representation of Women'. *The American Political Science Review* 75, no. 3 (1981): 701–716.

Sarkar, Sumit. 'Indian Democracy: The Historical Inheritance'. In *The Success of India's Democracy*, edited by Atul Kohli, 23–46. New Delhi: Cambridge University Press, 2001.

———. *Modern India: 1885–1947*. New Delhi: Macmillan, 1983.

Sarkar, Sumit and Tanika Sarkar, eds. *Women and Social Reform in Modern India: A Reader*. 2 vols. Ranikhet: Permanent Black, 2007.

Sarkar, Tanika and Sumit Sarkar. 'Introduction'. In *Women and Social Reform in Modern India: A Reader*, edited by Sumit Sarkar and Tanika Sarkar, 1–18. Ranikhet: Permanent Black, 2007.

Sathe, S. P. 'India: From Positivism to Structuralism'. In *Interpreting Constitutions: A Comparative Study*, edited by Jeffrey Goldsworthy, 215–265. New Delhi: Oxford University Press, 2006.

Scott, Joan W. 'Gender: A Useful Category of Historical Analysis'. *The American Historical Review* 91 no. 5 (1986): 1053–1075.

Seervai, H.M. *Constitutional Law of India*. 3 vols. Delhi: Universal Book Traders, 1991.

Sen, Sarbani. *The Constitution of India: Popular Sovereignty and Democratic Transformations*. New Delhi: Oxford University Press, 2007.

Shukla, V.N. *Constitution of India*. 10th ed. Revised by Mahendra P. Singh. Lucknow: Eastern Book Company, 2001.

Simon, Rita J. and Mohamed Alaa Abdel-Moneim. *A Handbook of Military Conscription and Composition the World Over*. New York: Lexington Books, 2011.

Singer, Wendy. *A Constituency Suitable for Ladies*. New Delhi: Oxford University Press, 2007.

Singh, Tripurdaman. *Sixteen Stormy Days: The Story of the First Amendment to the Constitution of India*. New Delhi: Penguin Random House India, 2020.

Sinha, Chitra. *Debating Patriarchy: The Hindu Code Bill Controversy in India (1941–1956)*. New Delhi: Oxford University Press, 2012.

Sinha, Mrinalini. *Spectres of Mother India: The Global Restructuring of an Empire.* Durham & London: Duke University Press, 2006.

Som, Reba. 'Jawaharlal Nehru and the Hindu Code: A Victory of Symbol over Substance'. *Modern Asian Studies* 28, no. 1 (1994): 165–194.

Srinivas, M. N. 'My Baroda Days'. In *The Oxford India Srinivas,* edited by Ramachandra Guha, 609–622. New Delhi: Oxford University Press, 2009.

Sundaraiya, P. *Telangana People's Struggle and Its Lessons.* Calcutta: Communist Party of India- Marxist, 1972.

Taylor, Charles. *Modern Social Imaginaries.* Durham and London: Duke University Press, 2004.

Tharu, Susie and K Lalita, eds. *Women Writing in India: 600 BC to the Present.* Vol. I. New Delhi: Oxford University Press, 1991.

Towards Equality: Report of the Committee on the Status of Women in India. Edited by Kumud Sharma and C. P. Sujaya. New Delhi: Centre for Women's Development Studies and Pearson, 2012; first published by the Department of Social Welfare, Ministry of Education and Social Welfare, Government of India, 1974.

Tushnet, Mark. 'The Possibilities of Comparative Constitutional Law'. *The Yale Law Journal* 108 no. 6 (1999): 1225–1309.

Velayudhan, Meera. 'Linking Radical Traditions and the Contemporary Dalit Women's Movement: An Intergenerational Lens'. *Feminist Review* 119 (July 2018): 106–125.

Verma, Dhirendra (ed.), *Hindi Sahitya Kosh.* 2nd ed. Varanasi: Jnan Mandal Limited, 1986.

Walker, Alice. 'In Search of Our Mothers' Gardens'. In *Within the Circle: An Anthology of African American Literary Criticism from the Harlem Renaissance to the Present,* edited by Angelyn Mitchell, 401–409. Durham and London: Duke University Press, 1994.

Wilkinson, Steven Ian. 'India, Consociational Theory, and Ethnic Violence'. In *Ethnonationalism in India: A Reader,* edited by Sanjib Baruah, 431–457. New Delhi: Oxford University Press, 2010.

Woolf, Virginia. *A Room of One's Own.* London: Penguin Books, 1945.

———. *The Common Reader,* Vol. I. London, Vintage, 2003; first published 1925.

Zelliot, Eleanor. *Ambedkar's World: The Making of Babasaheb and the Dalit Movement.* New Delhi: Navayana, 2013.

Index